INVESTMENT: A HISTORY

T0326912

NORTON REAMER
JESSE DOWNING

◆

INVESTMENT

◆

◀ **A HISTORY** ▶

Columbia Business School
Publishing

Columbia University Press
Publishers Since 1893
New York   Chichester, West Sussex
Copyright © 2016 Norton H. Reamer
Paperback edition, 2017

Library of Congress Control Number: 2015953162

ISBN 978-0-231-16952-3 (cloth : alk. paper)—
ISBN 978-0-231-16953-0 (pbk. : alk. paper)—
ISBN 978-0-231-54085-8 (ebook)

Columbia University Press books are printed on permanent
and durable acid-free paper.

COVER DESIGN: Jordan Wannemacher

To my wife, Rita, who "made" my life.
— Norton

For my parents, John and Ann-Marie, and my siblings,
Janelle and Brendan, for braising me in the stew of adventure,
affection, compassion, curiosity, and mirth over the years.
— Jesse

Contents

Acknowledgments

THIS BOOK IS the product of many hands, many minds, and many long hours. We began the project five years ago and have been actively pursuing it ever since. We are going to try to thank everyone seriously involved in it, but there will be inevitable lapses. For these we apologize.

The project has been an inspiring one. The canvas is vast; the subject more than deserving of a broad, detailed, and critical treatment. Everybody rejoices or complains about the role of investment in the world, but heretofore nobody seems to have acknowledged what it really is. We've tried to remedy that deficiency. Hopefully, we've made a credible start. The assignment is daunting, the work important and taxing, and the need, in our view, is great.

We have benefitted from a wonderful team of Research Associates, mostly economics majors at Harvard College but also undergraduates, graduate students, and recent graduates in other subjects and from other universities. They are: Yueran Ma, Rajiv Tarigopula, Xiaoxiao Wu, Charles Smith, Adam Chu, Amy Friedman, Mo Chen, and Albert Cui. They have our thanks for their substantial efforts.

Our last and longest-serving Research Associate has been Henry Shull. Norton has referred to Henry, not always out of his hearing, as our "vacuum cleaner." The truth is just the opposite. Henry was always adding, not subtracting, vital material. There is no counting how many times he has rescued us.

Katherine Walsh, our executive assistant for the last three years, has been a rock solid member of the team as well. Her cheerful efficiency and remarkable resourcefulness have underpinned a massive portion of our total effort. Before Katherine, Sandy Brewer was a wonderful and also upbeat mainstay of our early progress.

In addition, two consultants played important roles. Almost throughout the life of the project, John Butman, himself an accomplished author, counseled us on how to navigate book creation, publishing, and promotion. He has been a great adviser, collaborator on project management, and friend. Anna Weiss, who worked with John, is very talented and always helpful. Another indispensable consultant has been Alyssa Stalsberg Canelli, who helped us with editing, especially in the dauntingly immortal Chapter One, which covers, by some reckoning, more than 5,000 years!

Finally, we want to thank our team from Columbia including Myles Thompson, our publisher, who believed in us without undue coaxing and let us run, and our editors Bridget Flannery-McCoy, who was a tough task master, Stephen Wesley, and Elizabeth King who organized the production, copyediting, and page proof processes.

INVESTMENT: A HISTORY

The Investment Challenge

IN THE WAKE of the global financial crisis of 2007–2009, investment was on people's minds. From the fraud perpetrated by Bernie Madoff, to the mortgage crisis of 2007 and 2008 and the inadequate yields on "safe" bonds, it seemed as if no part of the economy had been more unsuccessfully managed or regulated than the part related to investing for our families' futures. And yet, in the ensuing years, the stock market was making new highs, borrowing money had never been cheaper, the credit and operating weaknesses of many industries were being corrected, and a sick economy seemed to be on the mend. Investments that had previously seemed menacing were beginning to appear more promising.

The crisis, and its eventual taming, sparked a national dialogue about these issues. However, this national dialogue focused primarily on contemporary financial, legal, and political contexts. Rarely were broader questions posed about the long-term history and mechanisms of investment that led us to the crisis. What is investment really all about? Who does it? Why do they do it? Is there a story that can be explored and understood? Are there lessons to be learned? It turns out that investment has a rich backstory that can serve to profoundly deepen, if not fundamentally alter, our grasp of the subject and the tasks at hand. Investment—the commitment of resources with the goal of achieving a return—is truly among the central themes in the story of humankind, and we must familiarize ourselves with its past to fully understand many of humankind's motivations, opportunities, and actions.

The task at hand is enormous in scope. Investment, after all, touches virtually every aspect of life today. Perhaps most obviously, investment underpins our entire economic engine. It is a vital determinant of what projects are funded; how individuals form collectives like companies, institutions, or unions; where in the world capital flows in and out; and when enterprises merge, disaggregate, or dissolve lines of activity. All economic entities are, after all, about investment. A business or institution is a collection of investment projects that grows or contracts based on the returns of those projects relative to its cost of funding.

But investment—one of the most fundamental of human activities—is more than its purely monetary manifestations. It is also intertwined inextricably with social ends: the prospect of homeownership, savings accumulation to finance education, and the health of the endowments of charities. There are very real repercussions on the political landscape as well. Investment affects unemployment, the ability of seniors to retire, the funds deployed to infrastructure and research, and the capacity of a government to access credit markets. Indeed, investment lurks in every corner of daily life and underpins issues of immense importance in both obvious and obscure ways. The fact that there have been few efforts to construct a genuinely comprehensive history of investment given its omnipresence is curious.

This book is not about how to manage investments; rather, as a history of investment and the activities related to it over the centuries, it adds vital perspective to issues in investment management. It traces the development of investment from the earliest civilizations where agricultural land, lending, and trade activities were the economic foundation; to the creation of basic financial, collective, and charitable investment forms; and through the innovation of a vast array of specialized vehicles and funds extending into the twenty-first century. Throughout the book, we trace the evolution of the single most important development in the history of investment: its democratization.

The democratization of investment—the extension of access to investment activities to the population at large—was the outcome of the advent of joint stock companies, the Industrial Revolution, and the development of public markets. It was, in time, the driving force behind the concept of retirement and its funding, the building of diversified investment portfolios, the expansion of securities regulation, the growing understanding of cyclical crises and investment theory, and the development of independent and entrepreneurial investment managers. However, we must qualify our use of the term *democratization*. This expansion of access to the populace does not mean that everyone's access to or sharing of the rewards is equal. Democracy does not necessarily entail complete equality. Nonetheless, taking a longer historical perspective reveals that the democratization of investment is indeed a transformative phenomenon in investment's history, and it is indisputable that investment access has expanded beyond the members of what in this book we call the power elite of premodern times. It also does not mean that investment's democratization is, or should be, over. Far from it. Investment's democratization is a project that should and will continue.

THE FOUR INVESTMENT PRINCIPLES

In order to set the stage for this vast story, our discussion begins with an explanation of the four unifying principles that support effective investment thinking. These four concepts are a basis for grasping the fundamentals of investment: real ownership, the importance of seeking value, the key role of financial leverage, and the crucial function of resource allocation in the success of an investment project.

These principles are introduced to frame the substance and mechanics of investment. They are thus intended to deepen the reader's understanding by whittling away at the marble block to slowly arrive at a concept of investment that is more sensitive to its nuances and complexities than any single pithy definition could be. After all, an insightful characterization of investment is a vital precursor to appreciating its long and storied history.

Real Ownership

Throughout the book, we discuss direct investment activities and investment in financial instruments that represent claims upon these direct investments. Although at first glance these seem to be very different types of investments, they are not. This view agrees with that held by the acknowledged dean of US investors of the late twentieth and early twenty-first centuries, Warren Buffett. Buffett has long contended that acquiring a company directly and purchasing the stock that represents a claim on that company are not substantively different.[1] This means that direct investment and investment in financial instruments should both lead to the same outcome: real ownership.

So, the first principle is that investment is *not* fundamentally different whether it involves open market purchases of public securities or private purchases of whole or portions of enterprises. The essential act of investment in both cases is still "the commitment of resources with the goal of achieving a return." Therefore, owning a business and owning its shares are basically the same. Throughout history there has been little practical difference between ownership and share ownership. The investor must act as if he or she has bought the business, not just a piece of paper. The appearance of distance from the actual business is illusory, for in both cases the investor must face the actual investment challenge at hand—namely, properly analyzing and valuing the business activity to which he or she is committing.

Fundamental Value

The second principle is the fundamental role of *value*. John Burr Williams, the twentieth-century American economist and author of *The Theory of Investment Value*, offers a concise but powerful definition of the investment value of a going concern: "the present worth of the future dividends." In other words, the value of an investment in the equity of a company is simply the present value of all future dividends, plus any predictable principal payments, also adjusted to present value.[2]

This definition is, and always has been, of practical importance to every investor because it delineates between sound investment practice and speculation. This is because a security purchased by an investor at a price below its investment value can usually yield a total return above its price. On the other hand, if an investor purchases a security at a greater price than its fundamental value, as described earlier, he or she is more likely to face a loss, unless the security is sold to another party willing to speculate on the swings of the markets (that is, the "greater fool"). As such, prudent investors often depend on estimates of investment value when making decisions regarding their transactions in the financial markets. Value provides an indispensable guide in terms of buying and selling.[3]

There have been countless examples of a failure to consider fundamental value in investing over the centuries. The most dramatic have been infamous "bubbles" involving gross overvaluation of securities or commodities that have led to calamitous market collapses and investment losses. Less chronicled are the great bargain opportunities that some of these crashes and other depressed conditions have created among investment choices. Value investing has on occasion been the dramatic source of almost unimaginable profits.

Financial Leverage

The third principle is the importance of *financial leverage*. Throughout history, people have secured credit for a variety of purposes, both personal and commercial. Borrowing for personal purposes was common to the ancients, just as it is to us today. Both ancient Greece and classical Rome employed loans broadly to finance profit-making activities as well. Since agricultural land was the foremost earning asset and enjoyed great prestige, the most significant productive borrowings were against this land, but borrowing to finance trade was also relatively common. As industry developed from the fifteenth century onward, credit also facilitated the financing of activities and assets for industrial development, growth, and achievement of a return.[4]

Financial leverage has long been an important contributor to the achievement of outstanding investment outcomes, as well as to disastrous ones. When an investment is a success, however, people do not generally talk about the role leverage has played. When it comes to failures, by contrast, leverage often takes the blame. This is precisely how most people understood the spectacular investment failure of Long-Term Capital Management, a large hedge fund management firm, in 1998. The firm, it was later discovered, had been magnifying its portfolio with leverage ratios as high as 100 to 1—that is, $100 of debt-equivalent employed for every dollar of equity committed.

Even though the firm was invested primarily in high-quality government bonds, its use of this extraordinary leverage created so much risk that even minor fluctuations in the value of its portfolio could cause extreme pressure on its available net worth. Had it not been for a government-organized bailout, Long-Term Capital Management would almost certainly have collapsed.[5]

On the other hand, there have been great investment successes over extended periods of time achieved by well-regarded investors (Warren Buffett again comes to mind) through the use of more moderate levels of financial leverage coupled with good asset selection and stable financing sources. Buffett's exceptional performance over the years can, in part, be attributed to a leverage ratio of about 1.6 to 1 and a low cost of debt financing.[6]

In sum, financial leverage magnifies risk exposure: it magnifies profits if the investment is successful and magnifies losses when the investment is badly analyzed or ill timed. Leverage is, therefore, the sharpest of double-edged swords. However, it has been strikingly important to both profound entrepreneurial success and dramatic investment growth.

Resource Allocation

Resource allocation—the process of allocating capital and human resources—in an investment setting began to emerge as far back as the Commercial Revolution and the successes of the merchant banks of the Italian city-states. Clear evidence shows that in fifteenth-century Florence, for example, the Medici and others who aggressively committed their financial and human resources to funding ventures in finance, textile fabricating, and trade had an acute awareness of the importance of resource allocation. They showed remarkably "modern" acuity by understanding the importance of analyzing available investment opportunities, matching them with capital and human capabilities, and applying these judiciously.[7] Indeed, we can even find this acuity in ancient Greek and Roman estate management, wherein estate owners selected managers who made decisions about agricultural resources and capital investments in order to maximize returns.

Although the modern concept of the CEO as an executor of management technique, objective setting, and implementation has continued to be dominant, another management model has gained traction in recent years. The success of CEOs who place emphasis on effective allocation of capital and people has led to a reappraisal of the hierarchy of management skills.[8] Noteworthy examples of these CEOs include Warren Buffett (Berkshire Hathaway), Henry Singleton (Teledyne), and Thomas Murphy (Capital Cities), all of whom have demonstrated the significant impact of CEOs as allocators of capital and human resources.

Often this focus on capital allocation is paired with an executive style that emphasizes meaningful decentralization in the management hierarchy. Decentralization provides substantial autonomy to carefully vetted division managers or subsidiary CEOs. Decentralized management approaches identify experienced, skilled, and accomplished leaders for different segments of a business network, allowing them to operate with relatively little day-to-day supervision beyond that exercised via control of major available resources. In the view of many management theorists, management control of this sort offers distinct advantages over the more minute-to-minute frenetic activity of dominating, control-oriented CEOs.[9]

Henry Singleton, the CEO of Teledyne from the 1960s to the 1980s, was a wonderful example of this management style. While there were earlier CEOs who focused more on resource allocation than on the more traditional management skills such as execution of management technique and implementation of day-to-day management plans, Singleton seemed to be the most striking contemporary departure from this dominant model. Among other things, Singleton was devoted to shrinking Teledyne's number of outstanding shares, often in lieu of potential acquisitions and substantial investments in plant and equipment. His focus was on return on shareholders' investment rather than on pure measures of revenue growth.[10]

THE ORGANIZATION OF THIS BOOK

The structure of the book is both chronological and thematic. We begin with accounts and narratives of investment in ancient times and continue to the present day. The historical content, however, is largely organized around our central theme: the democratization of investment. Over a three-hundred-year span, between 1600 and 1900, investment evolved from an activity exclusively benefiting the power elite to one that was also available to, and for the benefit of, the middle class: merchants, entrepreneurs, industrialists, and businesspeople.

In order to appreciate the historical significance of the democratization of investment, one must have an understanding of how investment was developed and organized in other eras and cultures. In ancient civilizations, agricultural land was the foundation of wealth and investment. Moreover, only members of the power elite—those with wealth and status affiliated with the leaders of government, church, nobility, or military—were landowners or investors. Commoners accumulated little, if any, surplus. This first chapter also explores the investment structures that supported the beginnings of global trade and commerce. As rudimentary as investment was in those times, however, we can see glimmerings of financial sophistication in the ancient civilizations of Mesopotamia, Egypt, Greece, Rome, and Asia. There we find instances of collateralized lending, forms of insurance, the concept of limited liability for investment partnerships, and profit-sharing arrangements. The history of investment is also intertwined with the history of lending at interest, and different religious and cultural attitudes about the concept of usury have influenced many investment and lending structures.

Chapter 2 picks up this historical narrative of investment in modernity by examining the three major developments that brought about a dramatic change in the participants in and activities of investment: the creation of joint-stock companies, the Industrial Revolution, and the advent of public markets. These developments created a middle class that could achieve surpluses and provided them with avenues to invest their new wealth. For the first time in history, investment and wealth-building activities were accessible to individuals who were not members of the power elite. The ascension of these nonelite investing individuals also brought into being another unprecedented development: the emergence of the concept of retirement and its funding.

Chapter 3 traces this emergence and explores the ways in which financing retirement has produced the largest aggregation of investment capital in the world. The focus on funding retirement has profoundly changed our institutions, the investment vehicles they employ, and also the people involved in managing retirement resources and funds. The idea that funding retirement is a major goal of investment has had important consequences for our society—such as the growth of pension funds and defined contribution retirement plans—and these concepts and instruments continue to evolve to this day.

This history continues into chapter 4, which explores the new clients and new investment forms that proliferated in the nineteenth and twentieth centuries. While individuals are the most important new client type, other clients like endowments, foundations, and sovereign wealth funds have become influential in the business of investment. What are now regarded as basic investments (life insurance, savings accounts, separate accounts, and mutual funds) came into being as a result of the demand from these new clients.

Chapter 5 turns from a relatively chronological narrative toward a thematic one: the history of fraud, market manipulation, and insider trading. These examples of malfeasance actually play only a small role in the history of investment, although they have received a disproportionate amount of attention. Furthermore, much of our contemporary regulatory structures were created in response to these incidents, and it is important to understand their origins. For instance, it is only in recent times that insider trading, once seen as an acceptable prerogative of those with wealth and access, has been targeted for prohibition. Market manipulation, too, was once rampant, and those with sufficient power could move markets to their advantage. In these case studies, we show how the government, its regulatory bodies, and the public have come to understand and react to these issues of fairness. Now, manipulation in major markets tends to be less flagrant and usually requires the collusion of an array of participants. These regulatory developments have given investors more confidence that they are participating in an equitable, more democratized market.

Chapters 6 and 7 delve into contemporary economics and investment theory. Chapter 6 explores the works of key economists like John Maynard Keynes, Milton Friedman, and Ben Bernanke. It argues that these economists have improved our ability to manage the economy for the well-being of all, partly by reducing the disruptive effects of cyclical crises. However, we have yet to fully extricate ourselves from unhelpful cyclical patterns of behavior—such as cycles of excessive confidence and appetite for risk—that still provoke these crises. Chapter 7 examines the twentieth-century emergence of a theoretical framework for understanding the fundamental investment principles. Scientists and economists worked to develop models to describe the movements of markets and articulated such concepts as randomness, the effects of diversification, and the impact of economics. Other new concepts such as the capital asset pricing model, beta, alpha, factor models, and mean-variance optimization also emerged and shed light on portfolio construction.

Chapter 8 is related in scope and structure to chapter 4 in covering investment vehicles, except that it discusses the much more recently developed—rather than the earlier and more basic—vehicles. These include alternative investments as well as low-cost index and exchange-traded funds (ETFs). Alternative investments—including hedge funds, private equity, venture capital, and a wide variety of other asset classes such as real estate, commodities, farmland, other natural resources, and infrastructure—are specialized investment vehicles mostly offered to sophisticated institutions and wealthy individuals. In most cases they offer the expectation of superior risk-adjusted performance, and in almost all cases they offer diversification in an investment portfolio. They also tend to come with higher, and often performance-linked, fees. Index funds and ETFs, on the other hand, are mass market, low-cost, and broadly diversified or sector-focused portfolios of mostly public equity or fixed income securities. They offer generally passive participation in investment markets. These two types of new investment forms are dramatically different but together offer investors the opportunity for employing modern investment techniques and theory-based improvements in constructing portfolios.

Chapter 9 argues that the rise of independent investment managers and entrepreneurial investors has transformed the landscape of investment. Most of the innovations in the field have been created by young and independent firms, and institutional clients have been receptive to the new vehicles, techniques, and fee arrangements they have deployed. The new and dramatic opportunities for business success on the part of investment managers have brought a vast increase in profitability and have established a new elite: those who manage money for institutions in the United States and abroad. However, the institutions this elite serves are largely engaged in the management of the assets of the general population—a reversal of the situation we saw in ancient times, when lower-class managers invested money for the benefit of only the power elite.

Future developments in investment management will involve broader application of investment theory and a change in our relationships with investment professionals. Successful investment managers will be the ones who focus on providing performance and counsel, rather than just selling products. Successful investors will be those who wake up to the fundamental truth that few managers and no single investment strategy can produce outsized returns persistently, and they will therefore pay less for advice or will seek out truly thoughtful investment approaches. And for investment itself, what was once a privilege of the few will have become a benefit to the many.

CHAPTER ONE

A Privilege of the Power Elite

THIS BOOK EXPLORES THE HISTORICALLY dramatic development of the democratization of investment. Simply put, this means that a much larger proportion of the population in advanced societies has been able to participate meaningfully in the enterprise of investment. This process of democratization has transpired as a result of several fundamental changes: the advent of collective ownership through the modern corporate form and public markets; the spread of investable surpluses beginning with the Industrial Revolution; the development of the concept of retirement, motivating the need for sizable savings; the enhancement of the regulatory environment that aided the leveling of the playing field; and the implementation of economic policy changes that has provided an improved safety net against market failures.

This chapter focuses on the ancient and premodern investment environment. Here the emphasis is on three areas: the basic investment media of early history; the extreme inequality of the distribution of investment opportunity and benefit; and the surprising sophistication of early investment vehicles, strategies, and purposes.

The modern corporate form is a relatively recent historical phenomenon. Its characteristics—shared ownership, permanent existence, transferability of possession, and limited liability—are the result of an entirely new form of ownership, one that is not necessarily dependent on elite familial or status relations. In order to fully appreciate the distinctly radical nature of this new ownership form, we must understand that for many thousands of years, agricultural land was the primary store of wealth, source of income, and reservoir of gains for investors in ancient and premodern times. From Mesopotamia to Egypt, Greece, and Rome, it was *the* basic investment medium in early civilizations.

While lending was another pillar of investment in premodern times, it was hampered in its development by its capital limitations and the taint of usury. Trade, based on exchange value and growing geographical mobility rather than use value, was the "sleeper" in investment influence and importance. But ultimately it has triumphed in a collective ownership world.

However, although in this chapter we identify precursors to modern forms, we are not hypothesizing causation, nor are we giving a comprehensive account of each society's history. Rather, we want the reader to understand that the arrangement of the investment landscape was historically contingent; the modern system was not necessarily "destined" to be, and there are other ways of organizing and approaching ownership and investment. That said, while there are multiple ways of conducting investment, the very existence of investment—defined as the commitment of resources for future returns—has been a universal phenomenon across history and cultures.

AGRICULTURAL LAND AND ESTATES

In many societies, land was literally intertwined with title, position, command, or rule. The major characteristic of land investors in ancient economies was high economic, social, and political standing. Given that many wealthy members of ancient societies associated agriculture with nobility and commerce or trade with low status, the preference for storing and accumulating wealth in land and estates is not surprising. While not always the most lucrative form of investment, it often bore lower risk than many forms of trade and commerce, and land-owners consequently accepted lower returns than might have been available in other economic activities.

Investment in land was also the primary mechanism for the inter-generational transfer of wealth. For example, in Arrapha in the middle of the second millennium, it was actually illegal to convey land title to anyone other than family members. But as long as motivations exist to bypass public policy, humanity has a way of concocting creative schemes to do so, and there is some evidence of landowners officially adopting prospective buyers in such jurisdictions.[1]

It was typical for elite landowners to avoid direct operating involve-ment even though they controlled the assets being managed. Many of those who owned land had other principal occupations, and pas-sive ownership often became the dominant form of ownership. For example, in the conquered provinces belonging to Athens and Rome, military men often owned land they had neither the skill nor time to manage. Landownership among the ancients was commonly deter-mined by noneconomic factors such as nobility, military rule, and claims to divine right. This policy frequently created a situation where the owners themselves lacked the knowledge to manage their assets and had to draw upon the talent of others to do so. Therefore, elite landowners often hired lower-status people, including slaves, to man-age their estates.

Mesopotamian Agriculture

The historical record on investment management seems to have begun in that cradle of civilization, Mesopotamia, tucked between the Tigris and Euphrates Rivers, now part of present-day Iraq, Syria, Iran, and Turkey. Mesopotamia, simply translated as "land between the rivers" in Greek, hosted an array of different civilizations. Sumer, the southern region of Mesopotamia, was the first widely known civilization, and Sumerian city-states are well known for early inventions, including the wheel and a writing system as early as the fourth millennium B.C. In Mesopotamia much of the land was owned by the temple or the state, even though private property did indeed exist as well, as evidenced by examples of wealthy urban Mesopotamians who were absentee owners of land in the countryside.[2]

As Mesopotamia was settled, temples grew in importance until they were the center of power.[3] Notably, the role of the temples in the north was less dominant than in the south. In terms of state or temple landownership, there were two priorities: first, the land had to be used for agricultural production; second, the land served as compensation for government officials.[4] The scale of these agricultural projects made state ownership advantageous. For instance, the early Sumerians needed to irrigate their land because of inhospitable climate and irregular river flooding. This large-scale effort required the labor of all citizens. By proclaiming the land to be the property of the gods, leaders were able to convince individuals to contribute to the collective labor.[5] It was the holy, and not the holy mina, that underpinned the Mesopotamian economic system at this time.

There is no proof that in these early periods land leases existed in these regions. However, in the third dynasty of Ur, farmers could rent land from the temple or the government.[6] Around 2250–2000 B.C., a strong religious system gave way to a strong state. The tight control of the economy passed from the temples to the government.[7]

Mesopotamia also saw the emergence of public asset management. Temple and state landownership was supported by a rather advanced bureaucracy, which dealt in part with determining when and how public land should be rented. It established provisions and rules to which employees had to adhere, with the objective of reducing fraud. These public investment managers functioned in the city-state of Lagash in Sumer, where there was a surplus of land with superb water supply. This land would be temporarily removed from the public stock to be rented out. Farmers would compensate the governing authority—in silver (called the *mas a.sa.ga*)—for the privilege of farming and for the use of water on the site.[8]

The Akkadian civilization was a rather advanced society that developed around 2330 B.C. and lasted for almost two hundred years. After the fall of the Akkad dynasty and the rise of the third dynasty of Ur, much of the state was partitioned into military governorships, each of which was required to pay the empire a tax known as the *gun mada*.[9] These military officials could structure land management in various ways: the household itself could farm the land with the aid of laborers or slaves, the landowner could hire a local manager who would superintend the cultivation, or the landowner could rent land to peasants.[10]

Babylonia was located in the central portion of the Fertile Crescent, and it was born out of the fusion of the Sumerian and Akkadian societies that had preceded it. Babylonia competed with Assyria, a society focused on expansion and conquest, which was located in the highlands of Mesopotamia. While records indicate that a few private owners acquired fields long before the Old Babylonian period (eighteenth and seventeenth centuries B.C.), as time went on more individuals and families in the south gradually began contracting to buy and bequeath fields as well. The land lease, which had become rare in the earlier Ur III period, became common once again. Written evidence appears widely around 1850 B.C., and the practice may have been widespread even earlier. Historical documents from cities and large towns provide information on the agricultural activities of wealthy citizens. Although it is clear that these landowners could till their own fields, lease their land to tenant farmers, or use slaves or hired laborers, surviving evidence unfortunately fails to show the relative frequency of these various landholding arrangements.[11]

From the Old Babylonian period until the late Persian, land leases became common and there were numerous records of farmland renting. Over time, practices evolved somewhat. The fields that were rented became bigger, for example. Compulsory labor became less common, most likely because this arrangement became prohibitively expensive when the harvest was weak.[12] Therefore, there was a shift toward the use of tenant farmers because the farmers were motivated to maximize production, as a portion of the production was theirs to keep. Further, this framework made it simple for the owner to shift previously untilled land into cultivable fields. This was done by striking agreements whereby the tenant farmer would not be liable for any rent for the first year that a new swath of land was farmed, and the tenant would face only a low rate in the second year, again creating an impetus for assiduousness not present in the salaried structures.[13]

In many ways, the salaried farmer and the tenant farmer structures are the ancient analogues to modern compensation regimes seen in finance, such as the fixed and performance fees levied by money managers today. In the former configuration, the fiduciary is paid no matter how the investments fare, and the principal keeps all the surplus; in the latter, the steward is induced to be more proactive by being granted a share of the return from the land.

Greek Estate Management

Estate management was also important to the Greeks—so much so that it was contemplated in philosophical terms. In the famous work on economics *Oeconomicus*—written in the fourth century B.C. in the Greek tradition of dialogues—Xenophon portrayed a conversation with Socrates about estate management:

> I once heard him [Socrates] discourse on the management of the household as well, in about these words.
> "Tell me, Critoboulus," he said, "is management of the household the name of a certain kind of knowledge, as medicine, smithing, and carpentry are?"
> "It seems so to me, at least," said Critoboulus.
> "Then just as we are at no loss to say what the work of each of these arts is, can we say also what the work of household management is?"
> "It seems, at any rate," said Critoboulus, "that it is the part of a good household manager to manage his own household well."
> "But if someone were to entrust another's household to him," said Socrates, "could he not manage that, if he wanted to, as well as he does his own? For the one who knows carpentry can do equally for another what he does for himself; and so too, presumably, can the skilled household manager."
> "It seems so to me, at least, Socrates."
> "Is it possible, then," said Socrates, "for one who knows this art, even though he happens to have no wealth himself, to manage another's household, just as a builder can build another's house, and earn pay for it?"
> "Yes, by Zeus, and he would earn a lot of pay," said Critoboulus, "if on taking over, he were able to do what's necessary and, in producing a surplus, increase the household."[14]

Given this focus on estate management, it is no surprise that Greek landowners did not farm the land themselves. The views of Ischomachus, another figure in Xenophon's *Oeconomicus*, have been explained by one scholar as follows: "Farming was a most delightful occupation and by no means difficult to master; you left it all to your bailiffs. True it was necessary to be about early, riding around your estate to see that your servants were busy at their tasks. But as soon as the morning inspection was over, the rest of the day was your own and could be employed by a visit to the city, to mingle with other gentlemen of leisure, and to talk to Socrates."[15] As this summary makes clear, Greek landowners were mostly privileged and well-born members of society. Aristotle further describes the extreme social stratification of Greek society: "Not only was the constitution at this time oligarchical in its every respect, but the poorer classes, men, women, and children, were the serfs of the rich." In addition to hiring bailiffs, some wealthy people who owned multiple estates used their slaves both to farm the land and to serve as managers to supervise the work of other slaves. Unlike the Mesopotamians, who had a strong preference for tenant farming, Greek landowners only rarely rented their land.[16]

Common output from the landed estates where cultivation was possible included barley, wheat, vines, figs, and olives as well as animal husbandry like the raising of sheep, goats, and cattle where the land could not be cultivated. In terms of the amount of cultivable land, since only 22 percent of modern Greece is cultivable, it has been surmised that a roughly equivalent proportion existed in ancient times. However, there are some excellent examples of people who engaged in farming for serious investment. For instance, Ischomachus's father ran an early distressed turnaround operation. Namely, he purchased problematic properties, implemented changes to improve them, and sold them to buyers who were happy to own productive land but who would never have purchased it before its repair.[17]

Roman Estate Management

Estate management rose to new heights in ancient Rome as it became more and more common for individuals in the rapidly expanding empire to own a handful of properties in a variety of regions. Investment in real estate was a key driver of wealth for many families in the Eastern Wars period (200–150 B.C.) and in the subsequent Gracchan period (150–80 B.C.). The Roman elite owned a large number of estates, farms, and ranches, whether awarded for military or political services or purchased as investments. Investments in the provinces—Asia, Greece, Gaul, Spain, and Africa—rose in number as the Roman Empire expanded.[18] The Roman elite were often absentee owners, and the management of their assets was an economic priority.[19] While family members often fulfilled this management role, the elite also made use of procurators, financial and property managers, who could oversee rural tracts. Procurators also often managed payments, lending, borrowing, and large purchases.[20] In other cases, financial managers would be the landowner's slaves, and some of the slaves assisted multiple masters and acted as professional managers.[21]

In some cases, members of the power elite assisted one another with these financial management tasks. For example, Cicero, the prominent politician, was known to receive help from Atticus, who was a banker and a noble himself. But Atticus himself was sometimes absent from Rome. In this case, Lucius Cincius would be in charge of Cicero's financial matters. However, there is no evidence of any regular payment for such financial assistance. Some managers did not provide financial services for a fee; rather, they wanted to prove they were capable of such demanding and high-level tasks. For example, Cornelius Nepos explained that Atticus chose to become a procurator in order to prove that although he did not participate in political affairs of the state, it was not because he was indolent but because he preferred other occupations. Atticus provided service not only for Cicero but also for Cato, Hortensius, Aulus Torquatus, and a number of Roman knights.[22]

During the Roman Republic (as in Greece), the estate managers were often slaves or hired freedmen who had been released from slavery. By the time of the Roman Empire, serving as an estate manager— at least as an estate manager for a prominent individual—was a more dignified and honorable position. Consider, for example, the estate of Aurelius Appianus, a councilor of Alexandria in Roman Egypt in the third century A.D.[23] Appianus was an absentee owner of many estates, including one in Arsinoe. A full-time manager by the name of Alypios gave orders to subordinate staff managers (*phrontistai*), who were each in charge of a unit of the Arsinoite estate. These managers were responsible for agricultural operations, maintenance of the estate property, and oversight of the permanent staff based in the area. Important decisions, such as harvest and produce sales, were made by the central administration and sent to the managerial units. Not only did Alypios manage and oversee the operations of the Appianus estate, but he was a large landowner in his own right and was very likely a councilor of Arsinoe. It is interesting to note that the historical record is inconclusive as to whether administrators of the Arsinoite estate were paid a salary. The estate's regular staff members were likely attached to the village in which their managerial unit was located, and the village provided them with a salary. Upper-level independent administrators, however, seem to have received compensation in various other ways, since a salary might have been seen as socially demeaning. Their primary reward was social status and power that derived from the prosperous Appianus estate.[24]

As the Roman Empire grew, other examples of land-based investment management emerged—the *ousiai* in Egypt in the first century A.D. being one of the most compelling. Ousiai were estates in Egypt owned by the emperor, his family, and his associates, and some were even owned by royal women and children. The ousiai generated income through renting out land, operating granaries, bottling wine, producing olive oil, and selling livestock. Ousiai owners tended to live in Rome, therefore entrusting their estate managers to be prudent stewards of the assets with minimal supervision. This is especially remarkable because management of the ousiai was not simple, as the estates were often highly fragmented, with small sectors of land spread out over considerable distances. The ousiai managers were most often freedmen, but in some cases slaves became managers as well, such as a man named Cerinthus who tended to the livestock in an estate in Oxyrhynchus (in upper Egypt south of Cairo). While the evidence is imperfect, Cerinthus may have been sent from Rome to Egypt, likely chosen because of the confidence his master had in him to do the job well without direct oversight.[25]

LENDING AND INTEREST

Along with agriculture and trade, the other historically relevant investment activity was lending. Lending was perceived as an activity of only moderate prestige and acceptability, but it was engaged in, either overtly or quietly, by many wealthy and privileged people. Most of this lending activity was financing for homes, land, and personal consumption, rather than for productive or investment purposes. While large individual loans were often undertaken directly by the elite, broad-scale lending as might be provided by ancient bankers was a low-prestige activity. While it might have been supported by the elite, the process of lending was practiced largely by much lower-ranking classes of society.

Gradually, as wealth came to consist of accumulations of coin, it began to be believed that this wealth should not be allowed to lie idle in the forms of treasures jealously hoarded in the temples or private fortunes locked up in cash boxes. In effect, coinage facilitated investment, and investment in lending came from the demand of borrowers. At the same time, the development of trade and industry drove manufacturers and merchants more and more to look for capital with which to procure materials, labor, or goods in the hope of making a profit from them.[26]

Interest rates varied widely across both time and geography. Sometimes non-interest-bearing loans were made to friends or relatives. On other occasions, particularly in ancient Greece during certain periods of its history, loans bore extraordinarily high interest rates. Often, however, lending was subject to government-established interest rate limits. Lending and interest go hand in hand, and in all of these societies the question of usury became of vital economic and religious importance.

Egyptian Lending

Egypt enjoyed a high degree of financial sophistication. The geography of Egypt, near both Europe and Asia, made it a focal point of international trade, and the flow of goods and money into the area aided in the development of the banking system. Early instruments included the simple letter of credit, whereby a borrower exchanged his liquidity for a promise from a banker so he did not need to endure the risks of theft or loss. These letters of credit appear on clay tablets as far back as 3000 B.C. in Egypt.[27]

Egyptian papyri written in Demotic prove that lending transactions were conducted for the period between 664 B.C. and 30 B.C., although Egyptian lending actually dates back far before this, beginning in the Old Kingdom (which stretched from approximately 2680 B.C. to 2180 B.C.). In terms of composition, Egypt's lending markets involved the supply of not just money but also grain and wine, moving surplus agricultural output to where it was needed.[28]

Lending in the early period relied heavily on the reputation of the borrower. Early borrowers were typically required to swear an oath to the region's patron god or goddess. Furthermore, borrowers were well aware that failure to pay could result in fines for double the amount of the loan and in physical beatings. Considering the pernicious consequences associated with failure to fulfill a covenant, it may be a surprise that there is no evidence for receipts being given to the borrower when he repaid the loan in the early period. Instead, it seems as though the lender would simply hand over the written document when the borrower paid back what he owed, discharging the debtor from any further payments by relinquishing access to the paperwork describing the pledge.[29]

Other cultures influenced Egyptian lending practices as well. For instance, the Persians instituted two consequential structures that influenced Egyptian lending practices: first, the contract was to be kept by the lender (for safekeeping in case enforcement proved necessary due to default); and second, a borrower's children could be used to pay down delinquent debt.[30]

In the third-century Egyptian *chora* (the countryside), bankers tended to be royal administrators or moneychangers working with the government. Despite the high regard these officeholders enjoyed, it was not a lucrative profession in these regions. In the chora, loans often went to individuals short on spendable resources rather than for the establishment and maintenance of new businesses.[31] In other words, the allocation favored consumption rather than investment. In many of the villages, securing a loan involved approaching someone within the community who was widely regarded as trustworthy and financially solvent. That person would, in effect, cosign the loan and agree to become liable in the case of nonpayment. The term for such a person in Demotic translates to "accept the hand."[32] Instead of resorting to credit scores and reporting agencies, these early Egyptian lenders used the social standing of the borrower and his family or his cosigner as the metric for default risk.

The primary term for "interest" in Egyptian Demotic is related to the verb for "to give birth." This linguistic connection is intriguing because the notion of interest being related to the "fecundity of money" also manifested itself in the Greek Aristotelian school with discussions of money's "sterility" and how interest ought not be charged. Interest rates in Egypt tended to be exorbitantly high. According to many of the surviving papyri, when the interest rate was recorded, rates from 50 to 100 percent seem to be the norm. Just as in many other ancient and modern societies, the Egyptian government intervened to cap interest rate. Through the reforms of Bocchoris in the eighth century B.C., the amount of interest collected could not be greater than the principal borrowed. During the reign of the Ptolemies, a maximum of 24 percent per year was instituted.[33]

Over time, Egyptian lending practices evolved away from the simplistic reputation system toward the regular use of collateral. The collateral offered was often one's residence, and at first it was legally unclear when the creditor would be permitted to repossess the collateral and inhabit the home in the case of a failure to pay. The solution to this problem was the development of a system of trusteeship, whereby the two parties signed a "letter of agreement" specifying precisely when ownership of collateral would be lost and establishing the conditions for the transferal of property to be overseen by a neutral third party.[34]

Lending in Ancient Greece

PERVASIVENESS OF LENDING

There are prolific references to lending and credit throughout Greek literature and rhetoric. For instance, the orator Demosthenes mentions credit arrangements some 150 times in his thirty-two extant speeches. Two Greek writers, Alexis and Nicostratus (son of Aristophanes), each wrote a play called *Tokistes*, or *The Usurer*. Plots of several other plays are also related to loans. For example, the dramatist Aristophanes wrote a play called *The Clouds* in which the protagonist goes under Socrates' tutelage to deceive his creditors. In another Aristophanes play, *The Birds*, a character comments on the universal quality of debt, saying to another character, "You were once a man, just like us. And you used to get into debt, just like us. And you liked to get out of paying, just like us." In a fragment from an unidentified play by another Greek poet, Philemon, being debt-free is remarked as the fourth important blessing, following good health, success, and happiness.[35]

More philosophically, the Athenians even thought about debt in metaphorical and religious terms. A widely held opinion was that life is a loan from the gods. An epitaph by the Greek lyric poet Simonides is said to include a line that "we are all owed as a debt to death." In his dialogue *Timaeus*, Plato explains that the gods "borrow" earth, air, fire, and water to create men and so, therefore, human life is part of a debt that has to be repaid.[36]

THE PROTOTYPE OF CREDIT RELATIONS:
INTEREST-FREE CONSUMPTION LOANS

A variety of credit relations coexisted in ancient Greece. The common form for consumption credit was an interest-free friendly loan among neighbors, friends, local businesspeople, and other citizens in general. For investment credit or for consumption credit that failed to be obtained through friendly loans, people would then resort to bankers, who usually made loans at relatively high interest rates and were, for this reason, generally the lenders of last resort.[37]

Among these various levels of credit relations, the interest-free loans seem to be the oldest and the most frequently used among commoners. These interest-free friendly loans evolved from borrowing and lending of tools and small amounts of money among neighbors and friends. In most ancient societies, interest was mostly associated with default risks rather than the opportunity cost of money. Because the two parties to the transaction typically knew each other well and were closely related in many other aspects of their daily lives, there was hardly any perceived need to require interest or a contract for enforcing repayment. Apart from the close interpersonal relations between the lender and the borrower, social norms also helped enforce the repayments. Greek society placed much emphasis on the importance of reciprocity and collaboration among neighbors.[38] For example, the Greek poet Hesiod wrote, "Take fair measure from your neighbor and pay him back fairly with the same measure, or better, if you can; so that if you are in need afterwards, you may find him sure." The small and tight community within a particular city-state thus formed a network of lenders and borrowers familiar with one another and cognizant of the nature of the transaction.[39]

GREEK COMMERCIAL BANKING

Two of the most famous Greek bankers were Pasion, who was said to be the "Rothschild of his day," and Phormion. Pasion was at first a slave for Antisthenes and Archestratus, two men who ran one of the earliest banks in Athens. However, Pasion was eventually freed and later gained control of the bank. Shortly before his death in 369 B.C., he retired from the banking business and rented the bank, along with a workshop, to his former slave and assistant Phormion.[40] Slaves and freedmen like Pasion and Phormion were the majority of employees and managers in the lending business, as banking was against the "work ethic" of the free Athenian citizens. The slaves not only carried out the instructions of their masters but were also able to make discretionary decisions, though some contemporaries expressed concerns about the legal implications.[41]

Both Pasion and Phormion are examples of enterprising individuals who were not originally part of the power elite rising to the rank of the very wealthy. When Pasion died, his total wealth amounted to 70 talents, 20 of which were tied up in landed property and 50 of which were invested in loans.[42] The historical record suggests this amount to be a very large sum, given that an Athenian laborer working five days per week could expect to earn just 1 talent after decades of labor.[43] After Pasion's death, Phormion married Pasion's widow and was appointed guardian to Pasion's younger son, who was not yet an adult. Phormion ran the bank and the workshop for eight years, paying rent to Pasion's estate. In 362 B.C. the younger son of Pasion reached adulthood; Pasion's property then reverted to his family and was divided between his sons.[44] Though Pasion and Phormion never jointly operated the bank, their collaboration was obviously substantial.[45]

In Athens this type of commercial banking activity, where we can see some investment management via partnership agreements, was relatively sparse. The legal framework present in Athens did not suit robust commercial banking because no money was allowed to be lent, for example, either to any ship that did not bring cargo directly to the city or to anyone who was not an Athenian resident.[46] However rare Athenian commercial banking, the collaboration between Pasion and Phormion demonstrates a remarkable degree of similarity to later forms of banking partnerships.

MARITIME LOANS

Maritime loans were actively used in ancient Greece, a society that thrived on its ability to take to the seas and trade with neighboring regions. The primary structural distinction between Greek maritime loans and modern lending is the absorption of the risk of catastrophic loss into the repayment terms. Today insurance markets exist to buffer the destruction or loss of assets, but for the Greeks, it was simply a natural part of these maritime, or bottomry, loans. In particular, in the case of sinking or shipwreck, the vessel operator was not held liable and the loss was borne in full by the lenders. On many occasions, the lender would accompany the voyage, and it is certainly apparent why the lender would not need to be repaid in the event of sinking in such instances.[47]

Maritime loans had the potential to be extraordinarily profitable for those supplying the funds. Typically, a rate of 22.5 or 30 percent was possible for voyages between Athens and Istanbul, depending on whether Athens was at war. Many lenders tried to position themselves potentially to earn on two loans per season, and bringing in more than 100 percent return was possible for the most aggressive suppliers of credit.[48]

GREEK REAL ESTATE LOANS

In the three centuries between 500 B.C. and 200 B.C., the region of Attica employed a remarkable system of indicating when real estate was serving as collateral for loans. The system used what were called *horoi*, or stones placed on the property that marked off the extent of the parcel. On these horoi would be written the terms and the amount of the loan so citizens would be aware immediately if the property had been offered to another party in relation to a debt contract. Around the year 450 B.C., a village in Attica requested that horoi be put on all properties of people to whom it had made loans, presumably as a method of protecting itself from attempts to transfer property illicitly and avoid obligations to the lender. In light of their importance, one would not be even remotely surprised that the penalties for altering the inscriptions on the horoi were extremely large.[49]

Today real estate transactions generally involve title searches to ensure that there are no liens or mortgages unaccounted for at the office of the municipality or deed registry, but in this period the horoi could serve as a rapid alternative to make such a determination.

Lending in Ancient Rome

In ancient Rome, equity finance flourished to a much greater degree. In addition, a noteworthy difference between the Greek and Roman banking systems was that Roman bankers innovated in their business by managing property for their clients under special mandates since their books kept the client's financial information, not unlike investment management services that many modern institutions offer.[50] This suggests that the Romans were actively practicing third-party investment management in a number of ways.

In Rome, even though interest-free loans continued to exist, the proportion was smaller.[51] In addition, compared to Greece and many other ancient societies, Rome seems to have been a society comparatively friendlier to financial activities. Not only do we see more complicated financial relationships, in addition to traditional banking, but also the financiers achieved a somewhat higher social status. Some bankers managed to raise their sons to become senators, indicating that they enjoyed much more social respect and acceptance than did their lower-class Greek counterparts.[52]

Lending money at interest was a business that seems to have been very profitable. The ancient upper class, including many senators and knights, participated in this business for centuries.[53] Noblemen who were politically ambitious, like Caesar and Antony, often were significant borrowers in order to finance their campaigns to gather support among eligible voters or otherwise elevate themselves politically. They were willing to pay a high price for this service, up to four times the legal cap of 12 percent interest. Those with spare capital readily participated in this scheme—bankers, for example, were able to loan not only their own money but also that of private individuals.[54]

Lending in China

Lending in China can be traced back thousands of years. Some of the earliest records of credit relations come from *The Rites of Zhou*, a Chinese classic about the political and moral systems of the Western Zhou dynasty (eleventh century B.C. to 771 B.C.), which mentions principles governing credit systems at the national level and among private persons. The book also mentions a governmental agency called *Quanfu* that lent at usurious rates. By the time of the following Spring and Autumn period (Chun-qiu, 770 B.C. to 476 B.C.) and Warring States period (Zhan-guo, 475 B.C. to 221 B.C.), lending was already flourishing and books of the time include detailed examples of usurious lending practices by aristocrats.[55]

For most of Chinese history, there were three major types of lenders: governments, monks in the temples, and private businesspeople, all of whom played important roles in the lending business. The government's participation in lending dates back far into antiquity.

The Chinese government was not particularly troubled by usury, and the loans it made were usually at very high interest rates and were very often forced on the borrowers. For example, in the West Han dynasty (202 B.C.–A.D. 9), people who did not need loans were forced to borrow at extraordinary rates. During the reign of the founding emperor of the Tang dynasty (A.D. 618–907), the state dispatched officials to make loans at 10 percent with profits helping to support large deficits.[56]

In the Song dynasty (A.D. 960–1297), the famous statesmen Wang Anshi enacted laws regarding the use of state-administered loans to subsidize agricultural production. Peasants borrowed in the spring to buy seed and repaid the loans after the harvest. It turned out, however, that in order to make money from this business, many local governments forced the peasants to borrow. The state did try to suppress usury for the sake of social stability but never seriously enforced these policies. In A.D. 701, the female emperor Wu Zetian of the Tang dynasty ruled that interest payments should not exceed the original amount of debt. This rule lasted, though not continuously, into the Qing dynasty (1644–1921). It was, however, often violated in practice, especially in state lending. For some time in the Qing dynasty interest rates were capped at 3 percent, but this rule was not strictly observed either.[57]

In most cases, governments operated lending businesses to generate revenues, sharing similar motivations with private lenders. For example, in the Song dynasty, the government earmarked specific funding for purchasing gifts and treating guests, and officials used these funds to lend and to open *Zhiku*, a type of lending institution. The government also inspected the inheritance of orphans and pooled their assets into public funds to help them preserve and manage the assets. These funds were called *Jianjiao-ku*. When the orphans reached adulthood, the government would then return their assets. People could borrow from the funds of *Jianjiao-ku*, and the interest was used to support the orphans.[58]

Monks in Buddhist temples were another group of active lenders. Their lending facility was often called *Changshengku* (long-life bank) or *Siku* (temple bank). The temple's banking business was supported by the idea of *Wujinzang* in Chinese Buddhism and was enabled by the surplus wealth accumulated in the temples. The phrase *Wujinzang* has its root in the Buddhist sacred text Vimalakirti sutra and was partly interpreted, since the Liang dynasty, as an encouragement for the Buddhist temples to gather wealth in order to help the needy. The temples gathered wealth from government funding, private donations, and sale of products produced from temple lands and temple properties. In some periods with incessant wars, people were so eager to join the temple communities that the temples became rich enough to invite jealousy and hatred from the emperors, which resulted in crackdowns on Buddhism. The monks were not shy about practicing usury as long as there was robust demand.[59]

Private persons engaged in lending included aristocrats, government officials, landlords, and businesspeople. They operated lending institutions commonly known as Zhiku or *Diandang*, although there are many names that refer to these financial institutions, varying with the dynasty in which they existed, the size of the loans, and the type of people running these businesses. Initially, their businesses consisted mostly of making loans against collateral. In the Song dynasty, their functions in accepting deposits and conducting money changing were substantially improved. During the Song dynasty, structures similar to joint-stock partnerships were also used for operating lending businesses. For example, a book written in the Song dynasty called *Literary Works by Mr. Huang of Jinhua* documents fifty people putting up capital to operate a lending business jointly. Besides the joint-stock partnership in which all parties provided capital, there were also partnerships in which some parties put up capital while others provided labor. The profit was shared by requiring the party without capital to pay a fixed interest, rather than by proportionately dividing the gains. This type of partnership was found in lending practices as early as the East Han dynasty and was extended to lending institutions like the Zhiku during the Song dynasty.[60]

In addition to lending based on land values with repayment dependent on crop production, Chinese lending increasingly migrated to the collateralized form of pawnshop lending, namely, loans collateralized by portable assets, almost always clothing. It is interesting that there was often little correlation between the amounts lent and the value of the collateral, implying either that loans were made with a variety of loan-to-value ratios or that estimations of the value of the collateral were not terribly precise. Default on a loan meant, of course, that the pledged goods would be forfeited. With the large volume of transactions that developed over time, pawnshops began, in effect, to become somewhat like a primitive form of bank.[61]

Chinese pawnshops seem to have dated from the last quarter of the fifth century A.D., initially restricted to Buddhist monasteries.[62] Beginning in the Tang dynasty, laypersons also began to enter this business, eventually in the Ming dynasty completely replacing the pawnshop activity of Buddhist monks and starting a phenomenal rise in the number of pawnshops.[63]

Lending in Japan

Japan had rather sophisticated money-lending institutions starting as early as the thirteenth century in Kyoto. These moneylenders were called *doso*, which is etymologically derived from a root word that references the storehouses that held deposits. The moneylenders operated almost as pawnbrokers; that is, loans were granted when items of value were presented as collateral.[64] Japanese money-lending practices were extremely widespread: an expert on Japanese medieval money-lending has noted that virtually all people, regardless of social class, comprehended and used credit in their daily lives.[65]

Through a means not entirely unlike the notion of usury in the West, the Japanese regulated interest rates in the *Bakufu* decrees based largely on the collateral surrendered for the loan. For instance, in return for silk or instruments, a borrower would receive a loan at an interest rate of 5 percent monthly; but in return for weapons or vases, the borrower would pay 6 percent monthly. These regulations were somewhat dynamic, however, with the original decree in 1431, new goods populating the lists in 1459 and 1520, and updates made again in 1530 and 1546.[66]

Many of the moneylenders had or achieved clerical status; in one list of lenders from 1425 to 1426, no more than 30 percent were laypersons. Further, many women were moneylenders as well. During the Muromachi shogunate, women performed a wide array of money-lending tasks, including suing those who did not repay their debts. One missionary named Luis Frois wrote about how women had the right to possess property and how women even lent their own funds to their husbands in the 1500s.[67]

USURY

World Views on Investment and Usury

Throughout ancient economic history, religion, morality, and ethics, as perceived by the leaders of the ancient world, played a substantial role in investment and commerce. This is not to say that the behavior of owners, investors, and businesspeople was necessarily more virtuous than it is in the twenty-first century. Rather, religious views, sometimes not aligned with the optimal course of action financially, were close to the surface of all economic activities undertaken in ancient civilizations. This was particularly true with respect to lending, which was usually burdened with moralistic concepts, sometimes unfortunate and economically counterproductive. As pointed out later in this chapter, blanket concepts of "usurious" lending often failed to recognize such now-basic issues as the time value of money and credit risk.

In addition, social standing and status frequently entered into economic transactions in ways that current civilizations ignore or explicitly reject. Further, at times religious groups and orders engaged in commercial activity in ways that are much less common today, bringing concepts of theology and morality to the forefront of economic dealings in ways that are no longer considered to be pertinent.

The historical record seems to indicate a widespread disapproval and censure of lending money at interest. However, this remarkable history of disapproval, restriction, condemnation, and punishment for charging interest, which in some cases focused on prevailing conceptions of excessive interest rates and in other cases involved rejection of all interest charges at any level, seems to ignore a basic fact of economic life: interest rates can properly reflect creditor risk and time value. The advent of laws and regulations against usury has been a striking and probably destructive element for investment. While there are circumstances that argue against permitting powerful lenders to take advantage of relatively weak and defenseless borrowers, modern Westerners do not usually object to incorporating proper credit and time value risk.

In our modern worldview, "time value of money" should have a price. Providing money to another person or organization means that the lender gives up access to that money for a period of time and accepts the risk of loss. Furthermore, the fairness of that price cannot be measured exclusively in proportion to the level of interest charged. We know from experience that widely divergent interest rates in different time periods, for different debt maturities, levels of credit exposure, and rates of inflation can all be fair. High rates might, in certain circumstances, be fairer than lower rates when considerations of fairness are expanded to include not just the borrower but the lender as well.

Over the last 300 years or so, this impediment has diminished in the West and in much of Asia, but it has continued to be a fact of life in Islamic societies, necessitating in some cases dramatically different forms of banking and lending, especially in consumer and small business contexts.

Historical and Religious Views of Usury

In ancient Mesopotamia, there were few official restrictions on interest rates. Interest rates usually varied from 5.5 to 25 percent.[68] However, we know of an Akkadian text saying, "Give the 140 shekels which are still outstanding from your own money but do not charge interest between us—we are both gentlemen!"[69] This text shows that although official interest rate controls were not established in that period, people already held the view that charging interest was ungentlemanly.

In ancient Greece, there were no legal limitations on interest rates either. The parties were allowed to agree on interest rates by themselves, and the interest rate was mostly determined by the loan's risk. In practice, interest rates in Greece reached 12 to 18 percent. In moral terms, usury—as in ancient Mesopotamia—was held in abhorrence. For instance, Aristotle held the view that money was created to serve the purposes of exchange, not for increasing wealth. He thought that money should be naturally "barren" and that it would be absurd for money to breed money and grow through a loan.[70] This view was later adopted by Thomas Aquinas and the Scholastic school.[71]

In ancient Rome, usury was treated as theft and frequently caused disturbances.[72] In 384 B.C. the 12 percent cap was revived by the Tribunes of the People, and then ten years later the limit was reduced to 6 percent. By 342 B.C., all interest rates were prohibited. As a result, lenders were reluctant to finance businesses as they had in the past; trade was disrupted, with wide-ranging economic consequences. In the sixth century, during the reign of Emperor Justinian, the Eastern Roman Empire restored the cap level to 4 percent.[73]

Christianity and Usury

The Catholic Church has had a long and complicated relationship with the notion of usury, manifested many times in Catholic canon. The Bible is quite clear and repetitive on the prohibitions against usury. Ezekiel 18:8 reads, "He [the righteous man] has not exacted usury, nor taken any increase, but has withdrawn his hand from iniquity, and executed true judgment between man and man." In Exodus 22:25, the practitioner sees the sentiment reiterated: "If you lend money to any of My people who are poor among you, you shall not be like a moneylender to him; you shall not charge him interest." This tenet survives into the New Testament, where the book of Luke directs its readers to refrain from charging interest even to one's adversaries: "But love your enemies, do good, and lend, hoping for nothing in return; and your reward will be great."[74]

It seems as though religious mandates in the early years of Christianity were consistent with these passages. At the Synod of Elvira in 306, the Church issued Canon 20, which read, "If any clergy are found engaged in usury, let them be censured and dismissed. If a layman is caught practicing usury, he may be pardoned if he promises to stop the practice. If he continues this evil practice, let him be expelled from the church." Shortly thereafter, at the Synod of Arles in 314, a similar decree was made.[75] In 325, the Council of Nicea proclaimed usury by clergy forbidden on the basis of Psalm 15. Saint Ambrose, one of the four original doctors of the Catholic Church who lived in the fourth and fifth centuries, supposedly decreed that usury should be permitted only for borrowers so nefarious that it would not be a crime to kill them. Charlemagne in the early ninth century proscribed the practice for all people and defined it so widely as to include all lending transactions "where more is asked than is given." There is even evidence of usurers being excommunicated in the ninth century.[76]

The outlawing of usury had not only economic but also cultural aspects, one of which was likely the fueling of anti-Semitic attitudes because Jews were often engaged in lending.[77] Catholics, who were not permitted to lend so freely, were less willing and able to supply loans than were the Jews, who were bound more by such provisions as those in Deuteronomy 23:19–20: "You shall not charge interest to your brother—interest on money or food or anything that is lent out at interest. To a foreigner you may charge interest, but to your brother you shall not charge interest."

Since usury regulations often capped interest rates far below their market equilibrium, the demand for loans far exceeded the supply. In order to compete for funds, the borrowers came up with many clever ways to get round the concept of usury. The simplest way is that the borrowers would give the lenders some "voluntary" gifts, in reality forced loans.[78] In other cases, a loan could be structured as a "repurchase agreement" with the borrower selling goods to the lender and buying them back at higher prices, sometimes with third-party involvement to disguise the nature of the sale.[79] Around the thirteenth century, usury came to exist alongside a somewhat similar, but this time legal, concept, *interisse*, which was revived in the medieval period from Roman law. Whereas the crime of usury centered on the lender making gain from a loan, interisse was a means for lenders to limit losses and allowed lenders to collect interisse due to defaults and late payments.[80] It was a fine line to walk, and there is some evidence of abuse. In some areas, "fictitious late payments became an accepted if disingenuous way of circumventing usury laws."[81] Equity finance was another prominent way of getting around usury laws.

With the rise in wealth that paralleled the cultural blossoming of the Renaissance, the larger banking houses took advantage of doctrinal "loopholes," allowing them to expand their business operations while still conforming to official Church doctrine. This resulted in the unequal imposition of punishment for usury on pawnbrokers and small moneylenders, who did not adapt such sophisticated banking techniques that would allow them to avoid officially usurious practices. While the small players were subject to these usury campaigns, the merchant banks with international connections were actually accepted by and worked with the Church itself. The moral issues were sometimes vague, however, leading to occasional doubts and confusion. For instance, when Cosimo de' Medici expressed concern that some of the bank's operations could potentially be considered usurious by God, the pope granted a papal bull saying that funding the monastery of San Marco could help bring him absolution.[82]

During the Renaissance, enforcement of usury laws in many other places also became much weaker, and disguise was unnecessary. In Venice, for example, lenders openly charged interest rates on loans. When Church pressure increased in the fourteenth century, the Venetian authorities interpreted usury as an excessive rate of interest that would be exploitive of the borrower.[83] In the Spanish city of Lérida, charging interest was an accepted practice from the mid-twelfth century and was legalized in 1217.[84] In Champagne, the payment of interest on debt was an acceptable practice so long as the interest was less than the lawful rate ceiling.[85]

Under the influence of the Protestant Reformation, usury laws were mostly replaced by interest rate ceilings in areas no longer under the authority of the Catholic Church.[86] For example, in sixteenth-century England, following the king's break with the Catholic Church in the late Tudor period, strict regulations on interest rates previously imposed by the Catholic Church became much looser and public opinion was liberalized. The Act of 1545 allowed lenders to charge up to 10 percent interest, and money-lending activity increased substantially. While it was repealed in 1552, the Elizabethan Act of 1571 once again allowed lending at 10 percent. With fewer restrictions on interest rates, activities of financial intermediaries grew rapidly.[87]

However, the influence of the concept of usury was still strong and lasting. Though fewer and fewer people continued to support a total ban on interest rates, there remained long debates, often among economists and economic philosophers in the eighteenth century, about whether interest rates should be set by a free market or be regulated with caps. In *The Wealth of Nations*, Adam Smith supported a cap on interest rates at around 5 percent. Smith feared that higher rates of 8 to 10 percent would mean that most of the debt would be issued to what he called "prodigals and projectors" (speculators), as few others would be willing to take on debt at such a rate. He believed that without such a cap on interest rates, the prodigals and projectors would outbid more rational economic agents, and as a result defaults and resource misallocation would be pervasive. Jeremy Bentham, however, argued against Smith from a laissez-faire perspective, pointing out that no rational person will purposefully take loans to harm himself. If a borrower thinks the interest rate is too high, he will not accept such a bargain.[88]

In 1744 Francesco Scipione, the Marquess of Maffei, wrote an influential work that suggested lending at moderate rates should not be illegal. Such an assertion was condemned by Pope Benedict XIV in an encyclical, *Vix Pervenit: On Usury and Other Dishonest Profit*, in 1745.[89] The encyclical stressed, in the scholastic spirit,

> The nature of the sin called usury has its proper place and origin in a loan contract. This financial contract between consenting parties demands, by its very nature, that one return to another only as much as he has received. The sin rests on the fact that sometimes the creditor desires more than he has given. Therefore he contends some gain is owed him beyond that which he loaned, but any gain which exceeds the amount he gave is illicit and usurious.[90]

This exchange made clear the opposition between those who judged lending at interest to be immoral and those who viewed charging interest as commercially necessary to ensure the supply of finance. Just decades later, in the early nineteenth century, the Church adopted a view similar to that espoused by Scipione and ruled that lending at interest was not a sin provided the rates were moderate.[91]

Islamic Societies and Usury

In the present day, some very mild regulations on interest rates still exist in countries like the United States, but Islamic culture retains the strictest prohibitions on charging interest. In Islamic societies, interest is called *riba*, meaning "increase" or "expansion" in reference to the earnings of the lender.[92] Like the Bible, the Qur'an explicitly bars followers from engaging in riba: Chapter 4, Verse 161, for example, states, "That they took riba, though they were forbidden; and that they devoured men's substance wrongfully. We have prepared for those among them who reject faith, a grievous punishment."[93]

To be clear, Islamic societies are not averse to profit, for Muhammad himself was a merchant and was known for being an honest and trustworthy businessman.[94] Chapter 2, Verse 275, of the Qur'an reads, "But Allah hath permitted trade and forbidden usury."[95] In fact, there is evidence suggesting that the Islamic banning of riba has only shifted how investments were structured, and many of the same activities persisted with simple organizational reworking. For instance, before

Islam, some Arab pagans (for example, those in the Quraysh tribe) engaged in trade enterprises, journeying with goods from one region to sell in others. Before the advent of Islam, these ventures relied on loans so that traders could procure large quantities of goods in one area before selling them at their final destination. After Islam, instead of extending loans, the financiers just took more direct stakes in the project so that they could share in profits rather than receive the illegal riba.[96] To some, the acceptability of profits on nonlending investments but the prohibition of interest seems quite arbitrary.

That said, there are several reasons the Islamic world insists on maintaining this principle. First, there is the long-lasting concern that interest would exploit the borrowers, who are often poor people, whereas the lenders are often richer. Second, some Islamic scholars think that income from interest payments decreases the working incentives of the creditor, since the creditor would find it easy to live just on the interest. Such a tendency is deemed undesirable for increasing the society's productivity. Third, there is a belief that if interest is illegal, people will abstain from borrowing and squandering money and will live with honor and respect.[97]

Many present Islamic societies have managed to do what seems almost unthinkable to the Westerner: establish interest-free banking institutions. The first full-scale modern interest-free bank was established in Malaysia in the mid-1940s; it was harmonized with Sharia, but it was unsuccessful financially. A larger interest-free banking institution began in the Nile Delta in Egypt in 1963, called the Mit Ghamr Savings Bank. Mit Ghamr flourished as a no-interest bank until the National Bank of Egypt and Central Bank of Egypt took over in 1967 and established the use of riba into operations at Mit Ghamr. Not until a few years later, in 1971–1972, did no-interest banks return to prominence when President Anwar Sadat founded the Nasser Social Bank, which operated entirely on an Islamic system, including the belief in interest-free banking.[98]

Asian Societies and Usury

In more religious Asian societies and countries, usury was similarly objected to but often to a significantly lesser degree. Usury regulation in India evolved in much the same way such regulations did in

Europe, moving toward a more moderate and relative view of lending and interest. The Vedic texts of ancient India (2000–1400 B.C.) had an all-encompassing definition of usury and identified any party who received interest at all as a usurer, or *kusidin*. Sutra texts (700–100 B.C.) and many of the Buddhist Jatakas (600–400 B.C.) were consistent with this interpretation and in their teachings began to cast a negative view of usury as a practice. By the second century A.D., however, the standard for judging usury became relative. In the *Laws of Manu*, usury occurred when loans were made at an excess over the legal rate.[99]

In ancient China, however, usury did not appear to be strictly prohibited or seriously sanctioned. A mostly secular society, Chinese culture was not constrained by religious codes regarding the immorality of usury. Therefore, governments, monks, and wealthy individuals often made loans at high interest, with the government even at times forcing people to borrow in order to raise revenue.

Contemporary Views of Usury

Currently, credit markets now mostly operate free of religious criteria, and this has created more economically appropriate pricing of borrowing in today's sophisticated markets. Overall, even though usury laws never entirely ruled out commercial lending, they did have substantial influence on the development of the financial system. In raising the transaction cost of lending and suppressing the growth of debt financing, usury implicitly encouraged equity financing and innovative business contracts and structures in societies that took strong stances against the practice.[100]

In recent decades, attitudes toward usurious interest rates seem to have changed completely—at times, it may appear that an insufficient premium and an unduly relaxed attitude is being taken toward higher-risk and lower-quality borrowers. The same has not been true, however, in consumer (as opposed to corporate and institutional) lending. Consumer credit continues to use rates that might be considered excessive, except for the inefficient size and high credit risk of these loans. Words such as *subprime* and the use of excessive leverage designate very risky types of lending, which in strained economic circumstances have led to large losses.

TRADE AND COMMERCE

Historically, trade was the riskiest form of investment of the three major forms in the ancient world, particularly long-distance and maritime trade. Returns could be very high, but risk of loss was often very great. In addition, trade, like the craft production of goods, was often left to outsiders and the lowborn and therefore rarely involved members of the elite, although they may have invested in maritime trade ventures.

While investment sophistication grew steadily from ancient Mesopotamia to the growth of the Roman Empire, much of this knowledge was lost or discarded in the medieval period. Around A.D. 1000, Europe began to emerge into a period of economic growth and modernization. The first steps toward urbanization and increasing commerce were demographic and agricultural. In order to support population and commercial growth, reclaiming the productivity of the land to create food surpluses and organizing the population to manage a sustainable form of agriculture were essential factors.[101]

In the eleventh century, a recovery in population, sustained by an agricultural recovery, set in motion a transition from investment leadership in agriculture to investment leadership in trade. In other words, the merchant began to innovate and develop more rapidly than the landowner. While still not the largest sector of the European economy, commerce grew vigorously, thus shifting the base of economic power closer to trade than it had been in the past. Merchants became increasingly dominant, not only with respect to the old agricultural leadership but with respect to the craftsman and the modest beginnings of industry as well.[102] This historical shift from agriculture to trade was a key precursor to the much later Industrial Revolution, which in turn heralded an economic shift into investment as a global economic engine. However, while the Dark Ages interrupted the development of investment and trade, it is important to understand the longer history of trade and commerce, as it set the stage for much later development.

Early Trade in the West

Even while social and commercial dealings and a basic division of labor were fundamental aspects of all ancient civilizations, philosophical systems that denigrated trade and its practitioners existed alongside these economic activities in some Western and Middle Eastern cultures. In fact, the philosophical ideal of a totally self-sufficient family unit had become a fiction and had been replaced by monetized transactions as early as the fourth-century B.C. in Athens.[103] Aristotle himself lavished considerable thought on the meanness of trading mentalities, with much anguishing over the merit of use value of goods and exchange value, which he considered a much less noble or meritorious basis for judging the intrinsic value of possessions.[104] While today we tend to reject these distinctions, it must be recognized that many ancient economies were not market economies, in which the exchange value becomes more dominant and commonplace in trade. A substantial number of transactions in these ancient economies were between people in a single, closed system where the provider of a good was transacting with a single related party as the buyer of that good.[105]

The documentation of trade in ancient Mesopotamia, even four or five thousand years ago, is remarkable, particularly because it was not limited to conventional trade transactions but also included activities that constitute investment in trading and commercial resources and systems.[106] Mesopotamian trade also shows extensive evidence of some governmental control and fairly elaborate bookkeeping, even of a rudimentary double-entry form that is generally not thought to have formally emerged until millennia later in Renaissance Italy. Evidence also indicates considerable activity by agents working on behalf of the king to acquire and transport goods for use by the royal family and the government.[107]

Trade in ancient Greece, Rome, and the Middle East was devoted to three main categories: foodstuffs such as grains, olives, and wine; high-value items such as decorative wear and wares; and extensive requirements to support military operations in far-flung locations. The location of many leading ancient civilizations on or near the Mediterranean Sea was more than fortuitous. While seafaring was limited to some extent by seasonality and the perils of piracy (until the large-scale suppression of piracy by the Romans in the first century B.C.), long-distance transportation over land in ancient times was much more inefficient and dangerous. The Mediterranean provided an invaluable reservoir of benign climate, rich resources, efficient and hospitable living, and most of all effective transportation. The Mediterranean and proximate waterways meandered along the territories of most Western and Near Eastern civilizations and wove them together for communication, trade, and conquest.[108] The transition from the Roman Republic to the Roman Empire spurred the development of a market economy with large transactions and distant trade across its vast, then mostly peaceful, expanses of territory.[109]

In the Middle Ages, beginning around the tenth century, more modern forms of trade began to be established and merchants began to conduct their long-distance trade at levels of organization and sophistication not seen before. Their culture was more peripatetic, economically astute, and detached from old agricultural and feudal norms. For example, it was difficult to place the new class of traveling merchant in the structure of slavery, selfdom, and control by the nobility. Merchants were not quite elite, but they were not obviously unfree either. The adventurousness and imagination of these merchants often garnered them wealth and influence despite their historical "odor" to the traditional landed nobility and the conservative Church.[110]

During this time, cities flourished as centers of trade, culture, and prosperity, not to mention safety and security. In fact, the emergence of cities meant the emergence of freedom for many individuals. City residents, called "burghers," were generally freed from serfdom after one year and one day, and therefore more and more serfs became free. The emergence of these new citizens led to the formation of guilds and merchant groups that challenged the old nobility. The management of the city and its taxes and tolls began to evolve into a municipal government supported and run by its citizens. Civil and criminal law also evolved in the medieval city, sometimes overly harsh but nominally more equal in treatment.[111] The intertwining development of the Commercial Revolution and cities became forces for modernism, freedom, and equality.

Italian City-States and Their Merchant Banks

By the tenth century, international trade and commerce began to emerge in several areas of southern Europe. Among the key participants in this Commercial Revolution were the Italian city-states, particularly Genoa, Venice, and, somewhat later, Florence.[112]

When the Commercial Revolution was born, the seeds of a new but basic form of capitalism were sown. Occasional or periodic trade fairs gave way to continuous commerce, including more sophisticated retail, wholesale, financial, and even manufacturing activities.[113] Trade in the Commercial Revolution also had a maritime flavor. The active port cities, first Genoa and Venice and ultimately others, experienced an explosion of trade and other commercial activities. This gave a distinct advantage to a port city in the development of trade beginning in the thirteenth century, one that, astonishingly, still has relevance in the twenty-first century, even if the leading participants have changed dramatically.[114]

To support these maritime trading activities, which required capital for the financing of cargoes and inventories as well as insuring risks, the role of merchant banks as financiers and investors became of supreme importance. Italian merchant banks aided the propagation of the Commercial Revolution, both in Italy and across Europe. The best known of these banks included the Florentine banks of Bardi, Peruzzi, and, of course, Medici. Each of these banks bore family names, and all of them became currency vendors, moneylenders, providers of bills of exchange, maritime voyage insurers, and in many cases sponsors of light manufacturing and other commercial enterprises.

The merchant banks were innovators in a variety of ways. In many respects they became the first to experiment widely with organizational structure. The Bardi and Peruzzi were geographically dispersed organizations yet remained organized around a single, integrated corporate structure and financial pool. In these banks, capital was divided into shares owned by members of the families and as well as outsiders. Sometimes outsiders technically had control of these businesses by owning more than one-half of the capital. In practice, however, a managing partner, usually but not necessarily a member of the family, took leadership of the bank. As time went on, more sophisticated formats began to emerge. By the time of the Medici in the fifteenth century, the widespread use of separate partnerships represented an attempt by a banking family to limit its risk from branch to branch and to draw leadership and a sense of responsibility from the managing partner at each branch more effectively. In this way, the managing partner participated in the successes or disappointments of the local bank even if he did not have much, or any, capital at risk.[115] The Medici bank, which operated with this decentralized structure, had investments beyond banking, including wool and silk factories. While these investments are important as evidence of the bank's diversified investment interests, they were never comparable to the size of the Medici's banking activities.[116]

The growth and diversification of these early banking and investment partnerships depended heavily on the commercial and merchant networks developed by the traders and businesspeople of the Italian city-states. These networks and their concomitant financing arrangements spread around the Mediterranean, into northern and eastern Europe and the Middle East.[117] While the merchant banks did have an understanding of diversification, many of these networked loans and investments involved very real risks; these merchant banks were not too big or too strong to fail, and there is no evidence that any government felt it had a responsibility to the bankers or their own economy to insulate these merchant banks against failure. A variety of risks may have accounted for the banks' eventual decline or failure. These included significant credit risks in certain loans and investments, the limitations of family-dominated organizations that were small by modern standards, and the impact of economic cycles or crises.[118]

The Italian merchant banks were often active in lending money to governments and sovereigns, although the outcomes of these credit relationships were often unsatisfactory and occasionally disastrous. For instance, large loans to England's King Edward III led to the mid-fourteenth-century collapse of the Bardi bank in Florence, which was, in its day, a larger bank than the Medici bank a century later. Even with the high risk of disaster, these lending relationships had more at stake than simply a desire on the part of the bankers to realize profits from interest returns provided by foreign kings and governments. These large loans also paved the way for important access to government contracts and other commercial concessions for the benefit of Florentine merchants, for example. In addition, since the Italian city-states had military, and therefore coercive, power, the political and business influence of loans to enterprises and even governments became an important political weapon. Of course, as is true even in the twenty-first century, the leverage of a foreign or even domestic lender over a sovereign state or ruler is distinctly limited.[119]

Trade in Japan

The relative isolation of Japan in comparison to the largely maritime trade societies in Europe and western Asia meant that Japan's rate of international exchange and mobility was not comparable to that of many Greek, Turkish, and Italian cities. Long-distance trade conducted by a class of mobile merchants drove the development of the investment partnership, and there was simply much less such activity in Japan. However, during the Middle Ages, there was indeed excess capital and financial sophistication in Japan, even if long-distance trade was a small factor.

For instance, the development of a remarkably sophisticated technological, business, and trade complex is illustrated by the oil dealers of Oyamazaki, a region south of and close to Kyoto, during the thirteenth to fifteenth centuries. The use of oil at that time was primarily for illumination. These dealers had to grapple successfully with issues of raw materials supply, extraction and manufacturing, distribution, and transportation. They also engaged in capitalistic activities such as commercial combinations and acquisitions as some members of the industry attempted to consolidate with others to dominate the trade. There is even evidence of prosperous oil dealers moving stored wealth into new investments in land and lending.[120]

The Japanese exhibited substantial financial sophistication again in the sixteenth and seventeenth centuries, with a rather large increase in the quantity of trade conducted within Japan's borders. In Osaka, for example, those who traded and brokered commodities soon began to specialize; for instance, traders who once simply traded fish now brokered desiccated fish, freshly caught fish, or just fluvial fish. As is typically the case, brokering a product, holding inventories, and meeting logistical demands arising out of a transaction required financing, and the boom in trade generated growth in this area as well.[121]

The development of financing in Japan can be seen in the trade centered on dealing with the taxes levied on the *daimyo* (a feudal ruler) by the *shogun* (the commander in chief). The tax was collected in cash, and financiers (*kuramoto*) often extended loans to the daimyo. When the daimyo required an even more substantial outlay of capital, he tapped groups of merchants for funds whereby each merchant would contribute a small part of the overall loan value and share some of his risk. There is evidence that families such as the Konoike accumulated vast wealth from daimyo loans.[122]

Beyond loan activity, trade developed through the efforts of the rice traders at the Dojima Rice Exchange in Osaka, who also drove the evolution of a vital instrument—a form of a futures contract—that would later bring improved stability to modern commodities markets. In the early eighteenth century, rice certificates were exchanged that entitled the holder to remove a contracted quantity of rice from a storehouse. Instead of transacting in physical property, the Japanese of this period were well acquainted with the concept of a separate "claim" on property that could be kept and transacted more easily. Also by this time, the Japanese city of Osaka had begun to outstrip Kyoto in commercial and financial activity. The vendors in Osaka became accustomed to dealing in short-term credit contracts on a regular basis, with promissory notes (*tegata*) becoming prominent. These tegata were generally collateralized by real estate or deposits made at some institution.[123]

Foreign Investment in Japan

Japan's relationship with foreign direct investment is fairly nuanced and interesting. It is well known that Japan had largely withdrawn from the outside world during a long period of seclusion (*sakoku*), but the effects this had on foreign investment in Japan is less understood. Japan was, in fact, quite open to the outside world until the early seventeenth century.[124]

The East India Company was involved in Japan for some time, and there are rather amusing anecdotes that convey the difficulty with principal-agent issues faced by those investing their savings from abroad in Japan some centuries ago. These include the tale of a certain Richard Wickham in the early seventeenth century in the employ of the East India Company and stationed in Japan to superintend trade and investment in a factory there. Wickham lived an extravagant life during his placement in Japan, consuming his meals on expensive china and drinking out of a silver teapot. His bathroom had abundant perfumes and fragrances, Japanese treasures adorned his walls, and precious stones were seen about his residence. Wickham had aggregated some £1,400 in possessions in Japan managing an investment in the Hirado factory. This was especially odd in light of the fact that he received compensation of £40 per year.[125]

Needless to say, he did not amass his fortune with great regard to frugal principles nor did he simply save his income—there was indeed foul play involved. In addition to managing the factory, Wickham traded for his own account and benefit as well. He also requested from friends shipments of certain commodities that were in especially high demand at certain times so that he could recover from some poor investments he had made. This was, unfortunately, a rather common problem that the East India Company faced in its international activity. Despite the fact that the firm had a policy that no individual dispatched to an overseas location trade for his personal benefit, there were many captains and shipmen who simply failed to heed the command.[126]

Another East India employee, William Keeling, actually demanded that he be given an exception to trade for his own account or he would resign. While those at headquarters were angered by this request, they ultimately agreed on one condition: that he ensure that nobody else in his crew was doing the same and to punish other offenders. It was a farcical but apparently successful way of dealing with the issue, and Keeling did enforce the company policy on his inferiors with great effect.[127] Indeed, the principal-agent problems and the issues arising involving fiduciary duty are nothing new today, but they extend in time and space to centuries past and to nations afar, as evidenced by the English involvement in Japan.

While many foreign companies did well there despite the issues with agency problems, Japan's days of financial openness were numbered. One of the longer-term causes of Japan's seclusion was the rise to power of Tokugawa Hidetada. Unlike his father, Tokugawa Ieyasu, Hidetada had a much more adversarial relationship with the foreign merchant class, thinking that they had mostly immoral tendencies. He also feared they would seek to influence the political environment in Japan, which certainly turned out to be true later. In 1638, the Portuguese had become heavily involved in the Shimabara Rebellion of Japanese Christians. The movement failed and unsurprisingly incited great animosity toward the Portuguese. The Japanese government issued an edict stating that all future vessels from Portugal seeking to trade in Japan would be summarily burned and their crews executed. The Portuguese seemed to hold the attitude that the Japanese would shortly get over whatever anger they had and sent along another crew in 1640. True to their word, the Japanese carried out the edict in full force, and indeed, the seclusion against the Western Europeans had begun.[128]

The Portuguese were able to recover some of the lost trading activity by shifting their focus toward India. The English were mostly denied access because of their robust ties with Portugal at the time.

The Dutch would simply not accept the severing of ties between Europe and Japan. The Dutch were so compelled by the prospect of trade with Japan that they set up a settlement on a tiny island off Nagasaki called Deshima and endured physical beatings at the hands of the Japanese. Each year when the Dutch ships came to Deshima, the officers were hit with sticks repeatedly.[129]

While it was an unparalleled persistence that kept the Dutch in Japan during the seclusion, there was one country that maintained formidable trading relations with the island nation: China.[130] China was not regarded with the same sense of distrust and suspicion as the Europeans, and consequently trade did continue in substantial volume.

Trade in India

As the medieval Indian economy developed, merchants and producers formed themselves into guilds in order to develop their resources and, presumably, restrict competition. Guilds and trade associations varied in influence throughout the early centuries of Indian economic history, but there was a marked shift from the initial relative balance of power. Specifically, the producer and manufacturer guilds held a powerful market position at the inception of these associations, but as people clustered into villages, merchants formed associations, grew in strength, and eventually gained the upper hand.[131]

In general, four main castes developed. At the top of the hierarchy came the *Brahmins*, a ruling and priestly caste. Then came the *Kshatriyas*, a military caste, the *Vaishyas*, a merchant or commercial caste, and a lower caste, the *Shudras*, who were serfs and laborers. After these four "*varna*" groups came the "Untouchables," as they were known colloquially, meant to perform only menial tasks and manual labor. Lower castes were looked down upon by individuals of higher caste, who claimed inherent superiority in all ways of life.[132] Thus, caste roles in socioeconomic affairs materially influenced occupations, opportunities for investment, and social mobility. Caste interactions and relationships were very complex in ancient Indian and Hindu traditions. They affected a wide variety of economic activity, including lending, trade, taxes, interest payments, mortgages, and even subsistence and resource allocations. In fourteenth-century Delhi, Brahmins were exempted from the poll tax that was leveled on all other castes of Hindus, an example of the upper caste receiving economic benefits.[133]

Lending relationships, for instance, developed according to the social hierarchy of caste. One study of eighteenth-century northwest India shows members of a given caste providing loans to one another out of a sense of "caste solidarity" or "communal identification."[134] Moreover, the pattern of development of guilds and trade organizations was influenced by caste roles.[135]

Foreign Investment in India

In the more modern era in the history of investment and investment management in India, the beginning of the British Raj in 1858 delineated a profound shift in both governance and economic affairs of the Indian subcontinent. In 1858, the East India Company's control of the Indian subcontinent ended with the establishment of British Crown colonial rule. This rule was not established easily, however; there was great expense (to the tune of £36 million) and bloodshed during the two-year period immediately preceding this formal establishment of Crown rule by the British, a period known as the "First War of Indian Independence."[136]

With these geopolitical changes, a marked change in commodities operations became apparent under British colonial rule of India. Now that a formal, stable geopolitical environment had arisen as a result of Crown rule, economic activity was facilitated greatly.[137] India served as both a market for British goods and services and an important defense asset in terms of the size of the standing British Indian Army. There remains great scholarly debate, however, regarding the economics of the Indian subcontinent under British Crown rule, mainly revolving around the central question of whether the British involvement in colonial India developed or hindered the Indian economy.[138]

Under Crown rule, India saw immense capital investments in infrastructure, including railways, irrigation canals, and mining. In addition, the British introduced an English-medium education system and strengthened the legal system, and they promoted India's integration into the global economy. At the same time, however, the British ransacked India of natural resources and wealth to pay for bloated bureaucracy, debt incurred, and military expenses; made the region more prone to destructive famine; imposed excessive cash taxes on the poor population; destabilized crop cycles and agriculture; and did not reinvest returns from capital investment into the Indian economy.

On balance, it is difficult to dispute that the economic gains and power remained primarily in British hands during Crown rule of India.[139]

EARLY COLLECTIVE INVESTMENT

Although many concepts related to ownership may have seemed rudimentary, we can see glimmerings of financial sophistication in the ancient civilizations of Mesopotamia, Egypt, Greece, Rome, and Asia via the emergence of different forms of investment. There were instances at various points in time of collateralized lending, early versions of insurance, the concept of limited liability, management partnerships, and profit-sharing arrangements. Surprisingly sophisticated arrangements and terminology were created in exploiting investments, recording transactions, and monitoring profits and cash.

Joint-Stock Companies in Rome

The complex social order of ancient Rome and the exigencies of empire produced the conditions for joint financial undertakings, speculation, and pooling of collective resources.[140] As Rome grew, government revenues and expenditures increased rapidly.[141] Like the ancient democracy in Athens, the Roman Republic avoided sponsoring powerful bureaucratic entities within the government itself. Public services were mostly put up for bid to private providers. These providers were, in effect, contractors or governmental leaseholders known as publicans. Eventually, the Roman state contracted out nearly every aspect of government service, most notably the collection of tax revenues, the provision of goods and services, and the operation of public property. The method of allocating these responsibilities was via public auction (*sub hasta*).[142]

A very large pool of capital was a prerequisite to participate in these auctions, which were held every fifth year. No single person had adequate funds to pursue such contracts, and so individuals joined together to pool their resources.[143] Two legal entities permitted individuals to join together in common efforts: *collegia* and *societas*. The former was limited to specific public or social activities, while the latter could execute a diverse variety of tasks that had business purposes.[144] *Societas publicanorum* were organizations intended to bid on and perform as government leaseholders and typically had characteristics similar to those of modern corporations in that their existence was not terminated by the retirement or death of partners and they could float shares with limited liability. According to Polybius and Cicero, societas publicanorum thrived during the Roman Republic but were eventually eliminated by the central bureaucracy of the Roman Empire.[145]

Roman citizens could actually participate in four types of societas, which could also include private transactions unrelated to performing state functions (such as wine or oil trade): (1) *societas unius rei*, which were designed for a single transaction; (2) *societas alicuius negotiationis*, which each undertook a single commercial activity but could endure over time; (3) *societas omnium bonorum quae ex quaestu veniunt*, which limited the property of the partnership to a certain purpose; and (4) *societas omnium bonorum*, which bound all the present and future partners' property to its purposes.[146]

These financial societies were joint-stock companies managed by publicans, including a manager in Rome, the *magister*, and managers in the provinces, each known as a *pro magistro*. The shareholders came from across the socioeconomic spectrum of Roman society, from senators and knights to common citizens.[147] By the second century B.C., share ownership had become quite widespread. In addition to their original purpose of raising funds for projects, shares also became objects of speculation based on political and economic events.[148]

Investment Partnerships

THE MEDITERRANEAN AND THE MIDDLE EAST

Although land was the dominant form of ownership and often the most coveted asset, there were other, even if more minor, forms of investment that transpired in these societies. There is a great deal of documentation on investment management for commercial and trade partnerships in Assyria. In Assyria, the word for financier was *ummianum*, and in the capital of Assyria, Assur, these individuals dominated the investment management market. The wealthy ummianum hired *mer ummianum* (son of ummianum), who journeyed around Anatolia to merchants, finding and managing ventures with them on behalf of the ummianum. Every merchant who had not attained the level of being self-financed had, at minimum, one ummianum.[149]

The Assyrians also had a rather advanced financial jargon. For instance, they had a word that essentially meant liquid assets—*saltum*, which translates to "uncommitted goods," or "cash on hand." They had a single word meaning total profit, *taksitum*, and one meaning net profit, *nemulum*. Further, they had a word describing a kind of long-term investment partnerships, *naruqqum*. These investment arrangements called for the investor to gain two-thirds and the manager (or merchant) to gain one-third of the total profit.[150]

The Byzantines—the civilization born out of the Eastern Roman Empire, lasting from about A.D. 300 to A.D. 1453—had an investment framework called the *chreokoinonia*. Modern knowledge about this instrument is derived from the *Nomos Nautikos*, an aggregation of maritime laws written sometime between A.D. 600 and A.D. 800, and the *Ecloga*, a set of laws compiled in the early 700s. The chreokoinonia exposed the agent to liability (his proportional liability in the case of loss was equal to his proportional gain in the case of profit).[151] The Byzantines' general form of the partnership, called the *koinonia*, featured the rather advanced elements of dissolution in the case of death and poverty. It is intriguing that some koinonia had clauses where the partners agreed to commit all future assets to the enterprise, such as property and capital they would inherit later in their lives, known as *totorum bonurum* provisions.[152]

Jewish societies at this time had the *'isqa* investment partnership. The key characteristic, compelled by rabbinical law (such as that described by Maimonides and written in the later portion of the twelfth century), was that the agent must be eligible for a greater percentage of the profits than he was liable for the losses.[153]

The Ottoman Empire also had its share of investment partnerships, dating at least as far back as 1480. They tended to be particularly complicated, involving a multitude of agents. For instance, a surviving document describes an event in which a man named Hace Şerefüddin el-Hace Yahya commanded his agent to deliver money to a third individual, named Hace Hüseyinşah. Hüseyinşah then gave the money to a man named Uğurlu Mehmed, who invested the money. When Mehmed's business made a profit, his own agent returned the principal and profit to the original investor, Hace Şerefüddin.[154]

ISLAMIC SOCIETIES

The salient investment structure in early Islamic civilizations was the *mudaraba*, which was a well-developed legal framework by the eighth century. The mudaraba was a contract between an investor and an agent (called the *mudarib*) who deployed the capital of the former to conduct long-distance trade. An essential characteristic of the mudaraba was zero liability to the agent. The agent was entitled to a percentage of the profits, but any losses were incurred solely by the investor. There were two levels of discretion associated with the mudaraba: one with limited permissible types of trade, and the other whereby the agent was not prohibited from any form of investment. This latter form was known as the *i'mal fihi bi raika*, translating as "act with it as you see fit."[155] Indeed, the notion of establishing levels of discretion for an investment manager has ample precedent in these ancient arrangements.

The mudaraba contracts were employed all across the Islamic world spanning much of Islamic history, from eleventh-century Egypt to seventeenth-century Turkey to nineteenth-century Palestine. The mudaraba manifested themselves in contexts beyond the classic desire for profit into the realm of charitable trusts. The second Caliph Umar (the head of the Muslim community who succeeded Muhammad upon his death), for instance, used mudaraba contracts to invest the resources of orphanages in trade between Iraq and Medina.[156]

In a slightly different arrangement, the *musharaka*, the agent could provide his own funds in the venture, thereby receiving a higher percentage of the proceeds.[157] The modern equivalent of the musharaka is the joint venture with one active and one passive partner, both contributing capital, but having differential involvement in the operations.

MEDIEVAL EUROPE

In medieval Europe, and especially in Genoa and Venice, there emerged two fundamental investment structures for overseas trade around the same period: the *commenda* and the *societas maris*. The commenda was similar to the Islamic mudaraba: it had the feature of an active and a passive partner, with no liability to the former. The profit breakdown was approximately one-quarter for the agent and three-quarters for the investor. These structures were prominent in trade with the East and among the very wealthy families of the Auria and the Spinulla, nobles, widows, and shopkeepers. The societas maris was slightly different. It permitted the agent to reinvest some of his proceeds earned from past voyages. The agent generally provided one-third of the initial capital and was entitled to half of the net gain (with the other half going to the passive partner).[158]

The agents (or investment managers) tended to be young merchants yearning for adventure. Sometimes the silent partners were older merchants, who had endured many long years of difficult long-distance trade and were happy to step back from the arduousness of the task. Many of the older merchants became partners and mentors to the young agents, either deciding or giving guidance on where to travel and what to trade.[159]

The use of the commenda and societas maris was widespread in the Commercial Revolution. The Italian merchant banks, for example, would invest in voyages and commercial enterprises through the use of a commenda structure, in which the agent might take one-fourth of the proceeds, or of a societas maris–like structure, in which the agent would take half the profits.[160] These forms of investment were all the more popular not only because they avoided the prohibition against the fixed charge of interest,[161] as discussed earlier in this chapter, but likely also because they encouraged entrepreneurial spirit and commitment based importantly on self-interest of the operating (but financially junior) partner. It is worthwhile to contemplate the utility of empowering a much more financially strapped but able operating partner to benefit in direct proportion to the effort and success in a dangerous venture such as transporting valuable goods over stormy and often lawless seas. In a similar but less dramatic sense, having a factory that is run by a skilled partner but primarily financed by a merchant banker, managed in such a way that the operating partner benefits in direct proportion to its profitability, is clearly desirable for both.

GLOBAL INFLUENCES ON INVESTMENT FORMS

There is an obvious question in this discourse about investment partnerships materializing in a wide array of medieval societies: did the development of one form of partnership in one society affect or even induce the creation of a different type of partnership in the next society? Abraham Udovitch has studied this question extensively. To be clear, with respect to Islamic societies, Udovitch uses the term *qirad* instead of mudaraba—in substance identical, except that the mudaraba is established by the Hanafi school of Islamic law and the qirad by the Maliki school.[162] Udovitch speculates about a likely connection between two forms of investment partnership: the qirad (or muda raba) and the commenda. He notes that the qirad came before the commenda, but they both had the vital characteristic of no liability to the agent. That fact, combined with the interaction between Christians and Muslims from the eighth to the tenth centuries, tends to support the notion that the Muslim qirad prompted the development of the European commenda.[163]

The complexity of the transactions in which the Ottomans engaged was made possible by the bestowal of a nuanced legal system by their Islamic forebears. The Ottomans termed the capital involved in these transactions *vedia*, and the transactions themselves resembled the mudaraba. The Ottomans did also use mudaraba alongside another contract called the *mufawada*, which had three vital provisions: the partnership terminated upon the death of one partner, the income was to be distributed in equal shares between two partners, and the capital contributions were to be equivalent.[164]

The mufawada was adopted by individuals of different faiths and nationalities because of the history of Muslim courts standing behind their stipulations. There are surviving documents proving that these Islamic mufawada existed even among such diverse parties as Greek sailors, Christians, and Venetians.[165] The logic of its structure and its well-established legal enforcement mechanisms inspired many to overlook cultural and religious differences and organize business ventures that relied on the mufawada.

TRUSTS AND CHARITIES

The sophistication of Greek and Roman trusts and charities is almost startling, not unlike early collective investments described previously. These ancient forms also demonstrate collaborative features, which are one of the key characteristics of more sophisticated investment forms. These were entities seeking to manage capital seeded by the state or wealthy individuals and organizations for the benefit of third parties.

Endowments and Foundations in Greece and Rome

Around the fourth century B.C. in the Greek world, the perpetual endowment emerged. Its profits were intended to be directed for specific goals and programs.[166] The perpetual endowments had great influence over many aspects of Greek society, including funding for the education of youth and the construction and maintenance of civic infrastructures.[167] Individuals founded most of the Hellenistic endowments overall, although endowments of the highest accumulation were mostly founded by kings.[168]

In the Roman Republic, public work was primarily undertaken by the previously discussed *societas publicanorum*, which raised funds by issuing shares. Endowments became mostly attached to collegia, associations with special functions. Members of the collegia and donors of endowments were mostly, though not entirely, made up of people in the lower classes.[169]

These endowments obviously served numerous purposes in the Western Roman Empire, as seen in the list below. Table 1.1 shows the distribution of endowments whose sums are known.[170]

PURPOSES OF ENDOWMENTS

38   Commemorative rites during certain festivals, esp. rosalia (May 13, rose festival), parentalia (February 13 to 21, festival commemorating deceased relatives), etc.

18   Celebration of the birthday of the benefactor

7   Maintenance of statues

2   Celebration of the birthday of (patron) deities

Reproduced from Jinyu Liu, "The Economy of Endowments: The Case of the Roman Collegia," in *Pistoi Dia Tēn Technēn: Studies in Honour of Raymond Bogaert*, Studia Hellenistica 44, ed. Koenraad Verboven, Katelijn Vandorpe, and Véronique Chankowski (Leuven: Peeters, 2008), 240.

The donations, as we can infer from the sums of the known endowments shown in table 1.1, were not very sizable. Compared with the estimated GDP per capita at the time, the endowments were not particularly large. Smaller endowments whose assets were often less than 100 times the average income were numerous. However, the largest endowments had more assets than many small ones combined because donors were more likely to give money to larger associations.

TABLE I.I

Distribution of Endowments Whose Sums Are Known

AMOUNT (HS)	ENDOWMENTS OF ALL CATEGORIES (DUNCAN-JONES 1982, P. 136)	ENDOWMENTS TO ASSOCIATIONS	
2,000,000–1,000,000	6 (5.4%)	0	
999,999–500,000	2 (1.8%)	0	
499,999–250,000	9 (8.0%)	0	
249,999–100,000	14 (12.5%)	1	
99,999–50,000	7 (6.3%)	4	
49,999–20,000	11 (9.8%)	9	
19,999–10,000	10 (8.9%)	7	
9,999–32	53 (47.3%)	8,000–5,000	8
		4,999–4,000	6
		3,999–2,000	16
		1,999–1,000	10
		999–80	7
Total	112	68	

Source: Reproduced from Liu, "Economy of Endowments," 235.

Note: HS is the abbreviation for *sestertii*, a Roman unit of account. We know that 1 denarius = 4 sestertii = 16 asses.

In return for their donations, donors often required the endowments to perform certain services for them. Records show that endowments had returns ranging from 5 to 12 percent annually. This required that the assets of the endowments be actively managed.[171] The management style varied across endowments, but in most cases the perpetual endowments were governed by management committees. The managers in these committees made most of the investment decisions. Evidence suggests that sometimes the same committee oversaw multiple endowments. In some endowments, the managers were elected; in others, the managers were appointed. Some endowments were mainly managed bureaucratically.[172] Limited by the available forms of investment at the time, endowments earned returns only through moneylending and real estate investments.[173]

Guardianship and Tutorship in Greece and Rome

Guardianship in Greece or tutorship in Rome was the legal system that provided for the care of parentless children. Besides their importance to legal history, guardianships and tutorships were, at their core, authorizations of third-party asset management, since the guardians and the tutors were charged not only with caring for the minors' living arrangements but also with managing their properties. In Greece, the guardian was normally appointed by the young person's father before death, but if the father did not make an appointment, guardianship would devolve on relatives in an order established by the law, mostly in the same order as succession.[174]

While guardianship in Greece was typically a privilege, tutorship in Rome was more of a burden, as the tutor had a greater liability for misconduct. At first, the regulations of tutorship simply proscribed fraud, but as the Roman Republic developed, the tutor came to be more responsible for good management of assets.[175] In order to ensure that the pupils received a safe income with a minimum degree of risk, Roman law required tutors to be very cautious in managing their pupils' wealth. However, in reality judges also understood the difficulty of making investments that were both safe and consistently profitable over a long period of time, so rules were established limiting tutors' liability in investment selection. The law also required that no funds be allowed to sit idle. A tutor's failure to follow this rule could result in penalties.[176]

Pensions in Rome

The first known pensions in history were for the military. In Rome, many legionnaires returned from battle having served valiantly but with little wealth. Gaius Gracchus in 123 B.C. came up with the idea of granting many veterans sinecures in Capua, Carthage, and Tarentum, which had the dual effect of marginalizing them politically (by lessening their ability to participate in the affairs of the republic) and giving them some financial stability in return for their service. Gaius Marius, Julius Caesar's uncle, helped pass legislation that gave his devoted veterans land in Africa and Gaul. The granting of land to veterans was unsystematic and arbitrary at times, which created a great deal of political resentment. When the Roman Republic fell and Augustus took over, he transitioned to a more systemic method of giving money to veterans through a formal pension system in 13 B.C.[177] The historian Suetonius described the systematization of the pension in *Lives of the Twelve Caesars*, where he notes, "Moreover, all the soldiers that were in any place whatsoever, [Augustus] tied to a certain prescript form and proportion of wages and rewards, setting down according to the degree and place of every one, both their times of warfare, and also the commodities they should receive after the term of their service expired and their lawful discharge: lest that by occasion of old age or for want they should, after they were freed from warfare, be solicited to sedition and rebellion."[178]

While Augustus instituted a formal military pension system, there is no evidence of investment management of the pensions. The funds required to meet Augustus's pension disbursements came from a 5 percent tax levy on bequests and a 1 percent levy on sales at auctions. However, evidence shows that Roman pension plans became overextended, and Augustus had to increase the years of service from sixteen years of active commitment and four years in the reserves to twenty years of active commitment and five years in reserves.[179] This pension dilemma is reminiscent of the present Social Security retirement age debate, and presumably this change was also controversial at the time.

CONCLUSION

While this historical overview cannot be complete, this chapter has focused on the history of a variety of financial and investment forms in order to illustrate four fundamental points. First, it is important to understand that while human civilizations have developed a wide array of approaches to ownership, trade, commerce, and lending, all of these approaches share a universal commitment to the concept of investment. At its most basic level, investment represents a commitment to an economic principle of increasing prosperity over time. This means that resources need to be allocated and managed so that despite Aristotle's distaste for the fertility of money, they bear fruit for the individual and collective future.

Second, the premodern period is undoubtedly profoundly "strange" in its economic organization and the resultant forms and practices of investment. As we saw, for instance, different societies struggled with how to ensure repayment of loans. The ancient Egyptians relied on oaths given to gods, the Persians made it possible to take a borrower's children as repayment, the Greeks made use of wealthy local cosigners, and the Chinese and Japanese were familiar with the concept of pawning collateral to receive a loan. When the Greeks made loans for property, they used horoi, or stones, on the property to note the amount of the loan and imposed substantial punishments if they were deliberately altered.

Furthermore, many ancient societies navigated complicated political and religious frameworks that governed their investment partnerships, whether it was the Jewish 'isqa, Islamic mudaraba, Byzantine chreokoinonia, or Italian commenda.

Various governments or religious organizations were intimately intertwined with the investment process. In early Mesopotamia, the centerpiece of the economic arrangement was around the temple and the tasks required for its upkeep and edification. The Chinese government was instrumental in the lending process, as were the Buddhist temples.

Across countless societies there was a heightened sensitivity to high interest rates that was made manifest in writings discussing the immorality of usury as well as laws or regulations against the practice. This was true as early as the Akkadians in Mesopotamia and extended to the ancient Greeks, the Christian kingdoms, and Islamic societies. The sheer breadth of this aversion across time and place is striking.

And yet for all its strangeness, and the third point of focus in the chapter, there were also remarkable parallels to today. The early modern period included ample examples of sophisticated organizational structures to enhance efficiency, such as the Medici bank's decentralized process of oversight. In addition, the Japanese had a highly functional and advanced commodities and futures market at the Dojima Rice Exchange and transacted regularly with paper representing a claim on goods stored in a warehouse rather than with the unwieldy goods themselves.

There were also investment and fund-raising programs undertaken for nonprofit causes or third-party beneficiaries under charitable arrangements. The Romans made use of collegia, often for religious purposes. The Romans also designed pension systems, though mostly for members of the military and even then for largely political purposes rather than altruistic ends. The Greeks designed a system to ensure that parentless children were supported financially.

The importance of relations across political boundaries to investment has not changed. The English, Dutch, and Portuguese did not take at all well to the isolation sought by Japan. The British Crown exploited India with respect to natural resources and other goods. Cross-border politics was already quite important to the way investment was, or was not, conducted.

Many premodern enterprises were also plagued by the very same problems faced in investment today, including fundamental principal-agent problems. The East India Company could not manage to prevent its employees from transacting for their own accounts when stationed abroad in Japan, and the solution (a rather comical one) was at times to allow a leader abroad to trade for his own account as long as he prevented his subordinates from doing likewise.

The fourth point of concentration, to be continued in chapter 2, is that the transition to the democratization of investment was a radical historical transformation. Land, lending, and trade have functioned as the major investment classes for most of human history. But in antiquity, ownership and investment activities were possible only for members of the power elite, even though the management of land and investment was often practiced on behalf of the elite by slaves or lower-status commoners. Today this dynamic has actually reversed: ownership and investment are available to the majority of people in advanced societies through savings, retirement vehicles, credit, and various investment products, while the business of investment is often managed by elites who have amassed great wealth through a system of fixed and incentive fees.

While investment and commerce did fuel the engine of historical progress, most of the population in premodern civilizations did not benefit directly from these activities. Rather, as will be evident in our discussions about the Industrial Revolution, commoners often paid the price with their exploited labor for historical and financial progress. That being said, the modern expansion of investment activities to a much larger percentage of the global population is no less remarkable, particularly when viewed through a longer historical lens.

CHAPTER TWO

The Democratization
of Investment

*Joint-Stock Companies, the Industrial Revolution,
and Public Markets*

THE SEVENTEENTH TO NINETEENTH CENTURIES saw the beginnings of powerful political democratization, as privileges and rights were extended to an ever-broader segment of the population. The kings and the landed class, who had ruled throughout the Middle Ages and the Renaissance, felt their previously tight grip on the reins of power slowly begin to slip away. Political rhetoric, armed rebellion, and wars of independence were the means of recrafting society and its institutions. The idea that society could be imagined anew became an invigorating source of human empowerment.

It is this political democratization that receives most of the ink of history, but there was another democratization afoot—an economic and financial one—that is often missed. The democratization of investment—specifically the expansion of the ability of those who were not members of the elite to participate in the enterprise of investment—had more subtle origins than its political counterpart. Revolutions, social and religious upheaval, and new political philosophies begat political democratization, but the democratization of investment was rooted in three crucial but quieter developments. The first was the emergence of the modern corporate form, with its key characteristics of limited liability, shared ownership, transferability of possession, and permanent existence. This new form of investment, which first manifested itself as the joint-stock company, had enormous flexibility, durability, and risk limitation that proved to be essential for financing and operating large and complex enterprises.

The second development was the Industrial Revolution. While it was a slow and painful transformation, often accompanied by urban squalor, wretched working conditions, and social strife, it forever altered the trajectory of the economic fate of nonelites. In particular, those beyond the landed gentry (notably, practitioners of commerce, manufacturing, and invention) at last began to share meaningfully in economic surplus. Gradually, there was an emerging trend toward meaningful savings that could be deployed for investment projects. In effect, it was the other side of the coin: the first development of the modern corporate form generated the seeds of demand for capital, and the long-term effects of the Industrial Revolution produced the means of satisfying these capital demands.

The third development was the construction of a means to connect empowered savers with these investment projects, which was accomplished through the emergence of public markets. The public market was, in the long term, the mechanism to join the two sides of the coin. Public markets offered liquidity, publicized value, broadcast availability, lowered transaction costs, and permitted investors to gain wide diversification with relative ease. Public markets, furthermore, aided in initiating the opportunity and need for regulation.

The democratization of investment is not a finished project. Just as the political democratization of the eighteenth and nineteenth centuries is still playing out (it left key demographics still disenfranchised and has not yet spread to all corners of the world), the project of democratization of investment is incomplete. A large swath of the population remains deprived of meaningful savings and thus is excluded from participation. Rules and regulations can still be enhanced to further level the playing field, and many international jurisdictions have yet to take up the banner of broadening investment opportunity. Nevertheless, the beginning of democratization itself has been a dominant force in the history of investment, and we can trace its lineage to these developments.

THE EMERGENCE OF THE MODERN
CORPORATE FORM

The advent of the corporate form, as embodied in joint-stock companies, was a vital precursor to developing capitalism, greater economic progress, and widespread financing and ownership of commercial and industrial enterprises. While the focus of this chapter will be on the first Dutch and English joint-stock companies founded in the early seventeenth century, recall that the *original* precursor to the joint-stock company appeared more than a millennium before—the Roman societas publicanorum. As mentioned in chapter 1, these entities were created to bid on and service the construction of public works, engage in tax farming (the government's sale of the right to collect particular taxes to a private enterprise), and provide goods and services to the Roman government. The societas publicanorum declined in popularity during the Roman Empire, as the government gradually inserted itself as the predominant player in these activities rather than outsourcing them to private concerns. After all, the Empire was not as interested in facilitating the decentralization of the activities of the state as the Roman Republic had been. And so this powerful form went dormant, and the elite maintained their exclusive right to the activity of investment.

It was not until medieval times that progress toward the modern corporate form began again. For instance, medieval commenda and *compagnia* were partnership forms that allowed the financing of commercial ventures—especially sea voyages for trade purposes—to be structured in ways that accounted for the economic differences between being an active participant in these ventures and merely providing financial support in the form of risk capital. This represented an important departure from a classical partnership in which all other partners had to agree to the sale of interests—and with good reason, as partners tend to be involved in the management of an operation and thus must ensure that the person to whom the interest is sold is actually effective and productive. In this new hybrid form, however, the use of shares opened new possibilities. With shares, consent is not needed, since the management of a shipping operation is not necessarily affected when one passive investor sells shares to another passive investor.

It was in the shipping industry that these arrangements were most common, and in twelfth-century Genoa, a major hub of shipping activity, it became more and more common to supply capital to shipping operations with *loca* (shares). Typically, the ship would be divided into somewhere between 16 and 70 shares, with the investment structure lasting just one voyage, rather than the life of the vessel. However, by the thirteenth century the use of loca began to decline as maritime insurance rose to prominence and it was no longer as necessary to spread risk and raise capital to undertake these voyages. For a brief time, though, loca were intensely popular in Genoa, and even investors who were not wealthy participated in the market.[1]

Finally, in the early 1550s the first joint-stock company, the Muscovy Company, appeared in England. It was started by English merchants and traders hoping to access wood, hemp, and construction materials in northern Europe. The earliest groups of traders were known as the Easterlings, and some etymologists believe that the term *sterling* comes from the name of these traders.[2]

The Muscovy Company came into being after a voyage to the White Sea. Although the first captain was lost, another sailor managed to navigate the vessel to Archangel (or Arkhangelsk) in order to parlay with Russia's Czar Ivan the Terrible. These sailors sought permission to engage in trade, and Ivan acquiesced, giving the sailors a missive to the English king as his official acceptance. Because King Edward VI died during the initial expedition, it was ultimately Mary I, Queen of England and Ireland, who issued a charter to the company in 1555.[3]

There are other early examples of joint-stock companies—for instance, one of the first investments by the European public in the natural bounty of the so-called New World was, in fact, a joint-stock company. On April 10, 1606, King James I granted a charter for the London Company. It was inspired by English envy of the Spanish, who found massive quantities of precious metals in the New World. As a condition of the charter, King James I sought to cash in on what he hoped would be abundant profits and stated that one-fifth of the metal discoveries be ceded to the throne.[4]

The company was composed of 145 men who sailed from England to the New World between December 1606 and May 1607, making port in Virginia (hence the company's later name, the Virginia Company). Investors who purchased shares in the enterprise capitalized the firm. The investor base was a motley lot: the upper echelons of civil society bought in alongside those with a thirst for adventure and speculation. Remarkably, these shareholders were fairly well organized. They created a "court" to manage operations, a body likely bearing some resemblance to what today would be seen as a participatory board of directors. This group proved to be reasonably effective when the venture failed to find the precious metals it had sought. It ordered a shift in operations away from locating metallic resources toward sustaining the colonizing population by selling rations, goods, and "patents" or "Plantations" (land deeds) to augment profits. It formed a subsidiary known as the Magazine to sell necessities, vestments, and rations to the colonists. This resourcefulness, while impressive, was not entirely popular with the colonists, who often found the prices to be outrageously high—an issue that was ultimately mitigated, to some extent, when the king placed a cap on net income from sales of provisions at one-fourth of sales. There are other examples of the shareholders' aptitude. For instance, when the shareholding body determined that the Magazine was not distributing profits fairly to the Virginia Company, it swiftly removed the manager involved. Despite the shareholders' relative success in exercising some control over operations, the company survived for only some eighteen years. The initial investors wanted to exploit gold and silver deposits, and without such a lucrative opportunity, the days of selling mostly to colonists were inevitably numbered.[5]

The Muscovy Company and the London Company had many of the characteristics that define the modern corporate form, but it was not until the seventeenth century that joint-stock companies started to exhibit the full range of modern corporate characteristics. Such companies included the prominent Dutch East India Company and the British East India Company, both founded in the seventeenth century. These two enterprises, both of which had relatively large market capitalizations, featured many shareholders who were not engaged in running the business and were created with limited liability in the modern corporate sense. Their mission was to finance long-distance and long-duration trade by committing capital for extended periods of time. The most striking corporate characteristics of these companies were their shareholder financing and their eventual permanent existence. In due course, the provision and withdrawal of capital to activities of the East India Companies became entirely separate from the acts of investment and disinvestment undertaken by their shareholders. These later acts were accomplished by the purchase and sale of the company's stock in the open market and originally, therefore, by transactions undertaken between existing shareholders (the sellers) and other existing or new shareholders (the buyers).

The South Sea Bubble

No sooner had the modern corporate form emerged than the need for its regulation did as well. The South Sea Bubble, economically ruinous to a host of early investors, highlighted the dangers of a lack of adherence to fiduciary duty and revealed some of the weaknesses of this new form.

The South Sea Bubble began with the South Sea Company, founded by Robert Harley and John Blunt in 1711. The company was given unrestricted and monopolized access to trade in South America in return for agreeing to purchase the public debt that resulted from the War of Spanish Succession. At the time of formation, it was not known how the War of Spanish Succession would end, and because Spain had control over South America, there was an embedded gamble on the outcome of the war. After all, the company would do well if Spanish control over South America waned because of defeat but would have limited access if Spain held control. The South Sea Company was to receive the interest from the government, and the company performed even more debt assumption from the government in 1719. Initially, all parties seemed content. The government was able to pay a reduced interest rate, and the funds directed toward the interest payments were to be raised from tariffs levied on imported goods from South America. The debt holders generally embraced the idea, as they had an opportunity to benefit from potentially very lucrative trade while continuing to indirectly benefit from their former interest payments as the entity in which they held equity now received them.[6]

There was one problem: the company actually did very little trade in South America, in large part because Spain had maintained control of its colonies after the war and was not keen on other empires gaining footholds in its lands. Indeed, the bet on significant British involvement in South America did not pay off for the South Sea Company. In fact, most of the South Sea Company's earnings were derived from the returns on public debt. The management wanted to push up the stock price, but clearly it could not do so by passing on the sad truth about its measly returns in South America. Instead, management decided to concoct a tale that it had made substantial sums from the South American trade. Investors believed the fabrication hook, line, and sinker, and the deception (along with a broader bubble in those trade enterprises that followed the lead of the South Sea Company in making extravagant claims of success) caused the share price to swell from £128 in January 1720 to £550 in May. The stock eventually collapsed from a height of £1,050 per share, and soon, after the ensuing investigations, it became clear to the shareholders that they had been swindled.[7]

The news, as can be imagined, did not go over well. One shareholder who lost a sizable sum was so incensed over the entire affair that he shot founder John Blunt for his complicity. The public rhetoric was equally charged. While a more unruffled member of Parliament called the event "a notorious breach of trust," another proclaimed that the fraudsters should be placed in sacks with snakes and loose change and thrust into the river to drown.[8]

The South Sea Bubble brought serious harm not only to much of the investing public but also to the broader English economy. One of the foremost ironies of the episode was the passage of the Bubble Act of 1720, which required all joint-stock companies to possess royal charters. Contrary to common conception, this was not passed out of a desire for reform; rather, it was passed prior to the collapse of the firm and was meant to aid and insulate the South Sea Company from competition for investors' funds by preventing other smaller entities from marketing shares, as they did not possess the required charter.[9] Nonetheless, the Bubble Act came to be used to regulate these early companies and made them less likely to do widespread harm. Ultimately, the South Sea Bubble reminded investors of exploitable information asymmetries between the body of shareholders and management, and it drove many to approach the task of allocating money with greater scrutiny and diligence. In the end, of course, the fraudulent activities of Enron and Bernie Madoff are echoes of this forerunner some three centuries earlier.

Adam Smith, the oft-cited "father of modern economics," took an entirely adversarial view of the structure of the joint-stock companies and the notion of investment management more broadly. Of course, Smith was highly influenced by the South Sea Bubble collapse, and in *The Wealth of Nations* he wrote, "Negligence and profusion, must always prevail, more or less, in the management of the affairs of such a [joint-stock] company." He claimed that the fiduciaries could not possibly be fully dutiful and completely concerned about the welfare of shareholders because the money is not their own: "The directors of such companies, however, being the managers rather of other people's money than of their own, it cannot well be expected that they should watch over it with the same anxious vigilance with which the partners in private copartner[ship] frequently watch over their own."[10] Adam Smith seemed to apply the famous principle of self-interest to the management of investment funds and, in so doing, deemed it a poor idea. His view of potential misalignment between owner and manager was not entirely misguided, but he did not appreciate that investors could develop more sophisticated governance and incentive structures to enhance alignment.

Naturally, a wide array of ownership structures developed throughout history, and the joint-stock company was the seed that would eventually blossom into the modern corporate form. These joint-stock companies first tended to involve trading firms: the Muscovy Company with English merchants trading in northern Europe and the London Company (later the Virginia Company) that aspired to enjoy the wealth of the New World and ended up transforming into an organization to profit from settlers. Over time, the sophistication of these trading companies grew with the East India Companies that were even more evolved, involving a clearer separation of ownership and management and an eased transferability of possession. The structure was, of course, far from perfect and had to experience an abundance of growing pains, of which the South Sea Bubble was perhaps the most obvious early manifestation. Adam Smith aptly pointed out the problem of agency—namely, how can the incentives of those who own the firm be well aligned with those who manage it? Of course, Smith believed this was a fundamental flaw, but as time would prove, it was an issue that could be addressed through more proper regulation, enhanced governance rights of shareholders, and castigation of managers who ignored their obligations to their stakeholders.

THE INDUSTRIAL REVOLUTION

Although Smith's protestations regarding joint-stock companies did not force them out of existence, in general his writings were quite influential. Indeed, his new economic theories, emphasizing strong market competition and laissez-faire economics as the means by which to innovate and prosper on a societal level, were particularly relevant as Britain and other European nations were increasingly turning away from mercantilism and embracing free trade. Starting with the First Industrial Revolution, from about 1760 to 1840, radical changes in iron production, the utilization of steam power, and the mass manufacture of textiles began to reshape the global economy and labor force. The Second Industrial Revolution, also called the Technical Revolution, involved the incorporation of new materials (most notably steel) on a massive scale, technologies (like the internal combustion engine and the radio), and electric power. Beginning in the middle of the 1860s, this second stage of the Industrial Revolution extended until World War I. This process of industrialization, one of the few times in history that humanity altered the very structure of existence under which it had lived for centuries, was a major accelerator of the democratization of investment. In fact, the Industrial Revolution would have been impossible without the evolution of the investment and banking systems. It also marked the historically critical inflection point in the trend of wealth generation and democratization. That is, it facilitated a slow retreat of nearly exclusive control of surplus resources by the elite to a slowly growing possession of surplus by broader swaths of the population.[11]

Of course, the Industrial Revolution was also enabled by earlier economic shifts, manifested at both a macro and micro scale. On the macro level, the commercialization of Europe in large part served as a contextual precursor for the Industrial Revolution. Many Europeans were already familiar with market production and were not manufacturing all of the goods they used individually but rather were obtaining them through means of trade and exchange. The role of the national banking system in England as a facilitator of sales and catalyst for the velocity of goods exchange was instrumental as well. And on a more micro level was the economic dynamism of individuals and their family units; much as in earlier European eras, prosperous merchant families and families of industrialists began driving their own economic success.[12]

The eighteenth century's demographic factors went a long way to catalyze the Industrial Revolution, and in Great Britain in particular. For one, there was a great deal of population growth, partly due to a break in the stream of plagues and disease outbreaks that had afflicted Europe for centuries. Coupled with this was the availability of resources, a willingness to innovate, and technological advances that together helped enable this transformation in industry. For instance, Johannes Gutenberg's revolutionary printing press of the fifteenth century clearly facilitated the diffusion of knowledge that made the Industrial Revolution—and its necessary technological innovations and inventions—possible in the first place.

Among the other facilitating technologies of the Industrial Revolution was James Hargreaves's spinning jenny, a spinning frame with multiple spindles that vastly increased production volume in the textile industry. Combined with the flying shuttle, the spinning jenny took the textile industry into the next competitive era. James Watt's late eighteenth-century steam engine changed most industries using mechanical power, especially transportation and agriculture, quite significantly. The previous costs of producing this mechanical power, no matter the application, were generally higher than the costs of heating water to steam, and thus enormous cost savings were realized and industrial and transportation projects became more feasible. All of these technologies of the Industrial Revolution made life easier for their innumerable users and facilitated much of the economic growth and societal advancement of the Industrial Revolution era.[13]

The Nature of Capital Demands in the Industrial Revolution

Over the long term, the Industrial Revolution influenced investment by creating a surplus shared by many beyond those in the upper echelons of society. The relationship between industrialization and public market investment, however, does not hold in the reverse. In other words, while industrialization may have produced surplus that could be invested in the long term, financial institutions beyond the banking system at the time were not really as crucial to industrialization in the first place as one might be inclined to believe.

To understand this, it is possible to bifurcate the capital demands of the First Industrial Revolution into fixed capital and working capital. Fixed capital requirements were low and were mostly met by entrepreneurs and their families, not by formal banking institutions. In fact, if one analyzed the division of the aggregate level of capital during the First Industrial Revolution, the share that belongs to fixed capital would have been between 50 and 70 percent of the total capital. However, this overstates the role of fixed capital in the actual industrialization process because the industries where industrialization began, such as textiles, did not require significant fixed capital.[14] For instance, perhaps the most significant fixed capital expense in an industry like textiles is the space where production occurs—a converted warehouse, most likely.[15] This would change by the time of the Second Industrial Revolution, which, by virtue of the specialized heavy machinery involved, necessarily required large quantities of fixed capital, but this was not yet the case in the initially industrializing sectors.

For those entrepreneurs and families involved, funding of fixed capital in the early industrializing sectors typically entailed reallocating the wealth derived from agricultural activities, ownership of natural resources, and other businesses toward these industrial enterprises. This tendency toward the self-financing of fixed capital also drove businesses to reinvest earnings in lieu of distributing them when a strategy of growth was pursued. Self-financing was also attractive to entrepreneurs as a means of keeping the requisite sources of outside fixed capital under control. Many perceptive business owners made decisions to keep fixed capital requirements low by renting rather than owning physical space, for instance.[16]

It is also important to note that working capital demands—unlike their fixed capital counterparts—were high. Working capital (or circulating capital) demands refers to the liquidity needs of the business for inventory, debt service, payroll, and other short-term financing requirements. The relative magnitude of fixed and working capital needs is exemplified by the northern and midland textile sectors before 1815, where the working capital commitments were three times the fixed capital demands. Given the greater requirement for working capital, it is believed that these demands were frequently too large to be satisfied by the entrepreneurs themselves and were met instead by banks. As we will see, the decentralization of banks contributed significantly to meeting this demand for working capital.[17]

The Banking Institutions of the Industrial Revolution

The role of the banking institutions—a source of capital supply—is also very significant to the Industrial Revolution. The eighteenth-century English banking system was run by three categories of players: the Bank of England, the private banks of London, and the country banks. The Bank of England was chartered in 1694, prompted in large part by the dismal state of affairs of the English navy, which had recently begun experiencing steep losses in battle. It was a wake-up call for Britain, and the English realized how sorely they required a revitalization of their maritime forces. This, however, proved to be a formidable challenge because King William III's ability to access credit (certainly not improved in the wake of such defeats) was limited, severely limiting how extensive this nautical overhaul could be. And so the Bank of England was born, with the goal of furnishing credit to William III. The Bank of England was not, at this time, a central bank wielding control over the supply of money, but it nonetheless became a national institution.[18]

The private banks of London grew throughout the eighteenth century, from a total of thirty in 1750 to fifty by 1770 and seventy by 1800. These private banks had two purposes. The first was to supply funds for short-term loans and to trade and help settle bills of exchange. The second, which became more important after 1770, was to serve as the intermediary between the Bank of England and the third type of banking entity, the country bank. These country banks, as the name would suggest, operated beyond urban London. The private banks helped move specie and banknotes back and forth between the country banks and the Bank of England to ensure the former were properly capitalized.[19]

While the growth of the private banks in London throughout this period may have been impressive, the number of country banks grew even faster. In 1750, they numbered just 12, but by 1784 they hit 120, by 1797 there were 290, and by 1800 there were 370 country banks. The number of country banks varied in proportion to the strength of the economy and the state of credit at the time. For instance, they tended to do well when the Bank of England suspended the ability of holders of banknotes to make conversions to gold during the wars with France in the late eighteenth century. Of course, the inverse held as well: when the economy was doing poorly, these country banks were quite vulnerable to bankruptcy. Of the 311 bankruptcies that occurred between 1809 and 1830, more than half of them happened in the crisis intervals from 1814 to 1816 and 1824 to 1826.[20]

Some of these country banks were created by families who accumulated fortunes in other trades and found themselves with adequate resources to capitalize a bank. Of course, these country banks accepted deposits as well, but the founding families' wealth made it possible to open the doors of the country banks in the first place. For example, Gurney's Bank (one of the banks that would merge into Barclay's in 1896) was started by the descendants of John Gurney of Maldon, who aggregated a fortune in the wool trade. As Quakers themselves, they attracted many of their early depositors from the Society of Friends, and over time, their reputation spread as a trustworthy institution.[21]

In addition to driving a change in structure toward joint-stock banks, the Bank Act of 1826 strengthened the scope and operation of country banks by granting permission to rural banking institutions (those beyond about sixty-five miles of London) to issue banknotes. One cause of this decentralization of banking in early to mid-nineteenth-century England was the refashioning of the international political landscape. During the reign of Napoleon, the English government had been particularly keen on ensuring that financing the national debt was a foremost priority of English capital markets. It was only with the defeat of Napoleon at Waterloo in 1815 that the English became less concerned with the prospect of a French-dominated Europe, and the government was able to relax its preoccupation with putting the national coffers among the first to receive service from banks and lenders.[22] Therefore, there was a resulting liberating effect on capital markets toward private enterprise. Beyond decentralization, the country banks served a fundamentally different role than did other types of banking institutions at the time. In fact, some of these country banks looked more like modern venture capitalists than conventional banks because country banks provided financing to the riskier, more entrepreneurial projects that the larger, more traditional banks tended to avoid.

Much of the nineteenth-century banking experience thereafter was marked by powerful consolidation. In lieu of a multitude of independent country banks, these establishments began to merge with other firms, acquire smaller players, and outcompete their peers that were slower to adopt this trend toward greater scale. Of course, the banks that became larger by way of acquisition still needed an instrument to exert wide geographic influence, which manifested itself in the phenomenon of branching. Banks could still penetrate provincial markets, but they now operated under a banner of other banks, enjoying a broader capital base, a wider diversification of loans, and economies of scale. Between 1825 and 1913, there was a precipitous drop in the number of banks in Britain, from 715 to 88. However, at the same time, the rise in the number of branches more than compensated for this, rising from about 850 to over 8,000 during this same period, indicating an even more extensive dispersion of banks integrated into fewer and more powerful corporate outfits.[23]

Long-Run Improvements in Wealth Generation

It is difficult for a modern person to understand how radical a transformation it was to have the generation of savings begin to spread from the prominent and landed gentry, first to merchants and manufacturers and later to others. Before the Industrial Revolution, the savings of most economies were held almost exclusively by a small elite class. Consider, for instance, the conditions of the poorest classes during the bubonic plague of the 1600s. Most became so desperate for food and clothing that they stole from the bodies of the dead, thereby spreading the disease. The town councils of many areas in Europe had no choice but to take notice and begin restrictions and provide aid for the lower classes.[24] The town councils were forced to provide assistance for the many who had no coinage to spare.

An analysis of GDP per capita leaves very little doubt that industrialization was transformative in bringing about sustained economy-wide growth in a manner that was essentially unprecedented in history (see table 2.1). The United Kingdom, for example, saw its GDP per capita approximately triple from 1700 to 1880. Considering the slow growth of the GDP in the years leading up to the Industrial Revolution, the new growth was indeed miraculous.

There are other metrics suggesting that the standard of living of the British was also slowly becoming better over this interval, consistent with the economic data. While perhaps today it would not be regarded as the optimal proxy for quality of life, rising sugar consumption typically implied a shift beyond sustenance and toward richer food. Between 1815 and 1844, the average person in England consumed less

TABLE 2.1
GDP per Capita from A.D. 1500 to A.D. 1890 in Selected European Countries (1990 International Dollars)

	AUSTRIA	BELGIUM	DENMARK	FRANCE	GERMANY	ITALY	NETHERLANDS	SWITZERLAND	UK
1500	707	875	738	727	688	1,100	761	632	714
1600	837	976	875	841	791	1,100	1,381	750	974
1700	993	1,144	1,039	910	910	1,100	2,130	890	1,250
1820	1,218	1,319	1,274	1,135	1,077	1,117	1,838	1,090	1,706
1830	1,399	1,354	1,330	1,191	1,328	N/A	2,013	N/A	1,749
1840	1,515	N/A	1,428	1,428	N/A	N/A	2,283	N/A	1,990
1850	1,650	1,847	1,767	1,597	1,428	1,350	2,371	1,488	2,330
1860	1,778	2,293	1,741	1,892	1,639	N/A	2,377	1,745	2,830
1870	1,863	2,692	2,003	1,876	1,839	1,499	2,757	2,102	3,190
1880	2,079	3,065	2,181	2,120	1,991	1,581	3,046	2,450	3,477
1890	2,443	3,428	2,523	2,376	2,428	1,667	3,323	3,182	4,009

Source: Angus Maddison, Contours of the World Economy, 1–2030 A.D.: Essays in Macro-Economic History (Oxford: Oxford University Press, 2007), Table A.8; Angus Maddison, The World Economy: Historical Statistics (Paris: Development Centre of the Organisation for Economic Co-operation and Development, 2003), 58–61.

than twenty pounds of sugar per year, but from 1844 to 1854, average annual sugar consumption grew to about thirty-four pounds per year, and by the 1890s, was around eighty to ninety pounds.[25]

Difficult Conditions for Laborers

The precise effect of the Industrial Revolution on labor and wages remains a contentious issue among economic historians, and clearly not all the nuances of the various arguments can be captured here. The view proposed here is that the Industrial Revolution was a process that induced substantial growth in the long run, though in the short run it produced very difficult living conditions for many urban laborers.

One debate among historians concerns the precise moment when wages for laborers themselves actually improved. A fair amount of compelling scholarship suggests that the period around 1820 represented an inflection point for labor, before which wages tended to stagnate and after which wages tended to march upward.[26] While wages for laborers did tend to rise after 1820, many laborers were far from being well off. Industrialization produced a larger concentration of the population in urban centers. Many who had worked comfortably in cottage industry and operated out of their bucolic homesteads found themselves plunged into urban squalor when they relocated to find work in the cities.[27] The influx into some cities was so great that the development of infrastructure (such as sanitation) and strong institutions (including law enforcement) seriously lagged behind what was necessary to keep a well-ordered metropolis.

Of course, efforts to remediate these hapless urban environments were not helped by the political climate at the time. Class conflict boiled over as laborers found themselves not sharing proportionately in the prosperity of the age, and the affluent often staked out an entrenched position to oppose meaningful political reorganization to that end. There was little interest by the latter in ameliorating the conditions the former were enduring. Indeed, one historian has gone so far as to assert, "No period of British history has been as tense, as politically and socially disturbed, as the 1830s and early 1840s."[28] The political movements collectively known as Chartism emerged beginning in 1838. These movements converged ideologically on a document known as The People's Charter that outlined a set of six proposals for reform to the political system to render it more accessible to the general population, such as extending the vote to all men and removing any requirements for the ownership of property for candidates running in parliamentary elections. Though Chartism began to fade by 1848, the class conflict prompted by the disproportionate effect of the Industrial Revolution in improving the lots of various income groups was far from over.[29]

One of the fascinating aspects of early English industrialization in retrospect was its highly controversial nature socially and abroad. The Germans reviled what they had seen in England during English industrialization. Many Germans cited the horrid urban filth, the rampant poverty, and the repugnant working conditions as the basis for detesting industrialization.[30] Indeed, many of the works of Charles Dickens, like *Hard Times* and *Oliver Twist*, dealt intimately with the subject and shared the wretched early consequences of British industrialization with the world.

There was also a significant contingent of the laboring class that certainly did not share at all in the growth—namely, those who remained on farms. Industrialization was a much more potent force in the city than it was in the agrarian setting. While nonfarm labor wages increased by some 80 percent from 1797 to 1851, farm labor wages actually dropped slightly over this period.[31]

White-collar workers did tend to outperform blue-collar workers in terms of income growth: blue-collar workers tended to see a doubling of wages from 1781 to 1851, whereas white-collar workers saw wages quadruple.[32] Indeed, the process of industrialization is linked inextricably to the phenomenon of increased urbanization from which a wide variety of occupations (and particularly white-collar workers, whose work is often tied to or done more fully in cities) benefited.

Ultimately, it is clear that wages did rise for many groups in the Industrial Revolution, but what was the effect on savings? Having an understanding of the changes in total savings is critical in thinking about capital formation, since the amount of savings determines the quantity of liquid resources available for investment. The methodologies employed to answer this question are far from perfect because they often involve making an assumption of an aggregate savings function that is not easily validated by the historical record. Nevertheless, there is reason to believe that much of the net growth in savings was due more to rising incomes than to a large increase in savings rates.

The observed savings rate increased from about 8.5 to 12.5 percent during the Second Industrial Revolution, while gross national income grew by over threefold in this same time period.[33] The previously lower wages left little surplus for discretionary activity at all, as little was left once housing, food, and other necessities were satisfied. The Industrial Revolution profoundly altered the landscape of investment because savings—the basis of all investment—increased as wages grew. Although not immediately, this put the economy on a trajectory toward a democratization of mass saving and investment by way of these higher incomes that would have otherwise been impossible for such a large swath of the population in the subsequent twentieth century.

Breadth of the Industrial Revolution

Although the Industrial Revolution did begin in just a few select sectors, it did translate into growth across a much broader portion of the British economy. Indeed, Britain saw strong increases in exports in a wide variety of industries beyond those touched directly by the radical innovations that brought on the entire industrialization process.[34]

However, while England is perhaps the most discussed and most studied nation when it comes to analyzing the transformative effects of the Industrial Revolution, the history of the experience of its northern neighbor, Scotland, is also quite rich. The experience of the Scottish during industrialization was inextricably linked to the Scottish Enlightenment, the period of intense intellectual and scientific achievement in the eighteenth century. The Scottish Enlightenment involved revolutionary thinkers like Adam Smith, David Hume, and John Millar, intellectuals who transformed economics, philosophy, physics, and chemistry. Though it is easy to identify a few key thinkers and their corresponding achievements, the Scottish Enlightenment had a more crucial and wider-ranging effect: a dedication to the improvement and reworking of society. Scottish intellectuals had a strong sense of the importance of infrastructure in greasing the wheels of the economy. An economy can thrive when infrastructure, like canals and roads, is constructed to facilitate the movement of products and labor. Many Scottish landowners were quick to utilize new agricultural techniques as well, which allowed Scotland to achieve self-sufficiency and reduced the transfer of capital abroad, leaving more for domestic investment.

There was also awareness that the institutional environment exerted a very tangible influence on the operation of the economy, and as such, many Scottish intellectuals began to advocate for the revamping of outmoded legal arrangements.[35] The legal framework in which this new commercial activity occurred needed to adapt to a changing world.

In terms of the mechanics of investment, Scotland also employed a rather different partnership structure than did England when it came to organizing an enterprise. Unlike the English common-law variety, the Scottish partnership was quite similar to the French civil law structure that emphasized the dissociation of ownership and management. In the Scottish arrangement, only the inside partners could make decisions on debt, contracts, or other major financing and operational decisions, while the outside partners were far more passive. On the one hand, the Scottish partnership still had the shortcoming of unlimited liability for all partners, including the passive outside partners, and thus created a strong incentive to ensure that partners with limited means were excluded from the acquisition of interests. This incentive arose because in the case of catastrophe where liabilities exceeded assets, partners would need to surrender their own outside resources, and if one partner was unable to do so, his share was borne by all the other partners. On the other hand, it does appear that the Scottish banks were, in fact, more stable than their English counterparts, as evidenced by the lower failure rates of banking institutions during periods of fiscal crisis in the early nineteenth century.[36]

Changing Modes of Capital Formation in the United States and France in the Second Industrial Revolution

Modes of financing changed over time in other nations as well. Many of these changes can be seen, for instance, in the markets of Cleveland, Ohio, which was a hub of innovation during the Second Industrial Revolution in the United States. However, these innovations during the Second Industrial Revolution were of a different flavor in that they tended to be much more capital intensive than their predecessors in the First Industrial Revolution. Many of the most transformative inventions could not be brought to market without substantial access to capital, and many entrepreneurs simply lacked the means to self-finance their new technologies. As a result of the greater capital demands, more innovation was localized within existing companies.

That is, instead of entrepreneurs or inventors conceiving of an idea and starting a firm to promote the commercialization of the technology, many of the larger existing firms spent handsomely on research and development, and more products came out of these efforts than before.[37]

To be clear, the days of the entrepreneur-led company were far from over; such entrepreneurship was just slightly harder to accomplish with the greater capital demands. Inventors were still most likely to grant their patent rights to a firm in which they possessed equity, rather than selling those rights to another firm. Entrepreneurs were still interested in preserving autonomy and control, and some still managed to do so despite the increased difficulties. As one can imagine, it was easier to attract capital if one had a history of successful inventions. This is evidenced in a variety of historical examples, including the story of Charles Brush, who invented arc lighting and founded Brush Electric. Even after he left that line of business and tried to pursue enterprises in other industries, his past success seems to have made it far easier for him to attract capital. Past successes gave firms a second immense advantage: the ability to attract talent. Many bright young scientists and inventors wanted to join Brush Electric ranks, well aware that they would be on the cutting edge and that they would work alongside brilliant colleagues.[38]

During this time, the operation of banking institutions also changed. Whereas during the First Industrial Revolution many families with wealth from preindustrial activities were founding and operating small banks, in the Second Industrial Revolution it was industrial magnates who were now operating many banks. For instance, Robert Hanna, who made a fortune in the Cleveland Malleable Iron Company, founded the Ohio National Bank.[39] It is very likely that these industrialists were more able administrators, for they were the products of the very industrial success in which they were intending to invest.

In France, though, many small banks continued to be run by older families with preindustrial wealth, even during the Second Industrial Revolution. In fact, many small banks were funded by these families and would deploy capital locally, much like the country banks of England. That said, these small banks funded by families had to share the market with a very adept financing institution: the merchant bank. Large merchant banks did quite well in capturing firms with international operations, as they were able to handle the settlements of funds across borders with ease. The small merchant banks, though, likely realizing they could not compete well in capturing large companies that traded internationally, tended to take more risk and invest in industries that were novel and growing, looking like modern venture capital firms.[40]

Thus, to summarize, the influence of industrialization on the character and practice of investment can be broken down into several lessons. The First Industrial Revolution was largely self-financed because there were low fixed capital demands. There was also a sophisticated network of banks emanating from London to the private banking intermediaries and ultimately to the country banks that financed higher-risk investment projects. The character of financing changed during the Second Industrial Revolution when high capital costs demanded external financing solutions that could no longer be accomplished through self-financing channels. Most of all, there are crucial lessons with respect to growth and wage improvements. The effect of the Industrial Revolution on wages was not immediate, and many people suffered from terrible working and living conditions. In addition, the effect of the Industrial Revolution on wages was not uniform across all types of labor, disproportionately affecting urban workers over farmers. The third lesson is that although not all workers benefited equally, the Industrial Revolution was also not just a phenomenon limited to a small portion of the economy. Finally, and perhaps most important of all, the Industrial Revolution did, in the long term, prompt the beginning of an unprecedented growth in wages for the average worker.

THE ADVENT OF PUBLIC MARKETS

To genuinely appreciate the emergence of the public market, it is necessary to look farther into history to examine how government lending and asset transfers occurred before this crucial development.

Before the Public Market

The earliest markets for securities resembling our modern system arose in twelfth-century Italy. While central governments and large corporations rule today's bond market, at that time most debt instruments were actually issued from local governments and landowners. The most notable innovations in debt issuance were in the city-states of early Renaissance Italy. Genoa in particular was a pioneer in securitizing public debt. As early as 1164, the city created a form of public debt in which members of an association, known as the *compera*, paid to receive a share, called a *luoghe*, or claim, on the debt. Venice, by contrast, tried to satisfy its debt requirements by asking wealthy citizens for voluntary loans. But eventually these loans proved insufficient, and the city turned to forced loans. In turn, as government spending grew larger and larger, forced loans failed to satisfy the city-state's credit requirements. Consequently, Venice consolidated all of its outstanding debts in one fund, the *Monte*, in 1262; all claims to debt were exchanged for shares in the Monte, which earned 5 percent interest. Florence and Genoa created similar mechanisms in 1343 and 1407, respectively. Most investors were wealthy citizens, though some middle-class citizens and some foreigners did buy the funds. Because shares of the Monte were easily transferable, a secondary market developed. Shares traded at market price, which depended on expectation of the government's ability to pay interest and the availability or reliability of other investments, demonstrating the influence of this secondary market on the exchange of securities.[41]

In addition to this trade in public debt was a growing use of private debt. This network of credits and debits was increasingly based on nonnegotiable bills of exchange. A bill of exchange is a promise by the signer to pay a certain amount of money on a certain date. A nonnegotiable, or nontransferable, bill of exchange is written to a specific person, and only that person can receive the money. A negotiable bill of exchange, however, is payable to the bearer, who is not necessarily the original owner of the instrument. This was a major improvement over shipping currency from place to place, a dangerous and unreliable practice. It was also an improvement over the system at the periodic fairs in Champagne, France, during the twelfth century, in which fair authorities and merchants simply recorded credits and debits accrued by the end of one trading period and carried them over until the next fair took place. The relatively widespread use of nonnegotiable bills of exchange in Renaissance Italy was also convenient because bills of exchange payable in a foreign currency presented a true risk, related to the rate of foreign exchange, thereby skirting the usury prohibitions of the period.[42] At the time, there was no secondary market in these financial instruments because they were nonnegotiable, but this period set the stage for the later securitization of debt in negotiable, or transferable, bills of exchange.

In the fifteenth and sixteenth centuries, the center of financial activity and power shifted from Italy to northern Europe, where various exchanges, known as *bourses*, developed. The most important of these exchanges in the late 1400s was Bruges, though dominance shifted to Antwerp in the 1500s and this city became very powerful by the latter part of the century. Other, less important bourses emerged in Paris in 1563, London in 1571, and Frankfurt in 1585. At first in these markets, commodities, crafts, and financial products were exchanged side by side, much as they were in the fairs of late medieval France. Increasingly, though, trade in goods and trade in securities became separated. In large part, the financial products exchanged at these fairs were currencies and bills of exchange, introducing new risks—exchange rate fluctuation and default, respectively—and increased liquidity to the market. To a smaller but still notable extent, debt was often exchanged at the bourses. Antwerp even had a notable market for municipal annuities. While most participants in the market were quite wealthy, likely nobility and landowners, some participants belonged to the "middle class." In 1545, an estimated 25 percent of purchasers were craftsmen, 21 percent were administrative officials, 17 percent were widows, and 16 percent were merchants.[43]

Despite all of the rather advanced features of debt in Italy and bourses in Antwerp and northern Europe, it is important to note that there was still no truly public market or stock exchange. At this time, there were few tradable financial assets, few people holding such securities at any given time, and few exchanges of those securities. As a consequence, no formal organization for trade in financial instruments existed, and there were no specialized intermediaries who facilitated such transactions. Instead, transactions were personally negotiated and executed at general mercantile exchanges. The supply of and demand for securities and the volume of trades simply did not yet support the creation of a public market.[44]

The Beginnings of the Public Market: Amsterdam

By the dawn of the seventeenth century, negotiable securities representing shares of a business or of government debt were gaining in popularity across Europe. As ownership of and interest in these securities became more widespread, formal markets were organized for their purchase and sale. As volume grew, those who facilitated these exchanges became full-time professionals who developed specialized techniques for the execution of transactions.[45] Thus began in earnest the stock exchange in its modern form.[46] As it did so, Amsterdam was established as the center of the European financial world in the first years of the 1600s.[47] The old center of Antwerp, now tarnished by sovereign debt default and beset by Spanish attack in the Eighty Years' War, was no match for the newly ascendant city.[48]

One major development cementing Amsterdam's important new role was the creation of the Amsterdam Wisselbank clearinghouse in 1609. While merchant banks in Antwerp, London, and Amsterdam had previously coordinated the flow of credit and debt in the European economy, the creation of a centralized location for account settlement represented significant progress over what had been a less efficient and less coordinated process.[49]

The next important step toward the development of the modern financial system was the creation of a joint-stock company whose shares were bought and sold on a public market.[50] Given that Amsterdam was the financial center of the Western world at this time, it is no surprise that this innovation took place there. The Dutch East India Company (Vereenigde Oostindische Compagnie, or VOC) was chartered in the early 1600s,[51] and by 1609 its shares were widely traded in a secondary market on the nascent stock exchange in Amsterdam.[52] Shareholder rights differed somewhat from today's expectations in that stockholders were not allowed to vote on the company's decisions, though they were paid a dividend. The dividend was often quite high, averaging 18 percent per year.[53]

Although Amsterdam was the first city to develop specialized intermediaries and many techniques that are hallmarks of the modern stock market, the city's stock exchange was not made a formal institution until 1787. As such, the first organized stock market was created in Paris in 1724, limited to sixty specialized intermediaries (*agents de change*) and self-governed with a written code of conduct.[54] Furthermore, Amsterdam lagged behind other cities in the development of a price list for securities. While a price list existed in London as early as 1697, such a list was not available in Amsterdam until 1795.[55]

London

Joint-stock companies had existed in England since well before the Dutch East India Company. However, the securities for these joint-stock companies, which were focused primarily on trading ventures, were not conducive to actual trading. Shareholders were subject to unlimited liability, and their numbers were few. Furthermore, though shares were negotiable, it was difficult to transfer them, so transactions happened almost exclusively among friends and family and no true public market developed.[56]

While the Dutch-English link was already strong in the mid-1600s, with connections through the trade of bills of exchange, it was the Glorious Revolution of 1688 that hastened the development of an English financial system resembling that of Amsterdam. In that year, James II was exiled from England and William of Orange, stadtholder of the Dutch Republic, became king, bringing his Dutch advisers with him.[57]

The first joint-stock company chartered after the Glorious Revolution was the Bank of England. Created in 1694, it was created largely to provide much-needed credit to King William III's government, as described earlier in this chapter. It was analogous in many ways to the Amsterdam Wisselbank, though it was also more efficient in some ways. One significant divergence from the most famous Dutch joint-stock company, the VOC, was that stockholders in the Bank of England were given voting privileges. However, this had no real meaningful impact because great wealth was required for effective voting.[58]

The English stock market began at the turn of the eighteenth century in the coffeehouses on Exchange Alley, a street near the Royal Exchange marketplace in London.[59] At Jonathan's Coffeehouse, John Castaing began offering a price list for securities that were being bought and sold privately in the city as early as 1698, bringing some order to the prevailing chaos and marking an important step toward the organization of trading in London.[60] Traders at the time were even licensed by the City of London.[61] Though several coffeehouses served as centers for information and financial transactions, Jonathan's became the most important and dominated the market for exchange.[62]

The stock exchange in many ways represented a social benefit. While the Bank of England was the original organ designed to help issue government debt, the stock exchange also helped England to borrow money at historically low interest rates and to raise substantial war money in the seventeenth and eighteenth centuries.[63] In turn, the need to raise these funds helped the stock market to develop. However, these new opportunities also came with challenges. The South Sea Bubble of 1720, as described earlier, rocked the English financial markets. As a result, the system, which was already under some measure of government control, became more strictly limited through the Bubble Act of 1720. Much government regulation at the time was fueled by anxiety rather than logic, and most regulations were weak. However, the Bubble Act was an exception to this rule. It significantly regulated the formation of joint-stock companies and curtailed issuance of equity, limiting market growth for over a century.[64]

In 1760 there were 60,000 holders of British government debt, indicating the level of public participation in the financial markets. There were even fewer joint-stock company shareholders, though trading in equity was more common than in government debt because joint-stock dividends were uncertain and subject to much speculation.[65] This figure represents just over 1 percent of the population of England, estimated to be approximately 5.75 million people at the time.[66]

Around the turn of the nineteenth century, the stock exchange underwent significant evolution. In 1773, the exchange moved to a new building and was reorganized as a joint partnership, briefly named The New Jonathan's and then soon renamed again as The Stock Exchange. Multiple price lists were consolidated into a new publication, the "Course of the Exchange," evidence of greater coordination and organization. In 1801, the group was reorganized again, this time as a joint-stock corporation. The new regulations and formalization associated with this transformation established the exchange in its modern form. The next year, the exchange moved to a new building. Finally, the Bubble Act of 1720 was abolished in 1825, accelerating the creation of new companies and fueling growth in the financial system. Apart from innovations within the financial system, the emergence of London as the new world financial center was fueled by the European political context. With the French Revolution beginning in 1789 and the Napoleonic Wars lasting until 1815, disruption and destruction in France and the Low Countries cleared the way for a rising England.[67]

The American Experience

In the United States, the federal government floated $77.1 million in debt in 1790 to pay back costs incurred by the American Revolution, giving birth to the first US public debt markets.[68] On May 17, 1792, the Buttonwood Agreement (so named because it was signed under a buttonwood tree by twenty-four stockbrokers) was executed. Soon, in 1793, the Tontine Coffee House in New York City became a forum for trading government debt and equities, while many of the stockbrokers' colleagues traded securities in the street nearby.[69]

The Buttonwood Agreement created what is today the New York Stock Exchange. It is of interest that the agreement specified that the brokers were to deal directly with one another and that commissions for trades would be twenty-five basis points (or one-fourth of 1 percent). The influence of auctioneers, who often charged very high fees and failed to create order in the transaction process, was curtailed within the exchange for the first time. The new organization was called the "New York Stock & Exchange Board."[70]

Three decades later, the traders who continued to trade in the streets of New York outside Water Street and Wall Street came to be called curbstone brokers. Typically, the curbstone brokers would be heavily involved in making markets in higher-risk firms, like turnpike or railroad companies. The California Gold Rush of the 1840s only drove business further for these curbstone brokers, with mining companies being added to the mix. By 1859, oil was discovered in western Pennsylvania and oil stocks began trading among the brokers as well.[71]

In 1863, the New York Stock & Exchange Board's name was shortened to the New York Stock Exchange, or NYSE. In 1868, membership became a valuable commodity—one could join the NYSE only by purchasing 1 of 1,366 existing seats on the exchange.[72] Meanwhile, the curbstone brokers needed better infrastructure. They formed the Open Board of Stock Brokers in 1864, merging with the NYSE five years later. However, the curbstone market continued to exist. In 1865, after the Civil War ended, these brokers began to trade stocks in small industrial companies such as those dealing in iron, steel, chemicals, and textiles.[73]

The turn of the twentieth century brought immense institutional change in the history of public stock exchanges in the United States. By this time, the NYSE had been recognized as a leading American financial establishment. Trading volumes skyrocketed in the second half of the nineteenth century, and the exchange saw average daily trading volume reach 500,000 in 1900 from 1,500 in 1861.[74]

At the same time, the curbstone brokers were moving quickly to institutionalize their own trading framework. Emanuel S. Mendels, a prominent curbstone broker of the time, began to organize the market and tried to strive for ethical dealings in trading shares of these companies. In 1908, he established the New York Curb Market Agency, which attempted to codify trading practices further and set rules by which brokers should operate. Seven years later, this agency created the constitution and framework for the New York Curb Market, which moved to a real building on Greenwich Street in lower Manhattan in 1921. In 1953, the New York Curb Exchange would change its name to the American Stock Exchange.[75]

The Effects of Industrialization and Technology on Public Markets

The late 1800s and early 1900s saw the emergence of the first truly global market, largely fueled by historical context and technological innovation. To start with, the Second Industrial Revolution during this period fueled corporate demand for capital that could be used for expanded business operations, primarily for investment in fixed capital such as machines and factories. Furthermore, many governments loosened restrictions on corporate formation at this time, making it easier for entrepreneurs to start their own businesses; these new businesses, then, issued debt or equity for the first time, further fueling financial markets.[76] As a result of these changes, the combined capitalization of these enterprises exceeded the gross debt of nations for the first time in the early twentieth century.[77]

Technology also played a vital role in the continued evolution of public capital markets. The most influential technologies were those that affected the spread of information, given the importance of accurate data in making financial decisions. The first in a series of such inventions came in 1844 with the invention of the telegraph, which allowed relatively convenient and immediate communication among markets and cities. In 1866, the first transatlantic cable was completed, allowing near-instantaneous communication between the key global financial centers of London and New York. The next year, the stock ticker was introduced. This specialized telegraph receiver, invented by Edward Calahan in 1863, printed stock symbols and prices on a paper tape, providing a mode of communicating financial data even more conveniently than the telegraph. Finally, the first telephone was installed on the floor of the NYSE in 1878, just two years after its invention.[78] In addition to these information technologies, the development of improved steamships and the creation of the Panama Canal also contributed to the globalization of finance.[79]

As a result of these changes, a network of buyers, sellers, and intermediaries constituting a global financial market emerged for the first time by 1870. Centered in London and Amsterdam—and with important hubs in New York, Germany, and France—this system lasted until 1914.[80] During these years, securities were more important in finance and investment than ever before. To quantify the extent of market participation at this time, one estimate suggests there were 20 million securities investors worldwide by 1910.[81] This number is likely larger than ever before; with a world population of roughly 1.65 billion people, it represented 1.7 percent market participation, and a much higher percentage of the population in the more developed economics.

Broadening of American Stock Ownership

At the beginning of the twentieth century, only about 5 percent of households in the United States directly or indirectly owned stocks. Because brokers would only manage large accounts and execute large trades, and because stocks often had to be bought in large lots, the markets were in practice accessible only to a small slice of society. In 1912, only 60,000 traded on the NYSE, and in 1916, only 13 percent of NYSE brokers would execute trades of fewer than 100 shares.[82]

Though investment was not actually widespread, stock markets captured the public imagination. Large numbers of Americans mimicked investment through so-called bucket shops, which arose around 1880 and remained popular for almost 40 years. In the bucket shops, participants essentially bet on the direction in which a stock would move in a very highly levered fashion, with small changes generating large profits and losses. Rather than watching horses race around a track, bucket shop patrons got their thrills by watching ticker tapes. Such gambling allowed people without real access to the market to participate in market hysteria.[83]

With a bull market in the 1920s, Americans began to participate more broadly in financial markets. A recent estimate suggests
that between 4 and 6 million Americans owned stocks in the 1920s,
accounting for 15–20 percent of households. However, most were not
active investors—about 1.5 million individuals, or 1.2 percent of adults,
likely had active brokerage accounts, while others simply acquired
shares through employee stock ownership plans and the like.[84] Other
estimates, based on federal income tax data, suggest there were 4–6
million shareowners in 1927 and 9–11 million in 1930.[85] When the
Great Depression hit, the broadening stock ownership of the early
1900s slowed, then stopped, then reversed. People lost trust in the
stock market, and investors no longer had as much extra money available to invest.[86]

In 1952, the Brookings Institution conducted a landmark study
of share ownership on behalf of the NYSE. The survey showed that
6.5 million Americans, or 4 percent of the overall population and
9.5 percent of households, owned stock directly.[87] When restricted
to adults, it showed that 6.35 million adults (6.4 percent of the adult
population, or about one in sixteen adults) owned shares.[88] It is
important to note the study's explicit focus on direct share ownership. It is true that most shareholdings at the time were attributable to individuals, with only 11.4 percent of shareholdings through
fiduciaries and less than 3 percent of shareholdings through institutions, foundations, insurance companies, investment companies,
and other miscellaneous corporations.[89] However, the distinction
between direct and indirect ownership is still significant. In addition to this focus, though, the study also examined the ownership
of other investments, finding that 67.1 percent of individuals had life
insurance, 34 percent had savings accounts, 4.2 percent had publicly owned stocks, and 1.9 percent had privately held stocks, with
78.9 percent of the population overall having at least one form of
investment.[90]

The Brookings survey showed differences in stock ownership
among segments of the American population. For example, older,
more educated, and wealthier individuals were more likely to be
shareholders. The number of men and women owning shares was
roughly equal, at 3.26 million men and 3.23 million women, and 33
percent of shareholders were housewives. However, women likely
came to be shareowners in significantly different ways than men did,

with 30 percent of female stockholders stating that their stocks were "inherited or acquired as gift."[91]

In the second half of the twentieth century, participation in the US financial system became more widespread. Some of the reasons for this upswing were out of the control of expert stakeholders, such as government regulators and financial professionals, and were due instead to the political and economic context of the period. For example, the long bull market following World War II made stocks seem like an attractive option for investing. In addition, the culture of the Cold War spurred the American public's eagerness to participate in the capitalist system and to support domestic industry. In contrast to the Soviet-style economic system, in which the means of production were taken over by the state, Americans hoped to show that workers could also own the means of production through equity shareholding in a capitalistic society.[92]

Other reasons for increasing market participation were more carefully constructed. The development of such investment products as mutual funds, retirement accounts, and equity derivatives offered new opportunities to investors. Greater regulation made investors more trusting of the markets and more willing to invest their money in securities. The federal government implemented several regulations during the New Deal years, and the Employee Retirement Income Security Act of 1974 (ERISA) ushered in a new era of pension investing. Similarly, the financial industry made some of its own rules more appealing to a broad investor base. For example, commission rate deregulation allowed brokers to individually set fees charged to investors for trade execution, making stock investing cheaper for retail and professional clients alike. Finally, public relations and marketing campaigns brought the market to the masses. Charles Merrill is perhaps the best-known figure in the development of the retail brokerage industry. The NYSE was also active in promoting share ownership during this time. From 1954 to 1969, its "Own Your Share of American Business" marketing campaign attempted to attracted small investors. New York Stock Exchange president Keith Funston expressed this objective clearly in 1951: "If we pursue our objectives with the strength of our convictions, we shall eventually approach our ideal, a nation of small share owners, a nation in whose material wealth every citizen has vested interest through personal ownership, a nation which is truly a people's democracy."[93]

By the early twenty-first century, 80 million Americans owned stocks directly or indirectly, accounting for approximately half of US households.[94] On the whole, then, the story of American investment in the twentieth century is one of broadening ownership. There is a much higher incidence of direct or indirect stockholding in the adult population now than there has been in the past—up from, for example, one in sixteen adults being an NYSE shareowner in 1952, to one in five in 1980, to one in four in 1990, to an impressive one in two and a half holding shares in the early 2000s.[95]

Many new investors, though, are not active participants in financial markets. Most American shareholders of the early 2000s held their shares through mutual funds or retirement accounts,[96] and although the direct owners of most shares in 1952 were private individuals, the direct owners became, to an increasing extent, institutions and intermediaries.[97] Furthermore, those who do participate directly in the stock market may participate in very different ways. In the early twenty-first century, about two-thirds of households held less than $6,000 in stocks. Many just held stocks through employee stock ownership plans, leaving a minority involved in active trading.[98] Most direct shareholders also did not have diverse portfolios. In 2010, of all families with directly held stocks, 29 percent held only one stock, and only 18 percent held more than ten stocks. Of the families that held stocks directly, the median stock portfolio was valued at $20,000, while the median retirement account of families holding this asset was valued at $44,000.[99]

Furthermore, while in aggregate the data suggest a public that is more engaged in the financial system, a closer examination of the data shows that certain groups of Americans are less likely to hold financial assets and, even if they do hold those assets, are less likely to invest much money in them. With respect to sex, the NYSE reported from 1952 to 1983 that the difference between the number of male and female adult shareowners ranged between 5.0 percent in favor of females and 5.4 percent in favor of males. A new survey methodology introduced in 1985 seemed to show that the gap was actually quite large, with 22 and 26 percentage points greater ownership for men in 1985 and 1990, respectively. (In 1990, 30.2 million adult men and 17.8 million adult women owned stocks.[100]) Not all data suggest such great inequality among demographic groups, however. For example, there is a distinct trend toward ownership of stocks by younger people. While the median shareowner age was fifty-one in 1952, it had decreased to forty-three by 1990, a trend that began between 1975 and 1980.[101]

Consolidation

In recent years, many exchanges, generally regional and relatively small exchanges, have shut down or been absorbed by larger exchanges as competition over cost, speed, and quality of execution has grown increasingly fierce. As laid out by economists James McAndrews and Chris Stefanadis, the main advantages of consolidation are threefold: streamlined technology, increased liquidity, and reduced fragmentation. First, when different exchanges use different trading platforms, they must each incur the fixed costs associated with creating and maintaining those platforms. Furthermore, investment banks and other intermediaries must maintain connections with multiple kinds of systems, leading to heightened complexity and cost. When a regional exchange is closed and trading is moved to a national or international exchange, or when a regional exchange is acquired by a national or international exchange system and integrated into that network, the costs of proliferating technologies are reduced. Second, as more and more buyers and sellers enter a single exchange, liquidity increases, meaning there is a higher likelihood that a match can be made between a buyer and a seller at a mutually suitable price. More liquid markets are more attractive to both buyers and sellers, creating a positive feedback loop or "snowball effect," in which the most attractive exchanges become even more attractive while the least attractive exchanges become even less attractive. Finally, exchange integration is beneficial because it reduces fragmentation of capital markets. It is inefficient to have the same stock trading at different prices on different exchanges. Under such a system, it is more difficult to discover the "true" price of a security.[102]

These three forces, along with some technological and regulatory changes, led to the decline of regional exchanges in the United States in the late nineteenth and twentieth centuries. The advent of cross-country telephone service in 1915 and the creation of a nationwide NYSE stock ticker network in the 1920s ended the regional exchanges' information advantage. In 1936, the federal government introduced unlisted trading privileges, permitting securities listed on one exchange to be traded at any other exchange. As a result of these changes, while the United States had over 100 regional exchanges in the late nineteenth century, that number had declined to eighteen by 1940, eleven by 1960, and just seven by 1980.[103]

Today, even the traditional giants in the stock exchange industry are subject to the forces of consolidation and technology-fueled evolution. The London Stock Exchange, for example, transitioned from a private to a public company in 2000. In 2007, the exchange merged with the primary stock exchange in Italy, the Borsa Italiana, to create the London Stock Exchange Group.[104] The NYSE itself has been involved in a number of mergers and transformations in recent years. In 2006, NYSE Group Inc., a for-profit public corporation, was created after the NYSE merged with a company named Archipelago Holdings. The next year, NYSE Group Inc. merged with the European exchange Euronext to create NYSE Euronext, and this group then acquired the American Stock Exchange in 2008. NYSE Euronext itself was acquired by Intercontinental Exchange Inc., based in Atlanta, in 2013.[105] There are some regulatory limits to consolidation of such larger mergers and acquisitions, however, as demonstrated when a proposed merger between NYSE Euronext and Deutsche Börse, a German exchange group, was blocked by the European Commission in 2012.[106]

Globalization

By the first years of the twentieth century, as mentioned earlier, a global financial network was emerging, largely enabled by new technologies that facilitated information flow among financial centers. Unfortunately, this development was stalled and reversed by the violence and financial turmoil of subsequent decades. World War I dealt a major blow to securities markets worldwide, and the Russian Revolution and the rise of communism led to the closure of stock markets in communist countries. Despite a minor recovery after 1918 and into the 1920s, the Great Depression stifled growth. Governments introduced new regulations in an effort to stabilize their economies, which led to further curtailment of the global financial network. And after all this, World War II caused even more destruction and even greater interruption of international exchanges.[107]

In the mid- to late twentieth century, the international flow of capital began to recover. While trade and financial agreements were limited and typically only bilateral in the 1950s, the next few years saw an increase in international capital mobility. By the 1980s, financial freedom of flows was finally at or above the level it had reached almost a century earlier.[108] Furthermore, new stock exchanges opened around the world, including New Delhi in 1947, Dhaka and Busan in the 1950s, Lagos and Tunis in the 1960s, Bangkok in 1974, and Kuwait and Istanbul in the 1980s.[109] Countries in Eastern Europe that had closed their exchanges in the 1940s began to reopen them after the fall of the Berlin Wall. For example, the stock exchange in Budapest reopened in 1990, and Warsaw's reopened in 1991. Even Shanghai reopened its stock exchange in 1990.[110]

Capital markets vary from country to country with respect to form and performance, suggesting that there is no single path to securitization and to the emergence of a public capital market. Scholarship on the subject suggests various factors that determine how market development unfolds, including a country's level of economic development, the amount and reliability of information available to investors, and whether a country has a common law or civil law system. Furthermore, governments play an important role in the process—issuance of public debt often sparked the development of markets, for example.[111] Legislation and other forms of government intervention also affect financial market formation.[112] As a result of these differences, the form and performance of markets can be quite different in different places. In relation to this chapter's focus on the broadening of share ownership, it is interesting to note a study from 1994 that found 21 percent of Americans held stock, compared to 35 percent in Sweden, 21 percent in the United Kingdom, 16 percent in France, and just 5 percent of the population in Germany.[113] At the same time, though, it is important not to overstate the differences among countries and to realize how interconnected various markets are.[114] For example, non-US and non-European stock exchanges were created and patterned on US and European stock exchanges as early as the nineteenth century.[115]

Ultimately, effective public markets for securities did not exist in substantial form before the 1600s. There were plenty of early glimmerings that had facets that were similar but lacked the essence of a public market: an organized forum for purchase and sale of securities that is reasonably straightforward to allow for ownership transfer and deep enough to provide liquidity. Before these public markets, capital formation for many groups, like governments, was difficult and often involved unusual means of procuring the needed funds like forced loans. Amsterdam saw the first real stock market with the trading of Dutch East India Company shares, though governance rights for such shareholders were poor. London saw a maturation of its financial centers with William III from the Dutch Republic taking the reins of English power after the Glorious Revolution, setting up the Bank of England. Soon, London coffeehouses served as primitive stock exchanges, equipped with licenses and price lists for securities. There were low participation rates in many of these public markets, of course, with an estimated 1 percent of the English public holding securities in English debt at the time. In the United States, the Buttonwood Agreement marked the beginnings of what would later evolve into the NYSE. Railroad, mining, and oil stocks were the flavor of the day by the mid-nineteenth century. These exchanges also underwent regulation, including self-regulation like that of the New York Curb Market Agency in 1908. Technology and globalization both facilitated the development of these public exchanges, including the increased speed of information transmission and the development of the ticker tape. Across many countries, stock ownership and utilization of these exchanges broadened widely. Whereas just 3 to 5 percent of adults owned stocks in the 1920s, about half of American households own stocks today. Of course, over time, the progress of public markets does not mean more public markets. There has been powerful consolidation afoot in recent years as network effects set in and there was more logic to having fewer exchanges, rather than a plethora of regional ones, list stocks.

FINAL COMMENTS

In the final analysis, the advent of public markets has significant implications for managed investments. As the final piece in the story of the democratization of investment, the evolution of public equity, capital-raising mechanisms, and strategy for professional money managers and individual investors cannot be ignored. It should not be lost upon observers that these modern developments are deeply rooted in the history of joint-stock companies and the democratization of wealth and resources that took place as a result of the Industrial Revolution.

As part of this clear trend of democratization, the introduction of joint-stock companies created a way for people and institutions lacking infinite resources to participate in investment as partial owners. Next, the Industrial Revolution was instrumental in creating surpluses for a much broader group of citizens than were included in the power elite, who were previously the only ones with real investable funds. This opened opportunity for investment to a vast middle class that included entrepreneurs, merchants, and manufacturers. Finally, the creation of public investment vehicles, both companies and funds, fostered a liquid marketplace in which a wide variety of people and organizations could participate.

After the creation, destruction, triumphs, tragedies, and economic catalysts of the Industrial Revolution, the advent of public companies brought dramatic breakthroughs, importantly driven by support from the broad population. Privately held equity stakes in business organizations and firms became publicly traded entities on what eventually evolved into high-volume public securities exchanges in the modern era. The emergence of public markets connected savers with investment projects all around the world, all the while providing liquidity, publicized value, broadcast availability, asset diversification potential, and lowered transaction costs.

Publicly traded companies arose largely as a result of the Industrial Revolution, drawing on the experience of the joint-stock companies that preceded them. They aided the pace and scale of growth in the era of nineteenth-century railroads and the twentieth century's automobiles, computers, airplanes, and industry. Retail investors and individuals saw new places to invest their capital and savings, and the world of business saw a level of transparency unparalleled in human history as a result of the regulatory framework that emerged in the public company era, in which we are still thoroughly immersed.[116]

In the decades to come, barring unforeseen circumstances, public companies and their equity shares will continue to dominate the securities markets, be the major element of the investing world, and remain a focal point of the bigger story of the democratization of investment—a theme seen time and time again through the tales of joint-stock companies, the Industrial Revolution, and the advent of public markets.

CHAPTER THREE

Retirement and Its Funding

ONE OF THE MOST PROFOUND MANIFESTATIONS of the democratization of investment is the emergence of the concept of retirement and its funding. Wider acceptance of "retirement" began to appear only 150 years ago and has expanded steadily since. Today, financing retirement has produced the largest aggregation of investment capital in the world. In the United States alone, retirement assets total an astounding $24 trillion.[1] The focus on funding retirement has vastly changed our institutions and the investment vehicles they employ, begetting the need for a new set of skills from people involved in managing retirement resources. The idea that funding retirement is a major goal of investment has had profound consequences for our society, including the development of pension funds, the burgeoning of retirement savings plans, and an unresolved national dialogue about the future of Social Security.

EARLY EFFORTS AT RETIREMENT AND ALMS

For many of us, retirement is seen as a cornerstone of modern life; the reward for decades of toil is unadulterated free time to spend with family, go on vacation, or engage in life's pleasures. However, the centrality of retirement in our contemporary lives obscures its modernity. While retirement was not wholly nonexistent for societies past, it tended to have a radically different character.

Of course, the inevitable march toward the frailties of the golden years is nothing new. What, then, did the masses of men and women of previous centuries do in the twilight of their lives? Most typically, there were two outcomes: either a man worked until the clutch of death plucked him from his labors or he ceased working and relied on the support of his family.

In the latter case, less altruistic progeny were not always thrilled to bear the burden of an elderly parent. Unlike today, however, many past societies actually required children to take care of their parents. This was certainly true of the United States (or more aptly, the then-British Colonies of America), where the values set in place by the English Poor Law of 1601 prescribed the family as the initial provider of support for parents and grandparents. This bred all manner of conflicts, and court dockets were often rife with claims arising out of some youth's failure to pay his due to his parents.[2]

For those without children, the English Poor Law had protocols for providing for them when they could no longer work. These protocols tended to involve ad hoc programs by public officials supported by "poor" taxes funding programs that coordinated transfers of wood or food. First, it was necessary for one to demonstrate legitimate need and to show that one had contributed in earlier years and was not deliberately seeking idleness. It was also essential to show that residency began long before the time of need. This requirement was generally strictly enforced. In 1707 the city of Boston, for instance, forced out a man of over eighty years named Nicholas Warner, telling him that he could not receive assistance in the city because he was not a long-time resident.[3] Communities were closer knit then and even the city of Boston had a population of a mere 7,000 in 1690, so it is unsurprising that while there were efforts to take care of one's own impecunious elderly, outsiders were viewed rather differently.[4]

Within one hundred years, however, the advancement of urbanization dissolved this kind of small-scale coordination and led to more institutionalized forms of public assistance for the involuntarily retired. Though the first almshouse in the British colonies was founded in 1664, such institutions were not commonly used at the time. By the mid- to late 1700s, however, rather than remaining in their own residences and receiving the requisite supplies for living, the poorly resourced elderly were very often forced into almshouses. When the almshouses were still novel and underused, they were not uncomfortable places to spend one's final years. However, that situation changed fairly quickly. As immigration increased and as rapid urbanization led to more squalid conditions for many, municipal administrators worked to control the rising costs of welfare by making it an unattractive option. By requiring residence in an uncomfortable almshouse as a prerequisite for any assistance, they hoped to curtail funds spent on welfare. The worst turn of events for the elderly in the almshouses was the relegation of orphans and released prisoners to their grounds, resulting in the old sharing residence with young children and ex-convicts, groups the community judged harshly as undeserving members of society. This unfortunate situation led the retired elderly to be seen as idle, despite their history of hard work. This view persisted until shortly after the Civil War when separate public programs were created for these demographics. The bottom line was that from the early seventeenth to the mid-nineteenth century there was a steady degradation in services provided to the elderly as many other marginalized demographics were consolidated into the almshouse. This "preretirement" era was simply not a pleasant time to be elderly and impoverished.[5]

EIGHTEENTH- AND NINETEENTH-CENTURY ACTIVITIES

The Presbyterian Church was at the center of much of the development of early versions of pension plans in the United States. There were two principal advances the Presbyterians made: one was a pension system supported by parishioners for the benefit of ministers, and the other was an insurance scheme paid for via premiums from the ministers themselves.

The first approach began in 1718 with the Synod of Philadelphia's introduction of the "Fund for Pious Uses," which had as its goal the extension of funds and relief of financial distress to Presbyterian ministers and their families. In 1759, this system was properly chartered, and though the name changed to the rather long-winded "Corporation for Relief of the Poor, and Distressed Ministers, and of the Poor and Distressed Widows, and Children of Presbyterian Ministers," its central goal did not. From time to time, money was spent on other causes as well. There were documented occasions of expenditures for an organ and even the payment of ransom monies for children captured in raids by Native American tribes. The funds were managed less conservatively than one might expect. For instance, there was a substantial $5,000 loan to the Continental Congress so that it could properly compensate soldiers during the American Revolution, a fairly high-risk investment, given the uncertainty of the very existence of a counterparty had the war gone differently.[6]

The second advancement—a more traditional insurance-style pension fund with revenues derived from premiums paid by ministers— began at the Presbyterian Ministers' Fund over eighty years before Mutual Life of New York, and it grew to be a tremendously well-run fund. It was, in many ways, the first real pension fund. With respect to the management of the fund's assets, both bonds and stocks were purchased. In terms of the cost of management, the fund outperformed its counterparts by a wide margin. While New York Life, for instance, had expenses per policy of about $20 in the early twentieth century, the cost per policy for the Presbyterian Ministers' Fund was a quarter of that.[7]

To be clear, it did have several structural advantages over later pension funds, including the fact that the majority of the fund's controlling directors were not compensated for their work. Furthermore, at that time the Presbyterian fund had never challenged a claim. In addition, and perhaps most salient of all, the Presbyterian fund faced a much more favorable actuarial schedule than did its fellow insurers, because it limited itself to a segment of the population that was better educated, more honest in making claims, and had much more predictable life spans, given a line of work with very low physical risk.[8]

The Philadelphia Saving Fund Society

There was another development during the time that enabled later-life leisure for those who were able to put aside money over the course of their working lives but did not have the sizable fortunes to which conventional banks tended to cater. Indeed, the wealthy and powerful had long had access to savings institutions to place their excess liquid net worth, but many of the less affluent had limited access to such services. From this need arose a new institution dedicated not just to generating profit but also to serving the social function of creating a place for the less moneyed to bank, called the Philadelphia Saving Fund Society.[9]

A close look at the early history of this fund reveals fascinating retirement planning among certain depositors—namely, female servants. Researchers who scoured data from the fund after 1850 found that female servants had a savings pattern resembling a deliberate attempt to store funds for retirement. Upon inspection, it is fairly straightforward to see why they were in a unique position to do so. Many were not married, were not anticipating the receipt of a sizable inheritance (hence their participation in the workforce), and all the while did well enough to meet their own expenses. Unlike males, for whom researchers found at best a tenuous relationship between the size of the balance and the age of the depositor, the trend of saving was clear among female servants. On average these women also withdrew from their accounts less often than males. This does not mean that males were not saving in some other capacity, but it does look as though male depositors used their savings as a highly liquid account, withdrawing money from it more regularly to pay off loans or provide for other, often familial, expenses.[10]

To summarize, the character of retirement before its modern incarnation broadly had three forms. The first was effectively involuntary retirement for those who were simply unable to contribute to the economic apparatus. This required the difficult and often ungenerous support of third parties. Retirement for this segment of the populace was not remotely liberating and rarely enjoyable. Retirement was not a much-anticipated stage of life as much as it was a mark of feebleness. Fortunately today's counterpart is far different. The second and third forms of retirement look much more modern in their character but were limited to a small segment of the population, notably either those who had the good fortune of significant wealth (or at least some disposable income to be able to put some aside regularly) or those who had developed a sophisticated mechanism of support from a much more generous community (such as the Presbyterian Church).

DEMOGRAPHIC CHANGE

What, then, precipitated the shift from this premodern retirement to today's form? The seeds were sown in large part by a series of changes, both economic and demographic. There is no clear consensus on precisely what drove the large increases in retirement rates observed from 1880 to 1940, though a variety of explanations have been offered. What is known is that the rate of retirement increased quite materially over this time period. In 1880, the labor force participation rate for males between sixty and seventy-nine years of age was 86.7 percent, and by 1940 this declined to 59.4 percent.[11] We offer two possible explanations for this important shift.

One trend that is partly responsible is the decline in the agricultural sector over this period. The argument in support of the importance of this explanation is that retirement is, on average, more of an urban industrial phenomenon than a rural farming phenomenon. Farmers generally participated in some capacity in the management or operations of farms until a rather advanced age. This suggests urban physical labor is somehow distinct from that faced in a rural setting; perhaps it is the reliance an older farmer could have on other hands or a transition toward overseeing his property rather than having direct involvement. Perhaps it is that urban labor caused more distinct physical strain than that faced in agriculture, or perhaps it is a greater breadth of opportunities available to an older individual in urban environments. Whatever the reason, it is true that the labor force participation rates for those on farms were higher than for those not on farms. As the number of individuals involved in the agricultural sector declined over this period, there was a resultant aggregate level increase in retirement. Estimating the degree to which declines in the agricultural sector were responsible essentially involves comparing the actual aggregate labor force participation rate to the theoretical value if the proportions of men in agriculture and nonagriculture had not changed from 1880 to 1940.

This exercise suggests that about 22 percent of the decrease in labor force participation rate among elderly males is attributable to agriculture, an important but not exclusive driver of this trend.[12]

A second explanation, and even more pronounced in effect, is that higher incomes over this period drove the ability of individuals to retire. There is strong evidence that the decision to retire, particularly in the mid- to late nineteenth century, was related to the ability to retire, whether through recurring income or accumulated wealth. Empirical work studying Union Army pensions as a natural experiment during this time suggests that economic shocks had a strong effect on retirement rates, indicating that the decision to retire is often distinctly financially motivated. Thus, during periods of rising incomes, retirement rates should naturally increase. It has been suggested that over the interval from 1900 to 1980, increasing wages could explain as much as 60 percent of the increase in retirement rates. It is interesting, though, that the effect of income on the retirement decision appears to have fallen after 1950 as individuals have come to see retirement as an "expectation" rather than a mere "option" and as an industry has developed to provide leisure for those in retirement.[13]

The decision to retire is not the sole change that has transpired over the last century and a half, however. There has also been growth in the length of retirement. This, too, is a worthwhile trend to study, as it is the length of retirement that determines what one needs to have saved. What has driven the elongation of retirement? Is it a drop in labor force participation rate at ever-earlier ages, or is it the decreases in mortality?

To begin to answer this question, there are two noteworthy points to consider: average total life expectancy for those who had reached twenty years of age grew from less than sixty-two years in 1900 to more than seventy-three years in 1990. Over this same interval, there was a drastic drop in the labor force participation rate of older Americans, from 65 percent to just 15 percent of men over the age of sixty-five by 1993. Both aspects—increased life expectancy and an earlier exit from work—have contributed to longer retirement. The increase in life expectancy was the more crucial factor from 1940 to 1990, with up to 79 percent of the increase in retirement length attributable to the drop in mortality over this period.[14]

It is likely that the growing length of retirement motivated significant savings at an earlier age. The economic explanation for this is life-cycle saving—or the idea of spreading one's means over the course of one's life by saving during employment and drawing down the accumulated sum during retirement. A simple computation suggests that a twenty-year-old in 1900 would anticipate a retirement equal to approximately 7 to 12 percent of the rest of his years, so he would need to save about 7 to 12 percent with zero return (and less if higher return assumptions are used).[15] Of course, the growth in retirement length would, by the same logic, necessitate ever-higher savings rates.

WEATHERING THE STORM: RETIREMENT THROUGH THE DEPRESSION

The demographic changes, however, only set the stage. It is then necessary to understand how the emergence of sound structures of retirement savings—both public and private—began to make the prospect of the golden years a genuine possibility.

Before the Great Depression, one contingent offering retirement plans was insurance companies, which supplied a small but robust customer base of clients. While the Depression wreaked havoc on trust companies, common stocks, and bond markets, insurance company–run pension plans actually fared extremely well. The total number of plans blossomed in the aftermath of the crash, as they were broadly perceived as among the few places to put money securely. In 1930, there were some 100,000 individuals covered by pension arrangements managed by insurance companies. Over the course of the following decade, insurers brought on 600,000 new covered employees.[16]

Insurance companies operated in a rather overtly oligopolistic fashion within the pension arena. Metropolitan Life was the most prominent player, underwriting about a third of the plans, followed by Prudential, Equitable, and Aetna, who together controlled about another half. The grip of these major players on the market was tightened by the creation of the Group Association, which largely standardized the rates paid.[17]

The major difficulty faced by these companies at the time was the Depression's effect on interest rates. The returns on investment were sharply curtailed by these low interest rates, and consequently, the cost to employers to provide for a given stream of payouts in retirement increased fairly drastically. A few insurers responded to the low interest rates by discouraging the sale of more plans, despite the new demand for them, because many managed their risk in terms of one company-wide interest rate being applied to all the contracts they insured. Bringing on new clients for companies with an overabundance of older plans would translate either into a dilution of their own earnings or into expected losses.[18] Ultimately, the fact that these structures did fare well through the Great Depression, inspiring confidence in both the purchasers and the broader public, laid the groundwork for many of the private forms of retirement savings.

THE FEDERAL RETIREMENT PLAN: THE ADVENT OF SOCIAL SECURITY

However, not all citizens had adequate wealth to tap into the private system. A public system soon grew up alongside it, and its own history is both fascinating and essential to understanding the course of retirement funding.

Franklin Delano Roosevelt, a staunch champion of public retirement support, was not the first Roosevelt to promote the potential benefits of implementing such a national system; Teddy had done so over twenty years before.[19] Of course, both Roosevelts were joining a long list of social advocates for these systems. Perhaps the most visible of all was Francis Townsend, who concocted a retirement plan during the Great Depression meant to entice less productive workers to retire and provide openings for younger, unemployed workers. Townsend was a physician who became thoroughly dedicated to the cause and continued to call for more benefits because the Social Security program that was eventually enacted fell short of his expectations. He sought a retirement system with a retirement age of sixty in lieu of sixty-five and one that would pay up to $200 per month (the average income of middle-aged workers), far greater than what would ultimately be enacted.[20] The Townsend proposal envisioned a 2 percent national tax on the sale of goods and services between businesses. He also suggested a requirement that pensioners spend the $200 within 30 days of having received it, thus combining a very progressive retirement system with a plan that Townsend hoped would aid in bringing the American economy out of the Depression. Townsend was certainly successful in marketing his message, joining forces with a real estate broker by the name of Robert Earl Clements, with whom he opened a headquarters for supporters of the plan on January 1, 1934. Within just one year, over 1,000 Townsend clubs were in operation across the country, and Townsend found himself with millions of supporters.[21]

Indeed, the time was ripe for Social Security, and over the decades of the early twentieth century, there grew broader political will to put it into place—attributable in part to the Great Depression, during which time the desperate need for solutions rendered flexible otherwise rigid institutions and made it possible for them to be molded into Roosevelt's progressive vision.

In 1937, there was essentially one hurdle left before the New Deal Democrats could enact the plan: the Supreme Court. It is interesting to note that the Supreme Court then had one of the most elderly compositions in history, with an average age of over seventy-one. The Court was divided, with three liberal justices and four conservative justices (no surprise why this, along with some federal courts, was subject to FDR's failed court-packing scheme) and two potential swing votes—Charles Evans Hughes and Owen Roberts. At first, the committee that had dreamt up the proposal, the Committee on Economic Security, was divided over whether it should invoke the commerce clause or the ability to levy taxes for "general welfare" programs. The program seemed to be in great peril when the Agricultural Adjustment Act, which claimed to have similar constitutional foundations as Social Security, was struck down by the Court in 1936. It was only an unforeseen change of heart by Justice Roberts that took the wind out of the sails of the conservative plurality and gave 5-to-4 support to the program.[22] History often has a tendency to naturalize pivotal events and to treat them as a chain of a multitude of causes, destined to happen. However, the truth is that this program that supports (or, for many, simply is) the retirement of countless Americans very nearly never existed.

The Bismarck Retirement System

Although Social Security may have seemed radical to politicians in the United States, the ideology behind it was far behind its more progressive counterparts of similar socioeconomics in Europe. Public insurance plans were seen as early as the late nineteenth century in Europe, developed first in Germany per an order from Otto von Bismarck. By the time the United States instituted its own scheme, it was behind over thirty other nations in doing so.

Remarkably, despite Bismarck's rather conservative political philosophy, he was quite forceful in his promotion of a retirement system in Germany. In the face of calls that his proposal was socialist, he stated, "Call it socialism or whatever you like. It is the same to me." He was, though, a subscriber to realpolitik, the doctrine promoting a pragmatically oriented decision-making process. And his dedication to the establishment of a retirement system was pragmatic indeed. There were calls in Germany by Marxist elements to implement a far more progressive system, and to some extent, this was Bismarck's attempt to quell those forces.[23]

There is a legend that America's retirement age of sixty-five is a vestige of Bismarck's retirement program. The lore has it that Bismarck chose this age and thereafter many other countries selected it as well, using Bismarck's model. However, Bismarck's program actually had a retirement age of seventy, an age likely chosen because few German citizens reached that advanced age. Although it is true that the German system did reduce the retirement age to sixty-five, it did not do so until 1916, many years after Bismarck's death.[24]

Whence, then, does the American selection of age sixty-five come? The Committee on Economic Security, charged with determining the proper retirement age for Social Security, drew on two antecedents. The first was a mosaic of state pension plans, which typically used either sixty-five or seventy as the retirement age, with approximately the same number of states using sixty-five as using seventy. Helping drive the committee toward sixty-five in lieu of seventy was the Railroad Retirement System, which made its way through Congress in 1934. The Railroad Retirement System used sixty-five as the age of retirement, creating a federal precedent for age sixty-five.[25] It was thus the retirement systems already in place within the United States that likely motivated the selection of age sixty-five, rather than the thinking of Bismarck.

The Effects of Social Security on the Private Pension Fund Market

There was an intriguing feedback effect on private retirement structures as a result of the rise of the public retirement system. One trend that evolved as a result of this New Deal legislation was that private plans increased coverage of white-collar workers and reduced it for blue-collar workers. The reasons for this were manifold. First, the concomitant increase in federal tax rates and a much more progressive distribution of the tax burden gave the higher-income cohort greater incentive to make use of the tax shelter the plans provided. Second, while Social Security would provide an adequate stream of payments for those individuals with a lower standard of living, those who enjoyed more disposable income found it insufficient to meet their lifestyle goals and had to supplement it with a private pension. Specifically, whereas blue-collar workers could typically expect Social Security to provide approximately 30 percent of their annual compensation averaged over the course of their careers, those who took home more than $3,000 per year would not receive a percentage of the excess paid to them through Social Security. Another possible reason, although frankly less compelling, was the friction between management and labor at the time. Companies felt the need to ensure that the managerial class was faithful to the firm at especially trying times and through some of the backlash many endured during layoffs of labor or cuts in wages. The net effect was a decline in total participation in private pensions in the short term. As a snapshot of the magnitudes involved, the coverage rates of the total workforce for a typical pension plan sponsor fell from 78 percent before 1930 to 41 percent in the late 1930s.[26]

Later, there was a push to return the protections and advantages offered by the pension fund to the public at large. For instance, the Revenue Acts of 1938 and 1942 included provisions that made pensions "tax qualified" and disallowed favoritism of highly compensated employees over labor, lest they jeopardize their protected tax status. Also, some firms cunningly sought to use the pension system to circumvent the price and wage fixing of World War II by increasing promised benefits rather than providing the often-prohibited raises. There were judicial changes as well that helped labor, such as the finding of the federal courts that pension plans could be part of the union negotiation process over employee salary and benefits.[27]

IMPERFECTIONS AND NEW LEGISLATION IN THE ERA OF CORPORATE-RUN PENSIONS

During this era of corporate-run pension plans, there arose some problems of inadequate funding. Corporations are entities that can fail when their financial obligations exceed their capacity to pay. A corporation's products may become less relevant, it may lose to certain macroeconomic shifts, and its management can be irresponsible or ineffective. Firms cannot print money and do not have tax-levying power (though as recent bankruptcies of American cities have shown, tax levying power alone does not make a municipal entity immune from the occasional need to restructure). So while the *management* of pension funds has long been reasonably successful, even during the difficult periods of the Great Depression, the *funding* of the plans by the corporations who sponsored them has not always been so commendable.

One of the first failures of unfunded pension liabilities was when the Studebaker Corporation closed its automobile-manufacturing plant in South Bend, Indiana, in 1963. While the retirees and those who had met the criteria for retirement but had been working until the time of the shutdown did receive their full pension benefits, the younger workers were almost entirely wiped out, with some receiving a cash payment worth a paltry percentage of the present value of the promised pension and another class of beneficiaries receiving nothing at all.[28]

This event, in concert with another instance in 1958 when the Studebaker-Packard Corporation reneged on a pension plan provided to employees of the Packard Motor Car Company,[29] put the issue of unfunded pension obligations on the radar of many Americans. The media picked up the issue as well; an *NBC Reports* special that aired in 1972 called "Pensions: The Broken Promise" received abundant press and was viewed widely across the country, spotlighting the issue during a divisive congressional battle over pensions.[30] Together, these events and the ensuing media coverage helped garner political support for pension reform.

Given their involvement in the early pension problems, the United Auto Workers (UAW) had an interesting position on the subject of pension reform. On the one hand, the UAW did not, of course, want to see labor suffer when firms were facing dire financial straits. On the other, because it had often pushed for retroactive increases in pension benefits, it did not necessarily want to require full funding of plans at all times because that would increase the push back against the UAW's negotiation of more pension benefits, since the firm would be required to make an immediate cash outlay to meet the liability after new benefits were set.[31] The thrust of the UAW's push for reforms was to establish pension reinsurance more than it was to create requirements for fully funded pension plans.

Congress responded with efforts from a variety of committees. The traditional view was that pensions were legislatively under the purview of the labor committees, but the Senate Finance and House Ways and Means Committees also played a role, citing the tax shelters that these instruments offered as the basis of their involvement. This multipronged legislative effort created ERISA in 1974, which materially improved pension fund solvency obligations, reviewed the limits on the tax deductibility of pension contributions, and implemented standards to assess whether plans were being too favorable to highly compensated employees at the expense of labor. The UAW's push for pension reinsurance materialized in the form of Title IV of ERISA, which created the Pension Benefit Guaranty Corporation, which pays out benefits up to a statutory maximum should a covered pension plan fail.[32]

Growing Sophistication of Pension Plans

General Mills was one of the first firms to move its pension away from the conservative management of insurance companies. The insurance companies generally saw invested funds through the lens of a conservator—to reduce risk but not necessarily to maximize return or generate excess returns. At a board meeting in 1965, the idea of ameliorating pension liabilities and improving the bottom line by taking advantage of a more aggressive investment approach was introduced with great success at the cereal and foodstuffs supplier. Of course, General Mills needed to conduct a selection process for a new manager, and the company ultimately settled on a group within Capital Research and Management Company, then run by Robert Kirby.[33]

Some within Capital immediately understood the potential of an entirely new type of client if other private firms were to follow suit in their decision to move money away from the insurers and toward investment management professionals. This type of client was more sophisticated than the average investor and, even more attractively, the client account could grow continuously rather than be spent down during retirement and liquidated at death by being paid out to heirs.[34]

The excitement some felt within Capital about securing this type of account was far from universal, however. Some of the most obvious candidates for running pension money—particularly those who would come from mutual funds—did not want to leave their positions because they were already earning healthy salaries and bonuses and saw the endeavor as risky. Others stayed away from the logistical challenges posed by pension fund management as compared to mutual funds, particularly travel to solicit new clients and maintain present ones.[35]

Although the independent pension fund management business may have had some trouble attracting personnel, soon the trend became undeniable. Municipalities, too, wished to put money with these managers. Once a California law changed to allow pensions to place up to one-fourth of their assets in equities extending their ability to be slightly more aggressive, many states, cities, and counties began to take the plunge.[36]

Defined Contribution Plans

While ERISA was a much-needed legislative achievement, in the period since, the private sector has largely begun a trend away from the defined benefit plan in the form of a pension to the defined contribution in the form of the 401(k) or 403(b). In the year following the passage of ERISA, there was approximately $186 billion in defined benefit plans and a significantly smaller $74 billion in defined contribution plans. However, in the late 1990s, defined contribution plans overtook defined benefit plans in terms of assets. That trend has continued since, and by 2006, private sector defined benefit plans had some $2.5 trillion in assets under management, compared to $3.2 trillion for defined contribution plans. The number of pension plans fell by over half from 1975 to 2004, while the number of plan participants increased by 26 percent. Defined contribution plans, by contrast, have seen participation increase about sevenfold over this same interval, with an approximate threefold increase in the number of plans.[37] Those numbers, along with funds in Individual Retirement Accounts (IRAs) and annuities, have continued to grow further at the start of the twenty-first century. As of the middle of 2014, employer-oriented defined contribution plans totaled $6.6 trillion, private sector defined benefit plans grew to $3.2 trillion, government defined benefit plans blossomed to $5.1 trillion, IRAs reached $7.2 trillion, and annuity reserves climbed to $2.0 trillion.[38]

Defined contribution plans have been a major vehicle for retirement investment and have further democratized investment. The penalizing of premature withdrawal by levying a 10 percent fee and making all taxes come due if the funds are removed early on retirement accounts holding tax-deferred savings has certainly provided a strong incentive to keep people invested in their retirement. The plans have also been effective in pulling a completely new type of participant into the investing world: the saver. According to a survey by the Investment Company Institute, over one-half of individuals who had IRAs and 401(k)s when polled about their reason for investment listed "general savings." These individuals see the market not so much as an opportunity for vast appreciation over the long term, but more as an alternative to depositing money at a bank. The tremendous simplicity in setting up 401(k)s and IRAs has certainly contributed to this trend.[39]

There is a broader history of people beginning to turn to the markets as another mechanism simply to save beginning with the inflation of the 1970s, when they were inspired by easy money and shocks to oil prices. Normally, the interest offered to depositors through savings accounts at banking institutions rises in line with the prevailing interest rates, so if the nominal interest rate rises along with inflation, so too will that paid by the bank. However, this state of affairs was prevented by an interest rate cap mandated by Regulation Q. Regulation Q was implemented in the depths of the Depression to prevent savings and loan institutions—many of which were then on the brink of collapse due to liquidity constraints—from competing against each other for deposits on the basis of interest rates and harming themselves in the long run by making payments to depositors unmanageable. Of course, this cap in Regulation Q was fairly innocuous in the decades after the Depression because it remained more or less dormant until inflation reared its ugly head. Once inflation exceeded the interest rate cap, savers watched the real value of their deposits being whittled away. Meanwhile, the stock market was ostensibly offering good bargains as equities declined, heightening the interest in alternatives to bank deposits.[40] This general trend fueled interest and participation in the equities markets, including through the use of vehicles like 401(k)s and IRAs in the late twentieth century.

HOME EQUITY AS A RETIREMENT ASSET

It is worth commenting on one final form of private retirement savings. Indeed, beyond managed funds, there is a prominent asset heavily involved in providing financial security during retirement: equity in the home. Often, individuals access this equity through a simple sale, deciding to move to warmer climates, downsize to smaller homes, or live in closer proximity to their children.

Home equity offers two significant advantages over conventionally managed retirement assets. First, one is forced to build equity by making mortgage payments month after month, so it is a structure that benefits materially from the "save the first dollar, not the last" effect. Whereas individuals might cut their contributions to IRAs or 401(k)s when expenses run high or during difficult financial times, they cannot cut a mortgage payment quite as easily (except, of course, through refinancing or electing to default). This effect has been particularly crucial in recent years, as savings rates have been low. Second, real estate normally offers good protection against inflationary risk, so whereas one's fixed income assets decline during times of rising price levels, homes are slightly more immune, and those individuals who have mortgaged their real estate with fixed interest rates usually fare particularly well in paying the lending institutions back in devalued dollars.

Housing wealth cannot be ignored in the present analysis, even if these assets are unmanaged, as it accounts for about one-half of total household net worth nationally. Furthermore, housing wealth represents about two-thirds of the wealth of the median household, given that other forms of financial wealth are not distributed evenly.[41]

ENHANCING PLANNING FOR RETIREMENT

One of the most troubling aspects about retirement saving today is the tendency of many individuals to procrastinate in their planning. In light of this, some companies have instituted automatic enrollment in 401(k) accounts, such that employees must opt out rather than opt in to the program. Although in models with perfectly rational agents and low switching costs the change from an opt-in to an opt-out design should have no effect, empirical findings suggest precisely the opposite: automatic enrollment seems to overcome many of the hazards of procrastination. One study followed the implementation of automatic enrollment in a large health care and insurance firm in 1998. It found that the automatic enrollment increased net participation from just 37.4 percent to 85.9 percent.[42] Furthermore, some of the greatest participation gains were for minority, young, and lower-income cohorts, suggesting that they were the most prominent beneficiaries of the plan change and perhaps among the groups most plagued by this indecision. This was not all the study concluded, however. The 401(k) plan had default contribution rates and a default allocation of funds. The institution of automatic enrollment caused most of the new plan participants to adopt the default contribution rate and the default allocation as well, even though both were uncommon before automatic enrollment when individuals made deliberate choices about how much to have deducted from their paychecks and which funds to purchase.[43]

Beyond highlighting some problems associated with delaying crucial decisions faced by a segment of the population in addressing their expected financial needs in retirement, this observation has critical ramifications for a policy that many touted in recent years—namely, private investment accounts in lieu of Social Security. First, it runs contrary to the most common benefit claimed by advocates for the reform, that of empowering individuals to take charge of their own retirement, as many do not spend adequate time mulling over the figures to optimize for their own needs. Second, it makes it abundantly clear that carefully setting default positions is vital, because many participants will simply stay with the default guideline, so either rates and allocations that best serve the greatest number of people or rates and allocations that change according to other participant dimensions (age, other savings, and income) seem appropriate.

CONCLUSION

The concept of retirement and the development of techniques to fund it have been the most striking single manifestation of the democratization of investment over the centuries. The newfound ability of the ordinary individual to look forward to, and eventually realize, an old age free of financial privation and loss of personal dignity has elevated the lives of innumerable members of the developed world's middle class.

It is impossible to overstate just how significant this recent growth in retirement assets has been. In 1974, the amount of assets dedicated to retirement in America was approximately $368 billion.[44] As of 2013, that number had grown to $20.8 trillion.[45] There was substantial growth across a wide variety of investment vehicle types—IRAs, for instance, had no assets in 1974 but grew to contain some $4.9 trillion in assets by 2011. State and local pension plans likewise grew, from about $88 billion in 1974 to $3.1 trillion by 2011, as did annuities, blossoming from $47 billion in 1974 to $1.6 trillion.[46]

How do these numbers look on an inflation- and wage-adjusted basis? Retirement asset growth between 1975 and 1999 translated into a fivefold increase in assets relative to income.[47] This, of course, meant that the stock of assets average retirees possessed could last them many times longer. This aggregation of investable assets constitutes an enormous pool of financial resources in the country. Similar proportions have been achieved in many other economically developed areas around the world, notably Europe, Japan, and other developed Western and Asian nations. Further, as more developing countries such as China and those in the Southern Hemisphere attain more mature economic status, the phenomenon is likely to extend toward additional segments of the world's population.

At the same time, despite this growth, the picture is not entirely rosy. Retirement savings are under pressure from another direction, which may be justifiable but threatens their mission to provide adequate resources to empower older citizens with a dignified, secure postretirement life. The replacement of many defined benefit pension plans by defined contribution plans is in many cases reducing the resources available to retirees and undermining their commitment to building adequate retirement savings. Many employers are off-loading the responsibility for these savings to their employees. There is also an off-loading of risk to retirees, who may be more susceptible to the shocks of investment declines because of their much shorter investment time horizon than that provided in a pension plan. The gap lies in the paucity of family retirement planning, rising income inequality, and the lack of investment savvy of the typical saver, who is not (and cannot be expected to be) a professional investor. This situation is then further complicated by the inevitable fluctuation of the financial markets in which the saver is invested. This is not to say that an injustice is necessarily being committed. It is simply to identify a funding risk lying ahead.

CHAPTER FOUR

New Clients and
New Investments

AS THE INVESTMENT LANDSCAPE democratized in the eighteenth century, new clients and new forms of investments began to emerge. These new clients included individuals who were not members of the socioeconomic elite and eventually their retirement plans, endowments, foundations, and still later, as mineral wealth discoveries became widespread in undeveloped and developing countries, sovereign wealth funds. The needs of these new clients were met by life insurance, savings accounts, investment advisers, and mutual funds. This chapter examines these new clients and the forms of investment that were developed to serve them. These developments represented a new form of economic freedom, one previously unavailable to the vast majority of people throughout history. This new freedom was supported by expanding the types of vehicles available to help these investors put their accumulated surpluses to work.

NEW CLIENTS

Individuals and Retirement Accounts

The investment history of the past 200 years is based fundamentally on the first steps of nonprivileged individuals toward becoming, for the first time in history, participants in the investment process. Individuals became participants slowly, haltingly, incompletely, and with notably mixed results as for the first time they emerged from economically disadvantaged roles into a modest but important entry into economic and political independence. Of course, many individuals still do not enjoy this opportunity, but the middle class has, over the past 200 years, begun to attain the benefits and burdens of participation in investment. Life insurance and savings accounts, along with the funding of retirement, has composed the historical foundation of middle-class investment. The existence of life insurance and savings accounts is directly linked to the democratization of investment, for these vehicles were developed to meet the investment demands and needs of this new type of less economically savvy client.

It is difficult to generalize about the investment activity of individuals because they are such a varied and heterogeneous group, but every individual is faced with a complicated series of investment constraints. These constraints include individual risk preferences, tax considerations, a need for accumulation early in life to support spending during retirement, a length of life that is limited and uncertain, and possibly the need to provide a bequest. To complicate matters further, different individuals also have different investment alternatives available to them. High-net-worth individuals, for example, have access to investment advisers and alternative investments, but those not meeting certain wealth or income thresholds typically cannot participate in certain investment structures.

The plight of the individual investor is distinct from the situation confronted by an institution or a corporation. Rather than facing the relatively straightforward fiduciary responsibility of a business or non-profit organization, individuals must consider a range of complications and uncertainties. In addition, the individual investor may be, or at least may feel, subject to duties that do not impinge on the operations of an institution or business. Unlike the officers of a corporation, the individual is personally liable if his or her assets are not sufficient to meet his or her liabilities. And entirely apart from contractual obligations, an individual may feel an obligation to support family or community financially beyond any extent implied by law. No dead person is required to provide money for his survivors, for example, but people still buy life insurance with survivor benefits. In the words of John Donne, "No man is an island, entire of itself."

A number of economic theories have been developed about how people choose to save and spend their money over time, taking into account the unavoidable humanness of the individual economic agent. These ideas provide insights into how finance can be and often is used to aid in solving life's challenges, and they plot out the foundational reasons for the retirement savings system described in the previous chapter and for the various instruments and institutions described in this book.

John Maynard Keynes included a basic theory of how savings and consumption are distributed across a lifetime in his highly influential *The General Theory of Employment, Interest, and Money* in 1936. He hypothesized that "men are disposed, as a rule and on average, to increase their consumption as their income increases, but not by as much as the increase in their income." Though accepted at first, new empirical studies in the years following publication cast some doubt on the accuracy of Keynes's theory.[1]

In 1954, Franco Modigliani introduced his life-cycle hypothesis of savings and consumption. He suggested that individuals choose to save their money for retirement to smooth their consumption levels across a lifetime, saving during their working years, hitting peak wealth just before retirement, and depleting their saved funds during retirement when they are no longer earning a full income. From this model, Modigliani sketched the macroeconomic implications of the life-cycle hypothesis. While it had long been known that saving money for advanced age is a prudent idea, Modigliani and his student Richard Brumberg expanded economists' understanding of savings by building a useful formal model and considering its larger significance. (Modigliani would later win a Nobel Prize, in part for the life-cycle hypothesis and in part for his work with Merton Miller on firms' capital structures, which is described in chapter 7 of this book.)[2]

Three years after Modigliani and Brumberg published their pioneering paper, Milton Friedman presented the permanent income hypothesis, a theory that disaggregates a person's income into "permanent and transitory" components. Friedman suggested that the permanent component determines a person's decisions about how to save and spend money over a lifetime, with temporary fluctuations not affecting those decisions significantly. In addition, he considered the investor's time horizon to be infinite and considered the investor to be saving for his or her inheritors, while Modigliani and Brumberg minimized the significance of bequests.[3]

More modern theories have built on the contributions of Keynes, Modigliani, and Friedman by incorporating other findings in economics and the social sciences, particularly regarding how people deal with the uncertainties of life and how they balance their short- and long-term interests, to build a more holistic theory of savings and consumption.[4] This survey of the most important theories of savings and consumption provides a framework for understanding when and why people choose to save and spend their money.

Now we turn to the details of *how* they accomplish these objectives. As members of the broader public have gained access to investment opportunities, they have been able to use them for more than just straightforward financial gain. Indeed, the modern financial system provides tools to help people navigate the messy and complicated economic aspects of human life.

As discussed at length in chapter 3, the emergence of the concept of retirement is entirely linked with the democratization process in which nonelite individuals were able to access investment and wealth-building activities. The rise of the individual as a new investment client also entailed the rise of retirement clients—notably, pension plans and defined contribution plans, which are among the fundamental underpinnings of modern retirement for millions of Americans. The 1974 passage of ERISA gave pensions favorable tax treatment in addition to creating the Pension Benefit Guaranty Corporation to provide insurance for plans that did not have adequate funds to disburse to beneficiaries. However, in the following decades, many employers shifted away from defined benefit plans and toward defined contribution plans. By the end of 2012, defined contribution plans held $5.1 trillion in assets.[5] These plans, such as 401(k) plans, 403(b) plans, and 457 plans, are not managed by a single sponsor managing one fund. Instead, each employee controls his or her own account; the individual makes allocation decisions in accordance with his or her own risk tolerance and savings needs. This mitigates the risks associated with unfunded pension liabilities in many defined benefit plans, but it shifts the risk of investment loss and the management of the assets to the beneficiary. Very likely defined contribution plans will continue to be the employers' retirement plan of choice because then employers are able to avoid the liabilities and risks associated with defined benefit plans.

While the cornerstone of this democratization process has been the participation of nonelite individuals, the proportion of capital contributed to many asset classes from individuals directly has been declining materially in recent decades. Instead, individuals are increasingly being replaced by either direct fiduciaries for their money or other institutional pools of capital from which the individuals benefit indirectly. New institutional clients like endowments, foundations, retirement plans, and later sovereign wealth funds came into being in order to support the collective investment needs of these individuals. As a specific example, institutions held a mere 6.1 percent of the public equity outstanding in 1950, but the figure had grown to 50.6 percent by 2009.[6] These institutions are the gatekeepers of a much greater amount of capital than they used to be; in part because of this, the growth in the investment management industry has accelerated as fiduciaries are hired to intermediate between individuals and their investments.

Investment has been professionalized, though the jury is still out on how much this professionalization has resulted in greater effectiveness. Although the vast scope of this professionalization is quite new, the process of hiring outside experts to manage asset holdings has a long history, as noted in chapter 1's discussion of Mesopotamian, Egyptian, Greek, and Roman estate and investment management. Defined benefit plans like pensions are normally overseen and managed by investment professionals who are charged with managing the assets exclusively for the benefit of the plan participants. To that end, there are regulations prohibiting the plan from owning too much of the stock of the company for which the employees work. In addition to a conflict of interest, this situation would expose beneficiaries to the risks of company failure and the potential inability of the firm to meet unfunded pension liabilities.

Endowments

As we have seen, endowments have been in use at least since the fourth century B.C. in Greece. Today, endowments take two forms:

the endowment for an educational institution and the endowment for a foundation. While slightly different in structure, they are quite similar in purpose—to enhance the mission of the organizations they serve. An endowment improves the flexibility and independence of the associated institution by allowing it to smooth its spending intertemporally, create new programs, and respond to shortfalls from student enrollments, donors, governmental grants, or other revenue-generating sources.

The amount of assets under management by the endowment does seem to matter in terms of investment success. There is an abundance of empirical research suggesting that the larger endowments outperform their smaller peers. There are likely a variety of reasons for this, including the ability to support a talented team of professionals, to diversify properly, and to access investments with higher minimum size requirements.[7] An endowment's investment profile tends to be one geared toward the preservation of capital; the goal is to generate consistent returns while avoiding substantial drawdowns. Endowments are also able to bear some illiquidity, investing in vehicles like private equity, venture capital, and other nonpublic opportunities. They are able to do so because their intended lives are often indefinite and their size relative to yearly spending tends to be large.

Endowments must weigh the trade-off between asset preservation and growing spending needs to support new programs and initiatives.[8] The question thus becomes how much is prudent to spend, given the uncertainty associated with future investment returns and capital inflows and the need to support later generations of beneficiaries. In 2011, the average annual effective spending rate for private colleges and universities was 4.6 percent, and for their public counterparts 4.3 percent.[9] In addition, educational endowments enjoy the benefits of tax exemption that allow them to compound their returns at a faster rate.

In 1972, a standard code of procedures and rules for the investment activities associated with managing an endowment fund was established in the form of the Uniform Management of Institutional Funds Act (UMIFA) by the National Conference of Commissioners on Uniform State Laws. Much later, the Uniform Prudent Management of Institutional Funds Act (UPMIFA) was passed in 2006 by the same body. UMIFA specified that assets should be deployed across asset classes (diversification) while UPMIFA updated those codes by additionally stipulating that investments must be executed in accordance with a prudent person standard and "in good faith."[10] Diversification is continuing to be a highly effective investment strategy for endowments. By way of example, as of June 2005, the average educational endowment held 53 percent in domestic equity, 23 percent in domestic fixed income, and 5 percent in cash.[11] Six years later, by June 2011, the average educational endowment's asset allocation was 16 percent in domestic equities, 10 percent in fixed income, 17 percent in international equities, 53 percent in alternative strategies, and 4 percent in cash or other general assets.[12] In short, endowment diversification is following the current investment trends by becoming more international, as well as taking advantage of more niche strategies.

Foundations

The foundation, in its modern form, dates back to the turn of the twentieth century, when many industrialists found themselves with enormous wealth they could funnel toward the improvement of society. Perhaps it was Andrew Carnegie who expressed most clearly the duty some of the more philanthropic industrialists felt at the time, noting that a fortunate person of wealth should "consider all surplus revenues which come to him simply as trust funds, which he is called upon to administer…to produce the most beneficial results for the community."[13]

One of the first modern foundations was the Russell Sage Foundation, created in 1907 by Margaret Sage with funds from her recently deceased husband, Russell Sage, who had amassed considerable wealth as an investor in railroads and telegraph companies. When he died at the age of eighty-nine, he left more than $63 million to his wife. In her lifetime, Margaret would give away $75–$80 million to various philanthropic funds. Much of her work was oriented toward the academic and the practical study of poverty and other social issues at universities and other institutions. Some of it was directed toward labor issues, including the Pittsburgh Survey, which analyzed the often ghastly labor conditions in the steel industry, resulting in the eventual alleviation of some of the most serious issues.[14]

Shortly thereafter, in 1911, Andrew Carnegie founded the Carnegie Corporation of New York "to promote the advancement and diffusion of knowledge and understanding." By the time Carnegie had established the Carnegie Corporation, he had already disbursed some $43 million for public libraries and another $110 million for other charitable uses. However, Carnegie wanted to transfer the power to make his philanthropic decisions to a permanent institution. Writing to his trustees, Carnegie explained, "Conditions upon erth [*sic*] inevitably change; hence, no wise man will bind Trustees forever to certain paths, causes or institutions. I disclaim any intention of doing so. On the contrary, I giv [*sic*] my Trustees full authority to change policy." To this day, the Carnegie Corporation of New York still exists and contributes money to a wide array of educational institutions, domestically and abroad.[15] Likewise, in 1913 John D. Rockefeller set up a foundation, which has given funds to medical schools, the American Red Cross, and other initiatives oriented toward medicine and health care around the globe.[16]

The relationship between foundations and the tax code was specified with the enactment of the Revenue Act of 1913, which made charitable foundations tax exempt. The Revenue Act of 1917 allowed individuals to make tax-deductible contributions, and the Revenue Act of 1918 reduced the tax burden associated with bequeathing assets to private foundations. The pace of the creation of independent foundations slowed during the interwar period, but after World War II, there was a considerable increase in corporate foundations, a fact undoubtedly linked to the country's return to greater economic prosperity.[17]

Soon though, in the 1960s, some foundations found themselves at the center of national debate because the regulations allowed them to be less transparent than other charities. Further, there were added concerns that some foundations were being used as tax shelters rather than providing real benefits for the community. The Tax Reform Act of 1969 required foundations to make payments to the federal government and also established a minimum annual percentage of assets that foundations had to distribute each year in order to avoid taxation and other regulatory consequences. These provisions were later altered to be more favorable for the creation and operation of foundations, contributing to their growth from the 1980s onward.[18]

Foundations are an important source of investment activity, due in no small part to the considerable assets they control: $622 billion as of 2010.[19] Trustees are tasked with managing budgets and with making investment decisions. Unlike the task of educational endowments, the task of foundations is slightly more complicated because of the minimum distribution foundations must make of their total asset base, lest they pay taxes and other penalties. As a result of this required minimum spending, trustees often focus on managing new contributions and being careful about investment activities in order to avoid having the foundation's asset base fall materially over time. The investing program of a foundation tends to otherwise look like that of an educational endowment, with an orientation toward capital preservation, broad diversification, and careful risk taking.

Like educational endowments, private foundations enjoy the benefit of tax deductibility of contributions as well as exemption from paying federal income taxes on investment earnings. While endowments usually directly benefit the institution's goals and programs, foundations often provide grants and other forms of aid to a charity that then distributes the funds to other programs.[20] In other words, foundations serve as the benefactors not just of the individuals they ultimately serve but also of the charities that assist the ultimate target population.

Increasingly, some foundations are attempting to marry their fundamental operational goals with their investment goals. The William and Flora Hewlett Foundation and the John D. and Catherine T. MacArthur Foundation, for instance, vote their shares of public corporations in a manner that reduces or avoids harm done (or ideally, produces benefit), and both foundations are led not just for financial gain but also for overall social gain.[21] Others make very specific mission-related investments, like microfinance loans to the impoverished, lending for affordable housing, purchasing assets or equity interests in clean energy, and investing in other endeavors with clear social goals. Although it is difficult to say precisely how widespread formalized mission-related investment is, the Foundation Center conducted a poll in 2011 of over 1,000 foundations and found that 14.1 percent were actively engaged in such investment.[22] It seems likely that this trend will continue as foundations find creative ways to deploy not just flows of cash but also their assets in ways that benefit their target populations.

Foundations are plentiful in the United States, with a total of 86,192 across the country as of 2012. They can be categorized in three general ways: independent foundations, corporate foundations, and operating foundations. Independent foundations are typically affiliated with one or several individuals who tend to be affluent philanthropists. Corporate foundations are associated with a company, and their budgets tend to be derived from that profit-earning entity. The last is the operating foundation, which directly spends resources. In 2012, foundations distributed a total of $52 billion—roughly 67 percent from independent foundations, 12 percent from corporate foundations, and 11 percent from operating foundations. The remaining 10 percent comes from community foundations, which are charities that draw funds from a wide array of different donors.[23] While the sources of foundation assets often originate from single wealthy donors, families, or corporations, their capital deployment strategies have contributed to the overall trend of democratization.

Sovereign Wealth Funds

The amount of attention sovereign wealth funds have received from the public in recent years is remarkable. Despite their size, sovereign wealth funds as a class of investment tended to fly below the radar of the public until 2007. Indeed, the term *sovereign wealth fund* was not even in modern parlance until about 2005, when Andrew Rozanov first used it in his article "Who Holds the Wealth of Nations?"[24] Sovereign wealth funds are another class of capital pool central to the modern investment scene, managing a total of $6.4 trillion as of March 2014.[25] Similar to endowments and foundations, sovereign wealth funds manage money for the benefit of the organization to which they are connected, the main difference being that the funds of a sovereign wealth fund belong to a nation or state rather than an institution. Their assets are derived not from donations or charitable contributions but, rather, from the sale or licensing of natural resources, excess governmental revenue, and foreign exchange reserves produced from positive trade balances.

Like endowments, sovereign wealth funds help manage money over time in two fundamental ways. In the short term, sovereign wealth funds serve as a buffer; when there is a shock in revenues or costs, the sovereign wealth fund can be drawn upon to normalize the budgeting process. This is especially crucial for nations that rely on natural resource sales. By smoothing spending, the sovereign wealth fund helps temper the damage done to the economy by adverse commodity price movements in exported goods. In the long term, the accumulation of wealth in a sovereign wealth fund ensures that subsequent generations can experience the benefits from the sale of resources that are, in most cases, finite.

There is some disagreement about which pool of capital was actually the first sovereign wealth fund. Some observers point to CalPERS, the California Public Employees Retirement System, established in 1932.[26] It was set up to manage funds for the benefit of the employees of the state of California. However, while it meets the IMF's definition of a sovereign wealth fund, it is unusual in several respects. For one, CalP-ERS has individual beneficiaries, whereas the beneficiary of a sovereign wealth fund is the state. Furthermore, a sovereign wealth fund does not generally have explicit liabilities as a retirement fund does; indeed, to the extent that sovereign wealth funds have genuine liabilities, they tend to simply be to another part of government.[27]

In light of this, most observers agree that the first true sovereign wealth fund was the Kuwait Investment Authority, which was created in 1953.[28] Today, one of the largest sovereign wealth funds with around $548 billion, the Kuwait Investment Authority is in charge of investing the assets of two funds: the Reserve Fund for Future Generations (into which a percentage of annual oil revenues is directed) and the General Reserve Fund (the general fund of the government that receives revenue and disburses expenditures).[29] This fund has fulfilled its mission of helping the nation weather difficult times. As Bader Al Sa'ad, managing director of the Kuwait Investment Authority, has pointed out, the sovereign wealth fund supplied funds for normal budgeting during the Iraqi occupation of Kuwait in the early 1990s.[30] Had the sovereign wealth fund not existed, Kuwait would have been forced to borrow expensively, tax heavily, or rely on other governments for assistance.

More sovereign wealth funds emerged in the 1970s, including the Abu Dhabi Investment Authority, presently one of the largest sovereign wealth funds in the world.[31] Many of these arose in the latter portion of the decade as oil prices climbed. This is a pattern that has continued—when commodities prices skyrocket or have sustained periods of loftier values, sovereign wealth funds are often formed to capture this profit. This has occurred not just in the case of oil but also, for instance, in the case of copper in Chile. In the 1990s, prices for commodities remained modest and few new sovereign wealth funds came into existence; but in the next decade, as commodities prices increased and as the merits of SWFs became more broadly understood, many new funds opened. Indeed, just between 2005 and 2012, more than thirty new sovereign wealth funds were born.[32]

There has been some anxiety, largely in the West, over the possibility that SWFs could be used to adversely affect financial markets for political purposes or to serve as a source of geopolitical leverage. The reality of the situation, however, is different. First, there has been virtually no evidence to date that sovereign wealth funds have any real interest in perpetrating such damage. Many sovereign wealth funds have proven quite economically rational and have operated with largely financial, not political, intentions. Second, if a sovereign wealth fund did seek to do serious political harm, it would generally harm itself in the process. For instance, if a fund initiated asset fire sales—the rapid unloading of assets to depress their prices—the fund itself would be seriously damaged. There would have to be a particularly potent motivation for a government to do this. Third, while sovereign wealth funds are an important source of capital, they remain a much smaller pool of capital than many other sources of institutional funds. Sovereign wealth funds are located in a wide array of nations, each with separate agendas, so coordination among them to do more serious damage seems like a remote possibility. The reality is that the evidence to date shows that the concern over sovereign wealth funds becoming political weapons has been a largely unfounded.

It is difficult to make rigorous and generalized statements about the investment strategies of sovereign wealth funds, given that they tend not to be transparent and that they are fairly heterogeneous. The lack of transparency is in part a function of their lack of individual beneficiaries. Sovereign wealth funds really answer only to the governments or the citizens (though indirectly) they serve, and thus many of them have no need to make significant disclosures.

That said, the individual investment mandates of sovereign wealth funds are often related to the source of the original funds. Middle Eastern sovereign wealth funds, for instance, often seek to diversify away from commodity price risk, investing in a wide array of other industries. Asian sovereign wealth funds, by contrast, have foreign reserves due to positive trade balances as their source; thus their focus is more about diversifying away from the currency price risk to which they are exposed.[33] The investment strategies of sovereign wealth funds also tend to align with the fundamental reasons for their creation. Most sovereign wealth funds tend to be slightly more interested in capital preservation, whereas ones that are centrally concerned with growing the assets often have a slightly higher risk tolerance. But in general, sovereign wealth funds are widely diversified and can manage a wide liquidity spectrum, since they do not have explicitly dated liabilities.

Given the historical trend and the broadening of the conviction in the merits of these funds, the future seems bright for sovereign wealth funds. They are likely to become more plentiful as countries seek to monetize their resources, diversify away risk, and orient the revenue of the country toward a wider stream of income sources.

NEW INVESTMENTS

The democratization of investment required the emergence of new investment vehicles that for the first time sought to meet the needs of the nonelite individual for financial security, accumulation, and management. Life insurance and savings accounts are two of the earliest and simplest vehicles. The development of life insurance includes comical legal strategies, actuarial mathematics, and ethical reactions to the very notion of betting on death. Savings accounts have an equally intriguing history—from the savings societies that were crucial for many working poor to the development of commercial banks that facilitate the transactions that propel the economy, and through the 1970s banking crisis, which required governmental intervention. Then there are the more complex, and often more risky, investments in the form of separate investment accounts and mutual funds. These vehicles are not prestructured and often have more ambitious capital appreciation goals and therefore must accept more exposure to losses as well.

Life Insurance

Life insurance serves the dual roles of allowing families to save money and to mitigate the financial effects of the demise of the family's provider. The structure of a life insurance contract typically involves outflows of cash, in the form of premiums, from the individual to the insurance company during the life of the insured and a one-time inflow of cash to the insured's beneficiary after the insured's death. Today, there are many manifestations of how premiums are paid, invested, and otherwise scheduled, as well as of the duration of the arrangement itself. This contract can be advantageous for both the insured and the insurance company; the former transfers the risk of unanticipated death, and the latter uses the incoming premiums as an inexpensive source of funds to invest. Insurance companies make a significant portion of their profit by investing the float.

One of the earliest records of a life insurance contract dates back to 1583. A life insurance policy was taken out on a man named William Gibbons for a duration of 12 months by several of Gibbons's acquaintances. The premium was a small fraction of the death benefit, with a payout ratio of 25 to 2. Gibbons died just twenty days before the end of the year, and the purchasers of the insurance contract believed that they would receive a windfall. The insurers, however, were far from pleased by this and concocted a rather creative legal defense, claiming that the insurance contract was for 12 months, and because the shortest month has 28 days, the contract was really for only 336 days, not 365 days, and thus they were not responsible for the claim. In the end, the court recognized the absurdity of this defense and the insurers were held liable, but the episode speaks to how nascent and often ill defined financial responsibilities in the insurance industry were at the time.[34]

While simple term life insurance had existed for some time, in 1756 the English mathematician and Fellow of the Royal Society James Dodson devised the level premium plan that allowed policyholders to pay a flat premium, and, in turn, they would receive coverage for their entire lives. With this idea, James Dodson became the father of whole life insurance. He created this system after he himself had applied for life insurance coverage from the Amicable Society, a group offering insurance chartered by Queen Anne in 1706, but was denied for being too old. The Amicable Society was willing to extend life insurance coverage, but only for young insureds.[35] Dodson demonstrated that a yearly premium could be charged to cover insureds that properly reflected the mortality risk to the insurer: an insured would pay more than his risk-neutral mortality risk in the early years of the policy but would pay less in the later years, thus creating the flat premium schedule. Dodson eventually solicited the government for a charter to create an alternative life insurance organization that could compete with the Amicable Society. Dodson would not live to see it, but Edward Rowe Mores believed strongly in the superiority of Dodson's proposal and finally managed to win approval in 1762 for what is called today the Equitable Life Assurance Society, the oldest mutual insurer in the world.[36]

Life insurance caught on quickly in Great Britain, but other countries were not so quick to adopt it. The notion of betting on death seemed inappropriate to many, as the timing of death itself was perceived to be God given and should be beyond human speculation. Some leaders of religious communities spoke out against the practice entirely. This initial religious reaction has been built into some forms of life insurance; many jurisdictions still have laws requiring the beneficiary to have "insurable interest," or a legitimate benefit conferred by the survival of the insured, at the origination of a new policy. In other words, to deter sheer betting on death—and of course, to prevent malfeasance—one cannot take out a life insurance policy on a stranger. Over time, we have come to recognize the importance of risk transfer around death, but few people remain excited about the prospect of broad wagering on the timing of any individual's death.

The religious climate in the United States was more moderate than in many European countries, and many people slowly began to appreciate the value of the product. By the 1840s, the life insurance industry in the United States hit a point of inflection, brought about by two structural changes in the industry. The first was to allow wives to be the beneficiaries of policies in which their husbands were the insureds. Before 1840, many married women were not permitted to sign insurance contracts themselves or to be a direct beneficiary of their husband's policy because the relationship of marriage itself was not at the time seen as necessarily constituting an insurable interest. Instead, the death benefit would be payable to the husband's estate, and thus creditors could access the proceeds before his widow. This changed when insurers joined forces with women's rights activists to promote the passage of laws like the Married Women's Property Acts, passed by a number of states starting in 1839 and 1840.[37]

The second structural change the industry experienced in the 1840s was the growth of mutual life insurance companies, or firms whose proceeds went not to shareholders but, rather, to the policyholders themselves. At the end of the previous decade, other life insurers had experienced difficulty accessing the capital markets in the wake of a financial crisis, so mutual life insurers fared much better because they required significantly less seed capital. Largely as a result of these two factors, the amount of life insurance coverage between 1840 and the end of the Civil War grew enormously, and the industry was fully integrated into the American economy.[38]

Today, life insurance is viewed as part of the bedrock of family financial security: a 2010 LIMRA market research study revealed that 70 percent of American families owned a life insurance policy.[39] The majority of life insurers fall into three categories. The first is the stock company, which is owned by shareholders and insures over $13 trillion in face value, or about 70 percent of the US market. The second is the mutual company, which is owned by policyholders and insures over $5 trillion in face value, or about 25 percent of the market. The third is the fraternal society that has a network of lodges and can offer insurance only to lodge members, and these collectively insure about $315 billion in face value, or 1.5 percent of the market.[40] The balance of the industry is insured by other groups, such as government agencies. The assets of life insurers are invested so that the insurers can meet their liabilities. Historically, most life insurance companies' assets have been held in fixed income securities. Early on, this typically meant government debt instruments, but over time it grew to include mortgage-backed securities as well as corporate debt. Over time, more public equities have been held by insurance companies (growing at a 5 percent annual clip from 2000 to 2010).[41] The establishment of insurance companies as investment vehicles is directly linked to the vast expansion of individuals who are participating in life insurance, savings, and investment activities.

Savings Accounts

Chapter 3 discussed evidence of life-cycle savings by female servants in the context of retirement. Here, the analysis broadens to the history of savings vehicles. Savings societies allowed the previously underbanked (most notably, the working poor) to access the benefits of a depository institution, and they grew in prominence in the early nineteenth century. The Philadelphia Saving Fund Society was the first American mutual savings bank, commencing its dealings in 1816. The first chartered US mutual savings bank was the Provident Institution for Savings in Boston, which began serving the public that same year. The number of savings banks grew rapidly, numbering just 10 in 1820 and growing to 637 by 1910, with total deposits growing from $1 million in 1820 to $3 billion by 1910. Their investment mandate was fairly broad, initially being confined to government bonds but later including mortgages, utility debt, and even the common equity of large corporations.[42]

These savings banks tended to be domiciled in the northeastern United States, where the demographics of a large swath of wage earners employed in industrial jobs were an appropriate match for their intended clients. Developing alongside mutual savings banks were the commercial banks, which were focused predominantly on making loans for profit maximization and had a strong foothold on the frontier portions of the country. The commercial banks required lower capitalization, and their governance structures were not as sophisticated as those of mutual savings banks, where prominent and successful trustees would oversee the soundness of the bank. Therefore, commercial banks tended to make more risky and potentially more rewarding loans, which meant that although they facilitated growth in many areas, they were less stable than their mutual savings banks counterparts.

As greater numbers of individuals were searching for institutions and vehicles with which they could grow their life savings, savings and loan associations (also known as thrifts) came into being. Their original function was to convert deposits into loans made for building, fixing, and refinancing homes, later expanding to include automobile loans and personal lines of credit. These banks were crucial to the construction and modernization of new cities across the United States while allowing individual savers to access a decent rate of return. These institutions allowed savers to make deposits in a variety of ways, including recurring payments at consistent intervals of time, dividend reinvestment programs, and irregular additional deposits to accounts. The depositors later enjoyed the backstop of the federal government when it created the Federal Savings and Loan Insurance Corporation to insure the deposits of these savings and loan associations.

Savings banks survived through the Great Depression and the succeeding decades, even though the banking environment did become more competitive. But the inflation of the 1960s and 1970s proved injurious to these savings banks with interest rate maximums in terms of what depositors could earn for keeping their money in the bank. A high interest rate environment drove depositors to move their money to funds where it could fetch a higher return.[43] As rates climbed in the latter part of the 1970s, many mutual savings banks failed. In 1982, annual losses at the mutual savings banks with FDIC insurance were running at a devastating 1.25 percent of total assets.[44]

At the same time, savings and loan associations were also suffering from the effects of high interest rates for similar reasons. The government's attempt to manage inflation caused short-term rates (the rates at which these institutions borrowed) to increase without the same increase happening to long-term rates (the rates at which these institutions could lend). Savings and loan associations were thus forced to borrow at high rates but to make new loans at lower rates. This situation was further exacerbated by the real estate investments of savings and loan associations, a sector that underwent a broad-based decline in the 1980s, thereby impairing both the collateral and the repayment rates of the underlying mortgages.[45] Furthermore, the governmental oversight of the associations was significantly deregulated, creating the conditions for very irresponsible lending decisions and, occasionally, outright fraud, including the looting of some associations' assets by management teams.

The FDIC deployed several different strategies to stem the tide of what would otherwise have been a widespread crisis within these institutions. Fortunately, by virtue of their structures, mutual savings banks did not have shareholders to worry about, and thus the central goal was to protect assets.[46] The introduction of certificates of deposit with longer maturities and the mergers of banks with other institutions had some positive effects on the industry. In addition, the Garn–St. Germain Depository Institutions Act of 1982 authorized the FDIC to acquire capital instruments from the bank, "net worth certificates," in order to aid their liquidity positions, which also helped the banks weather this painful inflationary period. With these interventions, the banking crisis of the early 1980s was contained. In total, between late 1981 and 1985, the FDIC aided with seventeen mergers and acquisitions of mutual savings banks involving total assets of nearly $24 billion, which translated into 15 percent of the total assets of FDIC-insured mutual savings banks as of year-end 1980.[47] At year-end 1995, the cost of all of the savings bank failures was estimated to be about $2.2 billion.[48]

Savings and loan associations fared even worse: from 1986 to 1995, over one thousand savings and loan associations with an excess of $500 billion in assets failed. The Federal Savings and Loan Insurance Corporation would later become insolvent and require a taxpayer bailout to the tune of $124 billion. In 1989, its responsibilities were subsumed by the Federal Deposit Insurance Corporation.[49]

Over time, savings institutions have come to account for a smaller and smaller part of the economy. Indeed, savings and loan associations and mutual savings banks today hold a much more limited portion of Americans' savings than they did in the past. A brief study of the quantitative sources demonstrates this transformation of the savings landscape. Data from the Federal Reserve show that although thrift institutions at one time held a greater amount of savings deposits than did commercial banks, this balance shifted decisively in 1982 and 1983. Today commercial banks hold almost six times the savings of thrift institutions.[50] In May 2014, 78.7 percent of savings deposits and small-denomination time deposits was held in commercial banks. Savings institutions, meanwhile, held 14.2 percent of these deposits, with the remaining deposits invested in retail money market funds.[51]

Investment Advisers (Separate Accounts)

Since the beginning of asset accumulation there have been investment clients—those who have acquired resources and have sought outside experts to manage all or part of their holdings. As discussed at length in chapter 1, ancient Mesopotamians, Egyptians, Greeks, and Romans employed agents to manage their agricultural properties, lending businesses, and trade activities. In many cases, these agents were slaves or commoners who possessed the expertise concerning the assets and activities involved and the time to devote to the task—commodities that the elite owners did not have. Agents were either directly employed by the resource owner or contracted, providing the service for some sort of fee rather than a wage or other form of subsistence.

Private wealth management in its modern form began to emerge in Europe at the end of the Middle Ages, when the traditionally wealthy members of the landed elite began to sell off their land. Likely originating during or after the Crusades, family activities designed for the purposes of preserving, managing, and growing a family's diversified wealth blossomed in Europe into the modern era. The historical role of separate account management is a critical one, because until the early twentieth century, this was the only way to manage individual or family wealth.

Today separate account management refers to a more modern practice, likely dating no further back than the eighteenth or nineteenth century, wherein a service provider—a bank trust department, independent investment adviser, or other contracting party—is hired to select and manage investments for a wealthy person or family or an institution. The service may include, in addition to specific asset selection, the setting of investment policy, the choice of strategies to achieve it, and the monitoring of the composition and risk profile of the portfolio.

In this case, the amount of assets under management must be large enough to justify an account that is not pooled with the assets of others—meaning that account management is limited to very wealthy individuals, families, or institutions. Whereas most institutions of any meaningful size can qualify for such a service, the vast majority of individuals, even among those who actually have assets to manage, cannot qualify for separate account management, which normally has a minimum asset threshold. Nevertheless, this form of management has existed for many decades and has attracted sizable sums of money.

Separate account management often utilizes the latest techniques from investment managers of all kinds. Yet surprisingly, it often does not benefit from the lowest fees or the best investment outcomes. These wealthy individuals or institutions are sometimes the targets of the most imaginative and adventurous of investment organizations. Separate account management is usually highly customized and responsively provided, which means that qualifying clients normally find such investment services attractive and convenient.

In the past few decades, a broad system of private wealth management has been created, bringing the features of a family office to a wider, albeit still limited, audience. This system takes into account the complicated needs of wealthy individuals, providing for estate planning and, importantly, keeping an asset base secure. Unlike a dedicated family office, private banking does not involve an entire organization devoted to the wealth of a single individual or family. However, private banking does require investors to have a high level of assets, and it provides personally tailored investment advising and other services that commercial bank branches and retail brokerages do not offer.[52]

J. P. Morgan's U.S. Private Bank, a division of financial giant J. P. Morgan Chase that is today America's largest private bank, provides a good case study for understanding the private wealth management industry.[53] The account minimums tend to be in the low millions, but its area of traditional focus and strength remains even wealthier investors, with most investors investing at least $25 million. In 2001, in fact, the average person or family invested in J. P. Morgan Private Banking had a net worth of around $100 million.[54]

Across all of its divisions, J. P. Morgan held $1.60 trillion in assets under management and $2.34 trillion in total client assets in 2013. The Private Banking division in particular held $361 billion in client assets under management (22.6 percent of total assets under management, or AUM), with a total of $977 billion in client assets invested in the division (41.7 percent of total client assets). These assets contributed significantly to the firm's revenues. In fact, J. P. Morgan Private Banking division generated $6.0 billion in revenues in 2013, accounting for over half of the Asset Management division's $11.3 billion in revenue.[55]

Mutual Funds

As the democratized investor base has grown, so has the variety of products that cater to it. One more recent innovation is the mutual fund—a vehicle that often involves higher risk and active management (that is, a professional or set of professionals actively making security selection decisions). Although the mutual fund has precursors dating back hundreds of years, it is the modern version, born in the 1920s, that has become the investment solution of choice for the savings and retirement assets of a large segment of the public. The current popularity of the mutual fund comes from a combination of three beliefs. First, individuals believe that mutual fund managers may be better and safer investors than the individuals themselves (in other words, a professional advantage). Second, mutual funds allow broader diversification than one can typically provide on one's own. Third, many individuals believe that active investors may be able to outperform a passive index by security selection, market timing, or some combination of the two. These beliefs, combined with the ubiquity of mutual funds in most individuals' investment strategies, illustrate the ways in which the democratization of investment has led to investment innovation and growing professionalism.

PRECURSORS TO THE MUTUAL FUND

An early precursor to the mutual fund was the depository receipt for government debt in eighteenth- and nineteenth-century Europe. In lieu of the modern large public auction, investors in government debt at that time gained exposure only through registration on a ledger. When funds were handed over and the investor was registered, he received a depository receipt that entitled him to go to the treasury of the country issuing the debt and receive interest payments at predetermined intervals of time. This process was cumbersome, particularly when an investor was giving money to another nation, as it would necessitate foreign travel just to collect interest. A Dutch firm by the name of Hope and Company made a successful business by issuing certificates to investors that allowed them to collect the interest from debt directly from the firm itself, which would in turn collect payments from domestic and foreign treasuries. This functioned similarly to a bond mutual fund because it allowed investors to access a previously unavailable asset class through an intermediary. Eventually these certificates became publicly traded too, enhancing their liquidity characteristics.[56]

A second vehicle that more closely resembled the modern mutual fund because it involved more asset selection rather than just convenient intermediation was created by Abraham van Ketwich in Amsterdam in the summer of 1774. Van Ketwich offered 2,000 shares of an investment pool to the public with the goal of investing in quality debt instruments of governments, banks, and plantations. In this way, with a single initial offering, van Ketwich essentially created an early closed-end mutual fund for sale to the public. All later liquidity was offered only through sale by the owner to another investor. The offering had a prospectus, an administrator of the assets, and a clear description of the two individuals involved in the supervision of the investment decisions of the fund: Dirk Bas Backer and Frans Jacob Heshuyen.[57] As it turned out, this initial foray was quite successful, and just five years later, in 1779, van Ketwich repeated the process by establishing a second trust with the name *Concordia Res Parvae Crescunt*, roughly translated, "In harmony all things grow," a motto that points to the growth of returns when the investors give managers a broader mandate to deploy capital. Van Ketwich preceded Benjamin Graham or Warren Buffett as one of the earliest value managers, noting in his prospectus that the fund would seek out securities priced "below their intrinsic values."[58]

THE GREAT DEPRESSION AND THE EMERGENCE
OF THE OPEN-ENDED MUTUAL FUND

Founded by Edward G. Leffler, the Massachusetts Investors Trust was the first open-ended mutual fund in the United States, and it remains active to this day under ticker MITTX.[59] Unlike van Ketwich, who sold a predefined number of units in a trust that could be liquidated only through sale to new investors, Leffler established a mutual fund that had no fixed number of shares and offered liquidity, not through a secondary sale, but rather through a redemption process. In other words, one could trade in a unit of the mutual fund directly through the issuer, who would then liquidate that person's share of securities and return the corresponding amount of cash. This fund was quite successful with 200 shareholders and about $392,000 under management after the first year, a much more sizable sum of money in 1924 than it is today. Just four months after Leffler's launch, Paul Cabot founded State Street Investment Trust, also in Boston.[60]

While these funds did have some early traction, the assets under management were miniscule in comparison with many larger closed-end funds and other investment companies in the 1920s. Indeed, in 1927, open-ended mutual funds were just 3 percent of all assets managed by investment companies.[61] However, the significant declines in value of closed-end funds during the Crash of 1929 made their open-ended counterparts seem more attractive, and by 1936 the Massachusetts Investors Trust had a staggering $130 million under management.[62] The Revenue Act of 1936 helped too, as it allowed open-ended funds to avoid taxation at the fund level.

Meanwhile, government regulators started to pay closer attention to the slowly blossoming universe of mutual funds as significant misconduct as well as poor performance was revealed in the wake of the Crash of 1929. The government's goals were to manage the alignment between the adviser and the investor, prevent malfeasance, and instill confidence in the public markets after the Crash and the ensuing Great Depression. A sequence of federal laws had some effect, though of varying degrees, on the industry. The first was the Securities Act of 1933 that required mutual funds to register with the federal government and provide updated versions of the prospectus to investors should it change over time. The second was the Securities Exchange Act of 1934, which mandated federal registration for the brokers (not just the fund itself) involved in managing the assets. This act also required mutual funds to file annual reports to the newly created Securities and Exchange Commission (SEC).[63]

These acts, while a positive step forward for the industry, did not eliminate all the malpractice of the bad actors. A study conducted by the SEC after the enactment of these laws found some instances of salespeople and managers transferring investor assets between different funds for the generation of fees, with no clear investment objective.[64] Even though Congress could have adopted a stricter disclosure rule within the framework of the Securities Exchange Act of 1934, it would not really have addressed the underlying problem of abuse by bad actors. Instead, Congress passed the Investment Advisers Act of 1940, which broadened the registration rules and, perhaps most important, included antifraud measures as well as strict custodial provisions. This law was followed later that same year by the Investment Company Act of 1940. It enhanced the precision of the existing law and is credited as the bedrock legislative achievement for the mutual fund industry. It called for clear disclosure of operational processes and fund structures as well as more frequent updates on the financial performance of the fund. It also prohibited affiliated party transactions that would disadvantage the investor by producing unnecessary fees.[65] In addition, the SEC was allowed to perform on-site inspection of fund financials. Furthermore, the law made it clear that the directors of mutual funds had the same legal and fiduciary duties as directors of other corporations and mandated that no less than 40 percent of the board of a fund be independent of the investment adviser (the SEC would later raise this percentage to 75).[66]

Notably, the law itself was given a mechanism by which it could evolve with the times; the SEC was charged with the power to designate rules and oversee the entities subject to the acts. Congress was aware of the speed at which this industry was growing—after all, its growth is what pressured Congress to act—and also knew it would be injurious to design a set of rules that would hamper investors' access to value-additive investment opportunities.[67] This is the hallmark of an impressive legislative achievement—the balance between protection for investors and the continued incentives for innovation and growth.

THE POSTWAR PERIOD

Two innovations in mutual funds arose in the period following World War II. First, Investors Diversified Services (IDS), one of the older mutual funds, pioneered the distribution of mutual fund shares through an internal sales group. Second, investors had increased access to funds with more sophisticated and more niche investment mandates, including those targeting international exposure, fixed income, and sector-focused funds.[68] These developments ultimately tended to favor multiproduct firms that could now offer investors a suite of products while leveraging an internal sales team that could tailor its product offerings to an investor's needs. With these developments underway, mutual funds thrived in the bull market of 1946 to 1958, when the gross sales of mutual fund shares exceeded $10 billion.[69]

It was at this point that the market sentiment toward mutual funds became exuberant. There was widespread enthusiasm about mutual funds even in publications that had little to do with finance, such as *Better Homes and Gardens*, which declared that "there is virtually no possibility that you'll lose your shirt" by investing in mutual funds.[70] This unfettered ebullience came to an end with the bear market beginning in 1969 and in the 1970s. Mutual funds did not remain unscathed by the general economic conditions and the oil crisis. Many investors saw steep declines in net asset values, often to the extent of being halved from their peaks. The public became so disenchanted by the decline in many mutual funds that *Business Week* noted that the fund industry had "an image problem."[71]

However, during this period, the first money market mutual fund, the Reserve Fund, was founded by Bruce Bent and Henry Brown.[72] The goal of this vehicle was to take very little market risk and preserve capital while earning a small but steady return. Investors were attracted to these funds because of their circumvention of Regulation Q that otherwise capped the interest rates savings institutions could pay, which was a large problem during this inflationary period. The central mission of these funds was to generate returns while not "breaking the buck," or having the net asset value decline below $1 per unit. Indeed, these funds rarely failed at their mission, with the exception of some funds during the financial crisis of 2007–2009, including, in fact, Bruce Bent's own Primary Reserve fund, which had some exposure to Lehman debt.

Mutual funds experienced vast asset growth in the 1990s because of three factors. First, mutual funds gained assets through price appreciation as well as investors' enthusiasm in the bull market of the 1990s. Second, 401(k) plans and IRAs gave much greater access to mutual funds. As defined contribution plans grew and the burden of investing shifted toward the individual rather than the company's pension plan, mutual funds were a convenient vehicle to which investors turned. Third, with better distribution systems, more product offerings, and fledgling competition from index funds, many mutual funds saw fees decline, particularly on the loads charged to get into or out of them.

THE MUTUAL FUND INDUSTRY TODAY

Clearly, the mutual fund industry has evolved over time. Today equity-oriented mutual funds have 45 percent of total mutual fund assets, and 33 percent of total assets are with equity-oriented mutual funds that invest predominantly in corporations domiciled in the United States. There is also a growing concentration of assets in the largest mutual funds. The ten firms with the most assets under management in 2000 managed 44 percent of total mutual fund assets, but by the end of 2012 the ten largest firms managed 53 percent.[73] At the end of 2013, US mutual funds reached $15 trillion of assets under management.[74]

The industry is also likely to see continued concentration in multiproduct platforms. Although it does seem at first glance that new product innovation and the ability of multiproduct organizations to offer a range of solutions are positive developments, there is a limit beyond which these may not prove additive for the investor. The purpose of the mutual fund, after all, is to simplify the task of security selection by shifting that burden to a professional manager. If the industry arrives at a point at which the investor has to choose among an endless number of funds, however, the simplification objective may not really be satisfied. Furthermore, within the multiproduct funds, there is a risk that the firm managing a given fund may not be as effective as a team with a single product. A team with a single product, after all, has its own fortunes tied to how each fund fares, whereas a multiproduct manager may be able to ignore or shut down a fund that does not perform well without significant impact on its overall business. These are fundamental but admittedly philosophical questions that will face the industry in coming decades, and only time will tell how they are resolved.

CONCLUSION

Investment clients, whether individuals or institutions, are driving the demand for new investment forms and products, which in turn has created the conditions for the business of managing investments to become an industry. Endowments and foundations, too, will remain key players with the infinite life span of enduring institutions and the virtue of philanthropic goals. Sovereign wealth funds, while not likely to drive political instability, are meeting new challenges and influencing investment innovations. Life insurance will likewise remain a staple of the investment landscape as families seek to shift the mortality risk of the breadwinner onto a common capital base managed by the life insurer. Savings accounts, in some form, are likely to remain an important basic vehicle. However, their purpose is likely to shift increasingly to managing short-term liquidity for spending rather than as an investment vehicle as it becomes easier to sweep funds in excess of near-term spending needs into mutual funds, index funds, and direct securities. The heart of the task for investment professionals falls to investment advisers and mutual fund leaders. The design and management of creative, superior vehicles to achieve adequate returns without unacceptable risk continues to be the challenge.

CHAPTER FIVE

Fraud, Market Manipulation, and Insider Trading

THIS CHAPTER IS ABOUT INVESTMENT'S unscrupulous: those who have committed fraud, engaged in market manipulation, or traded on insider information. While these three offenses do not encompass every form of securities violation, they most endanger fair markets and are highly covered in the media. Furthermore, these violations come with a clear intent to profit from malfeasance and unethical behavior. Indeed, the crafty and crooked operators who engage in this behavior inspire a sense of profound injustice, visceral indignation, and a desire to right the wrong. These strong emotions can drive a search for meaning: What can we learn from the deceitful? What are the general typologies of these bad actors? How has society adapted over time? Is any progress being made?

This chapter turns to the historical record to examine each type of behavior in turn—first fraud, then market manipulation, and last, trading on insider information—and looks at some of the pivotal cases in each category. In doing so, it enables us to reach a remarkable conclusion—namely, that as a society we have gotten much better at creating the legal framework to prosecute this behavior. The legal landscape has changed on several fronts, and we have substantially bolstered our ability to catch and punish offenders. Yes, the fraudster has always been around and always will be. If there is a dime to be made through deceit, there will be someone chasing it. But fortunately, those collecting the dimes of duplicity are now doing it in front of an ever-larger and ever-faster steamroller. Deception has become a dangerous business.

There are, in effect, three forces at play that are responsible for curtailing these actions. The first is legal: we have drafted new legislation to ban or prohibit certain behaviors, making certain actions illegal that were not previously so. The second is enforcement: we have improved our capabilities for detecting these transgressions and prosecuting them accordingly. The third is regulatory: we have enhanced the quality of the regulatory landscape to reduce the likelihood that these crimes even happen. In other words, we have reduced the number of circumstances that could potentially give rise to criminality, such as through better disclosures and practices for handling cash by certain investment advisers. To be pithy, the trifecta is improved laws, improved enforcement, and improved regulation.

Throughout the chapter, readers will see that while there has been broad-based enhancement on all of these fronts, there is still much work to be done, particularly on enforcement and regulation. There are cases (such as that of Ivan Boesky) where prosecutors were too lenient; this could jeopardize deterrent capabilities against future perpetrators and are a failure in enforcement action. The fact that Bernie Madoff went virtually untouched by the SEC for so long is indeed a blemish on the record of the agency and another failure of enforcement. Of course, the fact that he had such minimal constraint on handling funds and conducting proper audits speaks to a failure of the regulatory framework. However, we have made enormous improvements in the legal tools at our disposal to deal with fraud once it is brought to light.

This chapter therefore deals with successful democratization of investment along regulatory, enforcement, and legal lines with respect to these three behaviors. However, this is not merely a loud paean to the past, as the project is far from finished. We must, in short, be as creative and thoughtful in crafting our legislation, our agencies, and our regulatory bodies as are the very offenders they are intended to discourage, catch, and punish.

Before diving into the realm of bad actors in the investment world, it is important to recognize that the vast majority of investment managers are, in fact, quite ethical. The malicious characters, while they do a disproportionate amount of damage for their numbers, are truly relatively few and far between. We must keep in mind that these agents of malice are certainly not good for the ethical managers who have their profession tarnished as a result of the immoral behavior. We examine the nefarious as such, fully cognizant that they are not representative of the industry at large but must nonetheless be understood, given how much devastation and disruption they produce.

FRAUD

Bernie Madoff

We begin with fraud, or deliberate and premeditated deception undertaken for gain. Our first story starts in December 2008. It was the time of reckoning that Bernie Madoff, the man who has since become the modern embodiment of financial duplicity, hoped would never come. And yet, by July 2009 he would trade a life replete with Davidoff cigars, Patek Philippe watches, and fashionable digs in the Upper East Side for a prison cell in Butner, North Carolina.[1]

It was in this Upper East Side penthouse apartment that the conversation catalyzing his end took place the day before his arrest. Madoff explained to his wife and sons, Andrew and Mark, that his firm was completely insolvent and that the entire operation was a fraud. Andrew later quoted his father as having said, "It's all been one big lie. It's a giant Ponzi scheme and it's been going on for years, and there have been all these redemptions, and I can't keep it going anymore. I can't do it."[2]

The story goes that Andrew and Mark then brought their father to the authorities. However, this narrative of no culpability on the part of Andrew and Mark has been difficult to accept by some. In fact, the court-appointed trustee in the bankruptcy, Irving Picard, brought suit against the brothers. It is true, however, that the fraudulent investment advisory business operated on a different floor than the market-making side of the companies, which the brothers operated.[3]

There are scores of questions one could ask along these lines: Were they so incurious about what was happening on the other floor not to find out? Did they not hear from investors that their father was a supposed legend, and would they not want to learn how to emulate his prowess? Why were they not alarmed that they did not hear conversations about new strategies or novel investment theses on the advisory side? Or, even if curiosity did not motivate them, why did the simple realities of key man risk not spur them—for was it wise to continue having a man of seventy running a portion of this ostensibly very lucrative business no one else in the firm understood?

Shedding light on this question are Bernie Madoff's own contentions that it should have been abundantly obvious to the SEC that he was running a Ponzi scheme. Madoff said, "I was astonished. They never even looked at my stock records." He also noted that investigators did not check with the Depository Trust Company. "If you're looking at a Ponzi scheme, it's the first thing you do," said Madoff.[4] If Madoff believed that the commission, charged with overseeing thousands of firms, should have had no difficulty in ascertaining that a fraud was underway at his company, then surely his two sons, who spent their entire workweeks directing a part of the firm, had to have figured it out. It is also unconvincing to argue that Mark and Andrew were just too dimwitted to have asked such questions or made these observations. Andrew's educational pedigree, for example, suggests otherwise: he graduated from the Wharton School at the University of Pennsylvania.[5]

The investors who had put their money with Madoff for decades were perhaps less interested in speculation on the involvement of Mark and Andrew and more interested in what drove Madoff to do it in the first place. When pleading guilty to the charges brought against him, Madoff claimed that it was not until the 1990s that the fraud began. He stated that market conditions were such that it was too difficult to deliver the returns his investors had come to expect. In this account, Madoff seems to describe himself as a victim of his own success.[6] However, this story too seems to be just another drop in the deep stream of fabrication. The recent prosecution of David Kugel, a trader whose employment began at the firm in 1970, has indicated that there was, in fact, fraud going on in the 1970s.[7] Further, an expert investigator on the subject believes it could have gone on even before that, beginning around 1964 or 1965.[8]

Given both the number of people involved and the fact that the fraud was being perpetrated for decades, how was he not discovered earlier? First, Madoff's ostensible legitimacy was enhanced by his time serving as chairman of the board of the NASDAQ, a fact he placed right on the fund's website.[9] As evident in other cases, many fraudsters have benefited from affiliations with trusted individuals and institutions. Madoff was also well connected within the Jewish community, and many wealthy individuals as well as charities looked to Madoff to manage some of their funds. This religious and ethnic commonality may have given some investors a greater sense of trust than may be typical in a manager-client relationship. As Rabbi Yitzhok Breitowitz said, "I do think that psychologically in the Jewish community we often feel that our fellow Jew would never do that," and "I think that created an atmosphere of trust."[10] Surely, while many investors were not Jewish, having a close association with the community did help Madoff grow his asset base.

Further, Madoff largely stayed out of the major headlines talking about brilliant returns, lest some perspicacious soul would try (and most likely fail) to reconstruct how he achieved them. In a world where many investment advisers try to shadow the techniques and methods of other, successful firms, Bernie wanted to keep a low profile.

But even so, how is it possible that this fraud went on so long with nobody noticing? One seldom discussed but exceedingly strange angle on the Bernie Madoff fraud was the role of the auditor. The auditor, after all, is the last line of defense in such an investment structure with few regulations. The auditor is tasked with determining whether the assets claimed on the books are in fact present. Who was responsible? Surely a firm managing tens of billions of dollars in assets would have a well-known, highly reputable auditor with many capable employees. After all, it is no small task to examine the books of such a large firm with an array of different investments. And yet, defying all logic, Madoff's auditor occupied no such exalted status but instead was completely obscure. The entire firm, Friehling and Horowitz, had an office about 550 square feet in size.[11] Jerome Horowitz, Friehling's father-in-law, retired in 1998 and died in 2009, leaving Friehling as the firm's only active accountant. Someone working in the vicinity of the office in New York City suggested that Friehling would stop by the office for perhaps fifteen minutes at a time and leave again. For this, Friehling received payments of $12,000 to $14,500 per month. Friehling told the American Institute of Certified Public Accountants (AICPA), which oversees private auditors' compliance with standards, that the firm was not actually conducting audits. Firms that conduct audits are generally subject to a peer review process whereby external auditors look at the practices of an auditing company to see if they are up to par. As such, by Friehling and Horowitz's misstating that it was not conducting audits to AICPA when, in fact, it had been conducting the audit for the Madoff funds, the firm avoided the peer review process. Furthermore, at the time, New York was one of six states that did not even require these peer reviews to take place.[12]

The sad reality is that it seems Friehling had no idea Madoff was running a Ponzi scheme. After all, Friehling's family had money with Madoff. It seems that it was not complicity but incompetence that created a situation where the auditor merely rubber-stamped the financial statements. Friehling was quick to admit that he took these statements at "face value," not quite the standards one would expect of an auditor.[13] The takeaway is simple: if there are to remain relatively unregulated investment vehicles, it is absolutely essential that the function of proper oversight is at least supported by strong auditing and accounting standards. Someone somewhere must have an eye on the books, and if it is not a government agency, then there must be robust protocols for proper audits and very stiff penalties for noncompliance.

Curiously, many people did notice, and one man in particular was persistent in trying to get the Madoff operation shut down: Harry Markopolos. In fact, it was precisely in trying to emulate what Madoff was doing that Markopolos made his discovery. Markopolos came upon Bernie Madoff as part of an assignment from his employer, Rampart Investment Management, to deconstruct Madoff's returns.[14] The very essence of Bernie Madoff's fraud was that he contended he used a "split-strike conversion" strategy when in fact he was simply running a Ponzi scheme. Split-strike conversion is a trade where one buys an index (or some subset of it), sells call options, and buys put options. Put options increase in value when the index declines in price, so that serves to protect the portfolio against falling asset values. The sale of call options means that Madoff's firm would exchange some of the upside (if stock prices increased) for a fixed amount of money. This strategy, of course, should involve reasonably low volatility (as it is buffered on both sides by the options trades). The problem? Such an approach could not possibly generate the risk-adjusted returns (that is, the return per given unit of volatility) Bernie Madoff had claimed.[15] Analyzing Madoff's returns through one of the feeder funds that gave Madoff money to manage (Fairfield Sentry) reveals that Madoff claimed average annual returns of 10.59 percent with a volatility of just 2.45 percent (and a worst month of just—.64 percent) from December 1990 to October 2008. It is interesting to note that the average returns themselves were not outrageous—a split-strike conversion strategy over this period could have produced between 7 and 11 percent annually, but at four times the standard deviation of the returns (a measure of the volatility).[16] In other words, it was the consistency of the strategy that should have been seen as clearly fraudulent, a strategy different from the unbelievably high absolute returns claimed by Carlo Ponzi, examined later in this chapter.

Markopolos realized this and came to the conclusion that there were effectively two possibilities: either Madoff was unethically front-running his clients—meaning that because he was also their broker, he could see what his clients intended to buy and then simply buy some of those securities for his own book before executing the trade for the clients—or he was simply running a Ponzi scheme.[17] Markopolos wrote a detailed nineteen-page report with a succinct and explicit title: "The World's Largest Hedge Fund Is a Fraud." This report, too, was just one correspondence among many with the SEC that went back as far as May 1999.[18]

Markopolos, though, was far from the only person to figure this out. In that report, Markopolos also states that he spoke with many heads of equity derivatives trading desks (options are derivatives) at different firms and states that "every single one of the senior managers I spoke with told me that Bernie Madoff was a fraud." However, people did not want to jeopardize their careers by making public statements attempting to expose him earlier, suggested Markopolos.[19]

In the wake of the internal investigation to discover why the SEC failed to properly conduct an adequate review of the firm, it was revealed that other sources had submitted notes of concern and additional evidence pointing to the conclusion that Madoff was a fraud. The SEC had received a note from a hedge fund manager stating that Madoff's returns over the previous decade had no correlation at all with the equities markets and that it seemed unlikely he was transacting as many options contracts as would have been necessary to maintain a split-strike conversion strategy of that size. Another note received in October 2005 was from an investor in the fund who noted how suspiciously secretive the firm was and that he quickly decided to withdraw his own money.[20] There were ample warnings, but little was done. The SEC failed to properly conduct regulatory oversight, a fact to which we will return at the end of the chapter.

The Bernie Madoff fraud shook the foundations of the investment management industry so profoundly because of just how vast it was. It struck so many experienced professionals as shocking that a fraud of the order of magnitude of tens of billions of dollars could ever be pulled off.

There have been changes in the wake of Madoff's crimes. One has been implemented because Bernie Madoff failed to use an independent custodian, who is in charge of overseeing asset protection. After all, if Madoff had used an independent custodian, the only way he could have perpetrated this fraud for so long was if the custodian were either complicit or completely incompetent. In the post-Madoff world, registered investment advisers who do not use an independent custodian are subject to surprise exams where an accountant can show up to determine if the total asset pool is consistent with reported figures. Furthermore, the registered investment advisers who fail to use an independent custodian must have their protocols for managing asset flows reviewed by an independent third party.[21]

There were also reforms within the SEC, including enhancing the talent in units responsible for fraud detection, creating a single repository for all tips relating to potential fraud, and establishing responsibility for agency resources to triage and pursue these tips accordingly.[22] This was especially important after the clear failure to heed the work of Markopolos, who presented compelling evidence that something was awry as early as 1999. Of course, only time will tell how effective these reforms prove to be, and so much depends upon the quality and tenacity of the personnel at the SEC.

Allen Stanford

Bernie Madoff was not the only prominent and wealthy man operating a Ponzi scheme before the financial crisis. Allen Stanford also had a painful fall from grace. The billionaire who once occupied a spot in the Forbes 400 found himself convicted of a litany of crimes and sentenced to 110 years in prison.[23]

Stanford seems not to have been keen on legitimate business. Perhaps the fact that he failed early in his career pushed him toward making a business out of fraud. Indeed, he failed in a rather simple business, a health club known as Total Fitness Center in Waco, Texas. He grew the business by establishing other clubs in Galveston and Austin and attempting to establish a club in Houston. The business went bankrupt in 1982, however, precipitated in great part by the effect of a souring oil market on Houston. Stanford filed for personal bankruptcy in 1984, showing assets of less than a quarter of a million dollars and liabilities over $10 million.[24]

And yet, Stanford was undeterred. In 1986, just two years after filing for bankruptcy, Stanford established the Guardian International Bank, domiciled on the island of Montserrat. It was seeded by Stanford's father, who took the money he earned from some real estate investments and put it into the bank, becoming its chairman. The bank looked for customers in Latin America, running advertisements depicting large yields for certificates of deposit.[25] In 1992, Stanford founded the Stanford Financial Group in Houston, again selling certificates of deposit, and quickly the organization gained $3 billion in assets.[26]

Where did this money go? Not to liquid securities with low risk, as he told investors. Some of the money went into real estate and business investments instead. Much of it went straight to Stanford. During his high-flying days, Stanford funneled the money into purchases of enormous mansions, extravagant yachts, gifts for girlfriends, and patronage of cricket matches.[27] Some of his purchases seemed excessive, including spending over $100 million on private jets and helicopters within a three-year period and $12 million to add six feet of length to one of his yachts.[28]

Stanford's deception did not end with the funds he took from investors. Stanford also told tall tales about the origins of the Stanford financial institutions. He claimed that Stanford International was a family business dating back to his grandfather, who started it in 1932. He would insist as time went on that a picture of his grandfather be put in all of the firm's offices. Sadly, this was another notable misrepresentation. While Stanford's grandfather did indeed have a firm called Stanford Financial, it was a little insurance brokerage with no connection to the bank. Stanford would tell other lies, too, even when they were for no apparent gain except for some odd self-aggrandizement.

For instance, he claimed he was descended from Leland Stanford, founder of Stanford University, even though there appears to be no connection at all.[29]

The prosecution of Stanford's case depended in large part upon the testimony of James Davis, the CFO, who described at length the bribes given to Antiguan officials, the false documentation provided to clients, and the circumvention of US government scrutiny.[30] Davis's job was, in effect, to fabricate numbers, which he did for over 20 years from 1987 or 1988 until 2009.[31]

Even at the end, Stanford insisted that he was not insolvent and that instead the federal government was at fault for ruining his business, saying, "They [government officials] destroyed it and turned it to nothing."[32] He showed not even a tinge of remorse. When one victim asked all the other victims to show their pained faces to Stanford in the courtroom and the judge advised Stanford that he was not obligated to meet their stares, Stanford still did so without showing the slightest sign of contrition.[33]

It was in this environment of little regulation in the Caribbean that a man with no banking experience had an organization with billions in deposits. Stanford's episode is just another in a long string of individuals who seemed ill equipped to succeed in legitimate business but who remained fixated on creating great success and a lavish lifestyle. He found a little corner of the market to exploit by establishing a bank whose operations were mostly offshore and selling certificates of deposit to victims in Latin America and the United States. Perhaps one should not engage in comparing the insidiousness of one financial crime with another, but there are some noteworthy points of difference. Unlike Bernie Madoff's victims, who tended to be wealthy individuals and institutions, Stanford's victims were quite varied and counted among their ranks those of moderate to minimal means who purchased his certificates of deposit (CDs). Furthermore, a CD is supposed to be a minimal-risk asset in which one can place excess savings not intended to bear significant market exposure (unlike Madoff's scheme of supposedly investing in the stock and derivatives markets). Last, the purchaser of a CD should not have been expected to know that Stanford's operations were a scheme, since the purchaser was just buying CDs that did not offer egregiously high returns, whereas arguably a very sophisticated investor could have seen that Madoff's returns were too high to be true given their low volatility.

Even the very phrase "Ponzi scheme," used again and again in the headlines to describe the Bernie Madoff and Allen Stanford episodes, is eponymously named after Charles Ponzi, who even in his wildest dreams never thought that deceptions of such magnitude were possible.

Charles Ponzi

Charles, or Carlo, Ponzi immigrated to the United States from his native Italy in 1903 at the age of twenty-one. He would later declare, "I landed in this country with $2.50 in cash and $1 million in hopes, and those hopes never left me." In order to achieve his dream of affluence, Charles Ponzi would undertake one scheme after another. Though he initially landed in Boston, he went to Montreal, Canada, for a short time to be in the employ of Luigi Zarossi, who operated a bank known simply as Banco Zarossi. Zarossi ended up stealing from the bank directly. Ponzi, too, broke the law while employed at the bank; he was convicted of fraud, and he spent three years in a Canadian prison for his crimes.[34]

This episode certainly taught Ponzi a lesson—but not quite the right one. He learned that financial fraud was not terribly hard to perpetrate. In those days, regulators had neither the workforce nor the mandate to scrutinize the operations of every single firm in painstaking detail, so those running some institutions could easily abuse and exploit their positions of power. What Ponzi failed to learn was that eventually the commission of financial crimes tends to catch up with the perpetrator. And so, despite being caught and serving a prison sentence, Ponzi was already dreaming up his next scheme.

Ponzi went back to the United States in 1911 and participated in a scheme to shuttle Italian immigrants from Canada to America. This plot was short lived, and Ponzi was caught once more and sentenced to serve two years in a prison in Atlanta, Georgia.[35] Yet again, Ponzi seemed completely undeterred by his years in prison. It was at this point that Ponzi came across what was ostensibly a fantastically lucrative arbitrage opportunity that would catapult him into orchestrating his grandest scheme yet—and the one for which he would earn his infamy.

Ponzi's scheme relied on the market for the international reply coupon. An international reply coupon is a voucher for postage, allowing one to send mail to someone in another country and pay the cost of postage for the reply. By international treaty, a signatory country had to accept an international reply coupon sold in another nation. Ponzi realized that because of the weakness of the currencies of many European nations after the war, it was possible to acquire international reply coupons in countries like Italy for less than their value in the United States.[36]

It is important to note that though there was theoretically an arbitrage opportunity, it would have been very costly to exploit. It would require purchasing massive quantities of postal reply coupons in one country, shipping them across the Atlantic (if they were to be sold in the United States), and operating a business to sell the postage. Indeed, given how inexpensive postage was, generating the amounts of money required to keep Ponzi's scheme going would have necessitated the sale of an enormous number of international reply coupons, in fact many more than were ever printed.[37]

The key for Ponzi was that the idea was plausible enough (until one reflects more carefully on these complications) that he was able to convince many that he had the means to generate shockingly high returns. Ponzi opened a company known as the Securities Exchange Company, which offered a 50 percent return in ninety days (and later the same return in just forty-five days), and in 1919 the investors began pouring in. The inflow of capital was sustained by a large network of salespeople, who were paid 10 percent of the capital they managed to send to the firm. Ponzi wasted no time spending his newfound wealth, acquiring a mansion in Lexington, Massachusetts, a wide array of properties he could rent out in the Boston area, and expensive cars and apparel.[38]

The government began an audit of the scheme, and the *Boston Post*, which had initially written about Ponzi's operations and helped fuel its growth months before (when it did not know it was a scam), took up the task of investigating Ponzi as well. Soon, the *Boston Post* ran an article about how Ponzi had been prosecuted before for his previous scams, and at last, the government finished its audit and found millions of dollars missing, putting Ponzi under arrest.[39] Ponzi ended up serving over three years in federal prison for the crime and later more time in state prison, and even after that, he sought out new schemes (including one to collect capital for supposed property in Florida that was just marshland). Ponzi was eventually deported back to Italy, where he would become involved in an airline affiliated with the Mussolini government that essentially moved Nazis from Germany to Brazil, where they could hide out in relative safety.⁴⁰

With respect to the evolution of laws and regulations, it is worth noting that Ponzi was actually sent to federal prison for mail fraud. Shortly after his release, he was indicted by Massachusetts for larceny. A legal battle ensued over whether the Massachusetts indictment constituted double jeopardy, as Ponzi was being pursued for the same scheme. The Supreme Court of the United States ultimately spoke in the matter of *Ponzi v. Fessenden* in 1922 that serving a federal sentence does not make the individual immune from prosecution for other crimes (mail fraud and larceny being separate offenses) at the state level.⁴¹ Ponzi would eventually serve seven years in Massachusetts prisons before being deported to Italy, but the whole episode makes clear that the federal government did not have the legislative tools for dealing with financial crimes that it does today. The federal government relied on an indictment on many counts of mail fraud rather than a more sophisticated legal transgression that more appropriately described Ponzi's actions. Collectively, the federal and state governments may have punished Ponzi appropriately, but only because the state of Massachusetts became involved when it realized that the federal government's punishment was insufficient. This was arguably an inferior institutional design, as it required two governments processing evidence and investigating to formulate a case, leaving a gap in time during which Ponzi was able to commit further crimes in Florida and prolonging the restoration of justice for victims.

Ultimately, in comparison to Ponzi's scheme, Madoff's scam was actually much more impressive. Madoff sustained it for decades, whereas Ponzi lasted for just over a year. Madoff managed to cause losses of tens of billions, whereas Ponzi's toll would be equivalent to just hundreds of millions today. If schemers of yore could have idols, there is little doubt Madoff would have been Ponzi's.

William Miller

It is worth noting that while Ponzi has the distinction of having his name on this type of scheme of collecting from Peter to pay Paul, he was certainly not the first to orchestrate one. In 1899, William Miller, a bookkeeper in Brooklyn, opened the so-called Franklin Syndicate, where he offered astonishing returns on capital. He offered a miraculous 10 percent per week, a return that later gave him the nickname "William 520 Miller," for the 520 percent one could earn in the course of a year.[42] Miller claimed that he was able to earn enough return to pay out such exorbitant interest rates because he knew how to make tremendous sums of money on Wall Street.[43] Of course, he had no such abilities. All in all, he managed to steal some $1 million, or in today's equivalent some $25 million.[44] Almost comically, years later when Ponzi's scheme was still hot, Miller, who unlike Ponzi had learned the lesson to cease the constant scheming, remarked, "I may be rather dense, but I cannot understand how Ponzi made so much money in so short a time." Dense he was not, and just days later Ponzi's scheme collapsed.[45]

Madoff, Miller, and Ponzi, though, represent only one typology of fraud, that which begins or has long gone on as virtually pure, unadulterated deception. There are many episodes, however, where operations began as legitimate and legal but turned fraudulent when the technique proved to be too speculative and the manager hoped for a rebound but found himself permanently behind and unwilling to come forward with the truth of having sustained significant losses.

The history of these schemes makes another point clear: over time, the schemes have become far more sophisticated. Today, very few people would believe returns of 520 percent *per annum* were remotely possible in the case of William Miller or 50 percent returns in 90 days in the case of Carlo Ponzi. Today's fraudsters realize that the scheming has to be much more subtle to attract large pools of capital. In Madoff's case, the subtlety was in offering returns that were not completely outlandish but in offering a consistency of returns that was unbelievable. In Stanford's case, it was not even in offering CDs at very high rates of returns but rather in hiding behind an aura of security and personal fortune and selling a simple product to an audience who could have no way of knowing it was even a scheme because of regulatory failures. All of this means vigilance must be heightened—it is not enough to shy away from the simple huckster peddling eye-popping returns. One needs care and diligence to detect the modern financial fraudster.

Ferdinand Ward

Ferdinand Ward almost bridges the two typologies. He seems not to have started out with the intention of committing fraud, but when the time came and he suffered losses, it did not take long for him to resort to duplicity. In doing so, he claimed as his victim no less than former president Ulysses S. Grant.

Grant left high office in 1877 and embarked on a two-year tour across Europe and Asia with his wife. Though not doubting his fondness for travel, others too saw the trip as a means to garner more popularity at home and to position himself for a possible third term as president, an idea he had flirted with privately. Whatever the reason for the trip, it did claim much of the wealth of an aging Grant, and he returned home much wiser and worldly but also less affluent. The prospect of the third term not materializing, Grant set himself to the task of making money.

An attractive prospect emerged, or so it seemed at the time, when Grant's son Buck met Ferdinand Ward, a charismatic fellow who fooled Buck into believing he had far more skill in investment than he actually had. The two men formed a firm and named it Grant and Ward. Ferdinand Ward saw an obvious opportunity: if he could bring Ulysses S. Grant on as a partner in his firm, he could leverage Grant's popularity to gain legitimacy. Grant plunged some $200,000, a sum representing nearly all his wealth, into the firm.[46]

There was a major disconnect between what Ward was actually doing and what investors thought he was doing. Grant simply believed that Ferdinand Ward had some great financial prowess that would translate readily into financial gain. Meanwhile, Ward was actually telling other investors that the firm was making money by using Grant's influence to secure government contracts. Of course, Grant was far too noble to engage in such tactics, but investors believed Ward and thought it would be a straightforward and easy way to enjoy returns. In reality though, Ferdinand Ward took the cash from investors and engaged in simple speculation.[47]

For some time, new investors were attracted to the large dividends offered and the firm's capitalization grew steadily. Grant was quite pleased at the whole affair, believing his fortune to be in the millions of dollars, and would engage in leisurely talk with potential investors while leaving the complications of the operation of the firm to Ward.[48]

Unfortunately for the Grants, Ferdinand Ward was actually inept at speculation and lost a great deal of money. In April 1884, Ward asked Grant for a $150,000 loan. Rather than admitting that the firm of Grant and Ward was on the verge of collapse, he claimed that the loan was needed to bail out a bank doing business with the firm. Grant, still trusting Ward and hoping this could put an end to the catastrophe, brought himself to ask William Vanderbilt, who inherited his father's railroad empire, for a loan. Vanderbilt agreed but was quite clear that he did so not on the basis of the merits of the firm but rather because it was Ulysses Grant who was asking. "What I've heard about that firm would not justify me in lending it a dime," he said, but, he continued, "to you—General Grant—I'm making this loan."[49]

Grant returned with the money and gave it to Ferdinand Ward. The very next day Ward was gone, and it became clear to Grant that it was all over. Ferdinand Ward had lied and the whole firm was massively insolvent, with liabilities ultimately amounting to over $16 million, not even remotely offset by assets in the tens of thousands when the final calculations were made. Ward was swiftly caught, though, and brought to justice.[50]

Grant was swindled along with his investors and was left effectively broke. He was forced to take up his pen to write his memoirs, with an attractive royalty agreement with Mark Twain's publishing firm. It proved to be a lucrative endeavor, selling widely and considered by most to be written with impeccable clarity, though Grant would not be there to enjoy the fruits of his toils, perishing from throat cancer just days after he completed the draft.[51]

In the end, Ward was simply another charismatic character making use of powerful friends to perpetrate a scheme. Indeed, one could not imagine a better choice than a former president whose popularity, at least in the North, was still substantial. While it was not a Ponzi scheme from the very beginning, it did quickly evolve into fraud as Ward tried to recapitalize the firm with new investors who believed the mission and strategy of the company to be wildly different than it actually was.

Ivar Kreuger

Ward's fraud was certainly not the only occasion when a firm initially hoping to make money gradually came to the realization that it was continuing instead to register losses and resorted to fraud as a result. This was what occurred with Ivar Kreuger, who was singled out among larcenists by John Kenneth Galbraith as "the Leonardo of their craft."[52] As will be seen, Kreuger did have a legitimate business strategy—and, frankly, a far sounder one than the blind speculation to which Ward had resorted. He even executed it reasonably well for some time, but high expectations and economic conditions aided in the unraveling of the businesses.

Ivar Kreuger was born in Kalmar, Sweden, in 1880.[53] He was the oldest son in the family, and he gained control of the family's match factories by 1913. Kreuger aspired to much more than just operating a few match factories, however. In time, he saw incredible potential for the expansion of the family's holdings into a match empire that could span the world.[54]

The time was right in the wake of World War I. Many countries were devastated, having witnessed their capital stock depleted by a long and destructive war. Rebuilding of the capital stock was front and center, but many governments were hard pressed to find money to initiate efforts at reconstruction. After all, imposing high taxes on an already fragile economy as a means of generating the requisite revenue appealed to few. Enter Ivar Kreuger, who began offering loans to countries, sometimes as large as $125 million. What did he ask for in return? Complete monopolistic control over the countries' match markets. For many countries, it seemed like a small concession to make: they needed the funds, and the match market seemed like a reasonably innocuous segment of the economy to give away as a monopoly. Besides, the funds would be repaid through excise taxes on the matches, and the price of the matches would be agreed on in advance.[55]

Many countries took the plunge, and soon Ivar Kreuger's empire was growing, with complete monopolies in fifteen countries and enormous market share in nineteen other nations, serving a total of 75 percent of the entire European demand for matches.[56]

Of course, Kreuger could not simply make loans of this order of magnitude from company profits. He looked to the American capital markets for help, and he sold stock and bonds as a means of raising funds. However, some of this debt bore significant interest rates—often as high as 20 percent—and this generated a sizable financial burden. It is not precisely clear at what point Kreuger began to use fraud as a means of keeping the firm afloat, but there is no doubt that the stock market collapse of 1929 and the ensuing Great Depression created extremely adverse business conditions for Kreuger. In particular, the debt markets that Kreuger relied on not only to support loans but also to refinance existing debt began to dry up. Credit just did not flow as easily as it had in the 1920s. Indeed, just as Madoff's end was brought about by systematic calamity (in Madoff's case, the global financial crisis that motivated many of his investors to seek redemptions to bolster their liquidity), Kreuger's end was precipitated in part by the systematic seizure of capital markets in the early 1930s.[57]

While it would take a total of five long years to make sense of Kreuger's hundreds of companies and divisions, it was clear that he was altering the books to the tune of hundreds of millions of dollars near the end. Kreuger & Toll was engaged in the complete fabrication of Italian bonds supposedly worth $142 million, not to mention consistent attempts at double-counting assets.[58] In the end, Kreuger was found dead on March 12, 1932, in Paris, shot in the heart. It was ruled a suicide, though decades later Ivar's brother Torsten disputed this account, claiming Ivar had been murdered.[59]

The frauds that Ivar Kreuger committed during his life served in part to prompt reforms designed to prevent a recurrence of this sort of deception, including more rules on auditing and other accounting regulation.[60] In particular, Congress came to the conclusion that publicly traded firms must be subject to audits by trained auditors, but they could not agree on how this should be done. The two options at Congress's disposal were either to allow private accountants to be responsible for this task or alternatively to create a public corps of auditors. Ultimately, they decided that a corps of government auditors was not practical because the task was too large and, in the words of one partner at a prominent accounting firm of the day testifying in front of the Senate, the "type of men that are in the public practice of accountancy" would be unlikely to "leave their present practice to go into government employ."[61]

Richard Whitney

In the episodes of Ferdinand Ward and Ivar Kreuger, personal relationships were instrumental in perpetuating the fraud—for Ward, with former president Grant, and for Kreuger, the legitimacy he earned having served as an adviser to many prominent policy makers. The tale of Richard Whitney is similar in this respect. And, like Kreuger and Ward, he did not set out to perpetrate a fraud but, rather, fell behind on his obligations, ultimately resorting to all manner of illegal activity in an attempt to catch up with them.

Richard Whitney rocketed to fame on Black Thursday, October 24, 1929.[62] Panic had hit Wall Street, and the market tumbled as trading commenced. A private meeting of powerful financiers was called to react to the crisis, attended by such prominent figures as Thomas Lamont of J. P. Morgan and Charles Mitchell of National City Bank, who decided the best plan of action was to restore confidence in the market by placing bids above the then-going price on a number of major securities. There to execute the plan was Richard Whitney, the vice president of the NYSE, who marched out onto the floor and announced, "I bid 205 for 10,000 Steel," referring to United States Steel. He repeated the effort with dramatic flair with other stocks.[63]

The effort did work to push up prices in the short term, but of course there were structural issues in the market and the economy unbeknownst to the bankers at the time that were simply too deep to prevent a further slide. Nevertheless, for this and for his calm management of the exchange during the market crash of 1929, Richard Whitney garnered the respect and admiration of many, and he became president of the NYSE.[64] His service in this official capacity served to boost his reputation further (as Bernie Madoff's service as the non-executive chairman of NASDAQ, though less prestigious than the NYSE, certainly had).

Whitney ran a firm, named simply Richard Whitney & Co., a small brokerage firm that catered primarily to institutional clients. Whitney thought he had found a lucrative opportunity in Distilled Liquors, a firm Whitney surmised was poised to do well as Prohibition ended. To finance his acquisition of shares, he not only used his own money but also borrowed extensively, and he sunk the funds into Distilled Liquors. Whitney could have made a healthy profit if he had sold off his holdings shortly after Prohibition ended, as the price of Distilled Liquors did move up, but he was convinced the market would continue to put upward pressure on the price, and so he held on. The stock began to decline in value, and Whitney became increasingly unable to meet his financial obligations. He began to use his prominent positions to embezzle in order to cover his debts. First, it was from the New York Yacht Club, where he served as treasurer and removed $150,000 of the bonds owned by the club to collateralize a loan for his own debts. It is entirely possible that Whitney thought he could justify this action as a stopgap, for as it would later be learned, he did something similar in 1926 with his father-in-law's estate, removing funds temporarily but putting them back before anyone knew.[65]

Unfortunately for Whitney, this measure was not enough. The financial hemorrhage continued. The next victim was the New York Stock Exchange Gratuity Fund, a pool of money earmarked for paying death benefits to the families of exchange members. Here, when Whitney's firm was instructed to sell certain bonds and purchase others to replace them, he took the new bonds and used them to collateralize a bank loan (of course, with the lending bank completely unaware of what had transpired).[66]

Richard Whitney's firm was insolvent for several years before the embezzlement and fraud were discovered. The comptroller of the NYSE eventually figured out the fraud and made it known that the firm was deep in the red and had resorted to numerous illegal measures to prevent others from realizing it.[67]

Whitney was arrested. During his sentencing, the judge proclaimed, "To cover up your thefts and your insolvency, you resorted to larcenies, frauds, misrepresentations and falsifications of books," and he said that the "decent forces of America" were dealt "a severe setback" by Whitney's actions.[68] In the end, Richard's brother George, a partner at J. P. Morgan, paid off all of Whitney's debts, and Whitney faded from public view on a farm in Massachusetts after serving time in Sing Sing.[69]

The tale of Richard Whitney reinforces some of the recurrent patterns evident in other episodes of fraud. Whitney had a sound investment thesis, not unlike Ivar Kreuger, who tried to build a matchmaking empire. Whitney also had a stellar reputation from his performance during a previous crisis through effective management of the market collapse of 1929.

It is the very vagaries of the market that compel some of these individuals who never set out to commit wrongdoing to resort ultimately to fraud. The market moves up and affirms the original thesis, prompting the individual to think he is right. However, just as quickly as the market moves up, it can experience a reversal, and the buyer thinks, "Surely, the market will come to its senses soon." Eventually this line of thinking overwhelms sound reasoning, and some manage to cross the fateful line by thinking, "It will only be for a little while. When the market behaves rationally, I will make money and nobody will ever know." But when the losses grow, the fraud becomes unsustainable and it is no longer possible to reverse the whole affair. Hence it becomes obvious why reputation is so important to major frauds that do not begin as schemes: Those who are held in high esteem have so many opportunities to plug holes. They have ample access to credit because many are comfortable extending loans to these ostensibly worthy individuals.

The Richard Whitney affair had a comical and surprising effect on reforms. At the time, the SEC found itself at odds with the NYSE over instituting greater oversight and other regulatory enhancements, which the NYSE believed it did adequately on its own. The disagreement reached a fever pitch in February 1938, when SEC chairman William Douglas had a conversation with NYSE counsel William Jackson. The conversation transpired after an initial compromise seemed imminent over new regulations that stumbled over a failure to see eye to eye on the establishment of an outside president to supervise the NYSE, with Douglas commenting that he could simply take over the NYSE if they failed to come to an agreement.[70]

> JACKSON: "Well, I suppose you'll go ahead with your program?"
> DOUGLAS: "You're damned right I will."
> JACKSON: "When you take over the Exchange, I hope you'll remember that we've been in business 150 years. There may be some things you will like to ask us."
> DOUGLAS: "There is one thing I'd like to ask."
> JACKSON: "What is it?"
> DOUGLAS: "Where do you keep the paper and pencils?"[71]

The comedy that arose was that Richard Whitney, as a prominent individual associated with the NYSE, was ardently opposed to what he saw as SEC overreach. He believed that the NYSE was an effective self-governor. Whitney's crimes were the perfect fodder for Douglas to continue his campaign and bring both Congress and the broader public around to the necessity of a stronger SEC. After all, one of the NYSE's own had managed to wreak this much havoc. In the eyes of many, the Richard Whitney affair demonstrated that the NYSE could not handle its own brood, and from a policy perspective, Whitney became his own worst enemy.[72]

Tino De Angelis

This section on fraud concludes with the story of Tino De Angelis and the Salad Oil Scandal. This is not only one of the most infamous instances of financial fraud but also one that has meaningful implications about the appropriate nature of oversight.

Born in 1915 to immigrant parents in the Bronx, Tino De Angelis was initially far removed from a life of plenty. He seemed determined to rise above his humble origins, however, and to his credit he did not shy away from hard work. He spent the days of his early career butchering, curing, and packing meats. He rose quickly through the ranks and in 1949 became president of the Adolf Gobel Company.[73] It was during his presidency of this previously well-respected butcher that he exhibited a striking comfort with unethical business practices. Adolf Gobel won a contract to supply meat to schools as part of the National School Lunch Program, designed to offer healthy meals to students in need through partial or complete subsidy. De Angelis provided the program with meat not properly inspected for food safety and overcharged the government for the meat it received. This infuriated the supervising agency, and Gobel paid $100,000 in fines and lost its school lunch contract. De Angelis lost his post for a time, but he avoided personal fines or jail time, and he became president of the firm again in 1958.[74]

In the meantime, De Angelis started another project: Allied Crude Vegetable Oil Refining Corporation. De Angelis started the firm in 1955 with a simple thesis: there would be tremendous value exporting vegetable oil under the US government's Food for Peace program, which permitted countries deficient in food and funds to purchase subsidized American-grown agricultural products.[75] Operating out of northern New Jersey, De Angelis grew the company to considerable size, transacting in about three-quarters of US vegetable oil exports by 1960.[76]

It appeared at the time that he had earned his reputation as the "Salad Oil King" (so named, of course, because vegetable oil is the basis of salad oil).[77] Meanwhile, however, there was a sinister plot afoot.

What De Angelis really desired was to corner the market in vegetable oil. The means to manipulate the price, he figured, was by transacting heavily in soybean oil and cottonseed oil futures.[78] However, if he was to have any chance at seriously moving these markets, he needed substantial capital. Enter the American Express Field Warehousing Corporation, a relatively new player in the business of inspecting goods and providing owners of those goods with warehousing receipts, which certified the existence of that stock and which the owners could then use as collateral for loans. De Angelis saw an opportunity: he could use American Express's service, later provided through a subsidiary called American Express Warehousing Ltd., to inspect his facility and deliver warehouse receipts that he could then bring to brokers to extend him margin to participate in these commodities markets in an arrangement collateralized by the stored oil.[79]

There was just one problem for American Express: De Angelis simply did not have anywhere near the oil he said he did. Many of the storage tanks were filled with water rather than oil, completely unbeknownst to the inspectors from American Express who signed off on the warehouse receipts. There were a variety of tricks De Angelis deployed to maintain the façade of having far more oil than he did: using tanks with false bottoms, installing pipes to move oil from one tank to another during the inspection so the surveyors would be looking at the very same oil in the second tank, and putting a layer of oil on top of a tank full of water, exploiting the fact that oil is less dense than water.[80]

By November 1963 the game was over. De Angelis could no longer continue a successful manipulation and lost far too much money as the market moved against him. Panic ensued on Wall Street. Which firms had dealings with De Angelis? Which would be adversely affected indirectly as those that transacted with him directly failed? What would be the effect of the insolvency of brokerage houses be on other investors? The destruction was wide, motivating the bankruptcy of some two hundred firms, and it was lengthy, taking many years to settle the last of the cases.[81] Among the failures was the brokerage house Ira Haupt & Company, which failed in large part because it had allowed De Angelis to make large margin payments with warehouse receipts instead of cash, relying on the purported accuracy of the receipts.[82]

Of course, the inspectors themselves certainly deserve some of the blame for failing to adequately perform the audits. Indeed, in the wake of the scheme, it was revealed just how numerous the inspection errors were. Amex Warehousing believed De Angelis was storing an amount of oil far in excess (by about 425 million pounds) of what the tanks were even capable of holding.[83] Further, during the inspections, firm employees who were aware of the scheme (there were some) would get on the tanks, drop a tape measure into the oil, and announce a number for the inspectors to record, without the inspectors performing the procedure themselves.[84]

For these errors, American Express faced substantial legal liability. The company's stock was ravaged by the affair, falling more than 50 percent. It was at this time that Warren Buffett made his famous play in American Express, buying the stock with the thesis (later proven quite correct) that these liabilities would be small relative to what the company stood to gain by the trend toward broader credit card usage.[85]

And while firms failed and many employees lost their jobs, the perpetrator himself may very well have gotten off lightly. De Angelis served just seven years of his twenty-year sentence in a federal prison in Lewisburg, Pennsylvania.[86]

There are a number of valuable lessons to learn from the Salad Oil Scandal. For one, it reaffirms the obvious lesson (but one that we continue to have to relearn) that prominence does not assure legitimacy. First, the inspectors, knowing they were dealing with a large and ostensibly successful customer, assumed that he was acting honestly. Second, this case demonstrates that the answer to the oversight of financial activities at the regulatory level is not nearly as simple as privatization. American Express, a private firm, which had a tremendous amount of money on the line, failed in its inspection. Third, perpetrators of large-scale, successful frauds typically do have a history of operating in moral gray areas and breaking the law, as seen in De Angelis's attempt to scam schools into buying unsafe and low-quality meat early in his career.

To what degree does empirical work support the anecdotal conclusion of the relevance of a history of transgressions of law and ethics? This question, among others, has been studied in the slightly different context of hedge funds in recent years. Stephen Dimmock and William Christopher Gerken study characteristics of investment managers to see which traits are significant predictors of later fraud. In their paper entitled "Finding Bernie Madoff: Detecting Fraud by Investment

Managers," they showed that previous civil or criminal activity, past fraud, and past compliance issues were statistically very significant predictors.[87] There are, of course, practical policy implications: notably, that repeat offenses are common among those who commit fraud. This does not mean that an enforcement body should be lulled into concentrating only on those firms with past issues, of course, but that patterns of behavior are meaningful here and those entities should be treated with heightened vigilance. Undoubtedly, our enforcement efforts will be bolstered only by further empirical work into the mind and modus operandi of the individual who commits fraud.

Going Rogue: Trading Frauds

Before moving off the subject of fraud entirely, we consider another form of fraud of a rather different character than these other episodes: trading frauds. Commonly called rogue traders, these individuals fraudulently misrepresent or simply obscure their trading positions or the total amount of exposures from the bank or institution that employs them. These are different than the other forms of financial fraud discussed here, as they tend to be internal to a given organization rather than external to outside clients or individuals. They are still worth highlighting briefly, however, because there have been occasions when such frauds have crippled and even destroyed otherwise well-capitalized financial institutions. While there has been a litany of such episodes, two cases will be explored: Nick Leeson (Barings Bank) and Jérôme Kerviel (Société Générale). The Leeson case will be explored because of its role in the undoing of an old and venerable financial institution, and the Kerviel episode will be discussed because of its sheer size as one of the largest such trading frauds in history.

NICK LEESON AND BARINGS BANK

Nick Leeson was born in 1967 in Watford, England, a working-class town about seventeen miles outside central London. After a short stint as a clerk for a private bank and then Morgan Stanley, he joined Barings Bank in 1989. He made a reasonable impression on his superiors and, in 1992, was sent to Singapore to trade on the Singapore International Monetary Index (SIMEX), serving as the chief derivatives trader there. Leeson's desk was intended to generate profits for Barings in two ways: for executing trade orders from clients and for arbitrage. The arbitrage component was quite straightforward: there were identical futures contracts for the Nikkei index traded in Singapore and in Japan, and occasionally small price divergences occurred. This cross-exchange arbitrage is supposed to be relatively close to a free lunch in that it involves buying the contract that is less expensive on one exchange and selling its identical counterpart on the other exchange, waiting for the two to converge. This is what Barings thought Leeson was doing to generate profits.

However, Leeson was not just executing client trades and performing arbitrage; he made simple speculations on the direction of indices and currencies. Rather than performing small market arbitrages, Leeson put on trades that were entirely unhedged to attempt to capitalize on what he believed to be the direction in which the markets were likely to move. In the very beginning, Leeson appears to have made some money for the bank through these trades, which helped enhance his reputation internally and appears to have reduced suspicion now that he was well regarded.[88] However, this soon changed, and Leeson's losses began to mount. Although he would occasionally make the money back by taking on ever-greater amounts of risk, this was not a sustainable strategy, given that this was mere blind speculation.

Leeson covered up the losses through a variety of means, including entering nonexistent trades among the bank and its clients to make it seem as though the positions were all hedged, as well as having his personnel simply enter fabricated information into the system. Leeson also opened what would later become the infamous 88888 account—so named because of 8's representation of good fortune in Chinese culture—very shortly after Barings was admitted as a SIMEX member.[89] This account should, in effect, have been a bookkeeping account to net out the trading book as a result of trading errors, which in and of itself was permissible. However, this was the account in which he hid the gains and, later, enormous losses from speculation.

Leeson's losses were exacerbated by the Kobe disaster in January 1995, when a powerful earthquake claimed several thousand lives and caused widespread property damage, causing the index to fall when Leeson was on the wrong side of the move. In the end, Leeson's total losses were $1.4 billion, wiping out the capitalization of Barings. And so Barings Bank, founded in 1762, met its end as an independent institution in February 1995 and was swiftly sold to ING for a grand total of £1.

Leeson initially fled to Malaysia with his then wife, leaving a note on his desk stating, "I'm sorry," just days before he turned twenty-eight years old. Leeson wanted to get back to the West so that he could avoid serving a jail sentence in a Singaporean prison. He made it to Germany but was ultimately extradited to Singapore, where he served three and a half years.[90]

In the end, Barings exhibited some complicity not by action but by ineptitude. That is, there were a number of managerial errors Barings made that could have at least mitigated the likelihood that the losses would completely spiral out of control. Perhaps the most significant oversight was the failure to bifurcate Leeson's job responsibility of overseeing the trading and settling the trades. The reason this segregation between the front office and the back office is prudent is straightforward: an independent person should be overseeing the trade settlements to ensure that the trading is consistent with the guidelines and risk expectations of the bank. Because Leeson was given both functions in a single role, absent this independent supervision he was able to hide the enormous losses for an extended period of time. Further, Leeson continued to convince Barings headquarters that ever greater amounts of funds were needed for the normal course of business as the margin calls from the SIMEX exchange mounted. The fact that Barings believed that Leeson needed more funds as a normal course of business suggests that his superiors simply did not genuinely understand the mechanics of market arbitrage between Japan and Singapore. Last, the lack of robust and consistent auditing of Leeson's activities suggests an environment that was far too careless in managing its risk.

JÉRÔME KERVIEL AND SOCIÉTÉ GÉNÉRALE

Turning to a more recent incident that was at the time the largest rogue trading fraud based on total losses is Jérôme Kerviel and Société Générale. Jérôme Kerviel was born in 1977 and spent his childhood in Brittany in northwest France. He studied finance as an undergraduate and as a graduate student until 2000, when he joined Société Générale in the middle office. It was in this position that he likely developed expertise about how trades were overseen, monitored, and treated by the bank, along with gaining familiarity with their corresponding computer systems that help execute these tasks.[91] Several years into this job, Kerviel migrated toward the front office to the "Delta One" team, and his job was to help trade European instruments to arbitrage small mispricings across different instruments based on European stocks. "Delta One" refers to the "delta" in a derivatives context (rather than having a quasi-militaristic meaning), where delta is the sensitivity of an instrument to movements in the reference instrument (such as the sensitivity of options prices to changes in the corresponding stock prices).

Kerviel's actions were similar to Leeson's in that he was supposed to be engaged in arbitrage rather than taking outright positions on instruments on an unhedged basis. However, like Leeson, he put on trades that were entirely speculative rather than mere arbitrage. It is interesting that Kerviel's trades turned out to be massively profitable before 2008. In 2007, Kerviel made a staggering €1.4 billion in profits, but he reported only €55 million to his superiors knowing that booking such a monumental profit—equal to more than six months' revenues of the firm's equities group—would make it clear that he had taken on far more risk than he was permitted. In January 2008, Kerviel had a book with over €50 billion of exposure to stock indices, which soon resulted not just in his giving up the 2007 gains but in generating a loss of billions of euros. Société Générale officially became wise to what had happened when Kerviel tried to enter a fake trade for over €30 billion worth of exposure to the German stock index. The move raised a red flag because if the trade were real, the brokerage firm on the other side of the trade would have been required to put up an enormous amount of cash on margin for Société Générale, well in excess of what would otherwise be extended.[92] An internal group at Société Générale was put together to look into the trade and soon discovered that Kerviel was obscuring actual positions well in excess of this fake trade. Between the time the group got to the bottom of the trade at the end of the week and the time the market opened the Monday thereafter, equities markets in Asia were down and Société Générale exited the trades at unfavorable prices, with Kerviel's trading activities ultimately costing the bank €4.9 billion.

As investigations later revealed, Kerviel avoided earlier detection by manipulating inputs into the firm's risk management system—called Eliot—as well as booking hedges that did not exist against existing positions so that it appeared that all the exposures netted out.[93] Kerviel was convicted of breach of trust and forgery, ultimately receiving a sentence of three years but serving a total of only about five months before being released on the condition that he wear an ankle bracelet.

Like Barings, Société Générale shares some blame for such a delayed discovery of these unauthorized trades. The examination of the external auditor PricewaterhouseCoopers revealed failures in the trade clearing system to appropriately book and analyze transactions, overly manual processing by back office staff, and insufficient seniority in the back office to conduct the requisite oversight.[94] Kerviel has also long contended that senior personnel in the company knew about some of these nonarbitrage trades and looked the other way. This is entirely possible, but even if true, senior personnel would likely not have looked the other way on exposures of this immense scale that could jeopardize the entire business itself.

Ultimately, the prevention of rogue trading is difficult because such trading so often arises from cracks in the middle- and back-office functions that the trader learns to manipulate for an extended period of time. In some scenarios, the prescriptive is easier than others, such as with Leeson and the vital need to prevent a single employee from controlling both trading and settlement positions. But in most cases, prevention ultimately requires firms to understand that it is in their best financial interests to implement best practices to ensure that traders adhere to their job role and stay within their risk limits. Otherwise, as happens in many rogue trading situation, what begins as a small loss or gain quickly spirals out of control as the trader tries to cover his footsteps by taking on ever-greater amounts of risk, potentially jeopardizing the entire enterprise.

MARKET MANIPULATION

This next section deals with individuals who manipulated, or attempted to manipulate, markets. This was, of course, the dream of Tino De Angelis with the market in vegetable oil, as the fraud was meant only to set the stage for the price fixing, though in the end he only managed to commit fraud. We start with a look at the very early days of the United States, with the tale of William Duer.

William Duer

To suggest William Duer came from a family of means would be a gross understatement. His father, John Duer, was an affluent planter and controlled substantial holdings in Antigua. Born in 1743, William attended prestigious Eton, an English school whose attendees then almost invariably hailed from families of status and power. Despite this abundance of opportunity, there was one critical characteristic that would alter the course of his life: he was the third son. In the days of primogeniture, this meant he had little hope of gaining a sizable inheritance, as families did not want to dilute their holdings through the generations and accordingly gave the largest portion to the first son. If Duer wished to spend his adult years with the same standard of living as he had enjoyed during his childhood, he would have to accumulate his own wealth.[95]

Duer's rise to prominence began when he entered the timber business and established a sawmill near Albany, New York, the first in the region. Duer also began to express interest in advancing the cause of revolution. He served as a representative from New York in the Continental Congress and worked primarily on issues related to the purse. However, it became clear that Duer was in pursuit of profit above all and would sacrifice morality and allegiances to support that end. In 1783, after the American Revolution was settled, Duer won a contract to provide supplies for the remaining British forces, a prospect many loyal to the revolutionary cause flat out refused because it was seen as aiding a former enemy.[96]

Nonetheless, Duer managed to stay in the good graces of many of those overseeing financial matters for the new nation, and he was offered a position with the Treasury Board. It was in this capacity that Duer decided he could simply issue himself a warrant from the Treasury in order to secure a personal loan in 1788. Given this sort of questionable behavior, it is surprising that the ethically minded Alexander Hamilton extended Duer the opportunity to become assistant secretary of the Treasury, which Duer gladly accepted in 1789. Despite Congress's clear hope and attempt to prevent Treasury employees from engaging in public securities transactions during their employment, Duer could not resist the potentially extremely lucrative prospect of buying state debt, which was then trading at small fractions of its face value (as the market considered it exceedingly risky), on the basis that the federal government was considering assuming these debts. When Duer was caught, he resigned his post, but he still managed to make a considerable sum from the trade in late 1790.[97]

Duer made this unethical trade during his tenure, but his actual manipulation of markets would come later. Duer's first major act of market manipulation was in the strategic dissemination of information to the market regarding the plans of the Bank of the United States, which had equity that was publicly traded at the time. Duer bought this equity in massive quantities, securing an estimated 6 percent of the total outstanding issue. He then persuaded the bank's directors to announce at a meeting in Philadelphia the opening of many other branches all across the United States, realizing that such an announcement would drive up the price of the stock and thus the value of his holdings. When the price soared, Duer cashed in half of his position.[98]

Successful in this market manipulation, Duer set his sights on an even greater one: to influence the price of the stock of the Bank of the United States and of federal bonds by cornering the market for these securities. At first glance, the debt of the United States and the stock of the Bank of the United States should not be structurally related. However, Alexander Hamilton created a provision for buying the stock of the Bank of the United States that involved several payments in US bonds. Unlike today, when one must have the cash (or cash and margin) available to buy a security, the stock of the Bank of the United States could be purchased by making one payment in cash and three payments in US bonds, with the hope that this would broaden bond ownership. Duer thus realized that if he could buy up enough government bonds, he could manipulate the market for both the Bank of the United States stock and the federal debt. Duer borrowed tremendous amounts of money, first from banks and other institutional lenders. When that credit ran dry, he turned to a man by the name of Isaac Whippo to peddle notes to the general public, including the financially unsophisticated, who were paid an incredible interest rate of 5 to 6 percent per month.[99]

Duer's plot, however, was foiled by a major reduction in the money supply purposefully undertaken by the Bank of the United States. Hamilton realized that the headquarters of the Bank of the United States in Philadelphia had made too many loans too quickly, thus expanding the supply of money that was pushing up securities prices.

Hamilton was quick to realize the connection and on January 18, 1792, wrote to William Seton, who worked at the Bank of New York, "I have learnt with infinite pain the circumstance of a new Bank having started up in your City. Its effects cannot but be in every view pernicious. These extravagant sallies of speculation do injury to the Government and to the whole system of public Credit." It was ultimately decided that the way to induce the needed reduction of money supply was simply not to renew some of the recurring loans—and it did work, much to the pain of Duer. The market realized Duer was not able to meet his contractual obligations in early March 1792, beginning a panic and a spiraling downward of the market. (The debt market Duer tried to corner fell some 25 percent within two weeks of his default.) In the end, Hamilton was able to stabilize the situation brilliantly, but Duer's attempt at market manipulation was a significant contributor to Wall Street's first major financial crisis, thereafter known as the Panic of 1792.[100] Duer would live out his days in debtor's prison.[101]

The story of William Duer is critical for three reasons. First, it speaks to how early market manipulation manifested itself in the American capital markets. Second, it makes clear just how much a threat market manipulation was to the entire economy at the time. Third, the whole situation reveals how much of a Wild West early capital markets could be. There was an incredible insufficiency of regulatory control and institutional standards on what constituted proper and ethical behavior, such as the consequences of a Treasury official speculating in securities whose valuations his work would influence, the ability to sell notes to unsuspecting buyers to acquire more credit, and the failure of the government to respond directly to the prospect of price manipulation itself. As will be seen, though it is true that some market manipulation continues to this day, it is of a radically different flavor; it is generally far more subtle, usually involves collusion of multiple parties (as most markets are too large and deep to corner with one or two actors), and does not generally threaten the entire financial system.

Erie War

Even seventy years later, the regulatory system regarding market manipulation was still exceedingly weak, as is made clear by the infamous story of the so-called Erie War in the late 1860s. The Erie War—not an actual war, of course, but rather a financial conflict—was waged over who would own and control the Erie Railway, one of the main passages connecting New York City to other urban centers westward.

The story of the Erie War begins with Daniel Drew, a steamboat operator who acquired infrastructure on both the eastern and the western portions of the Erie Railway line and effectively forced the Erie's board of directors to grant him a seat. Drew proved very early on that he was ready and willing to manipulate the price of the Erie Railway stock for his own gain. For example, after taking a short position in the company, he began a rumor that the Bergen Tunnel construction project (part of planned improvements for the railway) was going to exceed the estimated costs and that the company might have to abandon the whole project. The manipulation drove the stock price down significantly, and Drew profited handsomely. He would take similar actions many times during his tenure on the board, as he admitted proudly in later writings.[102]

Drew would surely have loved to continue in this capacity of enriching himself at the expense of the company he supposedly served, but Cornelius Vanderbilt, the railroad magnate, set his sights on the Erie. Vanderbilt was far more adept than Drew at operating railroads, having run several others successfully, and he thought he could apply the same principles and add an attractive asset to his growing holdings. To do this, he started purchasing the stock discreetly and slowly gained enough shares to exercise control over the company. Drew finally learned of what was afoot and knew the board was about to be removed by Vanderbilt, so he went to New York to meet with him. Drew managed to persuade Vanderbilt to keep him on the board and to grant seats to two of his friends, Jay Gould and Jim Fisk.[103]

Vanderbilt did not realize how great a mistake he had made. Drew, aided by Fisk and Gould, plotted to retake control of the company. To do so, they came up with a list of substantial improvements that would have to be funded by raising new capital. Drew realized that bonds that were convertible into stock would be the best way to flush out Vanderbilt. Drew, Fisk, and Gould issued millions of dollars in convertible bonds and had many of them immediately exchanged for stock. Vanderbilt had given his brokers orders to purchase any shares they could, and seeing the new stock available, his brokers complied with his request. However, Vanderbilt quickly got wise to the scheme and learned that the perfidious Drew had been diluting Vanderbilt's ownership and control, effectively lowering the portion of the company owned by Vanderbilt.[104]

Thoroughly incensed, Vanderbilt sought legal channels to have the three men brought to justice. A warrant went out for Gould's arrest in New York, but the three simply moved across the Hudson River to New Jersey, where they could temporarily avoid capture. Using the extra time, they called upon the corrupt William Tweed, who was then at the head of Tammany Hall, the New York political machine that became infamous for accepting bribes and awarding favors. They asked Boss Tweed to help them pass legislation legalizing their attempts to dilute Vanderbilt's stake. After a bribe, the political boss complied.[105] Although Drew later settled with Vanderbilt, Fisk was murdered by his mistress's other suitor, and Gould was arrested and forced to return much of his earnings, this political manipulation helped the trio extend their extraordinary scheme a while longer.[106]

This episode speaks once again to the utter lack of an effective body of regulations against market manipulation. Not only was Drew able to manipulate Erie Railway stock, but he was also able to hatch a plan to alter its capitalization so radically that it diluted controlling interests and, further, to follow it up with a successful attempt to make the scheme legal ex post facto.

Walter Tellier

The foregoing two examples involved prominent individuals manipulating securities of real size. The next story is slightly different, involving a man manipulating many smaller securities through false information about the prospects of companies of more modest scale. Indeed, it could be said that most modern boiler room–style market manipulation has Walter Tellier as its historical forebear. Tellier was no master of finance, but he certainly was an aggressive and talented salesman. He spent his early years selling cosmetics but in the 1920s found himself turning to the securities markets, where he worked peddling securities for several decades.[107]

It was when the 1950s rolled around that Tellier really began his scheme. Tellier ran one of the first major boiler room operations, either taking a position in existing penny stocks or underwriting new issues entirely and by aggressively selling others on the supposed "merits" of a significant investment in them, pushing up their prices. When the stock price had been manipulated well over its fundamental value and well beyond where it had previously been trading, Tellier would exit his holdings for a tidy profit.[108]

Tellier was brilliant at it, taking out advertisements in major newspapers and on the radio, soliciting prospective buyers by having members of the public return coupons to his office containing their contact information.[109] A sense of his promotional techniques can be gleaned from one of his ads discussing Consolidated Uranium Mines: "No one ever made any money without taking some risk, so if you can afford to speculate and want a stock which has the best growth and profit possibilities we have seen in over twenty years of Wall Street experience—again we say, buy Consolidated Uranium Mines common stock now around 70 cents per share. Remember just two years ago the stock was around 15 cents—it's your guess what it will be two years from now."[110]

He also instructed his employees and affiliates to probe his prospects to discern their approximate net worth, thus enabling him to figure how much the prospects could afford to buy and how worthy they were of further pursuit. From this information, he built lists of potential victims on which he could unleash his marketing team.[111]

Just when Tellier was living the high life in a well-to-do New Jersey suburb, the government caught on to his schemes. As the government prepared to make its case on the basis of violations of the Securities Act and mail fraud, Tellier attempted to buy off a witness. It was to no avail.[112] At the end of 1955, Tellier was indicted on Securities Act violations and mail fraud, for which he was sentenced to four and a half years in prison.

Of course, similar schemes still persist today in the equities markets. Fortunately, most tend to be small. Indeed, current empirical work on market manipulation suggests that such schemes are largely limited to relatively illiquid markets. Work attempting to uncover market manipulation in equities markets suggests that it occurs mostly in very small market capitalization issues, such as those listed in the pink sheets and those sold via the Over the Counter Bulletin Board.[113] Regulators like the SEC, the Financial Industry Regulatory Authority (FINRA), and NYSE Regulation Inc. (a nonprofit subsidiary of the NYSE that helps to maintain the integrity of NYSE-listed securities and NYSE affiliates) are involved in the detection of market manipulation.

Guinness Share-Trading Fraud

One episode of market manipulation, known as the Guinness share-trading fraud, was a case involving a far more "liquid" security. However, the episode also underlines how subtle and often legally ambiguous certain types of modern market manipulation can be. Crucially, this contrasts remarkably with the stories of unfettered and straightforward manipulation of previous periods.

The scandal began when two British firms, Guinness and Argyll Foods (a large supermarket operator), went head-to-head to try to acquire Distillers Company, then the world's largest Scotch whiskey producer.[114] Argyll offered the equivalent of $2.74 billion for the purchase of Distillers in December 1985, and Guinness offered the equivalent of $3.2 billion a little more than a month later in January 1986.[115]

The basic plan behind the scheme was to increase the price of Guinness stock so that the proposed deal would be more attractive. Because Guinness's offer included stock in Guinness for owners of Distillers, the higher the Guinness stock price was, the greater the value the sellers of Distillers would receive if they elected Guinness rather than Argyll as the acquirer. As such, it was in the best interests of Guinness to pump up its stock's price in order to make the acquisition more likely. Guinness reached out to allies in both London and the United States, including Ivan Boesky (who would shortly thereafter go to prison for separate crimes of insider trading and who tipped off regulators to what was going on because he was already under scrutiny), to buy secretly millions of dollars in stock with the understanding that they would be recompensed for any losses they experienced. For their involvement, four businessmen were convicted. Three went to prison while the fourth, due to health problems, was only fined and stripped of his knighthood.[116]

Besides speaking to the fact that market manipulation is frequently subtler in the modern era than it was in the past, the Guinness scandal also makes clear just how iterative the process of improving securities law tends to be. It is often not until a practitioner or several practitioners push up against or cross the line of what is proper that the law changes. This lack of clarity was apparently obvious to those involved. As Gerald Ronson, who controlled two firms that received money for helping move the stock price (though Ronson quickly returned the funds once investigators announced that his companies were involved), stated, "This did not seem to me at the time to be in any way unusual or sinister."[117] Although it would, of course, be far better if regulators could identify weaknesses beforehand, this tale underscores how the securities law framework's flaws, ambiguities, and shortcomings are exposed when these episodes arise, prompting legislatures and agencies tasked with oversight, if they are responsive and adept enough, to rectify the situation.

The Guinness scandal had both immediate and longer-term effects on regulations. The set of principles that regulated these situations in the United Kingdom was the City Code on Takeovers and Mergers. The immediate effect of the scandal was to induce some changes in its list of principles. The item that remained the subject of long debate, however, was the precise enforcement of these rules. The takeover code was enforced by a voluntary panel, the so-called Panel on Takeovers and Mergers, which was assigned the task of ensuring that the codes were followed. However, this panel had no statutory authority at the time. It was, in effect, a form of self-regulation, and technically the panel possessed no legal powers of enforcement. It would not be given true statutory authority until the passage of the Companies Act in 2006, but the Guinness scandal was one piece of evidence that proponents of this statutory footing cited for years.[118]

LIBOR Scandal

One crucial exception to the idea that market manipulation tends to be limited to small, illiquid markets is the LIBOR scandal. The scandal did not come to public light until 2012, though evidence suggests that LIBOR rate fixing took place at least as early as 2005.[119]

LIBOR, the London Interbank Offered Rate, is intended to represent the interest rate major banks would charge each other for loans. The LIBOR system was implemented in 1986 by the British Bankers' Association, in large part simply to provide a benchmark that banks could look at in the process of setting rates. Currently, there are a total of 150 different LIBOR rates published daily for ten different currencies and fifteen different time horizons.[120]

The fundamental problem with LIBOR is that the number is calculated by a survey of the banking institutions themselves, not by analyzing actual transaction data. Indeed, the US-dollar LIBOR is calculated via a survey of major banks in which the highest four and lowest four values are discarded, with the remainder in the middle then averaged to get the rate.[121] If a bank has an interest in LIBOR being either higher or lower, it can manipulate the value it reports so as to influence the rate. Of course, if just one or two banks do this to the extreme, it should make no difference by design. However, if many banks are engaged in this practice of purposefully changing the reported rate, the process of removing the outliers may not be sufficient to arrive at an unbiased value.

This is precisely what happened repeatedly with many banks, as recorded in e-mails and other electronic communications among colleagues. For instance, at UBS a trader told an outside broker that if the broker held LIBOR constant that day, he would repay the favor by giving him tens of thousands of dollars.[122] At the Royal Bank of Scotland in August 2007, a trader told the head of yen-related investment products in Singapore that he could set LIBOR "where you would like it," given the firm's trading positions. Two other traders suggested it should be lower, so the first trader replied, "OK, I will move the curve down 1 basis point, maybe more if I can."[123]

Of course, the other reason the LIBOR scandal is so important is because so much money is tied to LIBOR. Indeed, as MIT professor Andrew Lo has pointed out, LIBOR was never intended to serve as the basis of such a large volume of financial contracts.[124] Among the contracts it affects are mortgages, interest rate swaps—where one party agrees to exchange a fixed interest rate for a variable rate that is a certain number of percentage points higher than LIBOR—student loans, and other debt arrangements. In all, some $300 trillion worth of contracts is tied to LIBOR, and, as such, a tiny manipulation of a single basis point translates into enormous transfers of wealth.[125]

The LIBOR scandal demonstrates another important feature of typical market manipulation today: in highly liquid markets, some form of collusion is typically required. Further, it demonstrates just how important an effective legal framework is to the proper functioning of markets. The LIBOR scandal underlines once again that when the incentives for even ever-so-slight deception are so great, some people will succumb to the temptation. It is thus critical not only to be vigilant about overseeing this behavior and administering punishment accordingly but also to be creative about redesigning contracts that are prone to manipulation so that the allure is reduced in the first place.

INSIDER TRADING

Using large buying power or collusion to influence the price of the market is certainly not the only way to get ahead in the market illicitly. This chapter concludes by exploring cases of insider information, where individuals quietly attempt to exploit knowledge of corporate events, earnings, mergers and acquisition activity, or other material and nonpublic knowledge to get ahead.

Ivan Boesky

We begin with Ivan Boesky, the man whose likeness was caricatured as Gordon Gekko in the acclaimed film *Wall Street*.[126] He was the man who famously proclaimed, "Greed is all right, by the way. I want you to know that. I think greed is healthy. You can be greedy and still feel good about yourself." The comment was met with some chuckling and an ovation when Boesky made it at the University of California, Berkeley, School of Business Administration in 1986.[127] Looking back, however, it is difficult to see precisely what "good" Ivan Boesky's greed has done society.

Boesky's father was a Russian immigrant who ran nightclubs near Detroit, Michigan. During his youth, Boesky sold ice cream out of a truck. He cut corners early in his life, not heeding the conditions of his ice cream vending license by continuing to sell past 7:00 P.M. He went on to college, but he failed to graduate from any of the three schools he attended: Wayne State, Eastern Michigan College, and the University of Michigan. He then went on to attend the Detroit College of Law, where no undergraduate degree was needed, and married Seema Silberstein, whose father, Ben Silberstein, was wealthy from real estate investments.[128] Ben Silberstein never thought particularly highly of Ivan, calling him "Ivan the Bum."[129]

Soon Ivan found himself in the securities business. He did not exactly have successful opening acts to his career. In his third finance job, one of his investments lost $20,000, and he was asked to leave. In his next job, he manipulated stock prices by buying up large volumes and received a $10,000 fine from the SEC for illegal short selling.[130] Time and again, Boesky seems to have sought the quick way to gain.

Boesky soon launched his own investment firm, the equity of which was funded primarily by his wife's family's money. This time Boesky found success. He was soon taking a limousine to work, living in a ten-bedroom home in Westchester County, New York, on 200 acres, and spending lavishly. Even more than lead an opulent lifestyle, Boesky also tried to cultivate an aura of great financial sophistication. He liked to claim that his success was due to mastery of strategies like merger arbitrage, a concept about which he had heard from a former class-mate. Later Boesky even published a book entitled *Merger Mania* with a subtitle of *Arbitrage: Wall Street's Best Kept Money-Making Secret*.[131]

The strategy itself was relatively simple. In the basic form of merger arbitrage, investors purchase debt or equity in a corporation that might soon be the target of a merger or acquisition. The investors do this in anticipation of a spread between the offer price announced in the deal and the price at which the target's securities were trading before the announcement. In the strategy's more complex form, investors buy and sell securities and derivatives related to a merger or acquisition after the deal has been announced, carefully evaluating the relative value of the various instruments and, above all, the risk that the transaction will not be consummated (due to failure to gain shareholder approval, regulatory sign-off, or sufficient financing for the deal or to another obstruction to the process).[132] Although this strategy is well known and well understood today, it was much more esoteric in the 1960s when Boesky first pursued it. The real secret to his wealth, though, was not brilliant utilization of a merger arbitrage strategy; it was instead a strategy as old as time—to play "hardball" to stay ahead.[133]

Boesky consistently relied on insider information and failed to dis-close who else was working with him to influence the market. Figures like Dennis Levine, Michael Milken, and Martin Siegel, whose firms had access to information—for example, by virtue of being retained in an advisory capacity on merger and acquisition deals—clandestinely and illegally worked with Boesky to pass along information on what to purchase so that they could share in the profits.[134]

Illustrating how Boesky's schemes worked, an early deal Martin Siegel fed Boesky involved Diamond Shamrock, a chemical company that was at the time interested in expanding its operations in oil and planning to do so through an acquisition. Siegel's employer, Kid-der, Peabody, served as the adviser and was privy to a list of possible companies Diamond Shamrock might attempt to buy. Siegel passed the name of one candidate, Natomas Company, to Boesky, thinking that Boesky could accumulate a sizable position well in advance of an announcement (because Diamond Shamrock was still in the phase of exploring acquisitions) and thus not raise red flags for the SEC. Boesky did precisely that and made millions when the deal eventually went through.[135]

The SEC became wise to all of these ostensible acts of prescience by Boesky when it charged Dennis Levine, an investment banker at Drexel Burnham Lambert in New York, with insider trading in 1985.[136] Levine cooperated, and the SEC was made aware of Boesky's involvement.[137] Boesky ended up getting a generous deal from the SEC in return for his help turning their attention to what the SEC seemed to regard as an even bigger fish: Michael Milken, also at Drexel Burnham Lambert. In the end, though he did pay $100 million for his transgressions, Boesky was even allowed to sell off his investments, saving him a great deal of money.[138] He was sentenced to only three years of jail time.[139]

Boesky managed to receive minimal punishment largely because of his cooperation. Although there is little doubt that the nature of financial crimes is typically sufficiently convoluted that cooperation does aid in the success of prosecutors bringing high-profile criminals to justice, undoubtedly more thought is required to determine how to balance the cooperation needed to make cases against others with a need to punish even the smaller offenders. Boesky's case might speak to a failure of striking the right balance, and though he ended up getting some jail time, the punishment may not have entirely fit the crime. There is some consolation in the fact that laws were passed in the wake of Boesky's crimes (and the 1980s merger mania episode more broadly) that give more teeth to prosecutors. Nevertheless, as the Boesky episode shows, prosecutors must possess the inclination to use them.

Raj Rajaratnam

Fortunately, in the years since Boesky was caught, enforcement bodies have made additional progress in prosecuting insider trading violations. In fall 2011, Raj Rajaratnam was convicted of insider trading and was issued the longest sentence ever before given in the history of insider trading: eleven years. However, given the number of distinct instances of acting on insider information, it could have been far worse for Raja-ratnam. His poor health seemed to inspire some leniency and lighten the sentence of up to twenty-four years and five months the prosecu-tors pursued in the case.[140]

Rajaratnam spent the beginning of his career studying technology stocks, and he quickly ascended the corporate ladder at the investment bank Needham & Co., landing positions as the head of research in 1987, COO in 1989, and president by 1991. He eventually broke away from the firm, and he started Galleon Group in 1997 with several coworkers from Needham. Galleon was extremely successful despite the bursting of the technology bubble. In fact, the firm was up over 40 percent from 2000 to 2002 when the Standard & Poor's 500 (S&P 500) was down 37.6 percent.[141]

And here is where Rajaratnam's story becomes so similar to many of those of others convicted of insider trading. The striking feature of almost all inside traders is that they were either already successful or seemed poised for success. They simply did not need to engage in insider trading to prosper. The question asked almost invariably is, why did they cross the line? Why were they dissatisfied with the returns they could earn legitimately?

Yet, though the question why seems so logical in retrospect, the answer is typically quite straightforward: they thought they had a "sure thing"—a sense of certainty about where the market was headed is normally elusive in the industry—and believed they would not be caught. Investigators relied on wiretaps to build the case against the offenders in this case, and the tapes reveal a tremendous arrogance among the actors. Danielle Chiesi, one of those convicted of having given Rajaratnam insider information, remarked about a conversation she had to acquire the information, "I just got a call from my guy. I played him like a finely tuned piano."[142] They saw themselves as slick and masterful at their craft, and the prospect of being caught seemed scarcely to enter the equation.

David Pajcin and Eugene Plotkin

The next tale deals with two relatively small-time characters. Though their gains were limited, the story speaks to another case in which those involved seemed poised for success but nonetheless looked for a series of complex, and often quite strange, shortcuts.

David Pajcin, the son of Croatian immigrants, earned a full scholarship to Notre Dame and achieved academic success there, graduating cum laude. After college, he found himself in a desirable Goldman Sachs position working on commodities, but he left after a few months to work in different firms in the industry. Eugene Plotkin transferred to Harvard from the California Institute of Technology after his first year. The two of them met at a Goldman Sachs training session and, despite being on trajectories for success, abandoned their upward paths to devise some of the most egregious schemes to acquire and trade on inside information.[143]

The first scheme began in 2004, when Pajcin and Plotkin placed advertisements online asking for factory workers and received a reply from a man by the name of Nickolaus Shuster of New Jersey. They wanted Shuster to get a job at Quad/Graphics, a commercial printing firm that printed *BusinessWeek*. According to plan, Shuster managed to get a job as a forklift operator. The target of the scheme was a weekly article, "Inside Wall Street," that gave analysis on stocks and was sufficiently widely read that the column's recommendations moved stock prices. The goal was to get an advance copy of the article so that Plotkin and Pajcin could establish positions before it was released to the public. The scheme worked quite successfully, and on Thursday mornings Shuster would take a copy of the magazine and contact the two with the contents. The group made over a quarter of a million dollars in the eight months from November 2004 to July 2005.[144]

The group did suffer some setbacks, however. One scheme to hire strippers to prevail upon bankers to give up information on pending mergers or acquisitions they knew about was completely unsuccessful. Another failure occurred when a long-time friend of Pajcin called him to say that he had been serving on a grand jury that was intended to get to the bottom of accounting anomalies and possible frauds at Bristol-Myers Squibb. The friend told Pajcin that a senior official at the company was likely to be indicted, which Pajcin figured would cause the stock to drop, and thus he took a short position in the stock. However, a deal with prosecutors was made and the indictment never materialized, causing the group to lose money.[145]

One of the most lucrative trades the two managed was sourced by Stanislav Shpigelman, a contact Plotkin had who was employed in mergers and acquisitions at Merrill Lynch. When Plotkin and Shpigelman met at a Russian bathhouse near Wall Street in late 2004,

Shpigelman began to boast about a corporate takeover he was helping with at Merrill. The takeover was the acquisition of Gillette by Procter & Gamble. Plotkin realized that the timing was not quite right yet, though, and he waited for a call from his contact when the deal was closer to being announced. About eight weeks later, Shpigelman told Plotkin that the time to act had arrived, and Plotkin started purchasing call options on Gillette. The group made a significant amount of money on this trade, and with other tips from Shpigelman, repeated this kind of success with at least three other deals. However, unbeknownst to Plotkin and Pajcin, they raised red flags when they attempted to do this yet again with Reebok. They purchased call options on Reebok that were not only close to their expiration but that were also far out of the money. This means that the position would profit only if Reebok moved upward substantially in a short amount of time. The SEC's Market Surveillance Unit found it unusual how many of these out-of-the-money calls were purchased and it tracked them, only to discover other anomalies. The group was using an account registered in Croatia but being accessed in New York. Plotkin and Pajcin thought they had covered their tracks, but their scheming caught up with them. Regulators realized the trades were too perfectly timed and, after an extensive investigation, uncovered many (and sometimes unbelievable) other instances of acting on inside information.[146]

In the end, it was remarkable that two successful men, educated at Harvard and Notre Dame and employed at one time by Goldman Sachs, would go to such lengths to procure inside information when they would likely have had bright futures if they had not resorted to this duplicitous behavior. Indeed, they made a whole business out of it. But, as Pajcin would confess later, he was looking for the fast way to wealth, much more pleasant, he believed, than the long hours that would be necessary for the legal path. As he explained to SEC regulators, "I was like, no, I can't handle this. I just didn't want to wait like four years and then still be on the floor."[147]

But just like Raj Rajaratnam, Plotkin and Pajcin never thought they would be caught. They thought they had been careful. Who, after all, could trace an advertisement for a factory worker back to them? Who would connect the dots between them and trades made in a Croatian brokerage account?

Today people like Raj Rajaratnam, David Pajcin, and Eugene Plotkin are convicted criminals. They broke the law, they undermined the principle of a fair market, and they enriched themselves at the expense of the law-abiding investors taking the other side of their trades.

It goes without saying that such behavior is unfair and deserves to be prosecuted. It is, in some sense, a reflection of the democratization of markets: everyone should be able to participate knowing that other actors will not be using material, nonpublic information. However, this used not to be the case. In fact, insider trading used to be legal. The road to its prohibition was a long one fought largely by academics and a few persistent regulators against a limited group of corporate titans and even Congress.

Albert Wiggin

The story of Albert Wiggin, the chairman of the board of Chase National Bank through the Crash of 1929, highlights the absurdity surrounding the historical lack of regulation of insider trading. Wiggin was a highly respected banker, ascending the ranks of the banking community and helping Chase expand.[148] Wiggin was not really an ill-meaning or nefarious character; he operated in an environment where transactions by insiders were effectively completely unregulated.

Wiggin formed three vehicles through which he could conduct his securities transactions: the Shermar Corporation, the Murlyn Corporation, and the Clingston Co. Inc., all of which were owned in their entirety by either him or family members. Wiggin traded the stock of the Chase Bank and profited handsomely from it, making over $10 million transacting in the shares of Chase companies from 1928 to 1932. The most egregious incident of all, however, was not just the trading of the stock while he was chairman but what transpired during the Crash itself. Just when the Chase financial institutions joined other banks in trying (though futilely) to inspire confidence in the market and started buying, Albert Wiggin sold his personal shares. He claimed that he sold them to reduce his family's exposure to the stock. That seems perfectly reasonable, but that was not all Wiggin did. He sold more stock *short* to profit explicitly from the decline in Chase stock. In other words, he sold more than he owned to take advantage of the decline. Wiggin profited handsomely from it.[149]

Wiggin's actions were not taken well by the general public when they were revealed by the Pecora Commission, a group devised to ascertain the fundamental causes of the Crash of 1929. Indeed, Wiggin decided under public pressure not to accept his annual pension of $100,000.[150] Of course, this was a small concession, given that he profited by more than $4 million from the short sales made at the end of 1929 alone.[151]

It actually was not illegal for Wiggin to transact in stock essentially whenever he deemed it beneficial to his financial interests. The value in the tale about Wiggin thus is not really about him, but about the nature of the time and just how far we have come. There was once an era when the only real remedy to actions thought to be unfair and dishonest, like insider trading, was public disapprobation and shame.

The Road to Making Insider Information Illegal

Remarkably, there was an 1868 court ruling in New York that stated that the directors of a publicly traded company did not actually have to make the market aware of nonpublic information (or otherwise await the time when that information would come to light) before acquiring or disposing of shares for their personal accounts.[152] This same idea was echoed in 1933 in *Goodwin v. Agassiz*, a Massachusetts case that would affect thinking on insider trading and information for several decades thereafter. In *Goodwin v. Agassiz*, the plaintiff had sold his stock in a mining company. The plaintiff learned later that the company's directors, meanwhile, had purchased stock in the open market after they had learned from geological studies that land the firm owned was likely to contain significant amounts of copper. The court ruled that the directors were not required to make this fact known to shareholders before trading.[153]

It was President John F. Kennedy's appointment of William Cary as chairman of the SEC in 1961 that would alter the trajectory of insider trading laws. Cary was a brilliant scholar. He graduated from Yale, where he was both an undergraduate and later a law student, followed by Harvard Business School. He served a short stint in intelligence during World War II, working for the Office of Strategic Services posted in Romania and what was then Yugoslavia. Soon, though, it was back to the law, and he eventually became a law professor at Columbia, the university where he would spend much of his career.[154]

To get a sense of how the man operated, consider a speech Cary made in 1962. To the chagrin of many in the industry, in the speech he declared that the NYSE, "though a public institution, still seems to have certain characteristics of a private club." Indeed, his success emerged from his fierce drive to reform the thinking on securities oversight, regardless of how much he ruffled feathers along the way.[155]

It would later be said that Cary had an exceptionally short agenda for the SEC, but among his goals was undermining *Goodwin v. Agassiz*.[156] The major blow Cary dealt *Goodwin v. Agassiz* was a decision in 1961 known as *In re Cady, Roberts & Co.* The *Cady, Roberts* decision involved a firm named the Curtiss-Wright Corporation, which was a publicly traded company. The board of directors of the Curtiss-Wright Corporation voted to curtail the dividend payment for the quarter. One of the men who sat on the board was J. Cheever Cowdin, a partner in Cady, Roberts & Co., which offered brokerage services and managed money for clients. Cowdin told Robert Gintel (also a partner at Cady, Roberts) that Curtiss-Wright had voted to cut its dividend, and Gintel, realizing this would cause the stock to drop, sold many shares of stock owned by his clients.[157]

The SEC maintained that Gintel's action was an infraction of SEC Rule 10b-5,[158] created in 1942 to prevent fraud in the purchase or sale of securities. At the time, it was obvious to the SEC commissioners that the rule should be instituted: it passed unanimously, and the only comment made was by Sumner Pike, a commissioner at the time, who remarked, "Well, we are against fraud, aren't we?"[159] It was William Cary who changed the interpretation of Rule 10b-5. The commissioners almost certainly never imagined that twenty years later this rule would be invoked by their successors to bring about an end to insider trading. However, Cary realized that congressional inaction meant he had to do something, and he made a vigorous and compelling case that the rule should be applicable beyond the most flagrant, cut-and-dried versions of fraud.[160]

The *Cady, Roberts* decision introduced two critical changes in the treatment of insider trading. First, it made it clear that "tipping," or the passing along of inside information to others for trading (as Cowdin did for Gintel), was illegal. The other change was that trading based on inside information was banned even for transactions on an exchange. It was previously thought that trading on inside information would be prosecuted only in cases of face-to-face transactions rather than "impersonal" transactions on an exchange. The SEC rendered invalid this line of argument. Corporate insiders who had inside information could thus not transact so long as the information was material and nonpublic.[161]

And so Cary had laid the cornerstone for modern regulation regarding insider information. Fortunately, this would be followed by a string of other victories improving upon his early success. The next major victory came in 1968 with *SEC v. Texas Gulf Sulphur*, again involving a mining company, just as in *Goodwin v. Agassiz*. Texas Gulf Sulphur was conducting a geological survey to assess the viability of a potential mine in Canada. The survey identified a region where it was possible there would be lucrative mineral deposits, and, in response, the firm ordered drilling there. It was determined that the potential site did, in fact, have extremely rich deposits. Without making disclosures to the public, officers within the company purchased shares. This, in turn, set off more buying by many members of the public who saw the insider activity and believed there must be a good reason for it. The officers then put out a statement to the public denying the discovery to try to stop the buying by outsiders, and this statement was later determined to have failed to properly represent the results of the drilling operation. Eventually, the correct results were released, but the appropriate disclosures did not happen until well after the insider purchases. The SEC brought suit, and the case went to the Second Circuit Court of Appeals, which found for the SEC. In the decision, the court stated that the law should ensure that "all investors trading on impersonal exchanges have relatively equal access to material information" and, furthermore, that "all members of the investing public should be subject to identical market risks."[162]

Enforcement of these regulations was given real teeth in 1984, when Congress passed the Insider Trading Sanctions Act of 1984. The law allowed the SEC to pursue treble damages, or three times the amount of money gained by trades based on inside information. The law came during the 1980s, a difficult decade marked by financial improprieties of many kinds. It was these laws that would aid in making examples of people like Ivan Boesky, Dennis Levine, and Michael Milken, who were extracting enormous fortunes from illicit informational edges and manipulation.[163]

CONCLUSION

The United States has made remarkable progress in democratizing access to a fair market by overhauling the laws and regulations against market manipulation, trading on inside information, and fraud. We have made behavior such as transacting on insider information, illegal where it previously had not been. We have recognized the damage market manipulation does to the fairness and proper operation of asset pricing. We have added teeth to the laws against fraud. That said, the system is, of course, not perfect. There are many improvements that can build upon what has already been achieved, most of which will be revealed only when new participants engage in behaviors not effectively covered by existing measures.

However, the concern today is of a very different character than it was decades ago. Then, it was that the regulatory framework was essentially absent: profiting from inside information was once regarded as the reasonable province of directors and officers of companies and their affiliates, and market manipulation was a well-understood phenomenon undertaken by highly capitalized groups to enrich themselves. That thinking, fortunately, has changed for the better. However, where we still often fall short is not so much in the framework of laws and regulations themselves but, rather, in their effective enforcement.

In recent years the SEC has consistently been denied adequate resources to do its job. Its mandate has only grown under the Dodd-Frank Act, and yet, as a study conducted by the Boston Consulting Group found, it is at least several hundred employees short of what it requires to properly oversee the markets.[164] It is no secret that vastly trimming the budget of the SEC has been a priority of some with a laissez-faire worldview. Almost comically, the House Appropriations Committee substantially scaled back the budget request for fiscal year 2012 and provided only the same amount of money as it had in fiscal year 2011, despite the new challenges presented by Dodd-Frank. Most puzzling of all, however, were some of the reasons cited by the committee for the decision, including that it "remains concerned with the SEC's track record in dealing with Ponzi schemes."[165] The solution to the commission's inability to properly identify and prosecute more cases of Ponzi schemes clearly was not to leave it even more bereft of resources than before.

The decisions to reduce the resources of the SEC are seemingly politically motivated attempts to limit the agency's reach. After all, legislators are wrong to cite the size of the federal deficit as a reason to curtail the SEC's budget so substantially, because the SEC's collection of fees and fines is greater than its own budget.[166]

The SEC is hardly a perfect organization. It needs to overhaul its managerial structure and deal more effectively with its unions to remove unproductive workers. Congress should also consider increasing the compensation of employees in the commission. There is serious concern that the disparity in wages earned by regulators and those they are regulating may not result in top talent being recruited into the agency. Despite these shortcomings, it is clear that the solution is not to slash the budget. The agency needs assistance, resources, and innovative thinking, none of which are normally encouraged by resource scarcity. If we are going to continue on the path of democratizing the landscape by way of enhancing our regulatory framework, we must tackle these challenges so that investors of the future do not have to suffer at the hands of individuals like Madoff, Ponzi, Stanford, Boesky, Rajaratnam, and Tellier.

CHAPTER SIX

Progress in Managing
Cyclical Crises

WE CANNOT CONSIDER INVESTMENT without placing it in the context of the prevailing economic environment. Every element affecting successful or failed investment activity is tied to economic support or obstruction. Economic developments condition the whole atmosphere in which investments grow and prosper. Without the support of economic nourishment, it is rarely feasible for investment plans to flourish.

The focus of this chapter is chiefly on comparing the effects of the policy response to two major economic shocks: the Great Depression of the 1930s and the Great Recession of 2007–2009. Although the precursors to and the characteristics of the Great Depression and the Great Recession were different, the profound economic dislocations of each and the policy responses to them portray eloquently the progress of economic theory toward more effective remedial measures. This direction of policy exemplifies to us the increasing democratization of the environment in which investment activity occurs and is evidence of the intent of twenty-first-century policy makers to protect the mass of economic participants from extreme dislocation in times of economic crisis.

Despite the popular opinion that there were clear excesses and ample warnings in the late 1920s that accurately foretold the great market crash beginning in October 1929, a more considered examination of the economy, the level of market speculation, and the degree of financial excess that preceded the 1929 crash fails to show clear evidence that an imminent profound collapse was precisely predictable. However, it appears that much more troublesome evidence of speculative excesses—notably in housing prices, credit standards, and the use of leverage—were demonstrated in the 2004–2006 period, which preceded the more recent financial crisis.

Nevertheless, the lessons learned from the Great Depression and the profound fiscal policy insights of John Maynard Keynes in the 1930s, importantly augmented by monetary policy lessons observed by Milton Friedman and Ben Bernanke and ultimately applied by the Fed beginning in 2008, led to a dramatically improved economic performance in the recent economic crisis.

This chapter offers insights into both events and draws lessons from them to present an enhanced understanding of their similarities, differences, and the strikingly divergent policy actions and outcomes that resulted. Let us begin with a look at the Great Depression.

THE STOCK MARKET CRASH AND THE GREAT DEPRESSION

To understand the origins of the Great Depression, one must consider the boom of the 1920s and the circumstance that created it—namely, the transition of the United States out of World War I.

As the 1918 truce approached, the political environment of the United States was marked by increasing resistance to the wartime command economy. The public had come to bemoan governmental involvement in private enterprise. In the United States, the secretary of the Treasury wasted no time writing a letter to the president of the Chamber of Commerce, remarking, "From the moment of the cessation of hostilities the Treasury of the United States has pursued a policy of looking toward the restoration as promptly as possible of normal economic conditions, the removal of governmental controls and interference, and the restoration of individual initiative and free competition in business." True to its word, the government started to lift many price controls within forty-eight hours once the cessation of hostilities began.[1]

The American economy sputtered at first. There was a mild recession as the economy emerged from the war, and there was a more severe recession from 1920 to 1921, although also minor in comparison to what would ensue in the 1930s. This recession, which began in January 1920, worsened over the course of the year; industrial production dropped by 7 percent by July and fell a total of 25.6 percent (from the January high) by the end of 1920. Unemployment, too, began to rise sharply. A mere 1.4 percent in 1918 and 1919, it rose to 11.7 percent in 1921. But the recession was marked foremost by the exceptionally powerful deflation that transpired. While estimates of the precise numbers vary, the price level, as measured by the GNP price deflator, is commonly estimated to have fallen from 13 to 18 percent.[2]

This is not an enormous surprise; moving from a command economy to a free market economy will never be perfectly smooth. But there are interesting differences in the views on why this deflation happened. The monetarists point to the powerful inflation that took place during World War I, due to a cooperative Federal Reserve lowering interest rates to ensure that the government still had access to inexpensive borrowing to finance the military buildup. This school argues that the Fed did too little too late when the war ended by increasing interest rates too slowly. Others, like many Keynesians, believe this deflation was caused by a return to fiscal sustainability by the government. The government balanced its books after the war, moving from a deficit to a surplus, resulting in a net decline in government expenditures and a reduction in aggregate demand.[3]

The truth is likely that some combination of these factors was involved—and that the deflation was partially monetary and partially demand driven. Whatever the cause, the recession, which finally ended in July 1921, made three facts abundantly clear. First, World War I left a deep mark on the economy (both negative and positive, as will be seen), and though the war's effects on the recession of the early part of the decade are more certain and measurable than its effects on the depression of the last part, its influences should not be underestimated. Second, potent recessions are possible without any major financial crisis, and we should not expect all recessions to be due simply to a collapse of asset values. Third, and most important for the content of this chapter, we did not have the tools or the wherewithal at the time to understand the importance of staving off deflation or drops in aggregate demand and supply, a fact that reared its head yet again at the end of the decade.

1920s Growth

Although the transition was not seamless, World War I did ultimately put the United States on a trajectory toward miraculous growth. In many ways, the United States was in a unique position in the war: its economy enjoyed the benefit of stimulus without the devastation of actual combat. The national economic output of France and Germany, on the other hand, fell by approximately one-third from the beginning of the war to 1920 as a result of destruction and steep loss of life (and the widely known economic punishment of the latter for its role in inciting the conflict). In Austria, Hungary, and Poland, the situation was even more dismal, as total output was halved over the same period.[4] Even the British would not experience the same rate of growth that the United States did in the 1920s, and the growth it did enjoy was mostly after 1924.[5]

Beyond the effects of the wartime destruction, the disillusionment with the heavy human toll of the conflict begot an isolationist spirit. Europe largely sought to withdraw from engaging with its neighbors, trying to curtail the economic linkages with them and imposing hefty tariffs on imports. Of course, the United States was by no means above this isolationism. It failed to join the League of Nations because of an effort spearheaded by Henry Cabot Lodge to oppose Wilsonian internationalism. The United States, so long a nation shaped by its immigrant tradition, crafted strict restrictions that prevented many Southern Europeans from coming to its shores. The number of total immigrants fell from some 1.2 million coming to the United States in 1914 to only about 150,000 per year by 1927 due to quotas put in place under the Immigration Act of 1924, with groups like Eastern and Southern Europeans disproportionately affected by a quota system.[6]

How, then, did the United States prosper, given that it too was awash in the spirit of isolationism? Partly responsible was its own geography. Whereas in Europe the tariffs diced the continent and partitioned its markets, cutting the access of many European firms to a larger base of customers, the vastness of the United States meant that firms had access to a large body of potential consumers that was unimpeded by these levies.[7] Given the smaller size of European countries and populations, the effect of these tariffs would be tantamount to cutting up different states and regionalizing the American economy.

This access to a large and undivided market was combined with another potent influence from the war—new capacities in mass production. The wartime demand for military hardware expanded many factories' production capacity as manufacturing firms sought to keep up with Uncle Sam's procurement needs. The automobile industry was certainly a beneficiary of this phenomenon, as the War Department ordered Liberty engines for aircraft, with contracts going to many automotive manufacturers. This stimulus of manufacturing facilitated the transition of the economy toward mass production, because the new capacity could then be deployed for consumer products once the factories underwent retooling.[8]

Benjamin Strong

Crucial to understanding the economic environment of the decade are the policy decisions that were made, notably at the Federal Reserve. Under the leadership of Benjamin Strong, the governor of the Federal Reserve Bank of New York from 1914 until he died in 1928, US monetary policy was generally expansionary during most of the 1920s. This helped to create a benign environment for economic growth, amplifying the country's economic resurgence. This dominance was supported by a rise in domestic consumer demand and a major impetus to American competitiveness from our lack of war damage at home coupled with the flourishing of mass production.

To provide a more complete view of how Strong affected the economy during his tenure, it is useful to give a better portrait of him and his activities. He would have a hard life, though in the beginning of his career it all seemed quite felicitous. He married, started a family, and began a strong friendship with a partner at J. P. Morgan named Henry Davison. He gained a reputation as one of the foremost bankers to help settle the Panic of 1907—a massive decline in stock prices due in large part to the stumbling of the Knickerbocker Trust Company, a large bank that had some of its funds backing a failed attempt to manipulate the copper market that in turn incited financial contagion among other participants who would no longer accept Knickerbocker as a counterparty. Davison was asked to help in the selection of candidates to fill the post of governor of the Federal Reserve Bank of New York, and he called upon Strong. Strong at first did not want the position, thinking the organizational arrangement of the Federal Reserve System to be under undue political influence, but ultimately he came around and accepted the role.[9]

By this time, Strong had remarried after his first wife committed suicide, but by 1920 his second wife had left him. Shortly thereafter, he fell victim to tuberculosis, and the rest of his eight years at the Federal Reserve were marked by recurring infirmity and weakness. He was occasionally confined to bed, and because of his sickness he offered his resignation, but the offer was declined as his contribution was regarded as crucial.[10]

Benjamin Strong's tenure and career dealt largely with managing the gold standard. There are many who lament the loss of the gold standard, believing that monetary systems were more stable and secure than under fiat systems. The vagaries of the 1920s, however, underscore the fact that the gold standard can, in fact, create a very unstable monetary framework whereby countries are forced to react to interest rate changes in other nations, often compelled to conduct policy severely averse to their own interests. In fiat systems, when two nations have different prevailing interest rates, the value of the currencies of those nations is expected to change so as to eliminate any gains that would be achieved by investing money in the nation with higher rates—a phenomenon known as interest rate parity. On the gold standard, however, the value of one currency is not supposed to change relative to the value of another currency, as both are fixed at a given rate of exchange to gold. As a consequence, investors seeking to maximize their return send money to the countries where it will return higher interest rates. The problem this creates on a national level becomes obvious: if one nation raises interest rates, other nations fear gold flight away from their own borders to the country with higher rates, and if the risk of gold flight becomes severe, it too will have to raise internal rates to prevent the exodus of capital. The need to raise rates may also be ill timed, as the economy may be weak and raising rates will harm total investment. This can result in "beggar-thy-neighbor" effects where countries engage in interactions that seem optimizing at the individual level but are quite damaging at the system level.

These beggar-thy-neighbor policies could be seen at play in France and Britain, which were competing over investing in Eastern Europe. The British thought Eastern Europe might represent a good market for loaned funds, with higher interest rates, but the French had the same ambition. As a result, the French sought to force the British to raise interest rates locally by exchanging £30 million they had in British banknotes for gold, the idea being the British would need higher gold reserves after such a depletion, which could be had at the price of increasing rates and inducing money to flow there.[11] French loans to Eastern Europe would enjoy a larger spread because British borrowing would come at a higher price.

This was the world Benjamin Strong inhabited, and it was the one his position forced him to navigate. Strong was criticized for his attention to the European plight with respect to these beggar-thy-neighbor policies and the instability of capital flows. In fact, he would later be derided by Hoover as "a mental annex to Europe." But in truth, Strong thought bringing Europe out of its postwar malaise was both noble and beneficial to the United States, given that no economy was completely unconnected. Strong was also close to Montagu Norman, the governor of the Bank of England, and so when Strong dropped American rates in the wake of this friction in Europe in order to keep Britain's gold supply strong, he was criticized for catering to foreign interests.[12]

When Strong died in 1928 and was replaced by George Harrison as New York Fed governor, the Fed's expansionist tendencies began to give way amid more concern about monetary ease and a developing trend toward restraint.[13] At the same time, fiscal policy needs were not yet well understood. Keynes had not yet made his seminal contribution to the subject, which, for example, was not actually expounded in book form until 1936. Therefore, the first reaction to a market crisis and an economic slump was to respond in a manner that might be appropriate for an individual, a family unit, or a private business but was not correct for a federal power. Unlike for a family unit, the appropriate response for a federal government is not as simple as cutting spending when income falls. In pursuing such a course of action, a federal government only adds to the reduction of aggregate demand and further impairs its economy. The government can instead step in to fill some of the void of private demand by increasing, not decreasing, its spending. Worldwide, this fiscal policy error was compounded by the international pressures of the lashing together of economies through the widespread commitment to the gold standard by developed countries. The result was an economic dislocation that took on global dimensions and progressed, largely unhindered, into a major depression, suppressing consumption, production, and employment, ultimately resulting in serial financial and banking crises, which were worldwide in scope.

The Crash of 1929 and the Depression

The structural shortcomings of the international monetary system were just the beginning. The financial system too was soon imperiled by one of the worst market calamities the United States has ever experienced: the Crash of 1929. The Crash commenced in the final hour of trading on October 23, 1929. Stock prices quickly fell, and nobody on Wall Street was completely certain of what had just transpired. Investors' anxieties were left to foment until the market reopened the next day, and the market fell again, this time not waiting until the end of the day.[14]

There was a small rally at the beginning of trading on October 30, driven by those who thought the market's problems were now fully discounted and they could buy in for some quick gains. There are tales of even those of modest means showing up to buy in increments of a few hundred dollars.[15]

The exuberance of these retail investors contrasted sharply with many who worked on Wall Street. After a week of running around to process the previously unseen volumes of stock traded, Wall Street traders and clerks felt lethargy and exhaustion set in. Many had slept at the office for some of the period, and the remnants of food and drink began to aggregate. The governors of the NYSE decided it would lack the labor force to run efficiently if these schedules continued, so it closed that Friday.[16] While the initial chaos had ended, little did those on Wall Street know the madness would continue for years as the market spiraled downward.

There is always great temptation to use the benefit of hindsight inappropriately when discussing the events leading up to the bursting of a speculative bubble. When hindsight is used in this fashion, causal explanations seem cleaner and neater. It seems as though every agent should have seen the crash coming, that it is difficult to sympathize with those who partook in the ostensible irrationality, and, most dangerous of all, that should bubbles of this sort repeat in the future, they should be easy to spot and prevent, given how tidily these histories may read.

The truth of the matter, however, is that the Crash of 1929 was tremendously difficult to foresee for those who saw the events unfold in real time. Even prominent economists, who had a longer view of history and were aware of the cyclical nature of markets, lost large personal fortunes in the crisis. John Maynard Keynes, perhaps the most influential economist of the period, if not of the last century, saw much of both his own savings and the endowment assets of King's College he helped manage lost in the Crash. Irving Fisher, too, suffered from the crisis. Not only was he bullish before the Crash, he published in 1930 after the events of October of the previous year saying that much of the manufacturing sector was undervalued. Paul Samuelson, too, conducted his own retrospective game in which he covered up the dates and looked at only the fundamentals at the time to see if he would have bought or sold. He has said, "I discovered that I would have been caught by the 1929 debacle."[17] Even the apparent market wizard Jesse Lauriston Livermore, the Great Bear of Wall Street, who had called the top and who made substantial sums shorting stocks ahead of both the Panic of 1907 and the Crash of 1929, would see his fortune wiped out some five years later from ill-fated speculative plays. In short, the reputed prowess of those who supposedly did see the Crash coming must be reevaluated and correctly contextualized.[18]

There was also no reason to believe that much of the market was overtly overvalued and that 1929 was a modern Tulipmania. There is some dispersion in the consensus estimates of the average price-to-earnings (P/E) ratios of companies before the Crash. Economist Harold Bierman calculated the averages of many such studies and disagreements, ultimately concluding that the most likely average P/E was around 16.3 based on 135 major companies and industrials in the summer of 1929. In addition, it was not the case that virtually every security traded at high premiums to fundamentals; indeed, most of the largest gainers preceding the Crash had operations in sectors that were expecting growth due to technological innovation such as airplanes, radio, telephone and telegraph, and chemicals. Furthermore, production and employment figures were quite robust, with the factory payroll index hitting a historical high in the fall of 1929.[19] The Crash itself caught most market participants by surprise.

Causality of the Great Depression

Having dismissed some of the mythology—namely, its predictability—around the causes of the market collapse, we can turn to thinking about the causality of the Great Depression. Understanding the investment environment in the 1930s requires comprehension of the causes of the Depression, and even more important, it requires one to be disabused of the notion that it was the stock market crash that caused the economic collapse.

Many of the results of the research program on the subject of the causes of the Great Depression can be described with relation to one of three schools of thought: the Austrian school, the monetarist school, and the Keynesian school. Although these are far from perfect and many Depression scholars today have views that bridge these admittedly crude divisions, visiting the central tenets of each in turn does help to ground the discussion of causality.

AUSTRIAN SCHOOL

The Austrian school was guided most prominently by the work of Friedrich Hayek and Ludwig von Mises. The Austrian school places the culpability for the Great Depression with the Federal Reserve. It claims that the Fed vastly increased the money stock throughout the 1920s, which resulted in a slew of market dislocations. These dislocations include an unsustainable growth in consumer loans and loans used to purchase financial securities, contributing to the bubble. It also drove up values of goods with higher durations in the market—most notably, capital goods—because the lower interest rates meant the net present value of cash flows with longer time horizons became much more valuable as the discount factor decreased. The so-called cheap credit also drove reorganizations of capital structure, and businesses issued more longer-term debt and equity financing. Firms that should not have been viable, in the Austrian view, were made solvent because of this inexpensive credit. The Austrian school also believes that these depressed interest rates caused a reduction in total savings, as the opportunity cost of consuming was lowered as the rate of return was less attractive, thus prompting more consumption.[20] The Austrian school views the death of Benjamin Strong, the governor of the Federal Reserve Bank of New York for 14 years, in 1928 as the end of this period of expansion, as his successor, in its view, tightened credit sharply and brought the house of cards to the ground. The overinvestment in capital goods over the course of the 1920s was realized by the end of the decade as firms saw projects to which they had committed capital prove uneconomic.

Many mainstream economists have voiced their disagreement with this framework, particularly with its highly one-dimensional nature of causality. These economists question how significant the increase in rates after Strong's death truly was and just how much the overexpansion in the 1920s was attributable to interest rates alone.

It seems that there were much deeper structural issues that were far more critical to causing the softness in the economy. Strong's supporters, such as economic historian and writer Charles Kindleberger, have said very much to the contrary—namely, that if Strong had been around through the Crash, the situation would have been much better because he was far more adept than George Harrison, his successor, who was unable to engage meaningfully with Europe before the crisis. In fact, Harrison exacerbated the situation by having a bidding war over gold and raising rates once the British raised rates in the wake of much gold leaving London for New York (and refusing pleas from Britain to cut rates at a summit).[21] Given all this, if Strong did contribute to the Crash, it was likely more through his untimely death than it was anything he did in life.

MONETARIST SCHOOL

The second school, the monetarists, also blame the Federal Reserve, but its arguments are more nuanced. The monetarist school's first comprehensive interfacing with history came from Milton Friedman and Anna Schwartz's *A Monetary History of the United States, 1867–1960*. The monetarists see the Great Depression as the result of a disastrous response by the Federal Reserve to what would have been a much more mild and normal drop in output, which is a natural and periodic result of the business cycle. The monetarists point out that the banking panics put strong downward pressure on the money stock.[22] However, the liquidity preferences of individuals did not fall at the same time (indeed, they increased), fueling the fire of the monetary contraction. The problem was that the Fed was unable to keep pace with this decline by expanding its balance sheet, and the size of the monetary base continued to cascade. The monetarists' explanation is compelling, but subsequent work on the role of the money stock has uncovered a strong role for the gold standard in contributing to the collapse. In the eyes of many, Friedman was not quite critical enough of the role of the gold standard in both inducing some of the deflation and tying the hands of the Federal Reserve.

KEYNESIAN SCHOOL

The third major school that sought to shed light on causality is the Keynesian. The Keynesian school has attempted to find a segment of the market that experienced a supply-and-demand disconnect—either oversupply or a fall in demand. The most challenging problem the Keynesian school has faced is identifying precisely where in the economy there was excessive supply or drying up of demand prior to the Depression. Perhaps the most famous market sector cited as a possibility for the demand-supply disconnect was the automobile industry. Edwin Nourse, the first chairman of the Council of Economic Advisers, did some of the first analysis in this field and ultimately concluded that the automobile industry had substantial excess capacity. Much of this work was later revised, however, because Nourse's study relied heavily on defining excess capacity in relation to what the manufacturer could physically produce. This is, however, the wrong framework because a firm's production decision seeks the minimum of the cost curve, so although a firm may be able to physically make more cars, doing so may be extremely uneconomic. Some academics, like E. H. Oksanen, however, have concluded that there is not much support for the idea of excess capacity before the Depression. Others have analyzed real estate to determine if there was a deficit or surfeit of housing available, and some scholars like Bert Hickman believe there was an overabundance, whereas others like Richard Muth claim there was a deficiency.[23] Although Keynesian theory does provide a very cohesive framework to think about a decline in output once it begins (such as sticky wages, excess savings, and the market for loanable funds) and a laudable set of tools to mitigate it, there remains tremendous division within Keynesian ranks in determining where precisely there was shrinkage in demand or overexpansion of supply before the Depression.

THE RELATIONSHIP BETWEEN
THE MARKET CRASH AND THE DEPRESSION

Clearly, a number of causal explanations have been proposed, some more compelling than others, but a critical takeaway is that it was not the stock market crash, as is often believed, that caused the Great Depression. That is not to say that the Crash of 1929 did not worsen the Depression. It most certainly did, as some of the work by prominent economists (including Ben Bernanke's academic research) makes clear. The Crash did exacerbate the structural problems within the economy that begot the Depression. The real economy and the financial sector are intimately tied together during crisis by the "financial accelerator," as described in the work of Ben Bernanke, Simon Gilchrist, and Mark Gertler. The essential idea of the financial accelerator is that the crisis harmed both the credit extension mechanism and the ability to post collateral. Credit extension is performed by banking institutions, which compile information to make estimates on the creditworthiness of borrowers and offer to lend at a rate that reflects that risk. The failure of many banking institutions, driven by runs and the sheer uncertainty of the future once the financial crisis set in, prevented them from performing their proper function. The second effect is the falling value of the real assets themselves, which becomes deeply problematic because the extension of credit is frequently dependent upon the posting of sufficient collateral (and the maintenance of certain loan-to-value ratios).[24] Although the Crash did make the Depression worse, it is not the case that the former simply produced the latter.

The Monetary and Fiscal Response

President Herbert Hoover entered office at the height of the greatest growth America had ever seen. Yet, months into his term the country would fall into depression and the blame would be based squarely on his office. During the first years of the Great Depression, Hoover repeatedly tried to balance the budget to no avail. When he left office in 1932, the country had amassed a deficit of almost $3 billion.[25]

Hoover's position on why a balanced budget was so vital is fascinating. He stated, "Nothing is more important than balancing the budget with the least increase in taxes. The Federal Government should be in such position that it will need issue no securities which increase the public debt after the beginning of the next fiscal year, July 1. That is vital to the still further promotion of employment and agriculture. It gives positive assurance to business and industry that the Government will keep out of the money market and allow industry and agriculture to borrow the monies required for the conduct of business."[26] Hoover's view, in short, was that deficit spending was harmful because it pushed up interest rates in the money market. We did not yet grasp the intellectual tools, nor have sufficiently refined institutional mandates to implement them, to parse out the appropriate fiscal and monetary response. Today this concern about deficit spending crowding out private demand for capital in the money market is mitigated as long as the Federal Reserve is adequately accommodative, buying securities in the open market to push down rates while the Treasury borrows.

To be fair to Hoover and his administration, there was not the same understanding of the theoretical underpinnings of deficit spending then. As noted earlier, Keynes's masterful exposition on the subject in *General Theory of Employment, Interest, and Money* was not published until 1936, and even then, it took the partial playing out of the Great Depression to foster more confidence in the plan.

Even Roosevelt's administration had to experience a rather painful education about the costs of pursuing austerity during economic crisis. In 1936, the fiscally conservative Treasury secretary Henry Morgenthau Jr., along with other members of the Department of the Treasury, persuaded Franklin Delano Roosevelt that it was time to pull back the reins on spending and balance the budget again. Roosevelt listened and on the campaign trail stated that he thought in 1936 the time was right to finally rebalance the budget, though he was clearly conscious of the fact that in previous years it would have been far too soon: "To balance our budget in 1933 or 1934 or 1935 would have been a crime against the American people. To do so we should either have had to make a capital levy that would have been confiscatory, or we should have had to set our face against human suffering with callous indifference. When Americans suffered, we refused to pass by on the other side. Humanity came first."[27]

Many other advisers to Roosevelt, however, took the profoundly different view that those so bent on austerity were premature and could impair the prospects for economic growth. This was the view of Harry Hopkins, Henry Wallace, and Marriner Eccles. Growth was underway—GDP grew 10.9 percent in 1934 and 8.9 percent in 1935—but they argued that it was too soon to cut back. Unfortunately, Morgenthau's views won the day, and Roosevelt began reeling in spending. It was much too early to do so. The economy needed the stimulus provided by the deficit spending, and the decision to cut spending prompted the so-called Roosevelt Recession from 1937 to 1938.[28]

And so the proponents of austerity inflicted great damage on the economy, and even many of those who had previously been pro-austerity began to call for a reversal of the decision to cut spending. In Roosevelt's address to Congress in 1938, he addressed the changing sentiments on the matter because of the recession: "We have heard much about a balanced budget, and it is interesting to note that many of those who have pleaded for a balanced budget as the sole need now come to me to plead for additional government expenditures at the expense of unbalancing the budget."[29]

It is worth pausing briefly to address a misconception about the Great Depression. There are some economists dogmatically opposed to deficit spending who claim that there really was no austerity in 1932 because governmental spending became a larger percentage of GDP. This argument is specious. It is, of course, true that government spending became a larger percentage of the economy, but only because the GDP fell so precipitously. In effect, it was the denominator falling—not an increase in the numerator—that drove the increase of government spending as a percentage of GDP. This argument misses the point of fiscal stimulus, which is to replace previous private spending that has evaporated with more public spending to insulate aggregate demand from cataclysmic decline. If public spending has not increased, it does not matter how much GDP it constitutes because it is clearly not making up for declining private spending. In the end, the fiscal response to the Great Depression was poor because we lacked the fully developed tools as well as the empirical evidence to gain confidence that implementing such proposals could be beneficial.

The Regulatory Response to the Crash and the Depression

The regulatory response to the market collapse of 1929 was, in some respects, less immediately crucial to the stabilization of the economy. This was because, as discussed, the stock market collapse did not really induce the severe economic contraction that followed. Furthermore, unlike the Great Recession, there were not the same widespread destructive behaviors that required regulatory intervention to curtail. Indeed, there was some fraud, manipulation, and deception that needed to be weeded out to improve the functioning of the market, but these behaviors were not truly jeopardizing the whole financial system. This differed from the Great Recession, where behaviors like improper risk exposures by extremely large, highly levered institutions needed to be addressed.

That said, the regulatory response—and particularly, the introduction of the Securities Act of 1933 and the Securities Exchange Act of 1934—did help create a freer flow of accurate information on firms as well as a body to oversee securities transactions. These may not have immediately stabilized the financial system, but in the long run they certainly improved it by establishing the grounds for greater investor confidence in the reliability of information.

The Securities Act of 1933 required firms to make far more disclosures about financials, business risks, and organizational health than before. The act is often referred to as the Truth in Securities Act, as it was intended to give investors adequate information to make informed decisions about securities. This changed the prevailing legislative framework from a mosaic of state-by-state legislation into one federal standard on disclosures for securities. To execute it, Roosevelt tapped Raymond Moley (a longtime speechwriter and supporter of Roosevelt's political philosophy who eventually became one of its harshest critics) to begin the process. Moley in turn solicited the assistance of Harvard law professor Felix Frankfurter, who would go on to serve on the US Supreme Court. Frankfurter brought on board James Landis (later the dean of Harvard Law School) and Benjamin Cohen, an attorney, to assist in the process. They drafted the bill in the Carlton Hotel with the goal of granting an agency some regulatory authority rather than defining explicit prohibitions.[30]

The Securities Act of 1933, while a significant legislative achievement, still left open the precise problem of exchange regulation and actual enforcement. During the initial envisioning of the legislation, the power to oversee securities transactions seemed destined to go to the Federal Trade Commission (FTC). Many corporations took immediate issue with this, however, as the FTC had a reputation of being fiercely independent, with enough radicals to make the prospect of burdensome regulation worrisome for some. As such, a new organization, what was eventually the SEC, was contemplated. Roosevelt initially would have preferred the power to remain with the FTC, but he ultimately decided to pursue the SEC plan, saying in the end it was "not a frightfully important thing, one way or the other."[31] And so, the modern SEC was born. Beyond the creation of the commission itself, the legislation also required many market participants, such as exchanges and broker-dealers, to register with the SEC. It also included rules on public disclosures through SEC filings if a single participant purchases 5 percent of an issue and created rules on proxy solicitations. In the end, Roosevelt's dedication to reforming the financial markets was critical in that it allowed a sufficiently broad mandate for agency oversight.[32] However, in the short run, the regulatory response did not generally involve correcting fundamentally unsound financial practices that threatened to take down the entire economic system.

THE GREAT RECESSION

Intercrisis Period

In hindsight, the years from the 1930s to 2007 now seem like an interlude between major financial and economic crises that was useful for the development of still "new" (and, for some, still controversial) economic policy techniques. Analysis of the events leading up to and during the Great Depression produced the beginnings of innovative economic thought and policy recommendations, most notably from John Maynard Keynes, concerning the causes and effects of financial and economic disasters.

As our previous examination has revealed, there were three important schools of thought in play: the Austrian school, monetarist theory, and Keynesian fiscal concepts. Over the years between crises, these different schools of thought produced a working body of knowledge that, at risk of oversimplification, has led to skepticism concerning the Austrian notion of unfettered free markets, a broader acceptance of activist monetary policy, and widespread but not complete agreement on the usefulness of Keynesian fiscal action to mitigate severe economic weakness.

During this period, economic policy emphasis has steadily shifted toward focus on employment management and a general dispelling of inclinations to simply accept dramatic economic dislocation as a natural and healthy purging of unfortunate excesses of speculative and greedy financial activity undertaken by business and the public.

Notwithstanding this generally constructive evolution of economic thought, policy, and tools, there is as yet little evidence of public restraint or caution once confidence and evidence of economic success have built up in the system. Unfortunately, it still appears that effective governmental regulatory and supervisory efforts are required for there to be any hope of the restraint to avoid ultimately disastrous risk acceptance once an economic cycle has progressed and delivered notable financial rewards to the business community and the general population.

During the years leading up to the Great Recession of 2007–2009, there were widespread attitudes in various administrations and Congresses that led to relaxation of some of the more restrictive prohibitions that were the legacy of the Great Depression and subsequent financial crises such as the savings and loan crisis of the late 1980s, various international crises of the 1990s, and the collapse of Long-Term Capital Management in 1998. One notable example was the repeal of Glass-Steagall in the late 1990s. The Glass-Steagall Act passed by Congress in the 1930s prevented commercial banks from owning investment banks in a post-Depression attempt to prevent deposit-taking institutions from engaging in high-risk financial transactions.[33]

Throughout the period, competitive regulatory agencies were allowed to develop, gaps in regulatory coverage occurred and were not corrected, clarity in regulatory responsibilities was not established, and lapses in regulatory enforcement occurred.

The Buildup

Thus the stage was set for various asset bubbles, which may have been further promoted by the relatively easy monetary environment supported by the Federal Reserve led by Alan Greenspan. These bubbles, which included the dot-com bubble of 1999–2000 and a much more consequential housing bubble in 2004–2006, seemed to grow largely unfettered. In hindsight, the dot-com bubble, which had substantial stock market impact, appears to have had much less systemic economic impact than the housing bubble that followed it.

A characteristic of the economy we do not yet seem to be able to address is the destabilizing element of economic expansion on participant overconfidence and speculation. The late economist Hyman P. Minsky addressed this tendency in various publications, including his 1986 book *Stabilizing an Unstable Economy.*[34] Minsky recognized an all-too-human characteristic of expanding economies that was present in the housing bubble of 2004–2006: excessive confidence, excessive greed, excessive speculation, and excessive carelessness developed in market participants. For all the actions, new regulations, bailouts, and other remedial efforts the administration and Federal Reserve lavished on the financial crisis of 2007–2009, it is far from clear that any material progress has been made in addressing these all-too-human tendencies of the economic cycle.

In addition, human psychology, policy errors, and regulatory mistakes were dramatically compounded by the advent of a hyperleveraged US economy. In this context it is critical to remember that the aggressive use of derivatives in market operations not associated with hedging constituted a dramatic element of leverage in the banking system.

The immediate precursor to the financial crisis was the run-up in housing prices in the United States with similar manifestations in other countries, one notable example being Spain. But the devastation that was sowed depended heavily on complex financial instruments that were created, sold to the public, and invested in by various individuals, companies, and institutions. All this was compounded by abundant use of leverage, including derivatives, which were laced throughout the United States and ultimately the international economic system.[35]

Housing, an asset that has over time appreciated at about the rate of inflation, suddenly became a growth dynamo with "cannot-fail" characteristics in the early years of the twenty-first century (from 2002 to 2006). Between 1947 and the mid-1990s, US house prices as measured by the Case-Shiller index remained relatively flat, with the index ticking up a negligible amount (86.6 in 1947 to 87 in 1996). However, between 1996 and 2006, the index soared from 87.0 to 160.6 and then dropped by fifty-five points to 105.7 by 2009.[36]

Valuing assets is often difficult, and valuing residential real estate is no different. However, in comparison to the average income levels available to support the investments homeowners were making and to typical rents that might have been paid as an alternative, housing had not just appreciated too rapidly but had also become too expensive for many of the market participants who were making the investment.

To sustain some of this feverish activity, market makers propagated the myth that there was no history of any appreciable national price decline in housing. Declines were thought to be local or regional and usually of limited extent and duration. The view was promoted that any broad investment in housing, or the financing to support it, would basically be immune to substantial economic cycle exposure. Of course, the signs were there. Robert Shiller, the Yale economist, posited in advance of the cataclysm that the boom in real estate values might be driven by these psychological factors. After all, one could not explain the rises in housing prices by decomposition of increases in rents or construction costs.[37] The practical manifestation of this was the boom in new construction, the growth in the phenomenon of flipping homes, and the increased tapping of built-up equity by homeowners.

In the course of the boom, financing was extended to buyers with poor credit in increasing percentages and with liberalized terms. The percentage of value financed, the level of care in determining the borrower's financial capacity, and the borrower's degree of exposure to interest rate increases were all significantly compromised over time. All this added to the risk. In our highly securitized financial markets, loans were often extended by entities that did not retain exposure to these loans and were often packaged into large portfolios that lacked adequate real diversification, compounding the exposure of investors.

The history of the ensuing crash is replete with examples of sophisticated contrarian investors capitalizing on these unfortunate financing techniques to create and bet against financing packages that were predestined from their inception to fail once economic stress ensued. The result, fully anticipated by few, was a chain of serial collapses in key financial institutions in addition to hundreds of corporate participants in this unfortunate daisy chain of shocking miscalculation compounded by excessive leverage.

The Crash

And in 2008 the crash finally came. A series of smaller detonations preceded the major, headline-making events. These were various explosions in mortgage financing, leveraged real estate, and various other, often subprime, arrangements. The signs of significant trouble, certainly including falling residential real estate prices, were obvious; what was not obvious was the depth and breadth of the problem facing the whole financial structure of the country.

When a financial crisis occurs, there are two kinds of emergencies, and frequently they are combined into one intractable disaster. These emergencies can be termed "liquidity" and "insolvency." In many cases they develop at the same time in a particular financial enterprise.

Liquidity problems are easier and less dangerous than insolvency for the Federal Reserve to address. The solution is for the Fed to become the lender of last resort and to act decisively and confidently to provide funds against good collateral. This role has been well understood by financial analysts and commentators at least as far back as Walter Bagehot in the 1870s writing in his classic book *Lombard Street*, which had reference to British banking.[38]

Insolvency is a much more troublesome problem. It is a situation wherein a financial crisis creates in a financial institution such a considerable reduction in the value of its assets that inadequate collateral is available to support safely solving its liquidity problems by a central bank such as the Fed. This condition was immeasurably complicated by the high degree of leverage that these institutions had undertaken. If an investor's capital is, for instance, 3 percent of his balance sheet and the value of his assets falls by only 5 percent, that investor (or institution) becomes insolvent.

It was conditions of this sort that occurred during the crash and, in the view of authorities, required bailouts, which led to the pejorative phrase "too big to fail" describing institutions that should have been allowed to fail but which the Fed, the Treasury, and the administration felt were systematically too important or too intertwined with other key economic players to be allowed to fail.

Exhibit 6.1 at the end of this chapter lists a series of major developments in the financial crisis, most of which occurred in the eighteen months from January 1, 2008, to June 30, 2009, which portrayed the falling dominos characterizing the crash.

The Response to the Financial Crisis

Beginning in 2008, a very different series of policy actions than those initially triggered by the Great Depression was set in motion and resulted in a very different outcome. In the six months from

September 2008 through February 2009, a series of corporate bail-outs and financial restructurings was engineered by the Fed and the Treasury, dampening the financial crisis. Simultaneously, the Fed and the Treasury orchestrated a sequence of powerful monetary steps (the Fed) and moderate fiscal actions (the Treasury and Congress). Taken together, these much more soundly conceived and vigorously executed policies largely based on the major advances in economic thought and social priorities of the previous seventy years served to abort a potential depression and initiate a sluggish but generally soundly based economic recovery.

Our interest now focuses on fiscal and monetary policy activities of the Treasury and the administration (fiscal policy) and the Federal Reserve (monetary policy) and, finally, on the regulatory response. Let us consider the Fed's actions first.

THE MONETARY RESPONSE

Although he was slow to grasp the full economic implications of the bursting real estate bubble and the financial crisis that followed, Ben Bernanke, who became chairman of the Federal Reserve in February 2006, may have been the perfect man for the job. Previously a Princeton economics professor and expert on the Great Depression, Bernanke had not only studied but also written extensively on policy issues related to the Great Depression and certain subsequent significant economic cycle disturbances such as the Japanese real estate collapse in the early 1990s that resulted in the so-called lost decade that followed in the Japanese economy.[39]

Bernanke, like Benjamin Strong, also turned out to be a willing and even courageous innovator in methods to advance monetary liquidity even after interest rates had been pushed to their "zero-bound." His approach of flooding the financial system with liquidity by undertaking several rounds of quantitative easing and by deciding to include mortgage-backed securities instead of just US Treasuries in open market operations received no shortage of bad press from a variety of politicians and commentators. And yet, slowly but surely, the credit markets were set back in motion, consumers experienced wealth effects from reflating asset prices, and firms that had access found themselves with inexpensive capital for investment projects and eventually had the confidence to use it when the smoke began to clear.

THE FISCAL RESPONSE

In terms of fiscal policy, the financial crisis triggered several important and substantial steps by way of fiscal stimulus from the Treasury. The Troubled Assets Relief Program (TARP) was launched via a brief Treasury memo on September 20, 2008. It is astonishing that TARP was actually passed by Congress only two weeks later in a much more complex form. The revised program had an initial authorization of $700 billion to a variety of financial and industrial recipients but ultimately deployed around 60 percent of that, or about $431 billion after the Dodd-Frank Act reduced the authorization to $475 billion.[40] Nevertheless, TARP can probably most accurately be seen as largely a liquidity supplement to the economy rather than a permanent fiscal stimulus. Although some recipients of TARP funds were either insolvent themselves or using the funds to acquire insolvent entities, TARP is now essentially repaid by the aggregation of its recipients.

More substantial and more enduring was the $787 billion economic stimulus plan entitled the American Recovery and Reinvestment Act and signed by President Barack Obama on February 17, 2009. This more conventional group of fiscal stimulus items was intended to be spent over a somewhat longer period in order to give the economic recovery additional force and duration.[41]

Even beyond these specific fiscal programs, because of a series of unpaid-for military and social initiatives, the economy as President Bush left office was strongly stimulated by a much larger federal deficit. As a result—and with great irony in view of the clamoring for deficit reduction from much of Congress and the citizenry—the financial crisis and accompanying recession were being substantially combated almost from the outset by a notably aggressive and stimulative fiscal response.

We know that both the enormous liquidity pool built by the Fed and the threatening budget deficit projections for the next twenty to forty years will have to be addressed. What we do not know is whether we have the political will to address them and what the consequences for the economy at large will be.

There were profound differences in the fiscal responses to the Great Depression and the Great Recession. By the time the 2008 financial crisis came, there was a much broader acceptance of the premise of increasing governmental spending to stimulate the economy. The response was there, even though it was probably too small in magnitude. The stimulus reached a height of only 1.6 percent of GDP and was spent in the brief window of a little over two years.[42] A further problem was that a significant portion of the stimulus was composed of tax cuts rather than direct spending. Fiscal stimulus can have a net effect on GDP that is greater than the initial outlay through the fiscal multiplier effect. The fiscal multiplier refers to the phenomenon that occurs during fiscal stimulus as initial spending is spent several times over. That is to say, if the stimulus gave $1 to Party A, Party A spends a portion of it by transacting with Party B, who then spends a portion of that by transacting with Party C, and so on, increasing GDP by a value greater than the initial dollars spent. The problem with tax cuts as opposed to direct spending is that there is one fewer iteration of spending, and so the fiscal multiplier resulting from a tax cut as opposed to direct spending tends to be smaller.

Fortunately, while the fiscal stimulus may have been too small, too short lived, and too oriented toward tax cuts, the monetary response was robust enough to aid the economy in moving out of the recession. In the end, though, it was quite different than the fiscal experience during the Great Depression because the issue was not the inadequacy of the development of fiscal tools but, rather, the lack of will of the political apparatus to stimulate more to facilitate faster growth (and reduced unemployment).

THE REGULATORY RESPONSE

The regulatory experience in the wake of the Great Recession has been rather different than that following the Great Depression. The ultimate effect of the bank bailouts during the Great Recession has been to introduce an essential and oft-discussed question: have banks become too big to fail? The concept of too big to fail is problematic for two reasons. The first is that if true, moral hazard may arise whereby exceptionally large institutions take on more risk than is prudent, thinking there will be a bailout in case the risk taking results in outsized losses. In particular, has the offering of bank bailouts to exceptionally large institutions altered their behavior in a way that has created moral hazard? Will banks now engage in risky practices in the belief that their risk is now limited by the federal government's safety net?

The second reason is that a bank bailout can create an unfair divergence in capital access between small and large institutions. For instance, large institutions may be receiving an effective interest rate subsidy because lenders to the more sizable banks feel greater confidence that some of the loan is backstopped by the prospect of a bailout in extreme distress. This issue has been discussed by some officials, including the former head of the FDIC, Sheila Bair, who stated, "'Too big to fail' has become worse. It's become explicit when it was implicit before. It creates competitive disparities between large and small institutions, because everybody knows small institutions can fail. So it's more expensive for them to raise capital and secure funding."[43] Indeed, by studying the effect of government guarantees on the cost of borrowing of large banks by looking at the credit default swap market before and during the Great Recession, academics at Oxford's Saïd Business School have found some evidence for the reduction in borrowing costs.[44]

The concept of too big to fail has been correctly understood to be a destructive force by many. There has been some progress toward mitigating the issue with the Wall Street Reform and Consumer Protection Act, more commonly referred to as Dodd-Frank. Title I of Dodd-Frank created the Financial Stability Oversight Council with the goal of monitoring and correcting the risk taking of large banks. It is a forum for many of the most senior officials responsible for financial oversight to discuss and decide upon financial regulations. It has ten voting members, including such officials as the secretary of the Treasury, chair of the Federal Reserve, comptroller of the currency, chair of the SEC, and chair of the FDIC.[45] Dodd-Frank also created an avenue for clearer stress tests for regulators to analyze. Bank holding companies with more than $50 billion in assets, as well as nonbank firms that the Financial Stability Oversight Council has decided to monitor, must perform their own stress tests semiannually and will receive additional stress tests directly overseen by the Federal Reserve once per year.[46]

One issue with which regulators will be forced to contend is where precisely to draw the line between issues of insolvency and illiquidity, both of which were discussed and defined earlier in the chapter. There are times when it is not completely clear when an institution is truly insolvent. This is due to two factors. The first is that the bank's assets on a liquidation basis can be rather difficult to value. In the midst of a crisis, the value of the assets shown on its books may differ wildly from what the bank could actually get in a liquidation event when it is forced to make distressed sales, worsened by the fact that it would be selling into an environment where other banks (the natural buyers) may have financial concerns of their own. The second is that regulators may be in a position where they hope that the insolvency is transitory. In other words, when the assets of the bank are studied, it may be that there is negative equity in the company but regulators believe there is a good chance of asset reflation that returns the institution to solvency in the near future. Simon Johnson, former chief economist at the IMF, makes the point that the experience of many banks in the crisis was, in fact, an issue of solvency but that many hoped that asset prices would rise again to reverse the issue.[47] As such, regulators will be forced to think through the question of solvency based on liquidation value as well as potentially transitory insolvency for banks that have slightly negative equity but have a chance of becoming positive in an improved fiscal environment.

One of the most promising ways of providing more stability to the banking system was the Volcker Rule, named after Paul Volcker, a previous chairman of the Federal Reserve. The goal of the original rule was to minimize or eliminate proprietary trading, or the trading of financial instruments with the firm's own capital.[48] It is a sound proposal, given that banking, in its most successful form, should be a rather mundane business. It should involve simple maturity transformation from short-dated depositors to longer-dated borrowers with sound asset coverage, the establishment of the appropriate collateral and covenants, and a close monitoring of borrower creditworthiness. Banking should not involve speculation in financial derivatives that can destabilize the financial system by quickly decapitalizing already highly levered institutions with financial losses. It is not that speculation should be banned in the financial markets more generally, of course, but that the speculation should be the domain of individuals, hedge funds, private equity firms, and other investors that can experience losses without inducing the seizure of the credit markets.

The rule's implementation took two years to clarify in the face of stark opposition. After all, proprietary trading is generally a profitable business for many investment banks. It is profitable, of course, until it is not. The original idea of the rule was threatened for some time, and Paul Volcker himself has stated, "I'd write a much simpler bill. I'd love to see a four-page bill that bans proprietary trading and makes the board and chief executive responsible for compliance." The final version, by contrast, was some 900 pages.[49]

The difficulty in designing the optimal legislation for financial regulation is that crisis is what prompts the appetite for change. It has historically been very difficult to pass landmark regulations in periods of non-crisis, as regulation's opponents often successfully curry favor by claiming that regulators are trying to create a solution for a problem that does not exist. Thus, when it comes to overhauling financial rules, there is very little ability to plug the holes tomorrow. We must approach financial legislation with the mindset of designing precisely the rules we want to have in the depths of the next crisis because the opportunity to tweak them in the intermediate period is elusive.

A similar phenomenon with which we must contend is risk-taking over the cycle. One troubling reality is the human tendency to accept greater business and personal economic risk as the economic cycle matures and more economic success is achieved. This human frailty does not seem to have changed, and the tendency for the system to become more permissive over periods of prosperity has not changed either. This proclivity shows in both legislation and regulation, with rules often pared back as the boom is underway.

Given both of these facts, the Dodd-Frank Act may be progress, but more could have been done to limit proprietary trading, enhance the accountability of top corporate officers, and design even tighter oversight controls. After all, we may not have another chance until the depths of the next crisis. And indeed, in the end only time will tell how successful this legislation is in enhancing the stability of the system.

The Interrelationship Between Finance and the Real Economy

One stark difference between the Great Depression and the Great Recession is the interrelationship between finance and the real economy. This chapter has discussed at length how the Crash of 1929 was not what set off the Great Depression. Surely, it did not help—the Crash drove negative wealth effects in some consumers as they saw an erosion of value of their assets, and that surely did not inspire confidence. Nonetheless, the Crash was not the cause of the Depression.

Today, however, the situation is rather different. Virtually all parts of the real economy are dependent to some degree upon the financial markets, and most important, the conditions of creditworthiness.

There is a little irony to the effects of financial innovation. Financial innovation, of which securitization is a part, serves to socialize risk. It spreads risk from the balance sheets of a few to the balance sheets of many. In this regard, financial innovation on the whole has been a positive force; it has been the force behind vigorous insurance markets and higher loan volumes.

However, in socializing risk, financial innovation has also done something else: it has created a *common source* of risk for many more economic agents than would otherwise be involved. This is perfectly fine as long as the potential risk is properly understood beforehand. If, however, the nature of the risk is not correctly comprehended, many economic agents can become distressed at one point in time because they are exposed to this common source of risk. This is precisely what occurred when the softness in the subprime-mortgage-lending market came to light. The question on the minds of many when it first arose was simple: who has exposure to this? Of course, because of financial innovation, the answer was that many more people had exposure to the risk who were otherwise far removed from the original lending apparatus: banks, foreign governments, municipalities, pensions, individuals, and other institutions. They all had to endure the financial shock at once because of this common source of risk. Financial innovation, for all the good it normally does, had now created a situation not unlike the outbreak of a deadly virus: at first, nobody was quite sure who may have contracted the virus, so agents tried to avoid contact with one another by ceasing to further interlink their balance sheets through the credit market. The lesson behind financial innovation is clear: there are many benefits of socializing risk, but if we are not exceedingly careful to understand the potential nature and magnitude of that risk, we may impair an array of institutions at once.

And so, we live in the age of a highly financialized economy. Now why, then, did the technology bubble not produce severe economic ramifications? After all, the disaster in the stock market surely should have caused the real economy to seize. Not necessarily. There were likely two related reasons why the technology bubble did not cause severe problems for the real economy. First, even though the risk of owning the technology enterprises was socialized through the stock market, the holders of the equity in these technology companies viewed it as being high-risk capital anyway. Economic agents knew enough not to view the equity of technology firms as low risk, and therefore agents generally did not assemble their balance sheets in such a way so as to have their financial obligations depend fundamentally on the value of those stocks. For the rational agent, then, the shock produced by the precipitous decline in the stock of tech companies did not induce severe distress. This was quite different than the highly rated tranches of mortgage debt (often having AA and AAA ratings), where agents believed in the soundness of the asset and often constructed their liabilities to depend fundamentally on their valuation not declining substantially. Agents thought, in short, that these mortgage assets involved their low-risk capital and as such could build more liabilities against them, and when that turned out not to be true, disaster struck.

Furthermore, the technology bubble did not trigger a major credit event. Surely, tech companies themselves had a very difficult time accessing any form of capital in the wake of the bubble, but beyond this sector of the economy, there was not a wide seizure of credit. Potential lenders were not wary of all potential borrowers because generally there was not a massive shock to assets consumed by ostensibly low-risk capital. As a result, financial innovation here did not induce a grinding halt to the real economy.

In short, the relationship between the real economy and finance was rather different in the Great Depression and the Great Recession. An explicit financial shock set off the woes in the real economy in the latter, but a more gradual structural softness—issues with either aggregate demand or aggregate supply or improperly set interest rates, depending upon which school one believes—was responsible for the Great Depression.

The Recovery

The result of all this substantial and feverish activity was an aborting of the financial crisis and what might have been a resulting economic depression. One trivial consequence has been the labeling of the economic collapse as the Great Recession to distinguish it from the Great Depression of the 1930s and to clarify that what we have experienced did not reach the scale of a depression. Looking back, we experienced the gravest economic setback since the 1930s, but one whose duration and magnitude fell far short of our experience in the 1930s.

The actions taken primarily by the Fed but secondarily by the Treasury were in the end a brilliant response to a truly frightening financial crisis and incipient major economic collapse. To use the vernacular, the financial crisis was "right up there with the best of them"; nevertheless, the economic impact, while severe, was clearly contained.

Given the still novel nature of many of the monetary responses and the almost accidental nature of some, but not all, of the fiscal support, it is unfortunate that a significant number of Americans seem to have drawn incorrect interpretations of the efficacy of what was done as well as the intended purpose.

Not surprisingly, in view of the research published by Carmen Reinhart and Kenneth Rogoff, the recovery has been slow and not extraordinarily dynamic. Through an exhaustive historical compilation of past economic crises, Reinhart and Rogoff seem to have established that a serious recession accompanied by a financial crisis normally results in a slow, drawn-out recovery.[50] In fact, that is what the United States appears to have experienced since 2009.

The more important lesson to be learned is that there is a place for activist monetary and fiscal policy in the face of severe economic crises, and there is evidence that the primary focus of the activist policies undertaken by the Fed and both the Bush and Obama administrations was on stabilizing employment. With the possible exception of the salutary effect of some of the bailouts on exposed creditor counterparties, the focus of these Olympian policy efforts has not been on saving bankers, senior executives, and tycoons. We have seen "democratization" at work in a way that a more hands-off approach, like that of the Austrian school of economics, would never have accomplished.

CONCLUSION

This chapter has examined what are, arguably, the two most significant economic cataclysms to befall the United States in the past century in order to draw conclusions about our efforts to manage cyclical crises and democratize the investment process for the benefit of the broadest possible segment of the population. The case made in this chapter is based on the belief that improved economic management aimed at stabilizing the economy's performance and, as important, employment and consumption levels is evidence of a more broadly democratic focus of national economic policy.

Putting these two crises in dialogue reveals that we have become more proactive and more effective in addressing cyclical economic problems. To examine this, this chapter has focused on developments in monetary policy, improvements in fiscal policy, and changes in regulation after the two crises.

There is striking similarity in our analysis of the monetary experience during the lead-up to the Great Depression and the management of the global financial crisis. This analysis reveals the critical role played by two radical, innovative central bankers: Benjamin Strong and Ben Bernanke. Both central bankers took calculated but bold steps to maintain order in the economy and the market, and in doing so, both often took no shortage of political heat. Sadly, however, Strong did not live to apply his skills to the 1929 and early 1930s crises. The detractors of both men claimed at best that their policies would not succeed and at worst that they would wreak irreparable havoc upon the financial system. As history is likely to have it, these detractors were shortsighted in their criticisms.

EXHIBIT 6.1 – KEY DATES IN THE FINANCIAL CRISIS AND GREAT RECESSION

February 1, 2006:	Ben Bernanke becomes chairman of the Fed
October 2007:	Bear market begins
December 2007:	Great Recession begins
March 16, 2008:	Bear Stearns sold to J. P. Morgan
September 7, 2008:	Fannie Mae and Freddie Mac put into government conservatorship
September 14–16, 2008:	Lehman Brothers fails
	Merrill Lynch sold to Bank of America
	AIG bailout
September 20, 2008:	Treasury first draft of TARP (three pages)
September 21, 2008:	Goldman Sachs and Morgan Stanley become bank holding companies
September 25, 2008:	Washington Mutual taken over by J. P. Morgan (largest US savings and loan)
September 29, 2008:	Congress rejects bailout
October 3, 2008:	Wachovia Bank sold to Wells Fargo
	Congress passes TARP (451 pages)
November 4, 2008:	Obama elected US president
November 23, 2008:	The Fed, Treasury, and FDIC bail out Citigroup
December 11, 2008:	Bernie Madoff arrested
December 19, 2008:	TARP loans to GM and Chrysler
January 2009:	The Fed, Treasury, and FDIC bail out Bank of America
February 17, 2009:	$787 billion Economic Stimulus Act signed
March 2009:	QE1 (first Fed quantitative easing)
April 30, 2009:	Chrysler files for bankruptcy
June 2009:	Great Recession ends
July 21, 2010:	Dodd-Frank Reform Act signed
November 2010:	QE2
November 18, 2010:	GM emerges from bankruptcy with IPO
September 2012:	QE3

CHAPTER SEVEN

The Emergence of Investment Theory

IT IS STAMPED ACROSS THE NEWSPAPER. It is mentioned in short sound bites among radio broadcasts. It is discussed at length in the nightly news. We are barraged by updates on how the Dow or NASDAQ or S&P 500 is faring on a given day; the fingers of the media do not slip, even for a moment, from the pulse of the market. As long as there have been financial markets, there have been commentators eager to interpret even their short-term movements—movements that are sometimes muted, sometimes violent, but rarely predictable.

All this leads to a central question: how does one make sense of the movements of the market? How does one sift through all the noise and reach meaning? That is the task of the investor, accomplished by deploying methods of valuation. Valuation is the process of finding logic amid this noise, hoping to uncover areas of the market where the price mechanism has failed—areas that are the exploitable opportunities and the bread and butter of the successful investor.

Investing and the companion enterprise of valuation have always been more of an art than a science. However, in the last century, there has been a burgeoning field of investment science that has profoundly shaped and guided the way practitioners approach their art. This effort has produced a toolbox of sorts for investment professionals. Of course, not all practitioners use all of these ideas. Some professionals use many of the tools in this toolbox with great frequency; others scarcely use them at all. But even those who never use the tools generally know of them—and often have strong opinions about them.

To extend the analogy, one could say that this toolbox of investment science has three drawers; that is, there are three different domains encompassing the output of this intellectual effort. The first drawer of the toolbox is the theory of asset pricing (the core of valuation), the second is the formalization of risk in the context of managing a portfolio of investments (the risks associated with valuation), and the third is measuring and evaluating the performance of investment managers (how well investment professionals perform valuation to exploit investable opportunities). Each domain will be introduced in turn. Along the way, the reader will note that some of these intellectual postulates are just formalizations of long-held understandings: the importance of diversification across many assets and the fact that some financial markets exhibit random processes at work. Other developments radically altered how we think about investing, such as how to allocate funds across an opportunity set of assets with different risk and reward profiles. All of it, though, has left an indelible mark on investment, as its totality relates to the very core of what an investment professional does, which is sorting out valuations and remaining deeply conscious of risk.

DRAWER 1: ASSET PRICING

The first domain, or drawer 1 of the toolbox, is asset pricing. What determines the appropriate price of a financial asset? As with any good, the price is determined by the intersection of supply and demand curves. The supply curve for financial assets tends to be reasonably straightforward in most instances, like shares outstanding for stocks and different segments of the capital stack for debt. However, for financial assets, the story for demand is not so simple. The demand for an asset is dependent on a host of factors such as the healthiness of the balance sheet, perspectives on the sector the asset is associated with, the consensus view of management of the firm, and interest rates (or, more accurately, discount factors applied to future cash flows). Indeed, the demand curve for a financial asset is far more complicated and subject to much greater change than it is, for example, for consumer goods, in which case it emerges out of simple human desires to consume certain quantities of the good at particular prices. What, then, is the appropriate way to think about pricing financial assets?

The Father of Mathematical Finance

It has been said that mathematical finance emerged largely out of Louis Bachelier's work on the theory of derivatives pricing at the turn of the twentieth century. Bachelier's father was a vendor of wine who also dabbled in science as a hobby. When Louis's parents died abruptly after he achieved his bachelor's degree, he found himself thrust into the position of steward of his family's business. He became quite fluent in finance as a result of this experience, and soon Bachelier found himself back in academia working under the polymath Henri Poincaré.[1]

He defended the first portion of his thesis, entitled "Theory of Speculation," in March 1900. In it, he showed how to value complicated French derivatives using advanced mathematics. In fact, his approach bore some similarity to that of Fischer Black and Myron Scholes many years later. Bachelier's work was the first use of formal models of randomness to describe and evaluate markets. In his paper, Bachelier used a form of what is called Brownian motion.[2] Brownian motion was named after Robert Brown, who studied the random motions of pollen in water. Albert Einstein would describe this same phenomenon in one of his famous 1905 papers. The mathematical underpinnings of this description of randomness could be applied not only to the motions of small particles but also to the movements of markets.

Bachelier's work did not seem to have an immediate and profound influence on those markets, however. Though it did have some effect, as it showed up in applied probability books and in some prestigious journals, it was really when Paul Samuelson came across Bachelier's work decades later that this contribution was appropriately appreciated by the financial community.[3] Bachelier, though not as lauded as he may have deserved to be among the financial community of his day, was the father of modern mathematical finance.

Irving Fisher: Net Present Value

Whereas Bachelier employed advanced mathematics to think about the price of a derivative, Irving Fisher used mathematics in an approach to a more fundamental question: how does one value the price of the underlying asset (that is, an asset that is not a derivative)?

Born in 1867 in New York, Irving Fisher was a prolific American economist who made contributions to indexing theory as it pertains to measuring quantities like inflation (James Tobin called him the "greatest expert of all time" in this topic), produced work distinguishing between real interest rates and nominal interest rates, and improved the quantity theory of money.[4] He also proposed debt deflation as the mechanism that wreaked havoc on the economy in the Great Depression. While John Maynard Keynes's economic formulations became largely favored over Fisher's in their own time, interest in debt deflation reemerged in the wake of the global financial crisis of 2007–2009. Given these achievements, it is not entirely surprising that Milton Friedman would call Fisher the "greatest economist the United States has ever produced."[5]

Fisher's primary contribution to investment theory was the development of a metric to assess which income stream represents the optimal investment: "rate of return over cost," a concept related to what is today referred to as net present value (NPV). Fisher, in *The Theory of Interest*, presents two principles that can be deployed to choose the best investment. First, he states: "The first (A) of the two investment opportunity principles specifies a given range of choice of optional income streams. Some of the optional income streams, however, would never be chosen, because none of their respective present values could possibly be the maximum."[6] Fisher is essentially calling for the investor to discard any negative NPV projects, as these would never have the maximum NPV because one would clearly choose to not invest rather than invest and receive negative NPV.

The second principle is as follows: "The second (B) investment opportunity principle, that of maximum present value, is of great importance. . . . Let us restate this maximum value principle in an alternative form, thus: one option will be chosen over another if its income possesses comparative advantages outweighing (in present value) its disadvantages."[7] Fisher instructs the investor to discount future cash flow streams and be aware that while some investment opportunities may have higher cash flows in particular years, it is essential to have a broader view and look at all of the discounted cash flows as the basis of comparison. Last, Fisher defines rate of return over cost as the discount rate that equalizes two possible investments in terms of present values.[8] New investment can occur when this rate of return over cost is greater than the interest rate.

The formula was simple, but powerful: one could assess the soundness of an investment project by finding the net present value of its future cash flows.

Discounted Cash Flow Models

Fisher helped devise the theory of discounted cash flow for any asset, but it was John Burr Williams who advanced this theory significantly. Williams spent his undergraduate years at Harvard studying mathematics and chemistry, and this mathematical frame of mind would serve him well in the years to come. In the 1920s, he worked as a stock analyst and witnessed firsthand the Crash of 1929. The experience motivated him to study the nature of economics further, and he returned to Harvard for a graduate degree.[9]

Williams's dissertation was on the subject of stock valuation and showed that a stock was worth the value of all future dividends discounted to the present. If a firm was not currently paying out dividends, then its value was the expected dividend distribution when the reinvested earnings eventually became dividends. Williams had built what today is referred to as the dividend discount model of stock valuation.[10]

Williams also believed that much of the market's fluctuations were due to the role of speculators who were failing to heed the proper valuation method of discounting future dividends and were instead interested only in forecasting the price at which they could later sell the security to another buyer.

It is amusing that given its eventual importance, the 1938 publication of Williams's *The Theory of Investment Value*—containing these beliefs and their justifications—came at the displeasure of two different parties, publishers and professors. First, both Macmillan and McGraw-Hill refused to publish the work, convinced that because it employed mathematical symbols in its arguments, it would not be of wide interest to readers. Williams could persuade Harvard University

Press to print it only once he said he would bear a portion of the costs of publication. Williams also received the disapprobation of his thesis committee for sending the work to publishers before it was reviewed and accepted by the committee itself as degree worthy.[11]

Despite being met with this initial displeasure, Williams set the stage for the modern school of financial academics who think in terms of cash flows and a discount factor to value stocks. In some ways, what Williams did was take a known idea of valuing a traditional asset, such as real estate or a bond, as the sum of discounted cash flows and apply it to the stock market, where dividends represented the cash flows. A simple application in retrospect, perhaps, but it was the forward march of intellectual progress.

The Effect of Capital Structure on Asset Pricing

Franco Modigliani and Merton Miller analyzed a rather different question relating to asset pricing: how does the capital structure affect the value of a firm? In other words, how does the breakdown of different forms of capital, like debt and equity, affect valuation? The origins of their collaboration are almost comical. As the story goes, they were both in the Graduate School of Industrial Administration at Carnegie Mellon and were supposed to teach a class in corporate finance. There was only one problem: neither was particularly familiar with the material. So, they worked together to get to the bottom of it, only to find that much of the earlier work was rife with inconsistencies and ambiguity.[12] They determined that new work was required, and that was precisely what they produced, publishing their results in the *American Economic Review* in 1958 with a paper entitled "The Cost of Capital, Corporation Finance and the Theory of Investment."[13]

The result was the Modigliani-Miller theorem, which was among the work for which Merton Miller would win the Nobel Prize in Economics in 1990 and would help Modigliani win the 1985 prize (along with his work on the life-cycle hypothesis).[14] The Modigliani-Miller theorem first established several conditions under which their results would hold: no taxes or bankruptcy costs, no asymmetric information, a random walk pricing process, and an efficient market. If these conditions hold, the value of a firm should be unaffected by the capital structure it adopts. In other words, the sum of the value of the debt and the value of the equity should remain constant regardless of how that sum is distributed across debt and equity individually. Given that these assumptions do not hold perfectly in the real world, there have been reformulations of the theorem to account for taxes. This was not an obvious result before its publication, and it ultimately generated a flurry of literature in the field of corporate finance on the role of capital structure and its interaction with asset pricing.

Paul Samuelson and Bridging the Gap in Derivatives Theory

We now come full circle within the discussion of the evolution of asset pricing theory and return to the pricing of derivatives. The man who, in a sense, connected the earlier work of Louis Bachelier to that of Black and Scholes, described later, was Paul Samuelson. Samuelson made a stunning breadth of contributions to economics until the end of his life at the age of ninety-four. Hailing from Gary, Indiana, he studied at the University of Chicago in the early 1930s, taking several classes alongside such distinguished classmates as Milton Friedman. After earning his bachelor's degree at twenty, he went to Harvard for his graduate degree and wrote *Foundations of Economic Analysis* in 1947, a piece of scholarship that won the David Wells dissertation prize and made Samuelson the very first economist to win the now-prestigious John Bates Clark Medal, earned by economists under the age of forty who have made significant contributions to the field.[15] He would soon go to MIT and work on diverse theories of consumer optimization, trade, growth, and equilibrium.

Samuelson was also responsible for bringing much more attention to Bachelier's work after L. J. Savage wrote postcards to a group of economists asking if any economists were familiar with Bachelier.[16] And Samuelson did rethink many of the assumptions Bachelier made, such as noting that the expected return of the speculator should not be zero, as Bachelier suggested, but should rather be positive and commensurate with the risk the speculator is enduring. Otherwise, the investor would simply either not invest or own the risk-free security (short-dated Treasury debt). He also redefined Bachelier's equations to have the returns in lieu of the actual stock prices move in accordance with a slightly different form of Brownian motion because Bachelier's form of Brownian motion implied that a stock could potentially have a negative price, which is not sensible, as the concept of limited liability for shareholders implies that the floor of value is zero.[17]

Samuelson helped motivate the work on derivatives pricing with a 1965 paper on warrants and a 1969 paper with Robert Merton on the same subject—although he did, as he would later note, miss one crucial assumption that Black and Scholes were able to make in their formulation of options prices.[18] Samuelson can be considered an intermediary in calling attention to the subfield of derivatives pricing, even if the cornerstone of the most famous final theory was not his own.

Black-Scholes Options Pricing Formula

Myron Scholes spent his graduate years at the University of Chicago, where he studied alongside Merton Miller and Eugene Fama. He went on to teach at the MIT Sloan School of Management, and during his time there he met his future collaborator in the theory of derivatives, Fischer Black. Black was a graduate of Harvard, where he had spent both his undergraduate and graduate years studying applied mathematics, and was working for Arthur D. Little Consultants when he met Scholes.

The revolutionary work of Black and Scholes was published in a 1973 paper, "The Pricing of Options and Corporate Liabilities."[19] There were two main ways the Black-Scholes options pricing scheme revolutionized the way that derivatives were understood. First, and what Samuelson had essentially missed, was that their scheme thought of derivatives with respect to a no-arbitrage condition. The version of the no-arbitrage condition Black and Scholes used was that of *dynamic hedging*, or the notion that one could construct an instrument with the same payoffs as an option contract by buying or selling different amounts of the underlying stock when there were moves in price (delta hedging), changes in the sensitivity of the contract with respect to price (gamma hedging), and swings in volatility (vega hedging). The hedging is dynamic in the sense that trading must be done any time these factors change.

Black-Scholes does make some unrealistic assumptions about dynamic hedging. First, it assumes that there are no transaction costs that would impede the constant trading required to maintain the hedge. Further, and perhaps even less realistically, there is an implicit assumption that markets follow a continuous pricing regime when they in fact follow a discontinuous one. That is to say, it is possible for a stock price, for instance, to fall from $7.00 per share directly to $6.75, missing all the intermediary values, and thus the dynamic hedging required for a true no-arbitrage condition is difficult to achieve. It turns out, though, that these assumptions are not outrageously unrealistic, as markets are sufficiently liquid to keep transaction costs reasonably low and do not generally experience gaps of such substantial magnitude so as to wreak complete havoc on the idea of dynamic hedging.

The second contribution Black-Scholes made was to one of the models that immediately preceded it: that of James Boness, whose work has since been largely forgotten by practitioners. Boness's model had a few vital errors that made the difference between his relative obscurity and a chance for enduring acclaim. The first error was the discount rate used.[20] The discount rate in the Black-Scholes model is the risk-free rate, again because of the no-arbitrage condition. Boness, though, used the expected return of the stock as the discount rate, but this is not logical in light of the dynamic hedging strategy. Also, Boness tried to incorporate risk preferences into his work, but Black-Scholes imposed the assumption of risk neutrality and did not distinguish between the risk characteristics of various parties.[21]

As for the equation itself, it is a partial differential equation—with partial derivatives that are now known as the Greeks: delta, gamma, vega, theta, and rho—that bears some semblance to thermodynamic equations. Of course, not all this was completely worked out by the actual 1973 paper. Robert Merton published a subsequent paper explaining the mathematics of the model (in which he also used the term *Black-Scholes* to refer to this equation for the first time). He described how generalizations of the results were applicable to a variety of other derivatives and markets using the same dynamics present in this model.[22] That said, the work of Black and Scholes rounded out that of Samuelson and Bachelier, for they had finally formulated a precise model of options pricing.

Black would not join his collaborators, Scholes and Merton, in winning the Nobel Prize simply because he did not live long enough. Having died of cancer in 1995, two years before the awarding of the prize (not generally awarded posthumously except in a few historical cases when the intended recipient died after being nominated), he was ineligible.[23]

Where Drawer 1 Has Taken Us

As asset pricing encompasses two fields, the theory of pricing of financial assets in general and the pricing of derivatives, there are two rather different answers to the question of where these achievements have taken us. When it comes to derivatives pricing, particularly the work kicked off by Merton, Samuelson, Black, and Scholes, as well as a flurry of important but less seminal work, the answer is fairly straightforward. The theory of derivatives pricing is largely resolved and can tell us quite successfully what the price of an option on a particular stock should be, given the stock's price. It is not to say that there is *nothing* left to do, but rather that we now more or less know what a solution "should look like." Typically, the modifications for derivatives pricing involve either alterations of some now well-known differential equations or, in the case where there is no explicit mathematical solution, the use of computer simulations.

Of course, upon reflection, it is no real wonder that the theory of derivatives pricing is in a much more advanced state than other theories of pricing of financial assets; it has the benefit of taking the price of the underlying asset as an *input*, whereas the nonderivative field of asset pricing faces the greater problem of asking what that very stock price should be.

This is also not to say that all market participants have learned to *trade* derivatives successfully. To say the theory is very successful simply means that inputs map to an output with a high degree of accuracy. This assumes, of course, that the practitioner used the right inputs—which certainly is not assured. Although the theory of derivatives itself is sound, the familiar mantra holds: garbage in, garbage out.

As for asset pricing more generally, there remains a great deal to be done on the academic side, but in truth, determining asset prices is effectively the bread and butter of the entire investment management industry. Some investors try to find value in the equities markets, looking at turnaround stories, improving management, or examining metrics and comparables to find "mispriced" assets. Others like to rummage through the garbage for distressed debt deals and find "diamonds in the rough." Still others find mispriced assets where there are massive dislocations. Investment management is all about asset pricing, and each manager brings to the task his or her own theories of value. So while there is more to do in the academic arena, we will never resolve a theory of value that is universal and perfect—that, after all, is the very art of investment.

DRAWER 2: RISK

Most of us know where we fall on the spectrum of risk appetites and how close to the edge we care to venture. Some of us are risk lovers, from the gamblers to the entrepreneurs to the adrenaline-loving sports enthusiasts. Others are profoundly risk averse; these are people who are fond of routine, safety, and predictability. Indeed, we know how we interface with risk in our own lives, but rarely do we pause to ponder the simplest questions of all: what is risk, and what is its origin?

Risk is a result of a basic fallibility. That fallibility is our incapacity to see the future. If we knew what tomorrow and every day thereafter would bring, there would be no risk. We could proceed about our lives making decisions whose consequences we knew precisely. We would not feel the trepidation (or, for many, the excitement) that arises from risk, and even more than that, we would not fall victim to the injuries risk delivers. It would be a perfect, though perhaps dull, world. And so risk is yet another burden we bear because of our epistemic limitations.

We are compelled then to walk through life in a certain probabilistic haze, ascribing to all future states of the world certain probabilities of coming to fruition. A collection of future states that is highly dispersed probabilistically with an array of varying consequences is risky, whereas a collection of few states with very similar consequences is not very risky. This is a correct, though slightly imprecise, way of contemplating the essence of risk. The following section traces the frontier of humanity's formalization of risk in a portfolio management context.

The Beginnings of Diversification

How many generations of parents have told their children some variant of the adage "Do not put all your eggs in one basket"? This pithy precept contains an extraordinary amount of wisdom. Diversification across truly unrelated assets forms the heart of risk management in investment. Virtually all investors would be well served to heed this concept. As it turns out, humanity has been well apprised of the notion of diversification of assets for many centuries. Sagacious advice about diversification appears again and again throughout the Western canon. It appears in the Old Testament of the Bible in the book of Ecclesiastes, which discusses the importance of diversifying: "Ship your grain across the sea, after many days you may receive a return. Invest in seven ventures, yes, in eight; you do not know what disaster may come upon the land."[24] Even William Shakespeare himself addresses the topic in *The Merchant of Venice.* Antonio declares in the very first scene of the first act, "I thank my Fortune for it, my ventures are not in one bottom trusted, nor to one place; nor is my whole estate upon the Fortune of the present year. Therefore my merchandise makes me not sad."[25]

From the Bible to the Bard, humanity has long understood the general notion of spreading risks over a diverse set of projects and ventures. So goes the oft-repeated reference to eggs and baskets. Despite this, there remains disagreement in the investing world as to the importance of diversification—largely because if the goal is extremely large wealth, another option is to embark on a path of nondiversification. In this case, the chances of success are presumably lower, but the payout is significant. As Andrew Carnegie's famous quip goes, "The way to become rich is to put all your eggs in one basket and then watch that basket." Bill Gates, too, accumulated substantial wealth early in his career by tying his fate virtually exclusively to that of Microsoft and would diversify only later once his fortune was already earned.

This disagreement regarding diversification hinges upon goals. If the goal is capital preservation and prudent management of funds, the ancient wisdom applies: invest widely. It enhances the probability that a large portion of one's wealth will remain intact over a variety of different states of the world. However, if one's goal is not capital preservation but rather extremely large wealth accumulation, diversification is, in many cases, inappropriate.

The source of the disagreement is in how diversification operates on expected returns. Imagine a bell curve sitting over a number line and centered on the expected return of a single asset. The bell curve represents the distribution of possible returns in the future. Adding more and more unrelated assets tightens the tails on the bell curve ever closer to the average expected return. In the process, one reduces the probability of massive loss (the size of the left tail), which is great for capital preservation. Of course, by the same token, one cuts down the size of the right tail, or the likelihood of enormous gain. And thus, both the adage and Carnegie are correct—it is just a question of purpose. Do you accept the left tail risk and swing for the fences, hoping to end up on the right tail with great riches? Or do you abandon the right tail and avoid the left tail, thus maximizing your chances of sitting somewhere in the middle?

Markowitz's Model and Tobin's Improvements

Although the concept of diversification has existed for some time, it was not until Harry Markowitz that the mathematical mechanics of diversification were worked out. Harry Markowitz was born in Chicago in 1927, and he stayed in his hometown as a young adult to attend the University of Chicago. Harry was interested in many subjects, including philosophy (having a special interest in David Hume) and physics.[26] He eventually gravitated toward economics and stayed at the university to pursue his graduate work under Jacob Marschak, a Russian American economist whose work advanced the field of econometrics. Markowitz happened to have a discussion with a stockbroker while awaiting an opportunity to speak with his thesis adviser, Marschak. The stockbroker seemed to suggest that Markowitz think about the portfolio selection problem in the context of linear optimization, and Marschak later agreed to his doing just that.[27] Markowitz was the man for the job; he knew the linear optimization methods, having studied with George Dantzig at the RAND Corporation.[28]

Philosophically, Markowitz realized that the theory of asset pricing was incomplete without a corresponding theory of risk. Markowitz reasoned that one can indeed perform a calculation of dividends (in truth, proxies for discounted cash flows), but those future dividends themselves are uncertain. And yet, the risks are not captured by the concepts of net present value of Fisher or the dividend discount model of John Burr Williams.[29]

Markowitz offered a technical solution. To give a slightly more modern version of some of his ideas, his approach involves plotting all of the assets available on a graph where the left axis is the expected return and the horizontal axis is the excess volatility, as measured by the standard deviation of returns of the asset (see figure 7.1). The approach is to consider the trade-off between return and volatility: less volatility comes at the cost of lower expected returns for a given

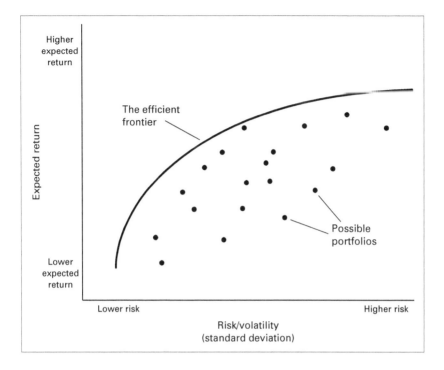

Figure 7.1 Contemporary Understanding of Markowitz's Efficient Frontier

Source: "Modern Portfolio Theory and the Efficient Frontier," Smart401k, accessed 2013,
http://www.smart401k.com/Content/retail/resource-center/advanced-investing/modern
-portfolio-theory-and-the-efficient-frontier.

portfolio, and achieving higher expected returns requires a portfolio
with higher volatility. Then, all possible portfolio risks and rewards
are mapped out.[30] The portion of the curve representing the highest
expected return for a given level of volatility is identified and marked
as the "efficient frontier."

One would want to invest only in a portfolio that is actually on the
efficient frontier with the following simple argument: if one is not on
the efficient frontier, one can move to an alternative portfolio that has
higher expected return for that same level of risk.

In a 1958 paper, James Tobin enhanced the value of the Markowitz approach by integrating the role of a risk-free asset (thought of
more practically as the T-bill), which is plotted on the left axis and

identified as having no excess volatility. A line is drawn from this point marking off the risk-free asset and is dropped down upon the efficient frontier to find the most efficient point on the frontier. This line is known as the capital allocation line and represents all possible combinations of the market portfolio and the risk-free asset. It is here that Tobin's famous separation theorem arises: the agent should hold some linear combination of the risk-free rate and the assets on the point of the efficient frontier that intersects with the capital allocation line (see figure 7.2).[31]

There is a remarkable implication of Tobin's separation theorem: the only difference in the assets every agent in the market should hold is just in the combination of risk-free assets and the tangency portfolio (assuming, of course, that everyone agrees on the risk and return

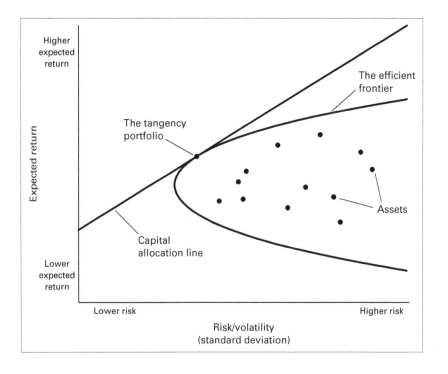

Figure 7.2 Tobin's Separation Theorem

Source: "The Capital Asset Pricing Model—Fundamental Analysis," EDinformatics, accessed 2013, http://edinformatics.com/investor _education/capital_asset_pricing_model.htm.

characteristics of all the assets in the opportunity set). Disagreement in these inputs, according to the model, is the only reason to have a portfolio whose components look any different from that of another rational investor doing mean-variance optimization. Which combination of risk-free asset and the tangency portfolio is selected is a function of how much risk one cares to accept. The most risk-averse individuals may hold only the risk-free asset, whereas the most risk-loving investors would theoretically borrow to leverage up exposure to the tangency portfolio.

There have been some criticisms of the Markowitz approach. For instance, some economists have pointed out that volatility may not be sufficiently described by the standard deviation of the returns. The notion of a skewed left tail on return distributions is absent in the Markowitz approach. Even more important, though, is the ability to forecast the expected returns and volatilities. How does one construct a model without knowing ex ante what these returns and volatilities are likely to be? Markowitz suggested using historical data. However, there has been an abundance of subsequent literature showing how notoriously difficult this problem of forecasting returns and volatilities can be (especially returns, as volatilities tend to be more precisely forecasted over short intervals). Nevertheless, despite its drawbacks, Markowitz's idea was a radical rethinking of portfolio design and allocation and paved the way for the next revolution in the intellectual theory of investing: the capital asset pricing model.

Capital Asset Pricing Model

The capital asset pricing model (CAPM), proposed by William Sharpe in 1964 and John Lintner in 1965, is an extension of the Markowitz model.[32] It assumes that investors are in agreement about the expected returns and variances of the assets in the opportunity set and, further, that capital for investment can be borrowed and lent at the risk-free interest rate. This generates the condition that all investors hold the same combination of assets in the same proportions, creating the market portfolio.[33]

The notion of beta is central in the capital asset pricing model. Beta is a measure of how responsive an asset is to a change in the value of a benchmark. A beta of 1 implies that an asset moves approximately in lockstep with the benchmark over time. A beta of zero, by contrast, means that an asset moves in a manner that is unrelated to the benchmark. More formally, beta is equal to the correlation between an asset's changes in price and the benchmark's changes in price multiplied by the ratio of the volatilities (as measured by the standard deviation of returns) of each, with the asset's volatility as the numerator and the benchmark's as the denominator.

The capital asset pricing model is of interest for several essential reasons. The first is in considering whether to add an asset to the market portfolio. More specifically, CAPM generates a condition on the minimum expected return, given the beta of the asset to the market portfolio. If the asset's expected return exceeds the minimum expected return, it is a worthwhile addition to the portfolio; otherwise, it should be avoided.

One radical implication of CAPM that almost universally proves initially uncomfortable is that sometimes it is in the interest of a portfolio manager to add an asset with a negative expected return. One can imagine, for instance, if the risk-free asset has zero return, then an asset that has a negative expected return may be added to the market portfolio if its beta is sufficiently negative. The reason this works is because introducing this asset reduces the total variance of the portfolio. Doing so is attractive because it stabilizes the rest of the blend of assets. It can be likened to vinegar: consuming vinegar on its own is usually undesirable. However, when combined with certain other foodstuffs, such as salad or sushi rice, it can be quite pleasant. CAPM instructs the practitioner that a portfolio analysis involves looking at more than just a collection of individually attractive assets; it involves, rather, a dissection of the blended whole.

The capital asset pricing model is also useful in corporate finance and in determining whether or not firms should invest in particular projects. A firm has a certain cost of capital that can be measured rather simply by beta. If a project has a rate of return on a given investment of capital that is less than the minimum return as prescribed by the CAPM, the firm should steer clear of the project, which would not entail an efficient deployment of funds.

Given this, one of the most difficult aspects of the capital asset pricing model is actually computing the forward beta, not unlike the problems of forecasting forward expected returns and volatilities discussed in the Markowitz model. By far the most common way practitioners

calculate beta for the next period is to take the most recent historical beta and use it as the most reasonable proxy. This is known as the
constant beta approach and is indeed the most straightforward way
to forecast beta, though there are more mathematically sophisticated
alternative approaches as well.

Fama-French Three-Factor Model

In 1992, Eugene Fama and Kenneth French wrote a famous paper entitled "The Cross-Section of Expected Stock Returns" that appeared in
The Journal of Finance, in which they said that beta alone is insufficient
to capture the risk-return trade-off. They introduced two additional
factors—size (as measured by the market capitalization) and value (as
measured by the book-to-market equity ratio)—as explanatory variables in the performance of stocks. They found that value firms (or
firms with low price-to-book value, as compared with growth firms)
and small firms (low market capitalization) have higher expected
returns in the aggregate but also have higher risk. That is, there is
generally a premium earned by holding value and small capitalization
stocks. This three-factor model was found to significantly enhance the
explanatory capacity of the model when compared to the pure capital
asset pricing model.[34]

This contention was of considerable practical importance. Fama
and French were suggesting that there could be other factors driving risk premia and that a single-factor CAPM may be insufficient to
adequately describe the risk premium the market offers. It also suggests that for those investors who had previously ignored the effects
of these potential sources of risk premia, the returns they experienced
in their portfolios may not have been only a function of the market
return and their stock selection skills but may also have been a function of exposure to different market factors.[35]

Where Drawer 2 Has Taken Us

When it comes to risk, we have made great strides, but there is still
work to be done. For instance, Markowitz and the later capital asset
pricing model suggest that risk can be effectively calculated with metrics like volatility as measured by the standard deviation of asset prices
and the betas of assets through time. But how well do these measures

really capture risk? To what degree can we rely on price action to tell us the real risk of our investments?

We also need to comprehend the nature of tail risks more effectively; that is, we need to understand how portfolios and markets behave under extreme scenarios. These types of outlier events have monumental consequences on all aspects of money management and lead to corresponding extreme shocks, from liquidity crises to credit crunches to fundamental changes in the economics of the underlying investments. Our failure to really conceptualize the nature of tail risk events has resulted in some investors and institutions becoming far too risky and some others, in truth, acting too conservatively. While the former is clearly worse, as this sort of aggressive behavior can jeopardize the very existence of the institution, being too conservative leaves returns on the table and can result in suboptimal performance.

Our failure to truly apprehend the nuances of tail risk has resulted in an even more pernicious and dominant phenomenon: participants are often too risky or too conservative *at precisely the wrong times.* When all is going well and it seems as if certain assets cannot possibly fall in value is precisely the moment when the greatest threats are lurking. And by that same token, when the despair seems most unbearable in a postcrisis atmosphere after enormous asset price erosion, many participants feel so pained by the prospect of further loss that they avoid even medium-risk assets. Of course, this is precisely when the market is offering bargains—and some of the best value investors have come to realize this—but much of the market is too shaken to take advantage of the possibilities.

The problem here is not so much one of theory but one of data; the truth is that there have not been an enormous number of these tail scenarios in major markets. In the last 25 years or so, we have seen the crash of 1987, the collapse of Long-Term Capital Management in 1998, the popping of the technology bubble in the late 1990s and into early 2000, and the Great Recession from 2007 to 2009. To build robust theories, or even effective working models, we require a broader set of data from which we can draw, synthesize, and eventually generalize. Of course, one does not want to overemphasize how problematic it is that there have been so few tail events in major markets—one certainly does not want to tempt fate and invite more. And fortunately, the quality of the data associated with the tail event does generally improve through time; for example, the quality of the data in terms of what is available to analyze from the Crash of 1929 is lower than that of the 1987 crash, though the former was arguably a much more monumental event. Because the crises are few in number and so different in content, it is not trivial to know how one should properly hedge a portfolio against extreme downside. All that said, the analysis of tail risk is an area within portfolio management of great practical importance.

DRAWER 3: THE PERFORMANCE OF INVESTMENT PROFESSIONALS

After asset managers estimate prices for individual assets, using the tools in drawer 1, and assemble them into suitable portfolios, with techniques from drawer 2, they can evaluate their performance with a third set of theories. Investment clients can also use these tools to evaluate the outcomes of decisions made by their money managers. As such, the third drawer is the one investment professionals open most fretfully. The theories contained in this third drawer are powerful but perilous. These theories are the yardsticks to measure the performance and value added by an investment manager. This is the set of tools, in short, that can be used to determine which investment professionals are wizards of their craft and which are just Wizards of Oz.

Cowles and the Analysis of Investment Forecasts

Alfred Cowles III was interested in the question of just how well financial forecasters performed. Like his father and uncle before him, Cowles III was educated at Yale, and he graduated in 1913. He found himself disillusioned by a number of financial practitioners who were in the business of forecasting the stock market after all of the projections he had read prior to the Crash of 1929 had missed the collapse. In 1932, Cowles founded the Cowles Commission for Research in Economics, now known as the Cowles Foundation, with the intention of making economics a more rigorous field. Having run his own research group in finance before that, he found himself able to leverage the help of academics, who became affiliated with the organization and took up the banner of studying issues in finance and econometrics.[36]

Cowles's most path-breaking research was published in a paper entitled "Can Stock Market Forecasters Forecast?," which was presented in 1932 and published in 1933. The paper effectively analyzed two groups: those who issued forecasts about particular securities and those who forecast the direction of the stock market as a whole. For the first group, Cowles analyzed four and a half years of data (from the beginning of 1928 until July 1932) from sixteen financial firms and four years of data (from 1928 to 1931) from twenty fire insurance firms that issued forecasts on particular stocks. For the second group, he looked at the projections from twenty-four financial publications on the general direction of the market from January 1, 1928, to June 1, 1932.[37]

In both cases, Cowles found that not only were their forecasts incorrect most of the time, but their forecasts were, in aggregate, even worse than random chance. With respect to the forecasters of particular securities, he found that the financial services firms tended to underperform the market by 1.43 percent annually and the fire insurance companies by 1.20 percent annually. As for the predictions of general market direction, he found that together, these predictions still underperformed random chance by 4 percent per year.[38] Indeed, according to Cowles, one was better off rolling dice than heeding these services. Although his focus on forecasters specifically was too narrow to represent an indictment of the industry of professional money management, it was the first step toward rigorously questioning the value added of some financial services.

The Application of Beta to the Formulation of Alpha

Cowles's work was a step in the right direction toward meeting the need to measure members of the financial industry, but it was the formulation of Jensen's alpha that really changed how well this measurement could be done for money managers themselves. In 1968, Michael Jensen created his metric of portfolio performance to determine if mutual fund managers were, in fact, adding value with their touted skills of stock selection.[39] The way this is done is to first use the concept of beta in the capital asset pricing model. One starts by calculating the beta of the portfolio compared to a relevant benchmark. A large capitalization US equity money manager might be compared with the S&P 500, for instance. Then, one does a straightforward calculation using the beta and the total return to back out the quantity of alpha, representing excess or abnormal returns. The excess return is Jensen's alpha. If positive, the alpha means that the manager has beaten the benchmark on a risk-adjusted basis. Positive alpha means the manager has added value. Negative alpha, on the other hand, suggests that an investor would be better off simply investing in the benchmark (fees aside). The manager who earns negative alpha has failed to add value from a performance perspective.

Jensen's initial study of mutual funds from 1945 to 1964 revealed that very few managers had effectively produced a greater return than one would expect, given the level of risk of the portfolio.[40] Investors finally had a mechanism by which they could parse out the risk-adjusted effects of active money management.

Samuelson and Fama: Formalizations of the Efficient Market Hypothesis

The question of whether managers can successfully add alpha remains a consistent and contentious debate in the academic literature. There are many who believe managers cannot consistently add value over the long term because markets are efficient.

One of the theorists behind this "efficient market hypothesis" was Eugene Fama, discussed previously in the context of his three-factor model with French. In his 1970 paper entitled "Efficient Capital Markets: A Review of Theory and Empirical Work," Fama effectively defined three different types of efficiency. The first is weak-form efficiency, whereby future prices cannot be forecasted based on current information. More practically, a corollary of weak-form efficiency is that technical analysis will not yield excess returns. The second variety of efficiency is semistrong-form efficiency, in which share prices reflect all publicly available information so that excess returns cannot be produced based on public information itself. Last is strong-form efficiency, which implies that all information, both public and private, is reflected in stock prices.[41] (Of course, a multitude of legal constraints exist in most regulatory environments to prevent the purest incarnation of strong-form efficiency, particularly laws prohibiting insider trading. Indeed, it is the divergence of the market from strong-form efficiency that makes insider trading profitable.) The critical implication of the efficient market hypothesis is that the market cannot be beaten if it is truly efficient.

To understand the efficient market hypothesis more completely, it is worth discussing perhaps one of its staunchest opponents: the school of value investing, which began with Benjamin Graham and David Dodd's publication of the famed book *Security Analysis* in 1934. Graham and Dodd posited that one could, in fact, outperform the market by concentrating on value stocks. These were stocks that had a margin of safety, or were protected by a fundamental valuation that exceeded the market's valuation. They also championed finding stocks that traded with relatively low price-to-book value or even sold at a discount to net tangible assets. The stock market, they believed, was irrational enough to push stocks out of favor and drive the price away from what it was actually worth based on an analysis of fundamentals.[42]

Graham would later discuss the short-run irrationality of the market by way of his analogy of "Mr. Market" in his subsequent book, *The Intelligent Investor*. Graham likened the market to a salesman who came around each day, knocked on the door, and said at what price he was willing to buy or sell, often at ridiculous levels. It was in this analogy that Graham acknowledged the randomness of the market, but he believed it was precisely this randomness that made the market exploitable if one used the right metrics of value. The markets were, in Graham and Dodd's view, anything but efficient.[43]

This was not the last word Graham would have on the subject, however. In the twilight of his career, Graham actually gave up most of what he championed in these books, saying that the market was no longer as exploitable as it had been when he wrote the books: "In general, no. I am no longer an advocate of elaborate techniques of security analysis in order to find superior value opportunities. This was a rewarding activity, say, 40 years ago, when our textbook 'Graham and Dodd' was first published." He went on to say that he agreed instead with those who believed the market had almost always priced securities correctly: "To that very limited extent I'm on the side of the 'efficient market' school of thought now generally accepted by the professors."[44]

While Benjamin Graham may have given up on his work, many adherents of the philosophy of value investing have not. One may consider Warren Buffett's primary objection to the efficient market hypothesis to illustrate this point: value investors, he claims, seem to have outperformed the market over time. The response of most proponents of the efficient market hypothesis has been that given the number of money managers in the market, statistically some will seem to outperform the market. Buffett's response in a 1984 speech to the Columbia Business School was to discuss the records of nine investors he had known since fairly early in his career who did value investing and who he said had consistently outperformed the market on a risk-adjusted basis. The essence of Buffett's retort is that it would be an extreme statistical anomaly not only to have seen this same group of investors beat the market in one year but to do so time and again over their careers, unless their strategies were truly adding value. And yet, supporters of the efficient market hypothesis are able to cast off these arguments as mere aberrations. Their argument is something along the lines of this: if 100 men spend an hour in Las Vegas, at least one of them should come out ahead. Of course, there is a problem with that sort of argument, because one could always claim that random chance is the source of one's success. Such a claim is not falsifiable in a scientific sense—it cannot be "tested," as one could always claim that random good fortune is at the root of it all. One is thus left with a decision to believe the claim that the success of the value school is due to just random luck or instead to notice that an array of investors subscribing to the philosophy from the very beginning of their careers (many of whom were eschewing such ideas as the efficient market hypothesis along the way) have produced terrific returns.[45]

Another Critique: Behavioral Finance

Beyond Buffett's more anecdotal and biographical approach, there has been a rich debate between efficient market supporters and other schools of thought over the last few decades. In particular, a large body of literature has developed that has come to constitute so-called behavioral finance. Behavioral finance essentially attempts to explain empirical anomalies and deviations from the classical risk models, including the efficient market hypothesis. Instead of considering market participants as hyperrational agents obeying arguably overly elegant utility functions, they are thought of as possessing biases, prejudices, and tendencies that have real and measurable effects on markets and financial transactions. Daniel Kahneman and Amos Tversky wrote a seminal paper in the field outlining what they call prospect theory, a description of individuals' optimization outside of the classical expected utility framework. Their pioneering paper noted many of the known behaviors that represent aberrations from expected utility theory, including lottery problems (in which individuals tend to elect a lump-sum payment up front even if that is smaller than the expected value of receiving a larger amount or zero when a coin flip is involved) and probabilistic insurance (in which individuals have a more disproportionate dislike for a form of insurance that would cover losses based on a coin flip more than the math suggests they should). Prospect theory contends that individuals' choices are more centered on changes in utility or wealth rather than end values; it also suggests that most people exhibit loss aversion in which losses cause more harm to one's welfare than the benefit from happiness one receives from gaining the same amount of reward.[46]

This theory may seem intellectually interesting, but how does it relate precisely to finance and investing? Since Kahneman and Tversky's seminal paper, subsequent work has made many connections to markets, one of which is the "equity premium puzzle." The equity premium puzzle was described first in a 1985 paper by Rajnish Mehra and Edward Prescott.[47] The central "puzzle" is that while investors should be compensated more for holding riskier equities than holding the risk-free instrument (Treasury bills), the amount by which they are compensated seems extremely excessive historically. In other words, it seems that equity holders have been "overpaid" to take on this risk. This paper set off a flurry of responses in the years after publication. There were some who suggested that it was merely survivorship bias that explained this phenomenon; that is, there were stocks that went bankrupt or otherwise delisted and so this high premium was not real after all.[48] Others suggested that there were frictions unaccounted for, such as transaction costs. The behavioral economists mounted a different set of explanations. One of the most cited and well-regarded explanations, put forth by Shlomo Benartzi and Richard Thaler in 1995, is "myopic loss aversion," a notion that borrows heavily from the concepts developed in prospect theory, including the fact that individuals tend to exhibit loss aversion and that they care about changes in wealth more keenly than about absolute levels of wealth. Investors who frequently look at the value of their equity portfolio—say, on a daily or weekly basis when the market behaves randomly over these short time frames, moving up and down—will thus experience more disutility on average, given that they derive greater pain from losses than pleasure from the same magnitude of gains. Over long evaluation periods, however, where market movements have a general upward trend, this feeling of loss aversion is reduced because equities tend to appreciate over time, so it is more palatable to hold on to equities. The size of the equity premium, then, is really due to loss aversion experienced by investors whose frequency of evaluations is too great; if investors looked at their equities portfolios over longer time frames, they would demand lower premiums and this puzzle would be resolved.[49] Other explanations that have been offered by behavioral economists focus on earnings uncertainty and how that influences investors' willingness to bear risk, and yet others develop a dynamic loss aversion model where investors react differently to stocks that fall after a run-up compared to those that fall directly after purchase.

Another place where this behavioral lens has been applied to financial markets beyond the equity premium puzzle is momentum. Recent work has looked at momentum in the markets by analyzing serial correlations through time. The idea is that a perfectly efficient market that incorporates all information in prices instantaneously should be a statistical random walk, and a random walk should not exhibit consistent correlations with itself, or "autocorrelations," through time. Thus, detecting serial autocorrelations may undermine the notion of efficient markets. The behavioral school has proposed two explanations for these results. First, it could be that there are feedback effects whereby market participants see the market rising and decide to buy in; or equivalently, participants could see it falling and then sell their own positions, a reaction also known as the bandwagon effect. An alternative explanation put forward for the momentum seen in markets is that the market could be underreacting to new information such that markets begin to move but do so incompletely when a news shock first occurs, only to continue to drift in that direction for a short time thereafter.[50]

The thrust of the efficient market theorists' response to these objections has been that while there may be momentum in some markets, one cannot truly generate outsized returns because of transaction costs. The work used to support these counterarguments by efficient market proponents has thus sought to compare those using momentum strategies to those relying on buy-and-hold approaches as a means of showing that the returns of the latter are greater or equal to the returns of the former. Other work that has sought to shake the foundations of the efficient market hypothesis has centered on predicting returns using various stock characteristics, such as dividend yield and price-to-earnings ratio. The empirical evidence here is also mixed, with some studies advocating such strategies as "Dogs of the Dow" (or dividend-based yield strategies) as generating outsized returns followed by responses showing how this does not hold across all periods, how it may hold for only select aggregations of stocks, or again how one cannot predictably get excess returns by adhering to it.

Where Drawer 3 Has Taken Us

Perhaps the best way to characterize the effects of drawer 3 is to say it has produced monumentally powerful but often underutilized tools. While many sophisticated institutional investors, like some endowment funds, constantly think about how much alpha a manager is producing as a yardstick for the manager's performance, others simply do not use the concept. Many investors put money with a manager and do not bother to think about how much alpha the manager is generating. This approach is especially disappointing when it comes to mutual funds, for instance, where price data are available each day and a precise alpha calculation can be performed. Alpha allows an investor to determine if a manager is earning his or her fees or not.

Beta, too, is powerful but underutilized. It may be that a manager has produced fantastic returns in an up market. However, upon close inspection with these tools, an investor may determine that the manager's portfolio is very high beta and that in a down market, the positions may be devastated. Investors should be apprised of how much systematic risk they are enduring, which is not obvious from the absolute return figures alone and requires closer analysis with these tools.

Most of all, though, these tools should inspire a certain sentiment in the investor—an educated sense of skepticism. Markets may not be as efficient as Fama suggests, but that does not mean they are necessarily easy to exploit. Furthermore, some markets are much more efficient than others. It is more believable that a very smart manager might produce more alpha in an unusual corner of the market with understandable dislocations and few participants than in markets that are well trodden and have countless eyes monitoring their frequent moves. Investors should approach managers with this skepticism and compel them to explain their edge, the reasons the pond in which they invest is attractive, their understanding of the associated risks, and the nuances of their investment approach. There are managers who produce alpha, but the bottom line is that many do not, and these tools can aid investors in identifying some shortcomings of manager portfolios as well as the health of their associated performance.

CONCLUSION

We have taken a gentle amble through the history of the theory of asset pricing, risk, and the measurement of manager performance. These stories themselves are remarkably human, often involving very good (or very bad) fortune, random encounters that altered life trajectories, and doubt about the applicability of a scholar's own work. There were those economists whose work was not understood for decades, like Bachelier, and others whose work induced an almost immediate and remarkable transformation in thought, like Black and Scholes. There were many who either came to these domains or worked on problems within them by chance, like Markowitz and his conversation with the stockbroker outside his adviser's office, or Miller and Modigliani, who collaborated because neither of them precisely comprehended the original material. There were those who ended up repudiating the value of their own work, like Benjamin Graham, who said his approach no longer applied in a world of so much information availability, only to have some of his ideas validated later (both anecdotally through Warren Buffett and empirically through Fama and French's recognition of a value factor as a source of excess returns). As much as we like to think science operates on a higher plane than the human world we normally inhabit, the historical episodes of the development of investment science suggest otherwise. Indeed, like the very markets these theorists sought to study, their own paths were fraught with tinges of the world's inescapable randomness, quirks, and caprices.

CHAPTER EIGHT

More New Investment Forms

THIS CHAPTER TRACES THE HISTORY of more recent and more novel investment forms—specifically, the class of alternatives as well as the low-cost passive vehicles embodied in index funds and exchange-traded funds (ETFs). In many respects, these two forms of investment are radically different. Alternatives (a class of investments that includes hedge funds, private equity, and venture capital) tend to be high-fee, relatively exclusive, and often institutionally oriented products. Index funds and ETFs, by contrast, are low fee, typically involve passive and rules-based ownership, and are available for retail investors and institutions alike. Debates have raged over the relative superiority of these as well as the ability to combine the two classes in a diversified portfolio. Few examinations, however, have sought to uncover their respective historical developments to unlock meaning and their possible futures. This chapter aims to do precisely that, unearthing the origins and evolution of these investment vehicles.

ALTERNATIVE INVESTMENTS: HEDGE FUNDS, PRIVATE EQUITY, AND VENTURE CAPITAL

The realm of alternative investments is vast and includes not just hedge funds, private equity, and venture capital but also commodities, real estate, and infrastructure. These investment vehicles have captured the attention of many, fueled in great part by stories of brilliant managers and stellar returns. Undoubtedly, the awe and reverence some investors have for these sophisticated vehicles derives in part from the fact that they have long been limited to high-net-worth individual investors and institutional investors, rendering them somewhat inscrutable to the public. The truth is more nuanced.

Snapshot of Alternatives

Alternative investments have been available to institutional and professional investors since the 1970s. While the term *alternative investments* generally refers to nontraditional investments in securities such as equities, bonds, property, or more esoteric assets, the term is a catch-all of sorts and can refer to investments made in hedge funds, private equity, venture capital, real estate, and other financial contracts and derivatives.

Alternative investments are usually less correlated with widely used indices and other assets, and they are often illiquid, a factor most commonly cited by investment professionals and market participants in justification *against* investing in alternatives. However, many major investment institutions, including university endowments such as those at Yale and Harvard, have praised the net benefits of alternatives, including their hedging potential and their ability to lower the volatility of the overall portfolio. The major investment categories within the sector of alternative investments are real estate, hedge funds, and private equity. The top 100 alternative investment managers in 2011 invested 78 percent of their total assets in these three investment classes.[1]

Alternative investments have continued to grow in popularity since their introduction almost 50 years ago. From the mid-1980s to the 1990s, aggregate commitments to the alternatives asset class grew by over 20 percent *per annum*. One 1997 report in the *Financial Analysts*

Journal corroborated a similar trend through the late 1990s, specifically among pension plans. Between 1992 and 1995, pension plans started investing a great deal more into private equity, with the more prominent funds increasing their commitments 92 percent to some $70 billion in total.[2] Some of this increase can be explained by the overall growth of pension fund assets under management, from $786 billion in 1980, to $1.8 trillion in 1985, to $2.7 trillion in 1990, all the way to $8 trillion in 2004. This growth has driven interest in alternatives, given the accelerating need for adequate returns on a vastly increasing stock of investable capital.[3]

The last few decades have also seen the expansion of alternative investments globally. In 1992, there was only subdued interest in private equity investment beyond the United States. However, in just three years, international private equity investment grew to comprise nearly 6 percent of total alternative investments. Experts generally agree that much of the growth in international private equity can be attributed to three factors: increasing investor interest in global publicly traded equity securities, the transition from government-controlled to market economies, and the privatization of industry that accompanied this around the world.[4] Accompanying these macroeconomic changes was the emulation of the structures of the private equity vehicles that had been successful in the United States. This led to the formation of large partnership legal structures around the world, many based in the United States but funded and invested all over the globe.

While the extent of institutional investors' support for the alternative investments available in the market is clear, it is not as easy to quantitatively determine how many individual investors invest in such assets. However, there are strong indicators that traditional retail investment in alternative assets is growing, with prominent fund managers and investment directors commenting that their own clients' perceptions are trending in this direction. For instance, bond fund manager Bill Gross asserted in 2012 that "the age of credit expansion which led to double-digit portfolio returns is over. The age of inflation is upon us." He argued that this would lead to the exploration of alternative assets, to increase returns and combat inflation, and to stalemates in the global equities markets.[5] Many fund managers do not have quite so negative a view, but they do believe that proper diversification may include capturing these asset classes.

One major barrier to traditional retail investment in private equity, venture capital, and other alternative investments in the United States involves several SEC regulations and congressional acts regarding "accredited investors," who, by Rule 501 of Regulation D of the Securities Act of 1933, must have a net worth of at least $1 million (not including the value of one's primary residence) or have income of at least $200,000 each year for the last two years, among other provisions, in order to invest in seed rounds, limited partnerships, hedge funds, private placements, and angel investing networks. As a result of these barriers to client acquisition, alternative investment sellers have shifted the burden of determining investment eligibility to clients themselves in most cases. Oftentimes, such notices will be accompanied by daunting *caveat emptor* (buyer beware) provisions warning potential investors of the inherent risks in such investments.[6]

All that said, the precise nature of the future of private placement solicitation rules is in flux. The JOBS Act of 2012 contained a section that broadens the ability of hedge funds to advertise to clients and lowers the standard of only speaking with accredited investors. It is up to the SEC to formulate a set of rules that is more detailed on what is permitted and what is prohibited. One of the staunchest opponents of this provision is the mutual fund industry.[7] It presently enjoys the ability to advertise and is not pleased by the prospect of competition from hedge funds.

Perhaps the most prominent concern regarding alternative investment advertising is the possibility for adverse selection. Many of the best funds may orient themselves primarily toward institutions given that, compared to individuals, institutions often have longer-dated capital and better underwriting and monitoring mechanisms by virtue of having full-time staff. As such, it is possible that there may be a disproportionate representation of lower-quality hedge funds that seek to advertise broadly because they have been less successful in raising money through traditional routes from sophisticated institutions. By targeting the lower end of the accredited investor pool en masse, they may find less sophisticated investors who do not have sufficient experience to conduct proper due diligence.

Although alternative investments are traditionally regarded as any investments having lower correlations with more conventional investments such as stocks and bonds, many analysts today take issue with this description. Indeed, one instance when correlations tend to be high across all asset classes is during financial crises. First, asset prices are affected more by broad macroeconomic factors (such as monetary policy announcements, trade numbers, or employment figures) than they are by idiosyncratic, asset-specific factors. Second, during a crisis, there is often a rotation toward cash and away from risk assets that drives prices down as market participants seek liquidity. These sell-offs often happen across many asset classes during a crisis, causing correlations to spike. Alternatives broadly are not immune from this phenomenon.[8] In truth, even private equity and venture capital, which do not have tick-by-tick prices, experience these declines in value as the price the companies could fetch in an exit decreases.

Having outlined this set of facts about alternatives, this chapter will now explore several of the major vehicles themselves, beginning with hedge funds. Hedge funds will be reviewed at slightly greater length, consistent both with the amount of attention they have captured and the extent of the care required for proper treatment of the subject.

HEDGE FUNDS

The hedge fund has found itself in headline after headline in recent years, and yet, the information disseminated seems to have produced little consensus on how these pools of capital have actually performed, how they should operate, and what role they should serve in both the wider financial landscape and within one's portfolio. Indeed, some investors have decried them as underperforming following the global financial crisis of 2008, and others have lauded them for providing relative stability during this tumultuous period. Some have condemned them as easily susceptible to fraud, and others have regarded them as relatively safe as long as essential red flags are avoided. Some believe ardently that more regulation is necessary, and others see such supervision as unnecessary and inconvenient.

There are broadly two reasons for this lack of harmony in public sentiment. The first is that the hedge fund is often cloaked in mystery. Some of this mystery is self-created, since many successful hedge funds have no interest in making their investment strategies transparent to the world, lest the investments become less lucrative as others emulate them. However, much of this opacity is due to the regulatory environment that allows hedge funds to avoid certain registrations under the

Securities Act of 1933 if they refrain from solicitation of unqualified investors. As a result, hedge funds sometimes appear evasive when in fact they are simply prevented from sharing particular information.

The second reason for the lack of harmony is that the very definition of a hedge fund remains exceptionally broad. As a class, hedge funds today invest in virtually every type of instrument, from derivatives to equities to corporate debt to private placements. Some funds exclusively establish long positions, whereas others complement their portfolios with short sales. Some decide to make consistent use of leverage, others make tactical use of it, and yet others avoid it entirely.

Almost comically, perhaps the most commonly shared feature among hedge funds has nothing to do with what hedge funds actually do. Rather, the most consistent element is how they charge clients for their services. Many hedge funds charge a combination of an asset management fee (most commonly a 1–2 percent fee on the total asset base, largely invariant with how well the fund does) and a performance fee of 10–20 percent of the returns of the fund above a high-water mark.[9]

Given this ambiguity and reticence, it is not easy to conduct a penetrating analysis on this investment vehicle. However, the questions posed are crucial: where did they come from, how justified are their fees, what are the various strategies employed, what common features do the outperformers have, and what does their future look like? With some persistence, though, these informational limitations can be overcome to generate satisfying answers.

The Origin of Hedge Funds

When it was conceived, the hedge fund was a far more specific and well-defined instrument than it is now. It was a fund that made use of "hedges" and, in fact, was termed a *hedged fund*.

The first hedge fund had a somewhat unlikely founder in Alfred Winslow Jones. Educated at Harvard as an undergraduate, he subsequently served in the American embassy in Berlin in the 1930s and later spent time in Spain during the Spanish Civil War. He went on to Columbia as a doctoral student in sociology, and after graduation in 1941, he turned his thesis into a book, *Life, Liberty and Property: A Story of Conflict and a Measurement of Conflicting Rights*. A passion for finance did not seem to manifest itself until Jones became a writer at *Fortune* magazine during World War II and eventually began to write about financial forecasting.[10]

It was through research for his financial articles that Jones came to the realization that one need not be fully exposed to the directionality of the market to produce returns. In fact, Jones thought he could produce more attractive returns by avoiding full exposure. He decided he would buy stocks he deemed to have compelling risk-reward characteristics and he would sell short stocks that were unappealing and overpriced. Jones was not typically completely beta neutral—selling short a volatility exposure that precisely matched the magnitude of his long positions—but he did use shorts to shave off some of the directional risk. In effect, Jones had constructed a long-short hedge fund.

In terms of operational control, Jones left the actual stock selection to managers he brought in to oversee portions of the portfolio.[11] These internal managers were given significant autonomy and were permitted to prepare the orders for execution. Once either Jones or his second in command took a look at them, they were given the green light. Jones did not use particularly active investment committees.[12] Meanwhile, Jones gave himself the higher-level task of trying to ensure that the managers were successful and determining if the entire portfolio was well diversified.

In return for his services, Jones charged his clients a performance fee that would eventually become the norm: 20 percent. He justified this number by referring to the Phoenician captains who took for themselves 20 percent of the gains from profitable journeys.[13]

The Growth and Development of the Hedge Fund

Two transformative changes to Jones's notion of a hedged fund followed rather quickly as a few other players joined the field. First was decreasing use of the hedge in the years that immediately followed. The reason was practical: the equities markets moved swiftly upward in the early 1960s and again in the mid- to late 1960s. Many managers saw their short positions as weighing down outsized returns on their portfolios.[14] In fact, many of Jones's own portfolio managers (who, unlike some of his competitors, continued to use shorts) remarked that it was much harder to find appealing short opportunities than it was to uncover alluring long positions.[15]

The second change introduced was leverage, and it was used for precisely the same reasons: to capitalize on the powerful upswings in the markets at the time. Gearing up the long bias via leverage proved crippling for a number of funds during the down markets of 1969, 1973, and 1974.[16] Some funds that utilized the most generous leverage were purged from the system. Many were caught in precisely the market-wide downdrafts that Jones's hedges were designed to mitigate.

Throughout this period, hedge funds did not attract much public interest. Indeed, an article appearing in a 1966 publication of *Fortune*, where Jones had previously been employed, was aptly entitled "The Jones Nobody Keeps Up With." The obscurity certainly was not for lack of performance: in the ten years leading up to the article's publication, Jones racked up total gains of 670 percent.[17] The paucity of public interest is attributable in part to just how small the universe of hedge funds was at the time. Even by 1984, the total number of hedge funds numbered in the sixties, and it was not really until the 1990s that the world of hedge funds began to flower.[18]

As the successes of hedge funds mounted in the 1990s, public interest finally picked up. One such successful fund was Julian Robertson's Tiger Fund. While Robertson's funds famously closed in 2000—his strategy of picking the best 200 firms to go long and the worst 200 firms to go short did not fare well in the distorted equities market of the tech bubble era—for years many regarded him as a wizard of financial markets. Other funds that gained media attention were much more exotic. For instance, the Quantum Fund, run by George Soros, gained high visibility when it "broke the Bank of England" by capitalizing on its expectation of a revaluation of the pound sterling.[19]

Indeed, for some of these funds, the more exotic nature of the vehicles they traded seems to have inspired a sense of awe. After all, stock selection within a hedge fund like Jones's did not look much different than stock selection within a mutual fund, with the major functional difference being the long-short approach. But with foreign exchange and derivatives, there was a sense of esteem for those who could monetize on far less comprehensible investments.

One overlooked contributor to the rise of the hedge fund and the rise in interest about hedge funds is the computer. The computer gave financial practitioners access to a wealth of information and data that was previously rather intractable to synthesize and without which it was virtually impossible to test rigorous models. Further, the very notion of a quantitative fund—a "quant" fund—or a quantitative strategy is simply inconceivable without the computer. Without the aid of the computer, one could not construct and back-test robust models or even generate signals where certain criteria were met.

The Hedge Fund Universe Today

As of 2014, the hedge fund industry had approximately $2.5 trillion in assets under management. Additionally, approximately $455 billion was in funds of hedge funds, a diversified investment vehicle designed to add value by selecting and overseeing other hedge fund managers that generate alpha.[20] Before discussing these funds of funds in more detail, let us consider the various strategies of individual funds. Despite the difficulty of categorizing hedge funds based on their strategies—many funds deploy a variety of approaches—the following list gives a broad overview of the relative composition of approaches.

ASSETS UNDER MANAGEMENT IN 2014

Hedge Funds	$2508.4 Billion
Funds of Funds	$455.3 Billion

SECTORS:

Convertible Arbitrage	$29.5 Billion
Distressed Securities	$184.9 Billion
Emerging Markets	$277.6 Billion
Equity Long Bias	$203.8 Billion
Equity Long/Short	$202.3 Billion
Equity Long-Only	$132.5 Billion
Equity Market Neutral	$42.6 Billion
Event Driven	$291.2 Billion
Fixed Income	$396.7 Billion
Macro	$204.0 Billion
Merger Arbitrage	$30.4 Billion
Multi-Strategy	$273.8 Billion
Other	$96.6 Billion
Sector Specific	$142.5 Billion

Source: "Hedge Fund Industry—Assets Under Management," BarclayHedge Alternative Investment Databases, accessed 2015, http://www.barclayhedge.com/research/indices/ghs/mum/HF_Money_Under_Management .html.

Today Jones's true market neutral, long/short style makes up only a fraction of hedge fund assets under management.[21] A closer look at some of the strategies can help illuminate the full range that hedge funds currently cover.

Merger arbitrage involves going long the equity of a firm that is the target of an acquisition attempt (and typically going short the acquirer as well if the acquisition is done for stock). Effectively, it represents a bet that the acquisition or merger will overcome any issues relating to shareholder approval, regulatory acceptance, and buyer financing. The merger arbitrageur collects a spread if the deal does ultimately close and takes the risk of loss if the acquisition does not receive approval or cannot be financed. This strategy can be attractive from a portfolio diversification standpoint, since the approval of a single transaction has little correlation to the market.

Event-driven strategies look for hard catalysts, or direct precipitators of asset price changes, most typically by explicit acts of a corporation's management or board. Such strategies may include capital structure arbitrage, where a hedge fund may analyze a firm, decide the firm is at great risk of bankruptcy, and invest along the capital structure accordingly. For instance, in a distressed situation, the hedge fund may determine that a corporation will have sufficient assets to pay the senior debt holders but that there will be minimal residual value left for the equity; the fund would then establish a long position in the senior debt and a simultaneous short position in the equity, expecting a bankruptcy to precipitate a revaluation of the different classes of securities and thereby creating a profit for the fund.

Convertible arbitrage is a strategy that generally attempts to be market neutral by buying long securities that are convertible to stock (convertible debt that has a coupon payment but also has an option to become equity at a predefined conversion factor) and selling short the equity. This strategy seeks to monetize on the fact that many of these convertible instruments offer less risky exposure to volatility. The strategy, however, is certainly not without risk. One of the most well-known disasters in the history of the approach involved securities of General Motors in 2005 and was precipitated by the confluence of two major events. In May 2005, Kirk Kerkorian made a tender offer for the equity of General Motors, offering about 15 percent above the previous day's close. The very next day, S&P issued a downgrade on the debt of General Motors.[22] This caused convertible arbitrage investors to endure losses on the equity side (which they had shorted), but also on the debt (which they were long).

Fixed income hedge funds differ fairly widely in the riskiness of the strategies employed. Some are rather risk averse, seeking to buy attractive debt securities that deliver healthy and uninterrupted payments. Others have far more complicated schemes to garner returns, such as exploiting aberrations in yield curves. This can occur when the yield curve adopts an unusual geometry (often a flat or steep slope at the extreme) and managers place long and short positions that profit when the yield curve shifts. One of the most common fixed income strategies is the "swap spread," which involves collecting the difference between Treasury rates and the swap rate. Others invest in mortgage-backed securities, like those packaged by Fannie Mae and Freddie Mac.

Macro hedge funds seek to anticipate major structural changes in an economy, either because of natural market forces (perhaps the market is grossly overheated and is due for a correction) or because of political circumstances. John Paulson of Paulson & Co., for instance, cashed in on the events that led the US economy into crisis by short selling subprime mortgage–backed securities. Because they seem to be predicting the future, many of the most successful macro hedge fund managers find themselves propelled meteorically into fame. However, there are abundant examples of macro managers who experience stumbling blocks to their prescience. John Paulson himself, for instance, experienced very poor returns in one of his funds in 2011, prompting some to question the persistence of the returns in the years that immediately followed.[23] Other macro managers—like Louis Bacon, who generated substantial returns in 1990 with a thesis that Saddam Hussein would attack Kuwait but that this would have minimal long-term effect on the market—found it difficult to maintain returns. Bacon announced in 2012 that he would be returning about one-quarter of his assets under management (or about $2 billion) because he found it too difficult to generate returns, given the magnitude of governmental intervention in the wake of the financial crisis. Some have cited this as a "victory of sorts for the technocrats" who were managing the governmental response to the financial catastrophe, and in many ways, these commentators are right.[24] This sheds light on another challenge of macro investing: the shifts that produce some of the most lucrative macro trades are typically quite extreme. Indeed, it is no surprise that managing a macro-oriented portfolio and having consistent success is no easy task: the identification of a *string* of exceptional shifts is what separates the one-hit wonders from the macro titans.

Relative value funds can encapsulate several different strategies. Some are engaged in what has been termed *pairs trading*, or the purchase of one security that has been deemed "cheap" on a relative basis and the sale of another that seems correspondingly "expensive." Relative value funds profit when the prices of the pair of securities readjust. Some funds use statistical arbitrage, often examining the behavior of the time series and making judgments as to relative value based on historical valuations. Others are more fundamentally oriented, believing that one well-positioned firm will outperform a competitor. The other common strategy employed by relative value funds is seeking value across the capital structure of a publicly traded firm. By way of example, a relative value fund may believe a publicly traded company will experience severe distress in the next six months. The fund may anticipate that the stock will be worthless when this distress comes, so it shorts the stock; but the fund may still believe that the senior debt is an attractive buy, as it may not be impaired because the firm's assets cover this tranche of debt. The fund would thus find relative value by being short the stock but long the senior debt.

Quant funds use quantitative factors in models to develop, buy, or sell signals for stocks, commodities, or currencies. These models have a wide spectrum of sophistication. Some of them are simple, trying to capitalize on well-studied sources of risk premium in the stock market like momentum, value, and small market capitalization. Others are more complicated, analyzing convergence-divergence patterns, steepness or flatness of yield curves or futures curves, or even sifting through press releases and conference calls for information on a stock that the market has neglected. The quant fund faces a few difficulties that the best groups are able to overcome. The first is to ensure that the models are not overfitted to historical patterns. In other words, if a strategy is designed or tweaked using historical price behavior, there is a temptation to retrofit a strategy that worked well in the past but may not be capturing the underlying dynamics that would cause it to be successful in the future. Second, no quant strategy, no matter how successful, will work in all market environments. There are many that work very well in certain market environments, but none that are foolproof all the time. The complication this creates is that if a given quant strategy is not working for some time, it is difficult to discern whether that strategy is failing to work because of short-term conditions in the market that may change or because there is actually a fundamental flaw in the model. It requires patience and resolve to ride out difficult market environments and await a market regime in which the strategy will prosper. Third, some, though not all, quant strategies deliver fairly small risk premia. Few quant strategies can deliver eye-popping returns on an unlevered basis. This means that many quant funds employ leverage to make returns more attractive. When prudent, this leverage can be perfectly acceptable, but it can also materially impair a fund if a strategy or set of strategies does poorly.

Given these myriad strategies (and many more not elucidated here), the natural question that follows is, which strategies are most successful? This is an enormously difficult question to answer, as one should really assess funds based on alpha and not simply returns. Furthermore, the best performers do change through time, since the market does not reward the same strategy all the time. That said, to provide some empirical insight on the matter of the more recent performance of these strategies, the aggregate risk and return figures from 1994 to 2011, assembled by KPMG and the Centre for Hedge Fund Research (table 8.1), show that relative value and event-driven funds have been the strongest performers on a risk-adjusted basis (as measured by their Sharpe ratios).[25]

By contrast, short bias funds have tended to have the least attractive risk-reward characteristics, returning just over 1 percent per year but

TABLE 8.1
Statistics for Hedge Fund Strategies

	EQUITY HEDGE	EMERGING MARKETS	EVENT DRIVEN	CTA AND MACRO	RELATIVE VALUE	MARKET NEUTRAL	SHORT BIAS
Annualized Mean	10.58	9.60	10.32	8.39	8.23	5.73	1.04
Annualized Std	9.49	14.25	6.97	6.69	4.35	3.30	18.96
Annualized Sharpe	0.74	0.42	0.97	0.72	1.06	0.65	−0.13

Source: Robert Mirsky, Anthony Cowell, and Andrew Baker, "The Value of the Hedge Fund Industry to Investors, Markets, and the Broader Economy," KPMG and the Centre for Hedge Fund Research, Imperial College, London, last modified April 2012, http://www.kpmg.com/KY/en /Documents/the-value-of-the-hedge-fund-industry-part-1.pdf, 11.

having the highest volatility of any of the categories listed. Much of this is due to the strong bull market of the 1990s and the run-up again in equities markets between the technology bubble and the global financial crisis. Timing shorts, as Jones himself found decades ago, is quite difficult. After all, if one's premise is that an asset is irrationally overvalued, it can be years before the market realizes its irrationality and trades the asset down accordingly. A short position may be sound, but it may be far ahead of its time, and one runs the risk of ever-increasing exuberance and the erosion of value by borrowing costs.

Characteristics of Strong Performers: Size and Age

Given this state of affairs in aggregate, another question is whether there are particular characteristics that are shared among the hedge funds that deliver persistent good returns. After all, an investor does not necessarily care if hedge funds, in aggregate, do not provide positive returns net of fees, as long as he or she is able to identify those that will.

One surprising finding, supported by a number of successful papers, is that smaller hedge funds tend to have better persistence of favorable performance than do larger funds. One study that has examined this has used the Lipper TASS database and looked at data from the late 1980s, including funds that continue to operate and those that have since closed. The study took pains to eliminate the backfilling of the database that can drive significant upward bias in aggregate returns. The finding is not that younger funds are explicitly better in terms of returns, but rather that of the funds that have a positive track record, the funds more likely to have those positive returns persist into subsequent years tend to be smaller. This finding does not seem to hold strongly for funds of funds.[26]

There are a number of causes that could explain this trend. The first and most apparent is that some small managers know a corner of the market so well that they are able to find inefficiencies easily, but that scaling up leaves them with more capital than they are able to successfully allocate. Second, it could be that some hedge fund managers are very good investors but are less successful at managerial tasks, so the organization itself is unable to scale appropriately. Further research is certainly needed to help determine why exactly small funds tend to have more consistent positive performance.

Funds of Hedge Funds

Funds of hedge funds—which hold a portfolio of hedge funds rather than investing directly in underlying securities—may have several notable advantages over individual hedge funds. The first and perhaps most pronounced is their ability to diversify across a range of hedge funds and strategies. In the absence of a fund of funds, achieving diversification can be elusive except for the exceptionally wealthy, since many of the best funds have fairly high investment minimums.[27]

Another important but less crucial factor is access to the most adept managers, which can come in two forms. One way is by identifying funds with good managers already in place, doing so through meeting with the managers periodically, determining if they are actually producing alpha by comparing returns relative to benchmarks, and conducting assessments not only of a fund's investment process but also of its business organization. This groundwork is crucial, since a hedge fund with material key man risk, difficulty in managing employees, or disagreements among partners over where the firm should be headed may see returns suffer in the long term. It is the job of the fund of funds to look at factors that could adversely affect their own investors but may not be completely obvious in quarterly letters or other investor communications. Second, some funds of funds have access to highly successful managers whose funds may be closed to further investment.[28] Sometimes, hedge funds close to new investment because managers have determined they would simply have too much capital for the given opportunities to exploit inefficiencies in the market. Although this decision may seem counterintuitive, it follows an often quite rational path. After all, while new inflows can increase the total earned on the asset management fee (the fixed fee on the total capital invested), they can also put the fund over its practical capacity, with returns suffering as a result. Funds of funds that have already invested in closed funds can provide additional slivers of exposure to otherwise inaccessible managers.

That said, the fund of funds structure is not without its disadvantages. For instance, at a certain scale, a fund of funds might be better off bringing certain strategies in-house by hiring managers directly and saving on fees. This would also grant the fund of funds the ability to scrutinize the trades directly and might support better control over liquidity and risk.[29] Indeed, there are some funds pursuing this

hybrid strategy, with internal capabilities as well as an external plat-
form to hire managers to invest in niche strategies that cannot be
executed successfully in-house. Some university endowments, such
as Harvard Management Company, pursue such a hybrid strategy,
keenly aware that there is logic to keeping much of its portfolio
in-house.

There is a second, more complex drawback of funds of funds—
one that, somewhat ironically, becomes worse the more diversified
the fund of funds becomes. In any given year, some strategies will be
successful and some will fail, but a diversified fund of funds must pay
performance fees on the strategies that are successful even if, in aggregate, the fund of funds does not have a positive return. Fortunately,
this problem with performance fees does decline the longer a fund of
funds is invested in its particular hedge funds, as funds must overcome
their high-water marks in order to charge the performance fee.

The third and perhaps most important disadvantage is the simple
fact that a fund of funds must clear two layers of fees: its own fees
and the fees charged by the hedge funds in which it is invested.[30]
This means that the value added by fund of funds managers must
be fairly significant for this to be a better enterprise than investing directly through underlying vehicles. Fortunately for funds of
funds, empirical research shows that these managers have indeed succeeded. One study draws data from a combination of two databases
(the TASS and the HFR) and performs an analysis of funds of funds
over an eight-year period. The study concludes that, in fact, funds of
funds do succeed, in aggregate, in adding value net of fees. Equally
interesting, however, is the performance attribution: the funds of
funds are successful because of sound strategic asset allocation rather
than tactical asset allocation. In fact, the study finds that on average,
the tactical asset allocation seems to add zero or negative value in
most years, though part of this may be due to the underlying managers' liquidity constraints (a fund of funds cannot reallocate funds
immediately, since the funds are often at the whim of redemption
windows).[31]

Illiquidity of the Vehicle

Hedge funds are less liquid than many other investment vehicles available in the market. Investors are often faced with initial investment

lock-ups (intervals of time during which they are unable to with-draw), and even after the lock-ups, investors subsequently face specific redemption windows during which they can elect to withdraw funds.

Taking advantage of the intrinsic illiquidity of the vehicle, some hedge fund managers position the portfolio to earn an illiquidity premium, or effectively, a return that is due to holding assets that cannot be rapidly sold without affecting the market price. In cases like these, unless it is clear to investors that the hedge fund is invest-ing in illiquid products and earning a return on illiquidity itself, it may appear that the managers are producing more alpha than they really are. Also, this illiquidity premium may be perfectly acceptable for funds that experience large net inflows of capital over time as new investors pour in, but it may devastate a fund that experiences a large flurry of redemptions and is forced to sell in high-illiquidity situations. This can be mitigated if funds have "side pocket" capa-bilities (that is, redemption requests involve transferring the inves-tor's share of the illiquid assets rather than selling and redeeming as cash) or gates the fund can use to slow down large redemptions at a distressed period. Indeed, one study has found that funds with a large net inflow of capital and with significant exposure to illiquid products outperform low-net-inflow funds by about 4.79 percent per year.[32]

This situation is seen more readily in funds that trade distressed credit, convertible debt, or other derivatives that have shallow markets or that hold private investments in addition to their public market activities. Long-short equity funds, by contrast, do not generally have this liquidity problem unless they deal with very low market capitaliza-tion or low-turnover stocks. So to some degree, the type of fund can shed light on how likely it is to benefit from the illiquidity premium. Whatever the case may be, investors must be aware of how changes in inflows could affect performance and how much of the performance could be due to the illiquidity of the market rather than the value-add of the manager.

Risks and Returns

One phenomenon that has been documented in the mutual fund literature but also likely holds for hedge funds is the increase in assumed risk during periods of underperformance. Researchers have found that many mutual funds that are underperforming within a year tend to take more risk before the reporting period is through, ostensibly in hopes of making up for the losses. One study with high statistical significance has looked at 334 growth mutual funds from 1976 to 1991 and found that volatility increases when performance is negative within a period.[33] It is not necessarily the case that these managers are being deliberately dishonest; they likely feel genuine responsibility to add value for investors. However, the way they go about it—by taking on more risk than usual—can prove even more injurious.

To be clear, one can only speculate that this is true for hedge funds, since we do not have the benefit of daily return data to actually measure volatility. But there are two good reasons to believe it might be the case. First, hedge funds often have the added benefit of not revealing the extent of the risks they took in the period, so their behavior is much more difficult to monitor. (With open-ended mutual funds, by contrast, one can simply take the standard deviation of the daily returns to calculate volatility and have a good proxy for risk.) Second, whereas the returns to a mutual fund benefit the mutual fund manager only indirectly (as higher returns often translate into higher net inflows and thus increase the asset management fee), the hedge fund manager earns a performance fee when returns are good. So hedge fund managers may have an even stronger temptation to make riskier moves toward the end of a bad period, given that this behavior will not be immediately apparent and that the payoff could be significant.

One final observation pertains to the difference between dollar-weighted and buy-and-hold returns. The returns one almost invariably sees from hedge funds are buy-and-hold returns, which operate on the assumption that the total dollars given by an investor to the fund does not change over time; that is, investors do not later decide to add more money to their position or, alternatively, withdraw existing investments. This can lead to the conclusion that hedge funds have generated more wealth than they actually have, given the reality that capital inflows tend to increase in the period after good returns because investors think the returns will persist into the future.[34] Likewise, funds often experience outflows after poor performance, so the dollar-weighted returns can be much lower than buy-and-hold returns if performance reverts to the mean.

Some studies have highlighted the fact that the harm to the hedge fund vehicle was likely far greater than it appeared in the global financial crisis, as capital deployed to hedge funds was at its maximum in 2007. As a consequence, the dollar-weighted losses were more significant than the buy-and-hold return metrics make them seem. Studies that attempt to measure how divergent buy-and-hold return measures are from dollar-weighted returns for hedge funds show that dollar-weighted returns tend to be 3 to 7 percent less than buy-and-hold returns per year (with the precise value naturally contingent upon the interval of time one chooses to analyze).[35]

Ultimately, the hedge fund is a much more complicated vehicle than is widely appreciated. This group encompasses a plethora of different strategies offering different risk and return characteristics. Although there are plenty of hedge funds that have performed terrifically, "tales" of truly phenomenal returns across the entire universe of hedge funds are precisely that: elusive fictions that are the result of generalizing the performance of a small class of stellar investors.

PRIVATE EQUITY, VENTURE CAPITAL, AND OTHER ALTERNATIVE INVESTMENTS

Next, we turn to the fields of private equity, venture capital, and other alternative investments. Just as larger institutions, investment banks, and wealth management divisions within private banking bodies primarily drove the world of investment management before the mid-twentieth century, the twenty-first century has been dominated by a wide range of alternative investment possibilities for both institutional and, to a lesser degree, individual investors.

Private Equity

Private equity, in the traditional sense, involves either purchasing or creating private companies with the goal of eventually selling to a strategic buyer, selling to another private equity firm, or listing the firm on public markets. A relatively new industry, it came to its current state only after a rollercoaster ride in the late twentieth century.

Central to the development of the early private equity market in the United States was a small firm founded by Georges Doriot (a professor at the Harvard Business School), Ralph Flanders (an industrialist and later a senator), Karl Compton (a president of MIT), Merrill Griswold (head of the Massachusetts Investments Trust), and Donald David (a dean of Harvard Business School). Established in Boston in 1946, it was called the American Research and Development Corporation, or ARD. In the wake of World War II and in an economy that had recently experienced a large upward shock in labor supply when millions of veterans returned from the war, ARD focused on both providing capital and enhancing the managerial skills of businesses.[36]

The corporation primarily sought institutional capital rather than capital from retail investors and as such was relatively unique in the asset management industry for at least a decade. It was successful in investing in a wide array of companies before ultimately merging with Textron in 1972. However, it was in the 1970s, when the first major shift in government regulations and investor perceptions of private equity funds occurred, that the industry really took off.

The regulatory change was prompted by the government's realization that there was a dearth of capital in private equity. So the Small Business Administration reexamined existing regulatory provisions and decided to try to reinvigorate private equity and venture capital deals by restructuring certain securities laws and rewriting the Employee Retirement Income Security Act. Between 1970 and 1980, and especially in the year 1980 alone, regulatory constraints were widely removed. For instance, the Department of Labor changed a provision that previously necessitated many private equity managers to be registered investment advisers. Further, in 1980 some private equity companies were recategorized as business development companies and thus were no longer required to comply with the Investment Advisers Act. This act had effectively limited private equity partnerships to fourteen partners; the rule change allowed private equity partnerships to grow without bound.[37]

With these key barriers to private equity market entry removed, the industry exploded. It happened almost immediately, with total commitments to private equity over the three-year period from 1980 to 1982 well over twice the total commitments throughout the decade before.[38] However, this seemingly unstoppable increase in the amount of private equity investment was not without considerable volatility. One reason for this was the surge in leveraged buyouts. Leveraged buyouts are a prime example of using leverage to improve returns on investment and typically involve taking a public company private. They are also characterized by a reliance on high amounts of leverage placed on the balance sheet of the firm being acquired. After deals are closed, private equity operating managers take over control of the portfolio companies and do not have to concern themselves with public company reporting requirements. The private equity firm can institute organizational changes, including strategic reorientations, personnel changes, and mergers with or acquisitions of other firms with the goal of achieving a future exit at a multiple of the original capital invested. The idea of the leveraged buyout was arguably thought of much earlier, by J. P. Morgan & Co. in 1901 when Morgan bought the Carnegie Steel Corporation for $480 million. The Glass-Steagall Act of 1933 virtually regulated away merchant banks like Morgan's by not allowing depository banks to act as investment banks.[39]

One of the first private equity firms of the post–World War II era was Kohlberg Kravis Roberts, or KKR, founded in 1978 by partners who left New York investment bank Bear Stearns. In 1988, KKR won the bid for the largest leveraged buyout in investment history to that point—that of RJR Nabisco for $25 billion, a storied investment transaction famously chronicled in the book *Barbarians at the Gate* and the film of the same name.[40] These firms of the 1980s were the first in the private equity world to use modern techniques of leverage, high-yield bonds, dividend recapitalizations, and new capital structures that have become so prevalent in the private equity world today. The inventiveness of the partners of the first movers in this industry allowed them to reach new levels of success and rewards.

However, while the significant use of borrowing is a vital component of the high return historically achieved by many private equity funds, it can also lead to serious shortfalls in outcomes when operations or the economic environment fail to unfold as expected. Indeed, from 1982 to 1993, the huge increase in high-yield and low-quality debt offerings led to substantial problems in the private equity industry.

The effect, though, was cyclical, and as the early-1990s recession led to undervaluation in the public equity markets, institutional private equity firms gained prominence and the industry was once again on an upswing—until, at the turn of the century, the technology bubble burst. This was followed by yet another upswing that culminated in, and contributed to, the 2008 financial crisis. Because many leveraged buyout private equity firms have performance that is intimately tied to public equities markets—after all, many of the exits are to the public markets through initial public offerings—it is not surprising that there is cyclicality in commitments and activity as the stock market experiences peaks and troughs of its own.

Since the 1980 boom in industry assets under management, the returns from the major private equity firms' funds have been considerable. That experienced fund managers could achieve consistent double-digit returns attracted investors and scholars alike. Some industry proponents continue to predict that with proper operational management and investment discipline, the successful major private equity fund managers may be able to achieve annual rates of return above 20 percent in the decades to come. However, some critics caution against being as bullish on private equity as an industry. Many believe instead that there is enough new competition in the realm of buyout private equity that the days of firms earning substantial premiums over the market may be largely over. What was once an exclusive and off-the-run asset class has seen much broader participation, and with it, the possibility of lower future expected returns in aggregate.

Venture Capital

Venture capital is really a subset of private equity, and the early history of venture capital goes hand in hand with the history of private equity. Venture capital tends to deal with high-risk, growth-oriented firms, often those in the various tech industries: information technology, biotechnology, energy technology, and computer technology. These venture investments frequently involve allocating capital to technologies that have yet to be proven or for products without an existing or well-defined market. Other industries, too, have historically been recipients of important venture funding. Starbucks and Federal Express, for instance, were capitalized early on by venture investors. Their success, while astounding and impressive today, was far from certain when the firms were in their infancy.

But it really was the technological revolutions in the twentieth century—opening the way for the development of powerful advances in computational power, medicine and health care delivery, data processing and analysis, and electronics, among other sectors—that spurred this new kind of investment as venture capitalists jumped at the opportunity to monetize many of these nascent industries.

It took several decades after the creation of the Small Business Act of 1958 for venture capital to really take off. Difficult conditions in equities markets, combined with a more complicated and expensive listing process, produced a barrier to initial public offerings, frequently the ultimate exit of a venture deal.[41] The National Venture Capital Association (NVCA) was founded as an industry association in 1973, and over the next several decades the dollar amounts flowing into venture capital as an alternative investment class ballooned significantly (see figure 8.1 and table 8.2). The industry is now seen as a leading alternative investment class for institutional and high-net-worth investors looking for ways to diversify their portfolios.

Venture capital is intimately tied to Silicon Valley in the San Francisco Bay area. This area—blessed with a confluence of some of the world's top research universities and technology companies—was a natural place for the venture capital industry to emerge and grow, given the initial near-synonymy of venture capital firms with

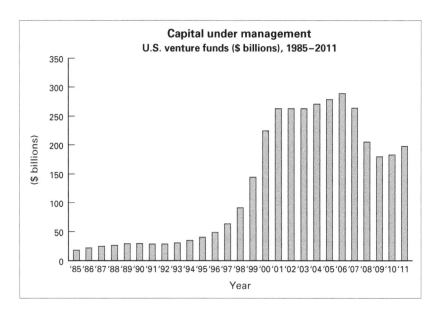

Figure 8.1 Capital Under Management U.S. Venture Funds (Billions), 1985–2011

Source: "2012 National Venture Capital Association Yearbook," National Venture Capital Association and Thomson Reuters, last modified 2012, http://www.finansedlainnowacji.pl/wp-content /uploads/2012/08/NVCA-Yearbook-2012.pdf, 10.

TABLE 8.2
Venture Capital Firms

	1991	2001	2011
No. of VC Firms in Existence	362	917	842
No. of VC Funds in Existence	640	1,850	1,274
No. of Professionals	3,475	8,620	6,125
No. of First Time VC Funds Raised	4	45	45
No. of VC Funds Raising Money This Year	40	325	173
VC Capital Raised this Year ($B)	1.9	39.0	18.7
VC Capital Under Management ($B)	26.8	261.7	196.9
Avg VC Capital Under Mgt per Firm ($M)	74.0	285.4	233.8
Avg VC Fund Size to Date ($M)	37.4	95.4	110.6
Avg VC Fund Raised this Year ($M)	47.5	120.0	108.1
Largest VC Fund Raised to Date ($M)	1,775.0	6,300.0	6,300.0

Source: "2012 National Venture Capital Association Yearbook," National Venture Capital Association and Thomson Reuters, last modified 2012, http://www.finansedlainnowacji.pl/wp-content/uploads/2012/08/NVCA-Yearbook-2012.pdf, 9.

technology. The first Silicon Valley initial public offerings were of Varian in 1956, HP in 1957, and Ampex in 1958. Sand Hill Road, in Menlo Park, California, became the hub for venture capital institutions, with today's quite recognizable firms (Sequoia Capital and Kleiner Perkins Caufield & Byers) coming to life in 1972. Furthermore, California has almost four times more venture capital–backed companies than any other state, with a focus in all sectors, but especially consumer Internet.[42]

Compared to venture capital investment in the United States, the amount of venture capital funds invested in other areas of the world does not reach the same level. For instance, Chinese venture investors in 2011 raised $16.8 billion, whereas US venture investment stood at $28.7 billion in 2011.[43] Furthermore, there are far more venture capital firms in the United States than anywhere else, with 770 as of 2014 compared to 50 in Canada, 75 in the United Kingdom, and 87 in China.[44]

From the venture capitalist's perspective, the economic alignment of the firm and its institutional investors with the entrepreneurs who are taking financing from venture capital firms is important. Such firms will often take seats on the boards of directors of the start-up companies they finance in order to play a key role in the guidance and development of the companies, to protect their investors' capital, ensure its best utilization, and be in a position to maximize return on investment. The investors in large venture capital firms are primarily institutional, though in recent years more and more funds are opening up for investment by high-net-worth individuals.[45] Like private equity, venture capital is a relatively illiquid asset class. Many firms have limited tangible value, and the ability to actually monetize on a venture capital investment depends, in large part, on successful growth of the firm.

Overall, venture capital is a significant subset of private equity investment in the United States and is a primary component of the alternative investment sector. The lucrative returns on the stellar growth companies that eventually have successful exits through acquisition by larger, more established firms or to the public through initial public offerings are what continue to attract investors to the industry. However, in recent years, critics and industry experts worry that declining returns, uncertainty regarding the existence of another technology asset bubble, and speculation regarding the level of market saturation in consumer Internet companies may all cause capital outflows in coming decades. Only time will tell.

Real Estate

Real estate products are a crucial part of the alternative investment landscape. Key among real estate products are real estate investment trusts, or REITs. These trusts were effectively created in 1960, when President Dwight D. Eisenhower signed the Cigar Excise Tax Extension bill that was sent to him by the US Congress. Originally, they were created to make a liquid and tradable form of real estate that could be accessed by not only large institutional investors but also retail investors with fewer resources. Much like today's REITs, the original trusts would accumulate capital from many sources, including debt from institutions and banks as well as equity sales, and then act as lenders to construction companies and real estate developers. Real estate investment trusts are quite versatile within the sector, being able to encompass commercial and residential categories as well as timberland, health care, real estate, and other buckets. In 2003, there were 170 REITs (134 of which traded on the New York Stock Exchange) valued at a combined $310 billion.[46]

Although liquid real estate vehicles, such as REITs, are extremely popular among investors, there are clear preferences among types of products. In one industry survey, some 68 percent of advisers responding said they had invested in such vehicles, but only 33 percent of them used nontraded REITs in their clients' portfolios.[47] This shows that liquidity preference, transparency, accountability, and ability to hold to a strict regulatory standard while still being able to achieve high risk-adjusted returns are important characteristics for investors in their alternative investment patterns.

In many ways, though, REITs and their publicly traded shares are not much different than more traditional public companies—they just happen to be in the business of financing real estate and have a different wrapper and management structure around the assets. They do have some favorable tax advantages, including avoiding taxation at the trust level if more than 90 percent of the income is distributed to unitholders. Compared to other classes of traditional and even alternative investments, real estate products and REITs are characterized as having relatively high yields, hence their inclusion in many alternative investors' portfolios.

Other Alternative Investments

Before completing the discussion of alternative investments, it is worth discussing a few other major categories, including commodities and natural resources, timber, agriculture and farmland, infrastructure, and currency.

COMMODITIES AND NATURAL RESOURCES

Investment in commodities and natural resources grew significantly in the twentieth century. One of the earliest commodities indices, the *Economist*'s Commodity–Price Index, was first published in 1864 and has continued publication for over 150 years now. This index, however, was among the first generation of commodities indices and was not investable, as it tracked spot prices for commodities and not real market bid-ask matches. Actual investable commodities indices are far more recent, coming into existence in 1991 with the Goldman Sachs

Commodity Index (S&P GSCI) and later in 1998 with the Dow Jones UBS Commodity Index.[48]

Commodities and natural resources investments include both traditional futures and collateralized commodity futures, as well as direct holdings of physical assets such as gold and other natural resources. Mineral rights and the licensing of revenue streams are also examples of real-world commodities and natural resources investments in the alternatives space. Commodity investments are an attractive way to diversify portfolios because they often have high returns and low correlations to equities and other liquid investable assets.[49]

TIMBER, AGRICULTURE, AND FARMLAND

The Employee Retirement Income Security Act of 1974 was a major catalyst for investment in timberland, since pension funds now had the ability to move into new and more esoteric asset classes.[50] Since the mid-1980s, institutional assets invested in timber have grown dramatically, from $1 billion to more than $50 billion.[51]

Asset returns were strong through the 1980s to the 1990s, resting in part on Japanese demand and pricing. Returns were helped again by the national forests reducing their output. These reductions in output were driven in large part by legal challenges around environmental concerns, including the destruction of the habitat of the endangered spotted owl. Institutions increasingly became owners of timber, purchasing from operators and owners in the foresting industry.[52]

Farmland (the land itself) and agriculture (the productive activity conducted on that land, such as the planting and harvesting of crops and grazing of livestock) are in much the same category. With most of the capital asset value deriving, likewise, from the real estate involved in these sectors, the history of alternative investment in agriculture and farmland is closely tied to the history of alternative investment in real estate, as discussed previously.

INFRASTRUCTURE, FIXED INCOME, AND OTHER ALTERNATIVES

Investments in infrastructure projects, around the United States and the world, are a small piece of the alternative investment asset class. These can take the form of investments by retail and institutional investors in listed infrastructure equities, which may be publicly traded, master limited partnerships, and open-ended funds.[53]

These infrastructure projects are often directed by local, state, or even the federal government. Consequently, one way in which infrastructure projects might find their way into an investor's portfolio as an alternative asset class investment is through government-issued fixed income securities such as sovereign debt or municipal bond offerings.

Global fixed income securities and products in general, including structured debt products, mezzanine debt products, and distressed debt products, are another type of alternative investment. Many large financial services firms in the United States have a department or group that deals with creating such structured financial products and marketing them to clients, institutions and high-net-worth individuals.

In addition to all of these other alternative investments, both professional investors and retail investors also invest a notable amount into more speculative assets such as art, stamps, coins, and wine. However, given the difficulty in quantifying the extent of such investment, the private market nature of trading in such assets, and the difficulty in drawing the line between investing to achieve superior returns rather than simply collecting "treasures" as a hobby, these alternative investments are not the focus of this section. Moreover, it is abundantly clear that listed and unlisted real assets, currency, and debt products make up the vast majority of investment in alternatives.

FINAL WORD ON ALTERNATIVES

The decades leading to the turn of the twenty-first century were instrumental in the evolution of the global capital markets, with many alternative investments—private equity, venture capital, REITs, commodities, and infrastructure—entering the arena. In some respects, the growth and proliferation of alternatives occurred because of the democratization of investment. The increases in wealth for middle-class people and the resultant institutional framework that grew to serve them (namely, pension funds, university endowments, and other forms of educational, charitable, and retirement savings) created a demand for management services for these pools of capital. As explored in the next chapter, the compensation earned for such management was far from egalitarian, as some management activities take a significant share of the economics. The next section turns to investment vehicles that are even more obvious manifestations of the trend of democratization.

INDEX FUNDS AND
EXCHANGE-TRADED FUNDS

We now consider radically different types of investment vehicles: the index fund and the ETF. Rather than being actively managed, with an investment professional making security selections through time, index funds and ETFs are passive and track a set of securities based on rules, such as sectors and market capitalization (the notable exception to this are the new active ETFs introduced after 2008, to be discussed later). This strategy allows the funds to charge fees much lower than those for actively managed funds. In recent years, ETFs and index funds have offered a major challenge to traditional mutual funds and to alternative investments as well and have a significant market presence. As of the end of 2012, there was a total of $1.3 trillion in index mutual funds and another $1.3 trillion in ETFs.[54] This section looks at both vehicles in greater depth and places them in the greater context of the investment management industry as a whole.

Index Funds

Until the 1970s, personal purchases of baskets of individual securities or separate investment in mutual funds were the primary methods of investing in the broader equity markets. All that started to change on August 31, 1976, when Vanguard and its founder, Jack Bogle, introduced the First Index Investment Trust. The central premise was that simply buying and holding the broad stock market (in their case, the S&P 500) could provide better results than trying to beat it by picking stocks. At the time, the idea was quite controversial and was derided by the general investing establishment for striving to be no more than simply "average."[55] The fund was slow to catch on, raising only $11 million in the early 1970s—far short of the $150 million Vanguard thought it needed to cover the transaction costs associated with owning five hundred stocks in a single fund. Later in the decade, however, it began to see meaningful asset growth. In March 1980, Vanguard changed the name of the First Index Investment Trust to the Vanguard Index Trust, and the index fund growth trend was on.[56]

Vanguard was not the only player. In 1984, Wells Fargo launched the second index mutual fund, the Stagecoach Corporate Stock Fund.

The fund had limited success—which, according to Bogle, was due to the fund's high fees. The very purpose of passive management through index funds, he contended, was to allow the investor to have inexpensive exposure to an asset class and to forego the high fees associated with active management And indeed, other early index funds with exceptionally high fees did not enjoy sustained success. Colonial Index Trust, for instance, generally involved a sales load of 4.75 percent and a running expense ratio of 1.5 percent. This fund lasted only 7 years, closing in 1993.[57]

It was not until the early 1990s that Vanguard started to see any meaningful competition. Vanguard had eleven different index funds by the end of 1992. That same year, thirty-five new index funds were formed by competitors, bringing the total number of index mutual funds in the investment market to just under eighty. The universe of product offerings also expanded. In 1993, Vanguard and some of its competitors offered the first bond index funds. With these, investors could get exposure to a wider array of investments than just equities. The bull market of the 1990s spurred continued growth in the industry, and many of the US equity index funds dramatically outperformed actively managed accounts during this time. Over the period from 1994 to 1996, some 91 percent of managed funds underperformed their index fund counterparts within US equities—a victory for the vehicle that was once derided as a recipe for mediocrity.[58]

Today there exist nearly 300 distinct stock and bond index mutual funds in the United States and over 1,000 American passive ETFs, and the world of investment has come a very long way toward not only accepting index funds as a fixture of investing but also fully embracing the power of indexing as one component of a strategy to outperform the market in terms of risk-adjusted return.[59] The first index funds were meant for passive investors who simply wanted a small piece of the larger pie of the equity markets. Modern index funds, however, cater not only to passive investors who are looking for a broadly diversified portfolio of securities but also to active investors who want to enhance their portfolio returns by investing in particular asset classes through indexing. For instance, there are index funds that specialize in timberland investment, leveraged index funds that attempt to double or triple the return of a common stock index such as the S&P 500 on a daily basis, and index funds that specialize in commodities. With the widespread proliferation of index funds through all potential asset classes and market segments, and as the industry becomes more and more aggressive in marketing in order to remain competitive, investors must apply ever greater standards of scrutiny to their investments.

Exchange-Traded Funds

Closely related to index funds, ETFs first became available to investors in 1993. At the fundamental level, an ETF is a publicly traded investment company that can be bought and sold through brokerage accounts. These funds have a sponsor (often a large financial institution or bank) responsible for ensuring the ETF tracks the appropriate index. This is done either by full tracking—having exposure to all of the securities in the relevant index—or by representative sampling, where a subset of all of the names is owned in a manner that closely, but imperfectly, tracks the index. The benefit of the latter approach is lower transaction costs, but it comes at the expense of the possibility of additional tracking error.[60]

The differences between ETFs and index funds are subtle. First, ETFs can be bought and sold throughout the trading day, whereas index funds are purchased or redeemed once per day. Second, index funds are intended to trade at the net asset value of the portfolio's underlying holdings, whereas ETFs can actually trade at a discount or premium to net asset value. Many ETFs do have mechanisms to prevent very large deviations in price from net asset value, but there is no structural reason that they have to trade at net asset value (as is the case for index funds). Index funds also reinvest dividends immediately whereas ETFs capture cash for distribution at a regular interval (often quarterly). There tend to be some tax advantages for ETFs over index funds because of how the shares trade and are redeemed, but the need to pay the broker and the bid-ask spread tends to result in higher transaction costs for ETFs. Although the differences between the two vehicles are nuanced, they are significant enough that when ETFs were first introduced, they had to receive exemptive relief from the SEC because the structure itself would not pass the provisions of the Investment Company Act of 1940.

The allowable mandates of ETFs broadened after 2008. Before 2008, ETFs were oriented around rules-based passive index tracking, but in 2008 actively managed ETFs emerged. Here, the role of the sponsor is a bit different. Instead of being charged with just tracking an index, the sponsor is responsible for active security selection. This process is complicated by a requirement that ETF managers provide a daily update of the securities the fund owns. As such, if an ETF is attempting to build a sizable position in a particular company, it runs the risk of other market participants front running it. Given how new this vehicle is, the jury is still out on what influence the introduction of actively managed ETFs will have on the industry.[61]

Exchange-traded funds, as an asset class, immediately caught on. Even with the collapse of the technology bubble and the dramatic fall in equity indices around the globe, assets in ETFs remained steady, and this growth accelerated tremendously at the turn of the millennium (see figure 8.2).

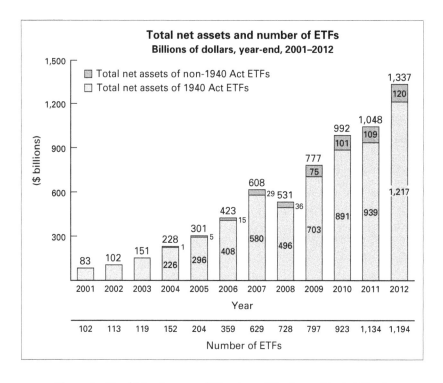

Figure 8.2 Total Net Assets and Number of Exchange-Traded Funds

Source: "2013 Investment Company Fact Book: A Review of Trends and Activities in the U.S. Investment Company Industry," Investment Company Institute, accessed 2014, http://www.ici.org/pdf/2013_factbook.pdf, 47.

Among the ETFs created during this decade were commodity ETFs. The first commodity ETFs were introduced in 2004, and they grew from $1 billion that year to nearly $120 billion by the end of 2012 on the back of both strong precious metals demand and performance.[62]

Index funds and ETFs have substantially changed the world of investment management. Their rise and near ubiquity across all asset classes are testaments to the diversification and liquidity benefits provided by these investment vehicles. From being called a recipe for mediocrity to being fully embraced by both retail and institutional investors, index funds and ETFs have both become major challengers to traditional mutual funds. These investment vehicles have primarily targeted passive investors, but the explosion in ETFs has been accompanied by an increase in the complexity and intricacies of ETF design, which has begun to appeal to active investment managers as well. In many respects, the index fund and ETF embody democratization, permitting even small investors to participate with ease in a source of diversified investment gain. The individual investor can put his or her money to work with this wide menu of options bearing relatively low fees.

The future of the index fund and the ETF will undoubtedly be marked by more product innovation to allow investors access to more esoteric and less traveled corners of the market. This development is already underway with distressed debt and merger arbitrage, for example. The rivalry between passive and active vehicles will continue as investors become ever more thoughtful about how to benchmark active return using alpha analyses.

CONCLUSION

The future of the alternatives asset class is an open question. There are two crucial factors that will affect the trajectory of alternatives. The first is regulatory. Governments and securities regulators will undoubtedly pay closer attention and give greater scrutiny to alternative asset classes in order to protect investors and consumers of such products, particularly in the wake of recent examples of fraud and other forms of malfeasance. However, if history is any indicator, it will take time for appropriate regulation that finds the balance between allowing for the benefits of a market to emerge without unfairly shutting down entire market segments. Experts who were surveyed regarding the challenges facing the alternative investment industry over the next three years cited transparency, regulation, investment performance, and operational risks as four of the major obstacles to growth.[63]

The second factor is performance related. There will be increased pressure on alternative managers to identify an appropriate benchmark and outperform it, net of fees, as institutional investors become increasingly focused on whether alternatives are genuinely providing greater risk-adjusted returns than investable indices.

Indeed, all active management, conventional and alternative, is being challenged by index funds and ETFs. The persistent claim of lower cost and competitive performance is creating a higher barrier for active and innovative managers to clear, not only with the investing public but with institutions and high-net-worth individuals as well.

Whatever the case, it is clear that the next few decades will bring a great deal of change: the reaction of the financial industry to the institutionalization of private equity, venture capital, and other alternative investments will carry significant implications as novelty gives way to widespread familiarity and greater liquidity.

CHAPTER NINE

Innovation Creates a New Elite

CREATIVITY IS CENTRAL to the investment process, whether it is structuring a unique deal with a borrower, hunting for the elusive diamond-in-the-rough investment, or cleverly determining the optimal capital structure of a business. It is little surprise, then, that the creative process practiced by successful investors was eventually turned not just to the sourcing and creation of investments themselves, but to the very *business* of investment management.

For most of the twentieth century, larger institutions and wealth management divisions within commercial banking bodies and investment banks primarily drove the world of investment management. Managing investments tended to be a large-scale corporate endeavor, involving the coordination of many individuals across a firm. While these corporate employees were reasonably well compensated, the days of astronomical compensation had not yet dawned. But during the 1970s, investment advisers and money managers began to leave larger institutions in order to strike out on their own. This move toward independence was coupled with an entrepreneurial spirit, and these two forces created the conditions for an era of financial innovation.

As these investment managers became equity owners of their own firms, the industry itself became larger and, in many cases, more lucrative for those who built these new investment management enterprises. These new independent firms attracted a great number of clients, often at significantly higher fees than were prevalent in the past. Within several decades, there was a profound shift in the economics and organization of investment management, which in turn would have a dramatic impact on the future of the industry. This trend toward a greater emphasis on the creation of wealth and true value in investment management expanded the innovative and entrepreneurial possibilities for individual managers.

Despite this sea change, these innovations are in many respects a byproduct of the democratization of investment, for many of the clients for alternative products are larger institutional clients like insurance companies and pension plans, whose assets come from a much wider percentage of the population. However, the investment of these democratized assets in new products and independent firms has also resulted in the creation of vast wealth for a "new elite" in the investment management industry.

INDEPENDENCE AND ENTREPRENEURSHIP: ENVIRONMENT, MOTIVES, AND BEHAVIORS

Economic leaders have long recognized the benefits of enterprise and independent action in producing superior outcomes and returns. Even the early history of agriculture in ancient Mesopotamia reveals the emergence of private farmers contracting with state-owned agricultural entities in order to improve their efficiency. In order to promote the growth and profitability of their operations, the merchant bankers of the Italian city-states, including prominently the Medici, created decentralized organizations and hired nonfamily partners who had wide autonomy. This decentralized management strategy is also followed by many successful modern industrial managers.

Investment management is not very different and has proven to be a fertile field for independence and innovation, attracting many entrepreneurial individuals. In fact, most of the newer styles of investment management developed in the last one hundred years have been created by new independent firms, which often launch entirely new vehicles in order to attract clients with the expectation of superior returns. The 1970s saw the advent of a new entrepreneurial trend in investment management, which was in part due to the rise in large institutional and wealth management accounts, client receptivity to higher fee rates, and growing asset flows. Investment managers left banks, insurance companies, and larger, more established mutual funds, becoming equity owners of their own firms following these emergent trends of independence, especially with respect to managerial incentives and decision-making processes.

At first, independent investment managers primarily dealt with long-only equity strategies for investing. Their management fees, a simple percentage of the total balance of assets they were managing, were arranged with no expectations of large performance incentives or stakes in client profits. Clients, too, had only modest expectations. However, once a critical mass of managers broke away from their firms, the industry began to shift toward creating inherent *value* in money management for the first time. They began to think as entrepreneurs, focusing on performance and revenue maximization, investment philosophy, style, products, and marketing. The development of innovative investment methodologies, best practices, and personnel management strategies also characterized this trend toward independence. Investment managers, long trained in the craft of assessing the prospects of other firms, became businesspeople themselves.

The Employee Retirement Income Security Act of 1974 was a key piece of legislation that helped pave the way for independence in investment management. It was passed by Congress in order to set minimum standards for private pension plans.[1] Its primary effects on the broader investment management industry were twofold. First, it provided investment managers with freedom to creatively fulfill their fiduciary duty to investors while acting responsibly within the confines of the law. This facilitated innovation by allowing independent managers to invest for higher risk-adjusted returns through a variety of means, most of which still fell under the definitions set forth by the government. Second, by establishing industry-wide standards for the new investment management firms to which it gave rise, ERISA encouraged many more managers to break away from larger institutions and pursue their own endeavors in the investing world. Coupled with the very low seed capital requirements of new investment management firms, ERISA created the conditions under which independent firms could flourish.

This synergy between independence, entrepreneurship, and innovation was highly valued by these newly independent managers for a number of reasons. First, they were able to manage money without being restricted by large institutional protocols and bureaucracy. They had the freedom to perform superior work in terms of making investment decisions and evaluating potential investments. Second, these managers gave priority to their client relationships, or at least they believed that as an independent firm, they could do a better job at this than the large institutions. Managers who broke away often felt that their unilateral focus on clients' results would prove useful in their independent endeavors, because many Wall Street firms seemed focused too much on firm results rather than on maximizing value for their clients, and this became a fundamental concern for these managers when the two objectives were not properly aligned.[2]

Clients have often agreed with this insight; many have felt that there are advantages to working with independent investment managers, including the incentives to maximize client gains. As history shows, busy individuals with investable capital have frequently hired money managers who have expertise in investment decision making. While the decision to hire a person to manage one's capital and investments is largely driven by the demands of time and skill, this motive does not explain why independent money managers would be preferred by the client over traditional institutional managers. However, the new independent firms were indeed promising superior returns and offering innovative investment products, which lured significant numbers of clients away from traditional institutions. A prominent investment adviser once declared that there are two ways a portfolio manager can outperform his or her peers, aside from sheer luck. The first of these is possession of or access to information superior to that which others have; the second is superior capacity to synthesize and draw conclusions from the information that is available to all investors.[3] In becoming independent, managers of their own firms strove to maximize returns for their investors, predicated upon the belief that they possessed such exceptional abilities (though at least a portion of the first kind of superior ability has been regulated away by securities regulators around the world with rules and enforcement related to material nonpublic information).

There was no stigma attached to the idea of breaking away from a traditional corporate financial services institution to begin work in an independent investment management firm. Rather, this move was encouraged by the growing culture of entrepreneurship and the allure of greater rewards—both financial and personal—through the means of creating value and wealth in a superior fashion for clients. This entrepreneurial streak continued in the investment management industry, and further innovative trends emerged with the advent of private equity, hedge funds, and other alternative investment managers.

As this independence trend took hold, various money management veterans at large institutions saw the competitive forces they were facing. Many who stayed with larger institutions echoed the independence rationale, advocating for the "relative charms" of leading a separate unit within an enduring, time-tested institution, with its involvement in many markets and a broader mandate than that of any independent management firm. Specifically, one Morgan Stanley investment management executive cited his ability to manage a top-notch investment management unit as part of a larger financial institution with a global brand as a reason for the supposed superiority of institutional money management over independent management. However, as the same executive conceded, the number of managers who have been very successful inside large institutions has been rather small in recent years.[4] The forces moving toward independence were too strong for the traditional money management industry to monopolize the new industry paradigm.

Of course, the lack of scale made breaking away more difficult, and asset management firms have a powerful ability to scale on the business side (though not on the investment side, where significant scale can make it more difficult to find pockets of great value). In particular, the back office (compliance, personnel, legal staff, and marketing) tends to scale quite well in asset management. The high scalability of the business means that costs of managing a fund as a percentage of assets under management tend to decline as the asset base grows.[5] This scalability made it more difficult for independent asset managers to instantly compete with their already scaled competitors within large institutions, but it also meant that running such independent firms would become less costly with new growth. Fortunately, for some newly independent firms, this scalability was reached rapidly because many clients of independent firms were actually larger institutional clients.

The creative impulse and the desire to move beyond the rigid bureaucracies of larger financial firms may explain why investment managers were eager to offer their services independently, but these factors do not account for why the trend toward independence began in the 1970s. For that, one needs to understand the sources of demand for these investment management services. This growth occurred largely because of demand driven by ever-greater savings for retirement, a subject covered at length in chapter 3. In 1974, retirement assets totaled about $370 billion, equivalent to more than $1.75 trillion in today's dollars.[6] As of the middle of 2014, total retirement assets numbered $24 trillion. Furthermore, IRAs as introduced by ERISA, which have $7.2 trillion in assets, were entirely new in 1974. Defined contribution plans, too, have grown materially in the past forty years as employers have tended to shift away from defined benefit plans, and this pool totaled $6.6 trillion in mid-2014.[7]

Increasingly since the 1970s, substantial new assets needed to be invested, and doing so typically involved a professional asset manager. In 1980, only 3 percent of American household financial assets was held by investment companies. By 1995, this number was greater than 10 percent, and in 2011, almost a full quarter of household financial assets was managed by investment companies, with retirement assets composing a large portion of the total. Mutual funds in household retirement accounts slowly escalated from 13 percent of retirement assets in 1991 to 55 percent of retirement assets by 2011 for defined contribution retirement plans, and 24 percent of retirement assets in 1991 to 45 percent of retirement assets by 2011 for IRAs.[8]

These new pools of retirement assets created increasing demand for investment management services, driving the revenues of the entire industry to new heights. It is difficult to overstate just how much growth the investment management industry has seen over this time frame. To consider just mutual funds, for example, the assets under management in equity mutual funds grew 135-fold from 1980 to 2010. The average annual expense ratio for a mutual fund grew by a total of 4.8 percent, so the resulting revenue to the equity mutual fund industry grew by over 141 times, representing a compounded annual growth rate of 17.9 percent.[9] Indeed, in just a single generation, mutual funds investing in equities experienced a rate of growth hard to fathom outside of high-tech segments of the economy. At the beginning of the independence trend, these growth rates were impossible to imagine. However, the rates make sense when one accounts for the fortuitous combination of independence and entrepreneurship with the growth of investment assets as a result of the democratization of investment.

THE RISE OF INNOVATION
AND ALTERNATIVES

Managers who succeeded in this new entrepreneurial era now included many who invented and exploited new investment approaches, techniques, and products that offered advantages in terms of performance, often at higher fees. The very first clients of hedge funds and private equity firms were those who had significantly more risk-tolerant profiles for their capital. This was understandable, as at the time there were often short, incomplete, or even nonexistent track records of performance for hedge funds or private equity firms. In fact, the justification for investing capital with such firms was largely theoretical.

After a few years, however, the "alternatives" and the innovative investment strategies employed by these new independent money managers started to demonstrate a marked ability to achieve improved risk-adjusted return in some scenarios. One of the very first institutional movers into this segment of alternative investments was the Yale University endowment, headed by David Swensen beginning in 1985. Yale began investing in alternatives shortly into Swensen's tenure in 1986. With Swensen at the helm, the Yale endowment jumped in value, overtaking that of Princeton and the University of Texas to be second in size only to Harvard University's. Average annual returns outperformed both the stock market and the average college endowment. Much of this success was driven by increased exposure and capital allocation to private equity, timberland, real estate, and hedge funds.[10]

State governments, such as that of Oregon, were also early adopters of alternatives. Entities created at the state level, such as the Oregon Investment Council, were mandated with investing all government funds, including those in public employee retirement funds and accident insurance funds, for instance.[11] All in all, it is clear that early conversion to alternative investments served the first movers well. Independent and alternative investment managers were to have a bright few decades, and those who got in on the ground level—as with many other innovations—reaped the profits accordingly. Clearly, these first movers were motivated by the prospect of improved risk-adjusted returns. Moreover, several observers of the investment world at the time remarked that traditional long-only investment strategies with stocks and bonds were viewed by some as less appealing than alternative investments, especially when it came time to raise funds or attract new capital into an investment fund. Over time, the first innovators and clients were joined by larger numbers of high-net-worth individuals and retail investors, leading to a correspondingly huge influx of capital into these strategies. Originally fairly simple, the strategies have grown and evolved over the last three decades to become increasingly complex and sophisticated.

In order to understand the "conversion" of investors to independent asset managers in general and to alternative investments in particular, we must fully appreciate the tremendous innovation employed by the creators, such as the private equity industry. Though the private equity investment management industry itself has been treated separately in the alternative investments section of this book, innovation *of* private equity itself was a truly dramatic inflection point of the entrepreneurial story of investment in the twentieth century. A look at the various strategies employed by hedge funds today, discussed in chapter 8, reveals how quickly fund methodologies aimed at generating superior risk-adjusted returns can evolve and develop. Most of these investment strategies, philosophies, and techniques did not exist even two or three decades ago.

Outcomes: New Clients, Performance Success, and Firm Size

As a result of the good performance of many of the early movers, a large segment of the potential client population became captivated by this success and was willing to pay significantly higher management and performance fees to get into the fray. The appeal of hedge fund and private equity firms soared, even as public scrutiny and media criticism of these alternative investment vehicles increased as well. By

the 1990s, investors, clients, and competing managers were all captivated by the potential success an independent manager could achieve,
both in terms of performance for the client and compensation for
the manager.

One central commonality among the independent firms that demonstrated remarkable performance in the early 2000s is the relatively
smaller size of successful managers. Economic theory and past academic consensus suggest that larger asset management companies
would benefit from economies of scale in technology, distribution,
hiring, and legal issues, as noted earlier. However, becoming too large
sometimes disadvantaged the investor or client when it came to performance, because performance of investments often does not scale in
the same way as costs do, as discussed in the context of hedge funds in
chapter 8.[12] Perhaps the most important reason for this is that smaller
investment management firms can often exploit undercovered or more
esoteric corners of the market. These may include smaller securities in
complicated situations that cannot accommodate exceptionally large
investments. When a firm grows too large and needs to invest beyond
its core areas of expertise, where its edge is not as pronounced, returns
may drop.

Very few areas within the financial services economy prospered in
the immediate aftermath of the 2008 financial crisis. Independent
asset management, however, was absolutely one of them. After the
crisis, some high-net-worth individuals and wealthy clients moved to
independent asset managers in order to avoid the tarnished reputa-
tions of many large institutions.[13] Some of this was likely a reaction
to revelations that some investment banks were selling to their clients
the very products they were betting against with proprietary capital.
At this stage of the game, of course, the rise of independent managers
was well underway, and the independent asset manager was a major
player in the financial services realm.

Independence Becomes Mainstream

A look at America's top 300 money managers in terms of assets under
management at the end of 2013 reveals the extent to which independence has defined success in the world of money management. In
fact, four of the eight largest money managers in the United States fall

under this "independent" classification if we define independence to include the following: unaffiliated mutual fund managers, independent investment advisory firms, largely manager-owned investing firms, and today's private equity and hedge funds (excluding large investment and commercial banks and departments within these institutions, such as bank trust departments, institution-owned hedge funds, quasi-independent advisories, and bank-controlled wealth managers).[14]

The largest firm in terms of assets under management is New York–based independent asset manager BlackRock, which controls $4.3 trillion. The second-largest is Boston-based State Street Global Advisors, which manages $2.3 trillion; but since it is under the control of State Street Corporation, a large institutional financial services firm, it is not an independent investment manager. Next on the list is the independent Vanguard Group, with over $2.2 trillion in assets under management.[15] Clearly, with two of the top three investment management firms in the United States classified as independent asset managers and together controlling over $6.5 trillion in assets under management, independent managers have come to define the very nature of investment management today.

In fact, comparing independent asset managers with affiliated asset managers by taking a closer look at the list of America's top money managers from today and years past, as compiled by *Institutional Investor*, reveals some interesting insights. For example, in 1991, the proportion of assets managed by independent managers among the top twenty-five money managers in America was at 24 percent. The next two decades, despite major global macroeconomic uncertainty in the aftermath of the 2008 financial crisis, saw a dramatic uptick of inflows into independent asset managers when it came to the top twenty-five money managers in the United States. By 2013, 51 percent of assets among the top managers were managed by independent firms (see figure 9.1).[16]

This trend, at first glance, suggests that independent asset managers are gaining popularity among clients and that capital inflows are favorable. Moreover, while many large banks and traditional financial institutions, such as divisions of Goldman Sachs and J. P. Morgan, are present in the top rankings of money managers by assets under management, most of the top three hundred asset managers are independently owned and managed entities.[17]

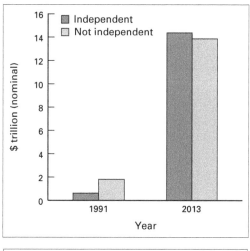

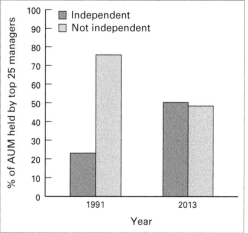

Figure 9.1 Title: Assets Under Management, Top Twenty-Five US Managers

Source: "America's Top 300 Money Managers," Institutional Investor, accessed 2013,
http://www.institutionalinvestor.com/Research/4376/Americas-Top-300-Money-Managers.html;
"Ranking America's Top Money Managers," Institutional Investor, August 1992, 79–83.

A wealth of data exists surrounding the dramatic surge in popularity of independent asset managers, indicating that the era of independent asset management is here to stay. Thus, innovation in investment management methodologies and in the organizational approach of independent investment firms laid a strong foundation for the independent investment managers of the twenty-first century.

A Contrary Movement: Market Efficiency and Indexing

While independent managers were breaking away from larger financial institutions and finding success in their own money management enterprises, a parallel movement driven by efficient market theorists and the phenomenon of indexing emerged. Indexing is the investment strategy of passively tracking collections of stocks and bonds that are represented in indices, or collections of firms that benchmark certain parts of the market. Two schools of thought on indexing and market efficiency have existed. The first, to which many of the independent investment managers presumably subscribe, is that active management can indeed add value for clients and investors in the medium and long term and that there is significant alpha to be gained over indexed investment portfolios.

The second, to which adherents of the market efficiency movement belong, holds that active management in the long term is usually not fruitful and that in general the capital markets are quite efficient in terms of pricing. Because of this, it has been significantly cheaper and much more productive for investors to select indexed vehicles. Some in this camp believe the origins of some of the best track records of active managers are produced by survivorship bias; that is, there are many failed investors for every great investor, and what separates greatness from failure is often luck or fortunate market tailwinds.

The fees on "tracker" or "passive" funds, which make no claims to beating the market and simply try to replicate it in most instances, are just a few basis points (hundredths of a percentage point)—a far cry from the "2 percent and 20 percent" being charged by active hedge fund and private equity managers in the independent investment management world (see figure 9.2). High fees can be a significant drag on compounded returns over time. One noted observer points out the dangers of such high fees and the potential benefits in investing in index funds by noting that investing $100,000 for thirty years at 6 percent, with annual charges of twenty-five basis points, and a portfolio will be worth almost $535,000; if the annual charges are higher at 1.5 percent, the portfolio will be worth only $375,000 after the thirty-year period. One prominent industry report in 2014 estimated that low-cost index funds, which appeal to those who believe in this alternative school of thought about market efficiency, were on track to experience a 100 percent increase in their market share globally by 2020, from 11 percent to 22 percent.[18]

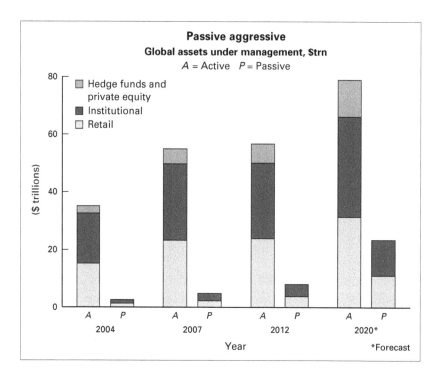

Figure 9.2 Passive Aggressive: Global Assets Under Management, $Trillions

Source: "Will Invest for Food," *Economist*, May 3, 2014, http://www.economist.com /news/briefing/21601500-books-and-music-investment-industry-being-squeezed-will-invest-food.

One analysis by the *Economist* in May 2014 argued that this more recent change—the shift toward more passive management—is happening for several reasons. First, more advisers are being paid fees by their clients *rather* than taking commissions from fund providers with whom they invest clients' capital. This approach aligns client and adviser incentives more appropriately and enables advisers to recommend a low-cost index fund or ETF, for instance, over a similarly exposed actively managed fund that might have higher fees. Second, "smart-beta" funds that use different metrics to assemble custom indices (aside from, for example, the classic market capitalization–based indices) have started to emerge and have grown in popularity. Finally, defined benefit pension plans are shrinking in terms of total managed capital and are giving way to defined contribution plans for retirement, thereby somewhat reducing the rate of growth of pension fund allocations to alternatives from what would have been the case if this rotation from defined benefit to defined contribution were not underway.[19]

Over the decades, the efficient market and indexing school of thought has experienced varying fortunes; with the performance success and enthusiasm generated by alternative investment managers and the subsequent "validation" of active management, some subscribers to this school fell away and paid the higher fees for the chance at higher return. However, the key is that the performance of passive indices is entirely a function of the market beta, or risk premium of a given asset class or other systematic strategy, rather than the active security selection of a manager, while superior performance by many alternative strategies is proving difficult to maintain over time.

Reward: Vast Revenue Growth and Wealth Creation for Investment Managers

Efficient market theory implies that no manager should be able to achieve outsized risk-adjusted returns consistently over time without a fundamental informational advantage, and much of the academic work regarding the performance of index funds, ETFs, mutual funds, and other investment vehicles discussed in this book seems to validate this thesis. However, this body of work seemingly fails to explain the phenomenon of a limited number of real-life, individual, independent money managers consistently beating the market or posting superior risk-adjusted returns year after year, at least for an extended period of their careers. It is worth turning our attention for a moment to the "ultrasuccessful" investment managers who have accumulated vast wealth and influence. In March 2014, the total number of American billionaires stood at 512. The total number of American billionaires in finance and investments was 128, meaning that they composed 25 percent of the total billionaires in the United States. This is, of course, in an industry that employs far less than 1 percent of the country's workers. The investment manager proportion of billionaires has been steadily increasing over recent decades, according to *Forbes*. This subset of American billionaires includes those whose primary means of accumulating wealth are listed by *Forbes* as investments, hedge funds, leveraged buyouts, private equity, and the like.[20]

The compensation arrangements that exist in the investment management world today are interacting with tremendous growth in investment assets under management and the changing business and legal structures that have allowed alternative investment vehicles to proliferate. These conditions serve as the primary means for their owners, shareholders, and executives to become part of a new elite. The rise of a new money-managing elite is also dependent on a variety of fee types and structures. While the compensation arrangements vary when it comes to hedge funds, private equity, mutual funds, and other vehicles for investment, there are management fees, performance fees, expense fees, event-based fees, carried interest, and other sources that all add to the potential compensation of an asset manager.

Management fees, or fees on assets under management, are period-based fees driven primarily by the size of the fund involved. These fees can vary from a few basis points to a few percentage points. A typical hedge fund fee structure is "2 and 20," or 2 percent of assets under management for the management fee and 20 percent of profits generated for clients by the manager for the performance fee. For a hedge fund, performance fees are also period-based fees, driven primarily by the return generated by a manager in a given period, usually a calendar year. For a private equity firm, the performance fee is levied on the returns of a given fund vintage and is typically subject to a hurdle, which is a minimum return the fund must post before the general partner is entitled to receive the performance fee. Expense fees are also period based and driven by the operating expenses of a fund or investment management firm. Active managers often charge high expense fees, whereas passive managers and some mutual funds can charge lower expense fees. Transaction fees are event-based fees driven primarily by the size of a transaction undertaken by a manager. Brokers and prime brokers generally charge small transaction fees for the individuals or firms engaging in securities transactions with them.

Soon, it was widely realized that the most compelling economic opportunity for an individual was to become one of the "hedge fund masters of the universe." Indeed, in 2010, the twenty-five highest-earning hedge fund managers combined made in excess of four times what all five hundred CEOs of the S&P 500 index companies earned combined. As recently as 2012, for instance, the ten highest-earning US hedge fund managers made over $10.1 billion in earnings from management and performance fees. The ten highest-earning corporate

CEOs, by comparison, made a "mere" $380 million.[21] These years of astounding compensation were not new. Well before the financial crisis, the average top twenty-five hedge fund manager made upward of $100 million a year. In 2007, just before the crisis, the average figure made by this super elite crowd was upward of *$1 billion*. In 2012, this figure stood at a relatively smaller but still huge $540 million.[22] To be fair, it is difficult to determine precisely how much the individuals themselves are earning, because some earnings may be shared with their teams.

No matter how one examines these compensation figures, it is indisputable that in the world of hedge funds, the performance incentives given to the most successful independent hedge fund managers have created a new elite. The rewards given—through voluntary contracts with investors—to the top hedge fund managers have driven vast fee and revenue growth for many independent investment managers in recent years, and this phenomenon seems far from over.

One should keep in mind that the earnings figures reported here are entirely cash compensation numbers; an examination of net worth increases in 2013, for example, including gains made in the value of equity owned and traded on the open market, shows that different individuals are on the list of highest earners. Warren Buffett, the acclaimed investor, tops this list, making on average $37 million a day in 2013 without being a traditional 2-and-20 percent hedge fund manager on the capital appreciation of his Berkshire Hathaway stock.[23] The other members of this elite cadre are primarily founders of now-large companies, whose market capitalizations increased dramatically in a year in which the S&P 500 stock index rose more than 30 percent.

In 2012, the highest paid hedge fund manager posted net returns of nearly 30 percent in his flagship fund and personally made $2.2 billion.[24] From one perspective, this income was well deserved for a manager who tremendously outperformed the stock market and the average hedge fund. From another perspective, however, the manager's clients were paying him a vast sum that may be inconsistent with the work required to achieve it.

Only very recently has discussion emerged about curtailing these remarkable earnings. For instance, in some cases investors have been able to push the average hedge fund asset management fee down from the traditional 2 percent of assets under management to 1.5 percent across a number of top asset managers. Even so, many hedge funds and publicly traded private equity firms are generating more and more of their revenue from fees even as this percentage goes down and do so because of the continuing increase in assets under management attracted to their strong returns in a zero-interest-rate environment.

This situation has created a remarkable dilemma for some asset managers: should they focus on maximizing returns or on increasing assets under management? Doing the first certainly helps achieve the second, as more investors will try to participate in a fund with a good track record. However, the managerial compensation incentive structure can become skewed because managers will often focus excessively on maximizing assets under management at the expense of returns—spending days on end meeting potential clients, for instance, rather than focusing on investment diligence and valuation.

In May 2014, the trend of top hedge fund managers becoming wealthier and wealthier was confirmed: the top twenty-five most highly compensated hedge fund managers earned $21.15 billion in 2013. This compensation figure is the largest such amount since 2010, and it represented a 50 percent increase in top hedge fund manager compensation from 2012. The manager who topped the list earned $3.5 billion, an amount that is $1.3 billion *more* than the top 2012 compensation (see figure 9.3). This increase was partly driven by a return of 42 percent to investors in two of his funds, which carry the typical fee structure described herein.[25] These returns were outstanding, but it is worth noting that not all of the returns achieved for investors by these top hedge fund earners were outstanding relative to the performance of widely followed market indices.

The year 2013, however, was the fifth consecutive year that, on average, hedge funds fell short of the performance of the broader stock market. This seems surprising for an asset class whose value proposition is to outperform the market in both good times and bad. The average hedge fund returned 9.1 percent in 2013, according to industry-tracking firm HFR after analysis of over 2,000 portfolios. In comparison, the S&P 500, one of the broadest American equity market indices, returned 32.4 percent after including dividends paid by component companies.[26] To be clear, it is not entirely fair to compare the returns of hedge funds directly to the S&P 500 for two reasons. First, the S&P 500 simply represents a single asset class (US equities), and hedge funds often have exposure to a wider array of asset classes. Second, hedge funds typically have a different (and usually lower) beta than the S&P 500 by virtue of hedging or having exposure to lower correlated

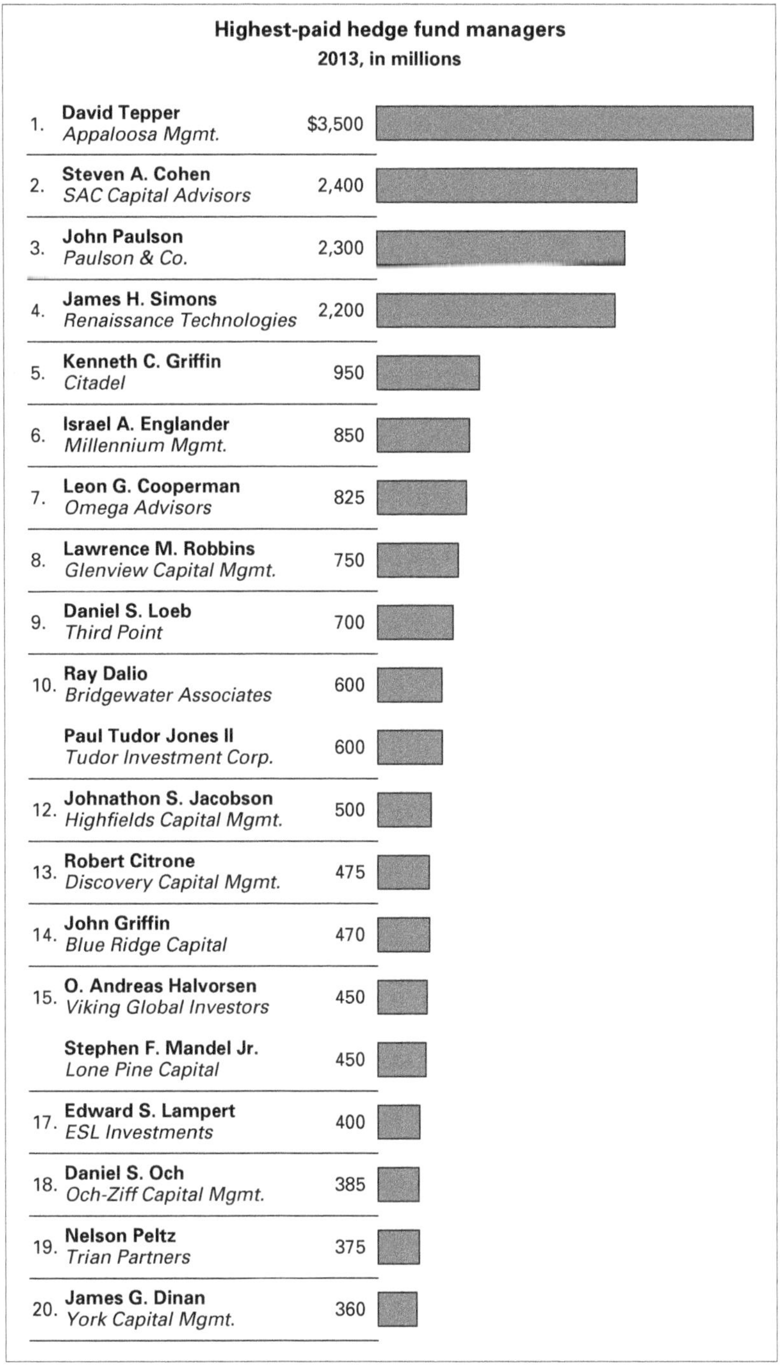

Highest-paid hedge fund managers
2013, in millions

1.	David Tepper *Appaloosa Mgmt.*	$3,500
2.	Steven A. Cohen *SAC Capital Advisors*	2,400
3.	John Paulson *Paulson & Co.*	2,300
4.	James H. Simons *Renaissance Technologies*	2,200
5.	Kenneth C. Griffin *Citadel*	950
6.	Israel A. Englander *Millennium Mgmt.*	850
7.	Leon G. Cooperman *Omega Advisors*	825
8.	Lawrence M. Robbins *Glenview Capital Mgmt.*	750
9.	Daniel S. Loeb *Third Point*	700
10.	Ray Dalio *Bridgewater Associates*	600
	Paul Tudor Jones II *Tudor Investment Corp.*	600
12.	Johnathon S. Jacobson *Highfields Capital Mgmt.*	500
13.	Robert Citrone *Discovery Capital Mgmt.*	475
14.	John Griffin *Blue Ridge Capital*	470
15.	O. Andreas Halvorsen *Viking Global Investors*	450
	Stephen F. Mandel Jr. *Lone Pine Capital*	450
17.	Edward S. Lampert *ESL Investments*	400
18.	Daniel S. Och *Och-Ziff Capital Mgmt.*	385
19.	Nelson Peltz *Trian Partners*	375
20.	James G. Dinan *York Capital Mgmt.*	360

Figure 9.3 Highest-Paid Hedge Fund Managers

Source: Alexandra Stevenson, "Hedge Fund Moguls' Pay Has the 1% Looking Up,"
DealBook (blog), *New York Times*, May 6, 2014, http://dealbook.nytimes.com/2014/05/06
/hedge-fund-moguls-pay-has-the-1-looking-up.

asset classes through distinct strategies, and thus for the most mean-ingful comparison one must compare risk-adjusted returns rather than total returns. Still, the comparison does hold in general terms with respect to the large performance discrepancy. Despite this lackluster performance record as compared to the broad equities market, record amounts of capital continue to flow into the hedge fund industry.

In recent years, the private equity industry compensation vehicle of carried interest (the profit share paid to the manager for performance) has also been the subject of much scrutiny. As a complex tax issue, car-ried interest has often been described as the primary means by which asset managers—including both private equity managers and hedge fund portfolio managers—rake in large amounts of compensation.[27] Because carried interest and performance fees represent the majority of the large sums earned by the top-performing independent asset managers, the taxation of carried interest has become a controver-sial political issue. Currently in the United States, carried interest has been defined as a capital gain for individuals receiving these payments, and as such it has been subject to materially lower capital gains tax rates. Supporters of characterizing carried interest as a capital gain argue that this policy encourages productive investment and economic growth. Detractors point to relative tax burdens and the undermining of a progressive taxation system. Whatever the relative merits of these positions, it is indisputable that carried interest and its capital gains treatment are certainly contributing to the rise and continued financial success of this new elite.

THE COMPENSATION STRUCTURE AND ITS NUANCES

The Problem of Bundling Beta and Alpha

Performance fees are almost always paid on return, not alpha. Alpha is the amount of risk-adjusted value, relative to the appropriate bench-mark, that a manager has added through investment management talent—that is, through some combination of security selection, tim-ing, sizing investments, or risk management. However, the return of a fund is a function of both the alpha and the beta. To give an example, imagine a long-biased hedge fund (meaning a fund that may do some shorting but tends to be "net long" the market), and imagine that because of this long bias its investments tend to move up, in aggre-gate, 60 percent of what the market moves up. If the market moves up 20 percent in a given year, the fund is expected to move up 12 percent from beta, or just by virtue of its market exposure. Assume that despite the market's move upward, the manager did not add any alpha and returned only 12 percent that year. In a traditional hedge fund, the investor would still owe 20 percent of the 12 percent move as a per-formance fee, leaving the investor liable for a 2.4 percent payment to the investment manager for beta alone.

However, the investor could just as easily have purchased that same market exposure by buying an equity index like the S&P 500 for a negligible fee. This is, in effect, the first problem with the performance fee: it is paid on a bundle of alpha (the manager's value-add) and beta (the market return), whereas it would be more logical for the fee to be paid on alpha alone to represent the excess returns the manager gener-ated. This problem plagues investors in funds that tend to have sig-nificant market exposure, like long-biased funds, private equity funds, commodities funds, and sector funds that tend to run net long. There should be a greater attempt by the manager and the investor to agree upon a benchmark and a methodology for calculating alpha such that the manager is paid only for "outperformance." To be clear, there are times when this would be advantageous to the manager too. If a fund is long biased, for instance, and the market moves down sharply but the manager is down less than the beta would suggest, the manager has outperformed and should be rewarded accordingly. The goal is to align the incentives of the manager and the investor appropriately such that the performance fee is paid according to how much the manager beats the market and not on market return, because an index that has the desired beta can be purchased much more cheaply through index funds or ETFs or through holding securities directly.

Fees as a Misleading Proxy for Quality

There is a comical corollary to the fact that the alternatives market standard is the 2-and-20 fee regime: if a hedge fund or private equity firm charges fees substantially below market in order to bring its com-pensation system into a fairer alignment, many investors will question this move. What is wrong with this group that it cannot charge full fees? Why is the manager leaving money on the table if it is otherwise competent enough to charge full fees? Usually, a fund offers below-market fees because it is a new fund launch or perhaps because the previous funds (in the case of a private equity firm) did not perform very well.

In this regard, there is a curious similarity between investment managers and, for example, surgeons. Imagine needing to have surgery performed for a dangerous medical condition. An individual may check various hospitals, receiving consultations and arranging for approximate quotes on what the surgery may cost. Consider the case where the individual receives the following price quotes from different doctors: $60,000, $55,000, $70,000, and $20,000. Unlike the market for many goods and services, the individual is unlikely to pounce on the opportunity to employ the low-cost provider. This is a service that requires a highly skilled practitioner, and without being a surgeon himself, the consumer has a very limited ability to make judgments about the relative skill and expertise of each surgeon. Therefore, the individual is inclined to believe that there must be a reason the fourth surgeon is so inexpensive—perhaps the surgeon has had poor surgical outcomes resulting in fewer patients, requiring discount prices to draw new patients, or insufficient training and experience to allow the surgeon to compete with more highly skilled and expensive surgeons. Thus, for some investors, price is seen as a proxy for quality. This may also mean that there may not be very high price elasticity among investors; thus, if a manager lowers fees dramatically, the fund's assets may not scale to the point where it is value additive to do so. In short, in this market, price discovery is an enormously difficult task, and those managers who cut fees materially are often met with reactions of suspicion or unease.

The Performance Fee as a Call Option

Furthermore, the performance fee is essentially a call option. That is, the manager receives 20 percent of the upside and none of the downside, so the fee has the same characteristics as a call option struck at the fund's net asset value (with a strike price resetting at the high-water mark each year). One of the determinants of the value of an option is volatility because the higher the volatility of the underlying assets, the more valuable the option. Managers are, in theory, financially incentivized to have higher volatility, as their expected payout tends to increase. In other words, there is an incentive to make riskier bets. To be clear, most managers are careful stewards of capital. Indeed, over the long term, it is rational for them to be because a significant drawdown can mark the end of a fund and damage the reputation and career prospects for the team involved. However, when looking at performance fees as a call option, managers who are not careful financial stewards could be tempted to take larger bets because "heads I win, tails you lose." Investors may thus need to pay attention to how much of the manager's own capital is in the fund and whether risk-control measures are well developed and properly overseen to ensure proper alignment.

An Implication of High Fees: Competitiveness of Alpha and the Brain Drain to Investment Management

Besides providing extraordinarily high compensation to the heads of the most successful firms, these fee structures have other effects on the labor market. Other employees of the firm on the investment team also enjoy very high levels of compensation. Therefore, successful investment management firms have the ability to attract top talent. Decades ago, the prevailing joke was that it was the "dumbest son" who would go on to manage the family's money because the job seemed dull and unchallenging. Today, to the contrary, investment management firms attract very accomplished individuals with physics, mathematics, statistics, and other technical backgrounds. Others simply pay top dollar for brilliant individuals who can do deep fundamental or statistical analysis. It is no surprise, then, that 15 percent of Harvard College graduates reported plans to enter finance immediately after graduation in 2013. This percentage is actually in decline, compared to the 2007 rate of 47 percent, prior to the 2008 financial crisis.[28] To be clear, the "finance" umbrella is much broader than just investment management and includes positions in banking or some corporate finance jobs. A brain drain is indeed underway; individuals who used to become scientists, doctors, engineers, and mathematicians are now migrating toward finance.

Some individuals, like Michael Mauboussin (the head of Global Financial Strategies at Credit Suisse), think an interesting phenomenon may be at play in the investment management industry. Mauboussin discussed the work of Stephen Jay Gould, who analyzed why Ted

Williams was the last Major League Baseball player to have a batting average exceeding .400. According to Gould, the quality of pitching has become better over time, which means that the level of competition is also higher. At least some part of Ted Williams's success, as phenomenal a player as he was, was because he was a big fish in a smaller pond. That pond has now become filled with other big fish, and the dominance of one player over another has thus been reduced. Mauboussin points out the irony here: "Absolute skill rises, but relative skill declines, leaving more to luck."[29] Likewise in the financial industry, it may be more difficult for individuals to outperform the average as the talent and skills of all managers are rising as the industry pays more to attract top talent.

Performance versus Fees?

Several questions emerge regarding the relative performance of various subsets of independent investment managers. For instance, are hedge funds adding value for their clients in aggregate, net of fees? Do private equity firms continue to generate superior risk-adjusted returns, or is the growth of private equity as an investment vehicle merely an influx of capital into an asset class that temporarily outperformed by accepting illiquidity when the premium for doing so was large?

Alternative investment managers today are enjoying a tremendously attractive compensation scheme in an era where returns for clients, net of fees, are not nearly what they were in earlier periods. The average hedge fund and average private equity firm are certainly not currently outperforming basic market measures of absolute return, and even many of the top performers are outperforming only in certain years and on an inconsistent basis.

Given these results, why does the marketplace support 2-and-20 fees? One contributing factor is the asymmetric process of setting fees. When clients really want a particular manager to run their money, few management or performance fees seem to be considered too high. The investor is excited about the manager, the strategy, and the prospective alpha. Conversely, when clients decide that a manager's performance, service, or investment style no longer fits their desires, they will not pressure the manager to lower the fees he or she is charging but will instead fire the manager and move capital elsewhere. The investor is dismayed and disillusioned because the strategy did not work, the manager did not execute, or the market soured. These reasons cause any initial excitement the investor may have had to dissipate, and the last issue on the investor's mind is reducing fees, which are seen as negligible relative to the subpar returns earned through the manager in the first place.

Thus, if one views the investment management fee market through the lens of traditional neoclassical economics, there is far less downward pressure on fees than one would think the basic laws of supply and demand should dictate. In this sense, the manager is the price setter and the client is the price taker. Clients who fall out of love with a manager and want to take their business elsewhere do not become price setters; rather, they shop around for a new manager instead of negotiating a lower or more advantageous fee structure. Thus, managers remain price setters in the industry. This dynamic has contributed a great deal to the rise of the new elite and the simultaneous decline in relative value for the end-client.

The other issue at play is the "easier" pools of capital that managers are able to capture. Certain very large institutions, from pension plans to sovereign wealth funds, have a strong need to allocate large amounts of assets in a short time frame and have to spend more of their limited resources identifying new opportunities than negotiating fees. Many times, these pools of capital do not put substantial pressure on managers to make their terms more client-friendly. If there are enough such investors a manager can capture, the manager has little interest in seeking capital from institutions that attempt to drive hard terms. These easier pools of capital effectively diminish the ability of other institutions to drive the proverbial hard bargain with a manager.

This situation, though, does seem to be improving over time. There are more sophisticated and better resourced pools of capital that are learning to drive fees. Although it is difficult to generalize, there is some evidence of fees slowly ticking down to the order of "1.4 and 17" instead of "2 and 20," as figure 9.4 illustrates. Some observers attribute this not only to the relatively low returns alternatives have provided in recent years but also to this increased investment savvy leading to greater negotiating power exercised by newer alternatives clients. The 2 percent management fee seems to be under the most pressure.[30]

There is, though, one other source of downward pressure that is probably underappreciated: the systematization of alpha delivered at lower prices. Recent years have also seen the systematization of once

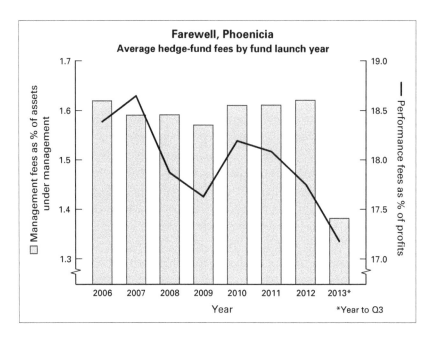

Figure 9.4 Farewell, Phoenicia

Source: "Down to 1.4 and 17," *Economist*, February 8, 2014, http://www.economist.com/news
/finance-and-economics/21595942-cost-investing-alternative-assets-fallingslowly-down-14-and-17.

"secret-sauce," alpha-generating strategies that previously required great specialization to achieve. For instance, merger arbitrage or momentum investing strategies were relatively rare before the late twentieth century, when hedge fund managers and others identified the alpha-generating potential of such methods. Now, after the turn of the twenty-first century, more capital flows into such investment strategies as a direct result of their success in creating value for investors. As a result, generalist portfolio managers are able to create funds around such special, historically successful strategies and capitalize on their mass-market potential. Also, multiproduct firms sell exposure to such strategies at lower fees than the standard 2-and-20 arrangement. Indeed, in recent years, merger arbitrage mutual funds have emerged, again attesting to the cheaper delivery of a once rare, sophisticated strategy. Hedge funds in particular will have to compete with these lower-cost providers of hedge fund–like alpha strategies in the future. Of course, the proliferation of a successful strategy that lowers fees may also impair its alpha by creating a growing pool of competitors.

CONCLUSION

It is clear that the second half of the twentieth century was of great importance in the history of global investment management. Investment management was thoroughly revolutionized by the creation of a class of independent investment managers who harnessed an entrepreneurial drive in order to produce sophisticated and innovative products. The rewards for this independence came to managers and clients alike: high-quality products for clients, the value added by particular managers, improved investment returns, and freedom to manage creatively. On the entrepreneurial side, issues of organizational leadership, profitability, business management, and microeconomics all contributed to the success or failure of individual independent managers.

Though the era of independent investment management began with individual managers breaking away from larger financial institutions, today's world of independent money management has a clear winner, at least in terms of compensation: the hedge fund and private equity "masters of the universe." These members of the new elite not only have benefited supremely from the last decades but also will probably continue to thrive in the future, as compensation trends and growth rates remain in only moderate danger of decline.

As the long history of investment through the ages seems to indicate, it is probably not possible to devise a single superior investment technique that works era after era after era. Like so many important innovations in the history of investment and investment management, competition and changing market conditions eventually moderate such high performance rates. However, this seems not yet to be clear to the client in the modern money management world—the limited partner (that is, the investor) of a hedge fund or private equity firm seeking to perform supremely well in all periods. Managers—those who consistently outperform and perhaps even those well-organized firms who do not add significant value for their clients—may continue to be well compensated, barring major changes in fee structures or introduction of exogenous downward pressure on fees to relieve the asymmetry issues discussed in this chapter. Thus, this era of vast earnings by top investment managers, while likely to moderate slowly over time, is unlikely to disappear completely.

At the end of the day, though, the next generation of financial innovations will likely take the spotlight. The changes may occur in niche corners of the market, like algorithmic trading, commodities strategies, or real assets, or they may involve a holistic approach like the endowment-style or multistrategy firm. Only time will tell what financial innovations the future holds.

Conclusion

Investment in the Twenty-First Century

THIS NARRATIVE HAS MADE IT CLEAR that investment is a fundamental human enterprise. It is not an overstatement to elevate it to be a basic element of the major economic and cultural activities of society: what individuals do for work, what they consume for physical sustenance, how they educate their youth and cultivate their intellectual interests, and *how they invest their resources.* Such an investigation unveils countless other facets of the society: how resources are allocated through time and across owners, what the responsibilities of the individual are vis-à-vis the responsibilities of the collective, who has the capacity to invest, and who is retained to manage the investments. In short, the act and form of investment are yet another pillar of society not unlike diet, health, physical comfort, and cultural aspiration.

For thousands of years, the act of investment belonged almost exclusively to those who had not only wealth but also great power. Only those with access to the powerful in society could possess and deploy resources in order to earn a return. The vast majority of individuals had neither wealth nor power and little hope of participating in the satisfying and rewarding activity of investing for the future. Today, billions of people have become investors, often in vehicles aimed at providing funds for a long and healthy retirement. The journey toward investment democratization has been complex, often difficult, and at times contentious, but the progress has been dramatic and rewarding. Lives have been ennobled and accorded a dignity that could not even have been imagined in the early millennia of civilization. The strands of innovation and entrepreneurship have been woven together to create a thriving, productive, constantly changing investment landscape that has delivered, and continues to promise, increasing opportunity and comfort for humankind.

Indeed, a dominant theme of this book has been the democratization of investment. Along the way we have examined the investment conditions and vehicles of ancient and premodern societies and the major investment forms and developments of the modern world. We have identified the crucial role of joint-stock companies, the Industrial Revolution, and public markets in creating the transition to a more egalitarian investment environment and then plunged into several of the most consequential outcomes of this democratization: the concept and funding of retirement, the democratization of the regulatory system, progress in managing cyclical crises, and the emergence of investment theory.

But the job is not done. The very process of democratization and increasing opportunity continues to present challenges, difficulties, and distortions to the progress of offering fair investment opportunities to all. The power elite of ancient times has been replaced by a new elite in the twenty-first century. They are men and women who have recognized and seized entrepreneurial opportunities in the investment firmament. For the most part, members of this new elite are not "to the manor born," but their vast financial success does reflect sometimes extreme opportunism vis-à-vis the inevitable vagaries of investment cyclicality, fashion, and emotion.

The corrective is not, for the most part, regulatory or proscriptive. The twenty-first century needs to bring with it an evolution in the understanding of investment truth such that the client, who is now everyman, can seize the enduring principles and realities of investment success.

Every individual client must also make investments in his or her own education, understanding, and confidence in his or her role as an investor. For most of us, investment success is not world-beating returns or get-rich-quick schemes. Rather, it comes when we recognize

our individual and institutional life-cycle needs and apply our knowledge, maturity, and realism to organize for a reasonable expectation
of their achievement.

A drive for independence and innovation that emerged among
investment professionals beginning in the mid-twentieth century has
led to a further explosion of new investment forms. These creative
and exciting vehicles, which largely arrived in the last forty years, have
made the field of professional investment management infinitely more
creative and complex, as well as profitable for its practitioners. In
many cases, it has also been rewarding for clients and other investing
participants, but this result has not been universally true or, inevitably, persistent and reliable. In addition, investment entrepreneurs
have implemented remarkable advances in applying theory, creating
technique, and disseminating imaginative investment approaches.
They have achieved dramatic and largely deserved rewards for their
imagination, courage, and skill. At the same time, those charged with
devising and leading economic policy and those responsible for market
regulation have made substantial, if at times slow and halting, progress
toward designing frameworks and guidelines for safer economic and
market environments. Although much remains to be understood and
accomplished, their success has been impressive.

But given the ever-changing and ever-competitive nature of the
investment process, the rewards to practitioners and the rewards to
clients have, with disappointing frequency, been misaligned. Investment innovations suffer over time from changing patterns of success
and crowding of the field. The rewards for innovation, well earned at
the beginning, can continue to grow even when the benefits to clients
have passed their peak. The idea that someone can produce prodi-
giously superior returns over extended periods and should be paid a
prince's ransom to do so is, to say the least, impracticable. The issue
is not the appropriateness or morality of the prince's ransom; the issue
is the difficulty of achieving vastly superior risk-adjusted returns from
one source over long periods. This is precisely the role of diversification. The lessons of investment theory have shown that diversification
is a powerful tool whose risk-adjusted benefits are often practically
free. Although putting all of one's eggs in one basket and choosing
the right basket are unmatched for maximizing returns, the risks to
all but the most brilliantly "correct" investors are usually greater than
one should accept because of the difficulty in selecting the single-
best basket. In addition to diversifying risks, most of us need to take

explicit note of the market volatility of the assets in which we choose to invest.

When an investor acts upon a realistic plan based on his or her resource availability and needs, then solutions can usually be structured without resorting to miracle-working investment talent. A thoughtful mix of investment classes combined with a careful choice of professional investors is the outcome of rational consideration of the odds of achieving certain returns and what is a sensible price to pay for the prospect of those returns. With a growing awareness of the long-term limitations of many aspects of active and innovative investment management, more conservative and cheaper "middle ways" such as indexing and ETFs are emerging as vehicles of choice for many clients and are helping investment become more beneficial to ever-wider swaths of people.

On the other hand, as we have learned, innovation is a powerful source of exceptional returns, but it can be a powerful source of exceptional risk as well. History seems to show, however, that innovation in investment is worth embracing on a controlled basis, that is, on a basis that does not invite an unacceptable level of failure. Institutional clients are normally adequately staffed to examine the choices among innovative investment options, but unfortunately, individual clients usually are not. This creates a difficult problem of finding an investment adviser willing and able to take on such a responsibility at what is often an inadequate level of compensation. It is on this conundrum that the frequently heard advice for the average individual client to limit himself or herself to low-cost index products rests.

Consequently, there is, sadly, no alternative to individuals' accepting some level of responsibility for their own asset allocation—a daunting task for all but a very few. For those still early in accumulation careers, a balanced approach, coupled with courageous dollar cost averaging appears to be required. But undertaking and maintaining such a strategy requires nerves of steel at certain times.

INVESTMENT AND SOCIAL CHANGE

Given that the powerful project of democratization is well underway, our expectations of it can be extended further. Investment has always been shaped and developed by the particular social, political, and cultural forms of contemporary society, and indeed, investment has driven many of the large-scale historical changes of modernity. In the current moment, we should consider how investment might be used to actually enhance the political and social realm. How can finance and investment be utilized to improve civilization?

An example of this influence of investment has already occurred in the case of the promotion of homeownership in the United States. Encouraging homeownership has long been a political priority in this country because of the belief that homeowners are intrinsic stakeholders in society and that growing this group enhances the social stability and economic aspirations of citizens. As early as 1918, the Department of Labor undertook an "Own Your Own Home" campaign, and in public-private partnership thousands of Better Homes committees promoted the advantages of home ownership in the 1920s.[1] However, the government was most effective in encouraging home ownership through the promotion of financial innovation in three different phases, leveraging the power of finance to accomplish this social and political goal.

The first phase was the encouragement of a new mortgage structure, brought about by the National Housing Act of 1934. It radically altered the terms by which mortgages were typically extended. Before this, most mortgages were short-dated loans, with maturities varying between just three and fifteen years. Some also carried bullet payments at the end, and since few people could afford such a large lump sum at once, most borrowers were forced to refinance the mortgage again when the bullet payment approached. This system failed during the Great Depression, of course, as lenders were less willing to extend credit, and thus homeowners were responsible for a payment they could not make. The National Housing Act introduced insurance through the Federal Housing Administration (FHA) mortgage insurance program and provided governmental guarantees for eligible borrowers with a corresponding amortizing loan—meaning it was paid down smoothly over time rather than relying on bullet payments—at 80 percent loan to value for 20 years.[2] Amortizing loans slowly became the market standard. This revolutionized the mortgage market as lower-income households who could not previously have afforded the high down payments were now able to afford mortgages.

The second phase was the division of the originator from the owner of the mortgage, aided largely by the creation of Fannie Mae and, later,

Freddie Mac. These too have their roots in the National Housing Act of 1934, which sought to develop a deeper, more liquid secondary market for mortgages than was then available.[3] Any mortgage has an originator—the firm that works with the borrower to assess collateral and creditworthiness—and an owner. In the early days, the originator and the owner were usually the same, for the local bank would both process the loan and hold it on its own balance sheet. But this arrangement was, arguably, not the most efficient design of housing finance, for two reasons. First, regions with better-capitalized banks could offer a lower interest rate on loans than could those regions where banks did not have as much capital. It therefore made sense to try to equilibrate the markets by having the owner of the mortgage be in an area different than that of the borrower and originator. Second, some potential owners of mortgages, such as insurance companies or pensions, have lower costs of capital, and though they could collect the proceeds, they did not want to run a mortgage origination business.

The National Housing Act of 1934 thus called for the creation of national mortgage associations, which would be private companies that could purchase these mortgages to provide for a deeper secondary market than existed at that time. But there were no takers; the private sector simply did not produce the demand needed to create such an association. So then in 1938 the federal government took matters into its own hands, establishing the Federal National Mortgage Association (Fannie Mae). Although Fannie Mae was a rather sleepy organization for some time, with a small market share relative to the shares of some other purchasers on the secondary market, activity increased when the government expanded both its mandate and its capacity for purchases in the wake of a crisis over housing funding in 1958 and 1968. The government then continued to support homeownership with the creation of Freddie Mac, an attempt to provide more liquidity while demonopolizing the market control of Fannie Mae.[4]

The third phase, facilitated by the separation of the originator from the owner of the mortgage, was securitization—the pooling of groups of mortgages for sale as financial products. By creating financial instruments that pooled mortgages across a wide array of states with a range of creditworthiness and collateral types, securitization accomplished what the original division of origination and ownership had started. Those entities with low cost of capital who wanted exposure to housing risk were able to become owners of mortgages more easily than before, as the securities would be bid up to equilibrium until those with the cheapest capital held them. Securitization drastically reduced transaction costs versus the whole loan market while enhancing liquidity because the instruments themselves were much more fungible and standardized than any given collection of loans. In 1970, Ginnie Mae, which was a wholly owned government corporation, unlike government-sponsored Freddie Mac and Fannie Mae, created the first "mortgage-backed" security—that is, a mortgage backed also by the full faith and credit of the United States. This move made mortgage-backed securities more prominent, as investors built an appetite not just for the lower-risk, federally insured product but also for other higher-risk, non–Ginnie Mae securities, including the private variety.[5] With this, the securitization market was born.

We now know that there are shortcomings associated with securitization. Their very purpose is to simplify and standardize, and they do inevitably rely on the originators to be responsible. As history has made clear, this is not always the case. However, the problems associated with the global financial crisis of 2008 did not inevitably arise out of securitization itself. Rather, at work were failures of oversight, misguided beliefs about the stability of collateral values, and perverse incentives on the part of originators to produce high-volume rather than high-quality loans. Regardless, the federal government was successful in converting the United States into a nation of homeowners. The very structure of our cities and suburban environments and the feasibility of the so-called American dream have been influenced materially by finance and investment.

As this short case study demonstrates, finance can be a powerful way to achieve a political and social objective. Finance and investment can be used to bring about bold political or social aims if the programs are broad based and carefully designed. The future of investment can and should involve a tighter connection between investments undertaken and social aims.

There are a variety of ways this objective can be achieved. One existing tool at our disposal is the public-private partnership. Broadly speaking, a public-private partnership is a joint venture between a government (local, state, or federal) and a private entity to serve a public objective. Historically, these have been employed in different contexts, particularly construction. The government engages a private firm, typically through a bidding process, to construct infrastructure like bridges, water treatment facilities, schools, toll roads, or hospitals. Governments engage in these relationships for a variety of reasons. One reason may be for financing purposes if the government already has too much debt and would prefer the private entity to bear the development costs in return for a future profit incentive (such as the operating profits that may arise from a toll road or a water treatment facility). Another may be for sheer efficiency purposes: the private enterprise may be properly incentivized to wring out excesses in the cost structure or to move more quickly than a public body otherwise would. The success or failure of any such partnership turns on how carefully the metrics of success are laid out, how meticulously the project is supervised, and how precisely budgets and timelines, along with specific contingencies for the inevitable unforeseen issues that arise, were designed in advance. Public-private partnerships could be deployed more broadly and more creatively to solve shortfalls in spending on infrastructure and facilities.

A second way public-private partnership can be promoted is through the expansion of impact investing. Impact investing, touched upon briefly earlier in the book in the discussion of foundations, is the deployment of capital not just for economic gain but for social advancement as well. Historically, charitable causes have benefited from a fundamental transfer of wealth from areas of high economic gain that had little or nothing to do with social benefit. For instance, an industrial magnate may build a fortune in one arena of the economy and decide in the twilight of his life to give the fortune to charity so that some aspect of civilization is improved. Impact investing changes the entire investment paradigm. It seeks to marry the economic and the social: capital can be deployed productively with gains that are both financial and societal. The charity thus becomes not just the recipient of capital transfers from other segments of the economy but, rather, an active recycler of capital that can be deployed and redeployed for humanitarian causes.

Impact investing has been imagined and implemented in various forms. In some contexts, it is conducted with returns that are less than the market would typically bear, but the impact investor's optimization function is now not just financial gain but also social enhancement. These forms may involve lending money at rates that are lower than one would receive from a strictly for-profit bank or receiving a share of equity capital at a price that is higher than one would get from another source. In other contexts, impact investing is still done at competitive rates of return either through novel structures or by pushing investors to be more creative in how or where their capital is used. It is not that impact investing with market-consistent returns is better than such investments that give up some return for increased social gain. Success does depend largely on the context. However, the ability to achieve market-consistent returns for impact investing can expand its potential enormously.

Impact investing can be utilized in a wide range of scenarios. Often, this type of investing will be a plug for spaces that traditional markets have failed to serve adequately. For instance, it can be used for research on novel therapeutics for orphan diseases or for ailments that plague only the developing world and so are untowardly neglected by traditional pharmaceutical and biotechnology firms. It can be used to design better health delivery systems focused on preventative care that traditional insurers have not been properly motivated to pursue. It can be used to provide microfinance for individuals and small entities in emerging markets that lack sufficient collateral or do not meet banks' conventional standards of lending. The way capital markets are organized leaves many such causes, individuals, and institutions deserted or overlooked that can become the domain of impact investing.

Indeed, from investment in education, inner-city schools, innovation, developing markets, new venture capital, and infrastructure, there are countless ways in which the power of finance to draw dollars into the appropriate places with proper oversight, clear goals, and appropriate metrics could be used. One need only look at the history of home ownership, previously discussed, to see how profoundly finance can shape our civilization and way of life if it is leveraged prudently and thoughtfully. We must learn to approach these new arenas realizing how potent a force finance and investing can be to achieving political and social ends.

FUNDAMENTAL ISSUES AND OPPORTUNITIES

There are several fundamental investment issues and opportunities for the future that are worth contemplating as we consider how the investment undertaking may unfold in coming decades. These issues and opportunities are distinct from the principles we elucidated in the introduction to this book and will reiterate shortly in this conclusion. The investment principles are essentially philosophy; they are techniques for soundly approaching investment. The fundamental investment issues are different; they are characteristics of investments and markets of which all participants should be aware. It is critical to remain cognizant of them and how they may evolve in the future.

Alignment

Alignment must be one of the focuses of the future of investment. Alignment refers to the degree to which the interests between the entity pledging funds and the entity deploying the funds are consistent. In other words, proper alignment exists when the desires of the investor and the incentives of the steward of the investor's capital are in agreement. If the steward receives financial windfalls from an investment and the investor does not, their interests are not aligned. Alignment is crucial in almost every aspect of investment. In public companies, the interests that must be aligned are those of the management of the company and those of the investors. In a fund structure, the interests that must be aligned are those of the investment manager and the fund investors. In real estate, the interests that must be aligned are those of the owner of the property and those of the property management company. Investing is never a one-player game, for it requires careful coordination and structuring between those who have the capital and those who are charged with putting it to work.

We have made significant progress through time. Indeed, alignment, or the lack thereof, has long been a central concern in the history of investment. The British East India Company, for instance, had a difficult time preventing teams stationed abroad from conducting trade to benefit themselves rather than the firm. Similarly, Adam Smith thought that joint-stock companies were destined to fail because management would not act to best advance the interests of the investors.

More recently, many mechanisms have been designed to aid in the alignment of interests. First, there are regulations that deem many fund managers to be legal fiduciaries and prohibit certain behavior that would put their own interests before those of their clients. Second, corporate boards of directors can act to limit abuses by corporate management, overseeing expenses on unnecessary purchases and ensuring that compensation is not excessive. Third, there are incentive arrangements that pay off to the stewards of capital when investors earn a return. In public environments, these incentives are sometimes structured as stock options for management teams to earn money when the stock performs well. In private equity environments, these incentives are structured as carried interest, a portion of the profits of the partnership that goes to the manager.

However, the future of investment must contemplate how some of these arrangements can distort behavior. Might the carried-interest feature cause certain stewards to treat it like a call option and invest in circumstances that are "heads I win, tails you lose"? Might there be opportunities for making corporate boards more shareholder friendly and reducing some cases of corporate abuses? Certainly, activist investors to some degree are pursuing such enhanced governance structures, but there is work that remains to be done. Small investors, too, must increasingly have access to mechanisms that ensure that their interests are aligned with either the managers they hire or the corporate heads who oversee the operations of the companies they purchase.

Liquidity

A second area needing greater focus is understanding liquidity. Liquidity is a measure of how quickly and cost-effectively an investment can be converted to cash. The fundamental liquidity test is to analyze how significantly one's sale price would be impaired relative to fair value if one had to sell an asset on a very short time scale. An investment that can be sold swiftly and with little transaction cost is deemed "liquid" (like large capitalization public stocks), and one that takes longer to sell and is often sold at a discount to fair value is illiquid (like houses and some esoteric financial instruments).

The first important focus for the future is who should actually care about liquidity. Commercial banks, for instance, that have to manage a fundamental maturity mismatch between short-dated deposits and long-dated lending investments have to care about liquidity to meet short-term obligations. A pension fund, by contrast, with long-dated liabilities should not care very much about liquidity because its future cash needs are known years in advance. However, there are many pension funds that care far too much about liquidity and there are banks that seemed to care far too little. This is also true of individuals: there are individuals who could bear more illiquidity than they typically care to and others who remain far too illiquid. The attitude depends on one's spending habits, stage of life, net worth, and financial dependents.

All this is crucial not just for maintenance of one's balance sheet but also for the very act of investment. There are times when being liquid is expensive; that is, there are market environments in which there is a real and substantial illiquidity premium. In such an environment, a pension fund or endowment should have little aversion to owning highly illiquid assets if those assets offer a substantial return premium over liquid assets with similar risk characteristics.

One of the great realizations David Swensen made about managing the Yale endowment is that there was excessive illiquidity premium early in the expansion of private equity. There were few participants and a broad opportunity set in the space in its early years, and the premium to bear illiquid equity over its liquid counterpart (the stock market) was high.

The importance of liquidity was highlighted again during the global financial crisis as banks dealt with liquidity shortfalls, funds sought to convert many of their holdings to cash, and other investors rotated out of risk assets. A liquidity shock to the financial system can cause assets to be sold at fire sale prices if the individuals and institutions that own the assets are determined to have them off their balance sheets. Becoming liquid shortly after the global financial crisis was actually fairly expensive, with many institutions in the market to sell their illiquid assets at a discount to generate that liquidity. And yet, many other market participants who could have absorbed these less liquid assets were hesitant to do so. In short, many market participants both misunderstood their own liquidity needs and failed to properly think about the costs of becoming liquid.

In the future, investors should come to understand increasingly that there is no silver bullet—that one should not be either liquid or illiquid. Sometimes one is compensated handsomely for owning assets that cannot be sold swiftly; at other times, it is not very costly to be liquid. A given market participant should instead be acutely aware of its own liquidity needs as well as the price of being liquid.

Benchmarking Performance

The future of investment, particularly when active management is involved (that is, the payment of investment professionals for portfolio construction), should involve more benchmarking. Investments should be benchmarked relative to the most pertinent index or set of indices available. The reason for benchmarking returns is simple: it allows the investor to flesh out a report card for the manager he or she has hired. A measurement of alpha allows disaggregating a manager's return stream into its two constituent parts, one due to market movement (for which the manager should receive credit only for market timing decisions) and one due directly to the manager's efforts to capture inefficient pricing (for which the manager should receive credit). Consider the example of hiring a manager to invest in Latin American small capitalization stocks. One year later, if the manager posts phenomenal returns, the investor should ask if those returns are due to the fact that Latin American small capitalization stocks as an asset class have done very well in the last year or that the manager actually added value beyond the market return of Latin American small capitalization stocks. It is possible that in this scenario, Latin American small capitalization stocks as a class had a terrific year and the "good decision"—that is, the decision to allocate to the asset class of Latin American small capitalization equities—was made not by the manager but by the investor who hired him or her. Alternatively, if the manager did very well because the manager elected to emphasize Latin American smaller capitalization stocks, the manager should be lauded for adding excess returns.

The ultimate goal of an investment manager is to generate alpha, or excess returns on a risk-adjusted basis, over time. Of course, this does not mean that one should expect an active manager to generate alpha every single year. There are vagaries to the market that make such a goal elusive. But over time, the manager should be expected to "earn his keep" or be fired.

If a manager does not generate alpha over time, the investor is better off simply buying the index. If the manager does generate alpha on a gross basis (before fees) but not on a net basis (after fees), then the manager is extracting the entire alpha and the investor is not receiving any of it, and the fee for the manager is too high. If the manager is generating alpha after fees, it is the investor's job to decide if the manager is likely to continue generating alpha. The investor should consider a number of questions: Is the space in which the manager operates just as inefficient? Have market conditions changed fundamentally such that they would impair the manager's ability to exploit mispricing? Or has the manager grown the asset base too much to reasonably extract the alpha in the corner in which he or she operates?

Alpha persistence is a much more difficult question and does require the investor to keep taking the pulse of the market niches where he or she hires active managers.

Market Inefficiencies

One would expect markets to become more efficient over time. Certainly, the growth of technology has enhanced the speed, quality, and breadth of information that has reduced the informational gaps among market participants over the years. However, there remain some sources of inefficiency that are likely to persist.

The first is distressed selling. Distressed selling refers to the disposition of assets, typically at prices below their fair value, because the financial or emotional condition of the owner is impaired. This often happens because of market shocks. These shocks could be systemic shocks like those that played out in the global financial crisis; they could be limited to more specific corners of the market, such as a shock in the form of low commodities prices for natural resources firms; or they could be purely idiosyncratic, as in a firm that became too levered, experienced significant litigation, or made a poor investment. It is possible that through time, cycles of distress do shorten as more capital flows into mandates allowing for the acquisition of distressed assets (for instance, if the number and size of hedge funds or private equity pursuing distressed strategies grows) and the competition for buying from distressed sellers heightens. However, distress is a normal part of a market that experiences disturbances and should offer inefficiency for those nimble and creative enough to exploit it.

The second source of potential risk premium for market structure reasons is mandate fragmentation. Every market participant has some mandate; that is, each participant has its own universe of assets in which the participant tends to transact. Some mandates have restrictions that are legal or regulatory, such as those of banks, insurance companies, or pension plans. Other mandates may simply be a matter of comfort and familiarity; thus a private equity firm that buys consumer companies may not be a buyer of coal producers, for example, as that is not its area of expertise. Mandates also may change through time: for instance, a hedge fund that was small ten years ago but is now large and has personnel with experience in new strategies may see its mandate grow. The market sometimes offers opportunities to exploit mandate fragmentation, opportunities for either owning assets or taking on risks that do not fit neatly into another market participant's mandate. For example, after the global financial crisis, there were reforms in regulatory capital rules in the United States and Europe. For certain assets, insurance companies received capital treatment different than what they had previously experienced and thus needed to enter into creative contracts with other market participants to lessen the burden of punitive capital treatment for those assets. Market participants with very flexible mandates were able to earn a premium for entering into the area of regulatory capital trades that few others could take on because of mandate fragmentation. To consider an alternative example, merger arbitrage spread—the premium earned by buying a firm that another company intends to acquire and holding it until the deal closes—sometimes grows when the volume of available deals grows. This is not because the deals have become more risky but, rather, because there is a limited amount of capital that buys in to merger arbitrage deals. In theory, the price of risk should be a function of just a few variables according to the capital asset pricing model, namely, the risk-free rate, the equity premium, the beta of the asset, and factor premiums like size and value. However, opportunities that arise because of agents' mandate fragmentation are fundamentally mispriced risk. These opportunities simply have nothing to do with these variables and instead arise from market structure.

Last are inefficiencies across geographies, though perhaps these are most certain to become more efficient through time. In developed markets, there tend to be sophisticated financial players combing over market opportunities regularly. In emerging and frontier markets, however, there are fewer sophisticated players trawling through the pond of opportunity. These spaces should offer less competition for deals and increased potential for alpha until more financial players arrive on the scene to close the gaps.

New Asset Classes

The future of investment will involve the creation of new asset classes, particularly for institutional investors. Over the course of history, the availability of new asset classes for investors has expanded. In the ancient period, land, lending, and trade were the primary investment activities. Over time, investors had access to more investment markets through innovation, including that involving joint-stock companies and public markets.

This trend has continued into the modern era. Some institutional investors have seized upon exotic asset classes, which are novel forms of risk that tend to bear low correlations with traditional asset classes. These exotic risks allow institutional investors to build more diversified portfolios. In their early years, however, these often also allow investors to earn outsized returns if they properly understand the emerging asset class.

This situation was certainly true, as discussed previously, of Yale's early adoption of private equity as an asset class. But it certainly goes beyond private equity. Harvard was a first mover in another exotic asset class: timber, which Harvard started purchasing in 1997. Over time, as more institutional investors have moved into timber, it has tended to offer less and less in the way of outsized returns. It is not as though there are no attractive opportunities in the space, but as these exotic asset classes become more widely understood, the returns tend to fall. This story has played out on many occasions in other exotic risks, like pharmaceutical and songwriter royalties and natural catastrophe bonds where the first movers did very well but the market has become more competitive through time. These exotic risks have a life cycle to them. They begin with "invention," a loose designation for first movers coming across and investing in the asset class and in which returns are often outsized for a given level of risk. Next comes "discovery," as more players see the success of the first movers and participate. Last is "maturation," when either more capital or those with a lower cost of capital enter the space and bid up assets, reducing returns. One has to be perpetually on the frontier of identifying and executing upon new exotic opportunities before they become mature. The future of investment will surely involve the emergence of new asset classes for the exotic risks that are likely to follow such a trajectory.

THE FOUR INVESTMENT PRINCIPLES

We conclude the book by revisiting the four basic investment principles that were enumerated at the beginning and that have been key to sound investments. One of the goals of looking at the history of investing is to better understand how to invest wisely and well, and thus in closing, we consider how *real ownership, fundamental value, financial leverage,* and *resource allocation* provide the foundation for a well-conceived investment process.

Today, real ownership seems more important than ever. In an era when much of public market trading volume is short-term oriented, momentum driven, or high-frequency enabled, leaving only a minor percentage to be based on fundamental analysis, the practice of regarding an investment not as a piece of paper but as a genuine commitment to an operating business is essential. This is an environment filled with opportunity and risk—the opportunity to bring a deeper level of understanding and evaluation to an investment and the risk of being steamrolled by a cascade of purchase and sale activity that has no more benefit of thoughtful analysis than an ocean wave breaking on the shore. But it is just this risk that creates exciting opportunities for investors who can resist extreme emotions and the "madding crowds."

It is in this environment that determining true fundamental value based on cash-flow projections is so crucial. At a time when markets are not only active but also no longer at extremely low valuations, maintaining the discipline of calculating expectable cash on cash returns is more important than ever. As some value investors observe, it is sometimes necessary to say that "very few investments meet my return criteria." In these situations, sitting out market activity or using hedges to reduce systematic market risk can be just as important as acting.

Financial leverage has come dramatically onto the scene in the last decade because of our propensity to pay attention to leverage when negative events are occurring, such as with the financial crisis and Great Recession of 2007–2009, but to ignore it under normal circumstances. But leverage is in use at all times, good and bad, and the investor must be aware of it. This is especially true given the easy money policy of the US Federal Reserve for much of the early twenty-first century. The availability of remarkably inexpensive borrowed risk capital has been very appealing as a wealth-multiplying tool for entrepreneurs. The skillful use of moderate amounts (and sometimes even seemingly immoderate amounts) of leverage can lead to significant investment returns, especially when the investment is not highly speculative. This thoughtful use of leverage to increase investment success continues to be a significant component of the tool kits of many, if not most, great investment performers.

Finally, resource allocation has gained prominence this century even though the exceptionally valuable skills of capital allocation and the allocation of human capability are still inadequately understood. The image of an outstanding manager as a feverishly busy and detailed director of day-to-day operations has been gradually replaced by the image of a largely hands-off, big-picture leader who delegates much of the day-to-day management but focuses intently on directing commitments of capital and selecting key executives. At a time when more and more corporate resources are coming under the control of decentralized Berkshire Hathaway–like enterprises and financially oriented private equity owners, this new focus seems to be thriving.

HISTORY

A history usually contains a story and a lesson. In this history, the story is of humankind's progress toward greater democracy, accessibility, and fairness in the activity of investment and its benefits. The lesson is somewhat different. It is that the right—the privilege—of being an investor has been proliferating dramatically, but with that right and privilege come responsibilities and challenges.

Investment is more available, but its practical requirements are not yet fully understood or accepted by most of us. Fairness and transparency are much greater, but the world of investment is still far from equal. Most crucial of all: study, understanding, and courage regarding investment are the duty of all of us who want to create the best, most comfortable, and most secure economic lives for ourselves and our families.

Notes

INTRODUCTION

1. Robert G. Hagstrom, *The Warren Buffett Way* (New York: Wiley, 1994), 75.
2. John Burr Williams, *The Theory of Investment Value* (Cambridge, MA: Harvard University Press, 1938), 5–6.
3. Ibid.
4. Richard A. Goldthwaite, *The Economy of Renaissance Florence* (Baltimore: Johns Hopkins University Press, 2009), 408–411 and 544–545.
5. Roger Lowenstein, *When Genius Failed: The Rise and Fall of Long-Term Capital Management* (New York: Random House, 2000), 191.
6. Andrea Frazzini, David Kabiller, and Lasse H. Pedersen, "Buffett's Alpha" (NBER Working Paper 19681, National Bureau of Economic Research, Cambridge, MA, November 2013), http://www.nber.org/papers/w19681, 4.
7. Goldthwaite, *Economy of Renaissance Florence*, 391–394.
8. William Thorndike, introduction to *The Outsiders: Eight Unconventional CEOs and Their Radically Rational Blueprint for Success* (Boston: Harvard Business Review Press, 2012), 5–8.

9. Ibid.
10. Ibid., 38–39.

1. A PRIVILEGE OF THE POWER ELITE

1. Marc Van De Mieroop, *The Ancient Mesopotamian City* (New York: Oxford University Press, 1999), 146.
2. Jane R. McIntosh, *Ancient Mesopotamia: New Perspectives* (Santa Barbara, CA: ABC-CLIO, 2005), 3, 62–65, and 349–350; Van De Mieroop, *Ancient Mesopotamian City*, 146–147.
3. Benjamin Foster, "A New Look at the Sumerian Temple State," *Journal of the Economic and Social History of the Orient* 24, no. 3 (October 1981): 226–227.
4. Maria deJ Ellis, *Agriculture and the State in Ancient Mesopotamia: An Introduction to the Problems of Land Tenure*, Occasional Publications of the Babylonian Fund 1 (Philadelphia: University Museum, 1976), 10.
5. Foster, "Sumerian Temple State," 226.
6. W. F. Leemans, "The Role of Landlease in Mesopotamia in the Early Second Millennium B.C.," *Journal of the Economic and Social History of the Orient* 18, no. 2 (June 1975): 136.
7. Foster, "Sumerian Temple State," 226.
8. G. van Driel, "Capital Formation and Investment in an Institutional Context in Ancient Mesopotamia," in *Trade and Finance in Ancient Mesopotamia*, ed. J. G. Dercksen (Leiden: Nederlands Instituut voor het Nabije Oosten, 1999), 32–37.
9. McIntosh, *Ancient Mesopotamia*, 130 and 351.
10. Ibid., 130.
11. Leemans, "Role of Landlease," 136–139.
12. A. Leo Oppenheim, *Ancient Mesopotamia: Portrait of a Dead Civilization* (Chicago: University of Chicago Press, 1977), 85; Van De Mieroop, *Ancient Mesopotamian City*, 147.
13. Van De Mieroop, *Ancient Mesopotamian City*, 147–148.
14. Xenophon, *Oeconomicus*, trans. Carnes Lord, in *The Shorter Socratic Writings:* Apology of Socrates to the Jury, Oeconomicus, *and* Symposium, ed. Robert C. Bartlett (Ithaca, NY: Cornell University Press, 1996), 39–40.
15. Humfrey Michell, *Economics of Ancient Greece*, 2nd ed. (Cambridge: Heffer, 1957), 38.
16. Ibid., 41–44.
17. Ibid., 39–41.

18. Tenney Frank, *Rome and Italy of the Republic*, vol. 1 of *An Economic Survey of Ancient Rome* (Paterson, NJ: Pageant, 1959), 208–214, 295–299, and 376–402.

19. Jean Andreau, *Banking and Business in the Roman World*, trans. Janet Lloyd (Cambridge: Cambridge University Press, 1999), 18

20. Ibid., xv and 18.

21. Ibid., 26–27 and 64–70.

22. Ibid., 18–19.

23. Dominic Rathbone, *Economic Rationalism and Rural Society in Third-Century A.D. Egypt: The Heroninos Archive and the Appianus Estate* (Cambridge: Cambridge University Press, 1991), xviii and 44.

24. Ibid., 58–87.

25. Dennis P. Kehoe, *Management and Investment on Estates in Roman Egypt during the Early Empire* (Bonn: Habelt, 1992), 16–20.

26. Jules Toutain, *The Economic Life of the Ancient World*, trans. M. R. Dobie (Abingdon, UK: Routledge, 1996), 246–250.

27. Agasha Mugasha, *The Law of Letters of Credit and Bank Guarantees* (Sydney: Federation Press, 2003), 38–39.

28. Joseph Manning, "Demotic Papyri (664–30 B.C.E.)," in *Security for Debt in Ancient Near Eastern Law*, eds. Raymond Westbrook and Richard Jasnow (Leiden: Brill, 2001), 307–308 and 312.

29. Ibid., 310 and 315.

30. Ibid., 308.

31. Sitta von Reden, *Money in Ptolemaic Egypt: From the Macedonian Conquest to the End of the Third Century B.C.* (Cambridge: Cambridge University Press, 2007), 8.

32. Manning, "Demotic Papyri," 310.

33. Ibid., 310–312.

34. Ibid., 320–321.

35. Paul Millett, *Lending and Borrowing in Ancient Athens* (Cambridge: Cambridge University Press, 1991), 5; Aristophanes, *The Birds*, trans. David Barrett (London: Penguin, 2003), 159.

36. Millet, *Lending and Borrowing*, 6.

37. Ibid., 3, 29, and 72.

38. Ibid., 27–52.

39. Ibid., 32–33.

40. Ibid., 24 and 247n21.

41. Edward E. Cohen, *Athenian Economy and Society: A Banking Perspective* (Princeton, NJ: Princeton University Press, 1992), 71–75.

42. Michell, *Economics of Ancient Greece*, 336.

43. Glen Davies, *A History of Money: From Ancient Times to the Present Day* (Cardiff: University of Wales Press, 2002), 75–76.

44. Millett, *Lending and Borrowing*, 24.

45. Cohen, *Athenian Economy and Society*, 76–77.

46. Michell, *Economics of Ancient Greece*, 335.

47. Sidney Homer and Richard Sylla, *A History of Interest Rates*, 4th ed. (Hoboken, NJ: Wiley, 2005), 35.

48. Ibid.

49. Ibid., 36.

50. Andreau, *Banking and Business*, 46.

51. Ibid., 142.

52. Ibid., 46–48.

53. Ibid., 2.

54. Toutain, *Economic Life of the Ancient World*, 246.

55. Jiaguan Hong, 中国金融史 [*A financial history of China*] (Chengdu, 1993); Qiugen Liu, "两宋私营高利贷资本初探" [A first look at usury capital in the Song dynasty], *Philosophy and Social Sciences* (Hebei University), no. 3 (1987): 11–17.

56. Hong, *Financial history of China*.

57. Ibid.

58. Liu, "First look at usury capital."

59. Hong, *Financial history of China*.

60. Quigen Liu, "论中国古代商业、高利贷资本组织中的'合资'与'合伙'" [Joint-stock partnerships in business and usury capital organization in ancient China], *Hebei Academic Journal* (Hebei University), no. 5 (1994): 86–91.

61. Valerie Hansen and Ana Mata-Fink, "Records from a Seventh-Century Pawnshop in China," in *The Origins of Value: The Financial Innovations That Created Modern Capital Markets*, eds. William N. Goetzmann and K. Geert Rouwenhorst (Oxford: Oxford University Press, 2005), 54–58; Homer and Sylla, *History of Interest Rates*, 614.

62. Hansen and Mata-Fink, "Records from a Pawnshop," 58–59.

63. Michael T. Skully, "The Development of the Pawnshop Industry in East Asia," in *Financial Landscapes Reconstructed: The Fine Art of Mapping Development*, eds. F. J. A. Bouman and Otto Hospes (Boulder, CO: Westview, 1994), 363–364.

64. Suzanne Gay, *The Moneylenders of Late Medieval Kyoto* (Honolulu: University of Hawaii Press, 2001), 37–40.

65. Suzanne Gay, e-mail message to author, March 30, 2011.

66. Gay, *Moneylenders of Kyoto*, 48–49.

67. Ibid., 40 and 45.

68. Franklin W. Ryan, *Usury and Usury Laws: A Juristic-Economic Study of the Effects of State Statutory Maximums for Loan Charges upon Lending Operations in the United States* (Boston: Houghton Mifflin, 1924), 38–39.

69. Oppenheim, *Ancient Mesopotamia*, 88.

70. J. B. C. Murray, *The History of Usury* (Philadelphia: J. B. Lippincott, 1866), 22–25.

71. Joseph Persky, "Retrospectives: From Usury to Interest," *Journal of Economic Perspectives* 21, no. 2 (Winter 2007): 229.

72. Murray, *History of Usury*, 28–29.

73. Ibid., 27–28.

74. The biblical references in this section are noted by Homer and Sylla, *History of Interest Rates*, 67, and by Sudin Haron and Wan Nursofiza Wan Azmi, *Islamic Finance and Banking System: Philosophies, Principles, and Practices* (New York: McGraw-Hill, 2009), 172–178. The translations provided here are from the New King James Version.

75. Jared Rubin, "The Lender's Curse: A New Look at the Origin and Persistence of Interest Bans in Islam and Christianity" (PhD diss., Stanford University, 2007), 31–32, ProQuest (AAT 3267615).

76. Homer and Sylla, *History of Interest Rates*, 68.

77. Ibid., 69.

78. Meir Kohn, "The Capital Market before 1600" (working paper 99-06, Department of Economics, Dartmouth College, Hanover, NH, February 1999), http://www.dartmouth.edu/~mkohn/Papers/99-06.pdf, 10–12.

79. Meir Kohn, "Finance before the Industrial Revolution: An Introduction" (working paper 99-01, Department of Economics, Dartmouth College, Hanover, NH, February 1999), http://www.dartmouth.edu/~mkohn/Papers/99-01.pdf, 10.

80. Homer and Sylla, *History of Interest Rates*, 71.

81. Persky, "Retrospectives," 227.

82. Raymond de Roover, *The Rise and Decline of the Medici Bank, 1397–1494* (Washington, DC: Beard Books, 1999), 10–14.

83. Frederic C. Lane, *Venice and History: Collected Papers of F. C. Lane* (Baltimore: Johns Hopkins University Press, 1966), 64.

84. Manuel Riu, "Banking and Society in Late Medieval and Early Modern Aragon," in *The Dawn of Modern Banking* (New Haven, CT: Yale University Press, 1979), 136.

85. Kohn, "Finance before the Industrial Revolution," 11.

86. Ibid., 11.

87. Murray, *History of Usury*, 45–47.

88. Persky, "Retrospectives," 227–236; Homer and Sylla, *History of Interest Rates*, 79.

89. Raymond de Roover, "Scholastic Economics: Survival and Lasting Influence from the Sixteenth Century to Adam Smith," *Quarterly Journal of Economics* 69, no. 2 (May 1955): 175–176.

90. Benedict XIV (pope), *Vix Pervenit*, [1745], EWTN Global Catholic Network, accessed January 2015, http://www.ewtn.com/library/ENCYC/B14VIXPE.htm.

91. Norman Jones, "Usury," in *Encyclopedia of Economic and Business History*, ed. Robert Whaples, Economic History Association, article published February 10, 2008, http://eh.net/encyclopedia/usury.

92. Shahid Hasan Siddiqui, *Islamic Banking: Genesis & Rationale, Evaluation & Review, Prospects & Challenges* (Karachi: Royal Book, 1994), 5–6.

93. Ibid., 9.

94. Haron and Azmi, *Islamic Finance and Banking System*, 48.

95. Ibid., 190.

96. Siddiqui, *Islamic Banking*, 21.

97. Anwar Iqbal Qureshi, *Islam and the Theory of Interest* (Lahore: Shaikh Muhammad Ashraf, 1946), 175–189.

98. Haron and Azmi, *Islamic Finance and Banking System*, 44 and 52–53.

99. Wayne A. M. Visser and Alastair MacIntosh, "A Short Review of the Historical Critique of Usury," *Accounting, Business & Financial History* 8, no. 2 (1998): 176.

100. Kohn, "Finance before the Industrial Revolution," 9–12.

101. Robert S. Lopez, *The Commercial Revolution of the Middle Ages, 950–1350* (Cambridge: Cambridge University Press, 1976), 27–30, 56–60, and 85–91.

102. Ibid., 85–91.

103. Cohen, *Athenian Economy and Society*, 6.

104. Scott Meikle, *Aristotle's Economic Thought* (Oxford: Clarendon Press, 1995), 6–21.

105. M. I. Finley, *The Ancient Economy*, Sather Classical Lectures 43 (Berkeley: University of California Press, 1999), 22–23.

106. Van Driel, "Capital Formation and Investment," 25–42.

107. Hans Neumann, "Ur-Dumuzida and Ur-DUN: Reflections on the Relationship Between State-Initiated Foreign Trade and Private Economic Activity in Mesopotamia Towards the End of the Third Millennium B.C.," in Dercksen, *Trade and Finance*, 45–46 and 62.

108. Colin Adams, "Transport," in *The Cambridge Companion to the Roman Economy*, ed. Walter Scheidel (Cambridge: Cambridge University Press, 2012), 218–227.

109. Elio Lo Cascio, "The Early Roman Empire: The State and the Economy," in *The Cambridge Economic History of the Greco-Roman World*, eds. Walter Scheidel, Ian Morris, and Richard P. Saller (Cambridge: Cambridge University Press, 2007), 621–622 and 626; Adams, "Transport," 223–224.

110. Henri Pirenne, *Medieval Cities: Their Origins and the Revival of Trade*, trans. Frank D. Halsey (Princeton, NJ: Princeton University Press, 1952), 114 and 123–124.

111. Ibid., 185–212.

112. Lopez, *Commercial Revolution*, 63–70 and 85–91; Richard A. Goldthwaite, *The Economy of Renaissance Florence* (Baltimore: Johns Hopkins University Press, 2009), 3–6.

113. Goldthwaite, *Economy of Renaissance Florence*, 9; Lopez, *Commercial Revolution*, 87–89; Pirenne, *Medieval Cities*, 114–119.

114. Goldthwaite, *Economy of Renaissance Florence*, 143–151.

115. Raymond de Roover, *The Medici Bank: Its Organization, Management, Operations and Decline* (New York: New York University Press, 1948), 5ff.

116. Ibid., 29–30.

117. Goldthwaite, *Economy of Renaissance Florence*, 143–151.

118. Ibid., 236–245.

119. Goldthwaite, *Economy of Renaissance Florence*, 230–245; Edwin S. Hunt, "A New Look at the Dealings of the Bardi and Peruzzi with Edward III," *Journal of Economic History* 50, no. 1 (March 1990): 156–161; Tim Parks, *Medici Money: Banking, Metaphysics, and Art in Fifteenth-Century Florence* (New York: Norton, 2005), 6.

120. Suzanne Gay, "The Lamp-Oil Merchants of Iwashimizu Shrine: Transregional Commerce in Medieval Japan," *Monumenta Nipponica* 64, no. 1 (Spring 2009): 2–31.

121. Nakai Nobuhiko and James L. McClain, "Commercial Change and Urban Growth in Early Modern Japan," in *The Cambridge History of Japan*, vol. 4, *Early Modern Japan*, ed. John Whitney Hall (Cambridge: Cambridge University Press, 1991), 542 and 562.

122. Ibid., 557–563.

123. Ibid., 562–563.

124. Christopher Howe, *The Origins of Japanese Trade Supremacy: Development and Technology in Asia from 1540 to the Pacific* War (Chicago: University of Chicago Press, 1996), 3–21.

125. Giles Milton, *Samurai William: The Adventurer Who Unlocked Japan* (London: Hodder & Stoughton, 2002), 301–302.

126. Ibid., 302–303.

127. Ibid., 303.

128. Howe, *Japanese Trade Supremacy*, 21–22.

129. Ibid., 22 and 26–27.

130. Ibid., 22–23.

131. D. D. Kosambi, "Indian Feudal Trade Charters," *Journal of the Economic and Social History of the Orient* 2, no. 3 (December 1959): 281–282.

132. Rosalind O'Hanlon, *Caste, Conflict, and Ideology: Mahatma Jotirao Phule and Low Caste Protest in Nineteenth-Century Western India*, Cambridge South Asian Studies 30 (Cambridge: Cambridge University Press, 1985), 4–5; Stanley Wolpert, *India*, rev. ed. (Berkeley: University of California Press, 1999), 119.

133. Shireen Moosvi, "The Medieval State and Caste," *Social Scientist* 39, no. 7–8 (July–August 2011): 5–6.

134. Nandita P. Sahai, "Crafts in Eighteenth-Century Jodhpur: Questions of Class, Caste, and Community Identities," *Journal of the Economic and Social History of the Orient* 48, no. 4 (2005): 535.

135. P. S. Kanaka Durga, "Identity and Symbols of Sustenance: Explorations in Social Mobility of Medieval South India," *Journal of the Economic and Social History of the Orient* 44, no. 2 (2001): 141ff.

136. Chandrika Kaul, "From Empire to Independence: The British Raj in India, 1858–1947," BBC, last modified March 3, 2011, http://www.bbc.co.uk/history/british/modern/independence1947_01.shtml.

137. Morris D. Morris, "Towards a Reinterpretation of Nineteenth-Century Indian Economic History," *Journal of Economic History* 23, no. 4 (December 1963): 611–614.

138. Kaul, "From Empire to Independence."

139. Ibid.

140. David McMorran, *The Origin of Investment Securities* (Detroit: First National Company of Detroit, 1925), 13.

141. Toutain, *Economic Life of the Ancient World*, 246.

142. Ulrike Malmendier, "Law and Finance 'at the Origin,'" *Journal of Economic Literature* 47, no. 4 (December 2009): 1085–1086.

143. Toutain, *Economic Life of the Ancient World*, 246.

144. Ulrike Malmendier, "Roman Shares," in *The Origins of Value: The Financial Innovations That Created Modern Capital Markets*, eds. William N. Goetzmann and K. Geert Rouwenhorst (Oxford: Oxford University Press, 2005), 35–36.

145. Malmendier, "Law and Finance 'at the Origin,'" 1088–1092.

146. Ulrike Malmendier, "Societas" (working paper, Department of Economics, University of California, Berkeley, CA, n.d.), http://eml.berkeley.edu/~ulrike/Papers/Societas_Article_v3.pdf.

147. Toutain, *Economic Life of the Ancient World*, 246.

148. McMorran, *Origin of Investment Securities*, 13.

149. J. G. Dercksen, "On the Financing of Old Assyrian Merchants," in Dercksen, *Trade and Finance*, 86.

150. Ibid., 88–94.

151. Abraham L. Udovitch, "At the Origins of the Western Commenda: Islam, Israel, Byzantium?," *Speculum* 37, no. 2 (April 1962): 201–202.

152. Olga Maridaki-Karatza, "Legal Aspects of the Financing of Trade," in *The Economic History of Byzantium*, ed. Angeliki E. Laiou (Washington, DC: Dumbarton Oaks Research Library and Collection, 2002), 3:1112–1115.

153. Udovitch, "Origins of the Western Commenda," 199–200

154. Murat Çizakça, *A Comparative Evolution of Business Partnerships: The Islamic World and Europe, with Specific Reference to the Ottoman Archives*, The Ottoman Empire and Its Heritage 8 (Leiden: Brill, 1996), 66–68.

155. Ibid., 4–5.

156. Ibid., 5–6.

157. Ibid., 4.

158. Max Weber, *The History of Commercial Partnerships in the Middle Ages*, trans. Lutz Kaelber (Lanham, MD: Rowman & Littlefield, 2003), 63–75; Florence Edler de Roover, "Partnership Accounts in Twelfth Century Genoa," *Bulletin of the Business Historical Society* 15, no. 6 (December 1941): 88.

159. F. de Roover, "Partnership Accounts in Genoa," 88.

160. R. de Roover, *Rise and Decline of the Medici Bank*, 237.

161. Weber, *History of Commercial Partnerships*, 137–139.

162. Sebouh Aslanian, "The Circulation of Men and Credit: The Role of the Commenda and the Family Firm in Julfan Society," *Journal of the Economic and Social History of the Orient* 50, no. 2–3 (2007): 127.

163. Udovitch, "Origins of the Western Commenda," 202–207.

164. Çizakça, *Comparative Evolution of Business Partnerships*, 67 and 77.

165. Ibid., 78.

166. Joshua Sosin, "Perpetual Endowments in the Hellenistic World: A Case-Study in Economic Rationalism" (PhD diss., Duke University, 2000), 17, ProQuest (AAT 9977683).

167. Ibid., 28–29.

168. Ibid., 23.

169. Jinyu Liu, "The Economy of Endowments: The Case of the Roman Collegia," in *Pistoi Dia Tèn Technèn: Studies in Honour of Raymond Bogaert*, Studia Hellenistica 44, eds. Koenraad Verboven, Katelijn Vandorpe, and Véronique Chankowski (Leuven: Peeters, 2008), 233 and 239.

170. Ibid., 240.

171. Ibid., 239 and 244–245.

172. Sosin, "Perpetual Endowments."

173. Ibid., 2.

174. A. R. W. Harrison, *The Law of Athens*, vol. 1, *The Family and Property*, 2nd ed. (Indianapolis: Hackett, 1998), 99–100.

175. Adolf Berger, Barry Nicholas, and Susan M. Treggiari, "Guardianship," in *The Oxford Classical Dictionary*, eds. Simon Hornblower, Antony Spawforth, and Esther Eidinow, 4th ed. (Oxford: Oxford University Press, 2012), 637.

176. Dennis P. Kehoe, *Investment, Profit, and Tenancy: The Jurists and the Roman Agrarian Economy* (Ann Arbor: University of Michigan Press, 1997), 35.

177. Robert L. Clark, Lee A. Craig, and Jack W. Wilson, *A History of Public Sector Pensions in the United States* (Philadelphia: University of Pennsylvania Press, 2003), 24–26.

178. Suetonius, *Lives of the Twelve Caesars*, trans. Philemon Holland (New York: Holland, 1965), quoted in Clark, Craig, and Wilson, *History of Public Sector Pensions*, 26.

179. Clark, Craig, and Wilson, *History of Public Sector Pensions*, 26.

2. THE DEMOCRATIZATION OF INVESTMENT

1. Meir Kohn, "The Capital Market before 1600" (working paper 99-06, Department of Economics, Dartmouth College, Hanover, NH, February 1999), http://www.dartmouth.edu/~mkohn/Papers/99-06.pdf, 14–18.

2. Robert Gibson-Jarvie, *The City of London: A Financial and Commercial History* (Cambridge: Woodhead-Faulkner, 1979), 24 and 98.

3. Ibid., 24–25.

4. Mira Wilkins, *The History of Foreign Investment in the United States to 1914*. Harvard Studies in Business History 41 (Cambridge, MA: Harvard University Press, 1989), 3–4.

5. Ibid., 4–5.

6. "South Sea Bubble Short History," Baker Library, Harvard Business School, accessed 2014, http://www.library.hbs.edu/hc/ssb/history.html; Joel Bakan, *The Corporation: The Pathological Pursuit of Profit and Power* (New York: Free Press, 2004), 6–8.

7. "South Sea Bubble Short History."

8. Bakan, *The Corporation*, 6–7.

9. Colin Arthur Cooke, *Corporation, Trust and Company: An Essay in Legal History* (Cambridge, MA: Harvard University Press, 1951), 83.

10. Adam Smith, *An Inquiry into the Nature and Causes of the Wealth of Nations* (New York: Modern Library, 1937), 334–335.

11. Peter N. Stearns, *The Industrial Revolution in World History*, 3rd ed. (Boulder, CO: Westview, 2007).

12. Ibid., 34–37.

13. Ibid., 17–26 and 79–83.
14. Meir Kohn, "Finance before the Industrial Revolution: An Introduction" (working paper 99-01, Department of Economics, Dartmouth College, Hanover, NH, February 1999), http://www.dartmouth.edu/~mkohn /Papers/99-01.pdf, 5–6.
15. Joseph E. Inikori, *Africans and the Industrial Revolution in England: A Study in International Trade and Economic Development* (Cambridge: Cambridge University Press, 2002), 315.
16. Kohn, "Finance before the Industrial Revolution," 2–4.
17. Inikori, *Africans and the Industrial Revolution*, 314–316.
18. Richard Brown, *Society and Economy in Modern Britain, 1700–1850* (New York: Routledge, 1990), 198.
19. Ibid., 200.
20. Ibid., 200–201.
21. Ibid., 293.
22. Richard Price, *British Society, 1680–1880: Dynamism, Containment, and Change* (Cambridge: Cambridge University Press, 1999), 76–78.
23. Michael Collins, *Monday and Banking in the UK: A History* (New York: Routledge, 1988), 57.
24. Carlo M. Cipolla, *Before the Industrial Revolution: European Society and Economy, 1000–1700*, trans. Christopher Woodall, 3rd ed. (New York: Norton, 1994), 30–33.
25. Eric Hobsbawm, *Industry and Empire: From 1750 to the Present Day*, rev. ed. (London: Penguin, 1999), 55–56.
26. G. N. von Tunzelmann, "The Standard of Living Debate and Optimal Economic Growth," in *The Economics of the Industrial Revolution*, ed. Joel Mokyr (London: Allen & Unwin, 1985), 207; Peter H. Lindert and Jeffrey G. Williamson, "English Workers' Living Standards During the Industrial Revolution: A New Look," *Economic History Review*, n.s., 36, no. 1 (February 1983): 1–2.
27. Hobsbawm, *Industry and Empire*, 54–55.
28. Ibid., 58.
29. Ibid., 55–59; Price, *British Society*, 275–276.
30. Martin Kitchen, *A History of Modern Germany, 1800–2000* (Malden, MA: Blackwell, 2006), 39.
31. Lindert and Williamson, "English Workers' Living Standards," 4.
32. Ibid., 7.
33. Sutapa Bose and Ashok Rudra, "Quantitative Estimates of Primitive Accumulation and Its Sources," *Economic and Political Weekly* 29, no. 4 (January 22, 1994): 200.
34. Peter Temin, "Two Views of the British Industrial Revolution," *Journal of Economic History* 57, no. 1 (March 1997): 63–64.

35. David McNally, *Political Economy and the Rise of Capitalism: A Reinterpretation* (Berkeley: University of California Press, 1988), 156–158 and 177–179.
36. Brown, *Society and Economy*, 192–193.
37. Naomi R. Lamoreaux, Margaret Levenstein, and Kenneth L. Sokoloff, "Financing Invention during the Second Industrial Revolution: Cleveland, Ohio, 1870–1920" (NBER Working Paper 10923, National Bureau of Economic Research, Cambridge, MA, November 2004), http://www.nber.org/papers/w10923.pdf, 1–2.
38. Ibid., 10–20.
39. Ibid., 5.
40. Hubert Bonin, "'Blue Angels,' 'Venture Capital,' and 'Whales': Networks Financing the Takeoff of the Second Industrial Revolution in France, 1890s–1920s," *Business and Economic History On-Line* 2 (2004), http://www.thebhc.org/sites/default/files/Bonin_0.pdf, 9–14.
41. Kohn, "Capital Market before 1600," 9–13; Larry Neal, "On the Historical Development of Stock Markets," in *The Emergence and Evolution of Markets*, eds. Horst Brezinski and Michael Fritsch (Cheltenham, UK: Edward Elgar, 1997), 61–62.
42. Maurice Obstfeld and Alan M. Taylor, *Global Capital Markets: Integration, Crisis, and Growth* (Cambridge: Cambridge University Press, 2004), 17.
43. Ranald C. Michie, *The Global Securities Market: A History* (Oxford: Oxford University Press, 2006), 21–23; Kohn, "Capital Market before 1600," 6–7; Obstfeld and Taylor, *Global Capital Markets*, 18.
44. Ranald C. Michie, "Development of Stock Markets," in *The New Palgrave Dictionary of Money and Finance*, eds. Peter Newman, Murray Milgate, and John Eatwell (London: Macmillan, 1992), 662; Michie, *Global Securities Market*, 21–23; Obstfeld and Taylor, *Global Capital Markets*, 18.
45. Neal, "Historical Development," 63.
46. Michie, "Development of Stock Markets," 662.
47. Obstfeld and Taylor, *Global Capital Markets*, 18.
48. Michie, *Global Securities Market*, 24.
49. Obstfeld and Taylor, *Global Capital Markets*, 18.
50. Ibid.
51. Kohn, "Capital Market before 1600," 20; Neal, "Historical Development," 62.
52. Obstfeld and Taylor, *Global Capital Markets*, 19.
53. Neal, "Historical Development," 62–63.
54. Michie, "Development of Stock Markets," 662–663.
55. Neal, "Historical Development," 63.

56. Kohn, "Capital Market before 1600," 20–21.

57. Obstfeld and Taylor, *Global Capital Markets*, 20; Neal, "Historical Development," 65.

58. Neal, "Historical Development," 62–65.

59. Obstfeld and Taylor, *Global Capital Markets*, 19.

60. London Stock Exchange, "Our History," accessed October 2014, http://www.londonstockexchange.com/about-the-exchange /company-overview/our-history/our-history.htm.

61. Neal, "Historical Development," 65.

62. Obstfeld and Taylor, *Global Capital Markets*, 19.

63. Ibid., 20.

64. Neal, "Historical Development," 64–71; Obstfeld and Taylor, *Global Capital Markets*, 22.

65. Michie, "Development of Stock Markets," 662.

66. Julie Jefferies, "The UK Population: Past, Present and Future," Office for National Statistics (UK), last modified December 2005, http://www .ons.gov.uk/ons/rel/fertility-analysis/focus-on-people-and-migration /december-2005/focus-on-people-and-migration---focus-on-people -and-migration---chapter-1.pdf, 3.

67. Neal, "Historical Development," 71–74; Michie, "Development of Stock Markets," 663; London Stock Exchange, "Our History;" Obstfeld and Taylor, *Global Capital Markets*, 19.

68. Joseph J. Ellis, *His Excellency: George Washington* (New York: Knopf, 2004), 303–304.

69. Stuart Banner, "The Origin of the New York Stock Exchange, 1791–1860," *Journal of Legal Studies* 27, no. 1 (January 1998): 115.

70. Ibid., 115.

71. Robert Sobel, *The Curbstone Brokers: The Origins of the American Stock Exchange* (London: Macmillan, 1970), 24–29.

72. New York Stock Exchange, "New York Stock Exchange Ends Member Seat Sales Today," December 30, 2013, http://www1.nyse.com /press/1135856420824.html.

73. Matthew A. Postal, "New York Curb Exchange (Incorporating the New York Curb Market Building), Later Known as the American Stock Exchange," New York City Landmarks Preservation Commission, June 26, 2012, http://www.nyc.gov/html/lpc/downloads/pdf /reports/2515.pdf, 2–3.

74. Jerry W. Markham, *A Financial History of the United States*, vol. 2, *From J. P. Morgan to the Institutional Investor (1900–1970)* (Armonk, NY: Sharpe, 2002), 3.

75. Postal, "New York Curb Exchange," 1–3 and 7.

76. Daniel Verdier, "Financial Capital Mobility and the Origins of Stock Markets" (working paper, European University Institute, San Domenico, Italy, February 1999), 4 and 11.
77. Michie, "Development of Stock Markets," 663
78. New York Stock Exchange, "Timeline—Technology," accessed October 2014, http://www1.nyse.com/about/history/timeline_technology.html; David Hochfelder, "How Bucket Shops Lured the Masses into the Market," BloombergView, January 10, 2013, http://www.bloombergview.com/articles/2013-01-10/how-bucket-shops-lured-the-masses-into-the-market.
79. Obstfeld and Taylor, *Global Capital Markets*, 23.
80. Ibid., 22–24.
81. Michie, "Development of Stock Markets," 663–664.
82. Hochfelder, "Bucket Shops."
83. Ibid.
84. Janice M. Traflet, *A Nation of Small Shareholders: Marketing Wall Street after World War II*, Studies in Industry and Society (Baltimore: Johns Hopkins University Press, 2013), 3 and 179n15.
85. Lewis Henry Kimmel, *Share Ownership in the United States* (Washington, DC: Brookings Institution, 1952), 137.
86. Traflet, *Nation of Small Shareholders*, 3–4.
87. Ibid., 4.
88. Kimmel, *Share Ownership*, 89.
89. Ibid., 125.
90. Ibid., 118.
91. Ibid., 90–98 and 121.
92. Traflet, *Nation of Small Shareholders*, 5–12.
93. Ibid., 1–12.
94. Ibid., 1.
95. New York Stock Exchange, "Highlights of NYSE Shareowner Census Reports (1952–1990)," accessed October 2014, http://www.nyxdata.com/nysedata/asp/factbook/viewer_edition.asp?mode=table&key=2312&category=11.
96. Traflet, *Nation of Small Shareholders*, 1.
97. Kimmel, *Share Ownership*; New York Stock Exchange, "Major Sources of NYSE Volume," accessed October 2014, http://www.nyxdata.com/nysedata/asp/factbook/viewer_edition.asp?mode=table&key=2641&category=11.
98. Traflet, *Nation of Small Shareholders*, 1–5.
99. Jesse Bricker et al., "Changes in U.S. Family Finances from 2007 to 2010: Evidence from the Survey of Consumer Finances," *Federal Reserve Bulletin* 98, no. 2 (June 2012): 28–34.

100. New York Stock Exchange, "Shareowner Census Reports."

101. Ibid.; New York Stock Exchange, "Selected Characteristics of Individual Shareowners," accessed October 2014, http://www.nyxdata.com /nysedata/asp/factbook/viewer_edition.asp?mode=chart&key=51&ca tegory=11.

102. James McAndrews and Chris Stefanadis, "The Consolidation of European Stock Exchanges," *Current Issues in Economics and Finance* 8, no. 6 (June 2002): 2–5.

103. Ibid., 4–5.

104. London Stock Exchange, "Our History."

105. New York Stock Exchange, "Timeline—Events," accessed October 2014, http://www1.nyse.com/about/history/timeline_events.html; Robert E. Wright, "The NYSE's Long History of Mergers and Rivalries," BloombergView, January 8, 2013, http://www.bloombergview .com/articles/2013-01-08/nyse-s-long-history-of-mergers-and-rivalries.

106. Deutsche Börse Group, "Company History," accessed October 2014, http://deutsche-boerse.com/dbg/dispatch/en/kir/dbg_nav /about_us/10_Deutsche_Boerse_Group/50_Company_History.

107. Michie, "Development of Stock Markets," 665; Michie, *Global Securities Market*, 12–14; Neal, "Historical Development," 77; Obstfeld and Taylor, *Global Capital Markets*, 15–16.

108. Obstfeld and Taylor, *Global Capital Markets*, 15–16.

109. Michael Gorham and Nidhi Singh, *Electronic Exchanges: The Global Transformation from Pits to Bits* (Burlington, MA: Elsevier, 2009), 67–71.

110. Michie, "Development of Stock Markets," 665–667.

111. Verdier, "Financial Capital Mobility," 6–10.

112. Michie, *Global Securities Market*, vi.

113. Neal, "Historical Development," 60.

114. Michie, *Global Securities Market*, vi and 334–340.

115. Michie, "Development of Stock Markets," 663.

116. "The Endangered Public Company," *Economist*, May 19, 2012, http:// www.economist.com/node/21555562.

3. RETIREMENT AND ITS FUNDING

1. LIMRA Secure Retirement Institute, "Retirement Plans—Investment Company Institute: Retirement Assets on the Rise in 2014," October 2014, http://www.limra.com/Secure_Retirement_Institute/News_Center /Retirement_Industry_Report/Retirement_Plans_-_Investment _Company_Institute__Retirement_Assets_on_the_Rise_in_2014.aspx.

2. Carole Haber and Brian Gratton, *Old Age and the Search for Security: An American Social History* (Bloomington: Indiana University Press, 1994), 118.

3. Ibid.

4. Lawrence W. Kennedy, *Planning the City upon a Hill: Boston since 1630* (Amherst: University of Massachusetts Press, 1992), Appendix A.

5. Haber and Gratton, *Old Age and Security*, 118–123.

6. Historical Center of the Presbyterian Church in America, "January 11: Presbyterian Ministers Fund," January 11, 2012, http://www.thisday .pcahistory.org/2012/01/january-11; Richard Webster, *A History of the Presbyterian Church in America, from Its Origin to the Year 1760* (Philadelphia: Joseph M. Wilson, 1857), 92.

7. "The Oldest Life Insurance Company in the United States," *New York Times*, November 19, 1905, http://timesmachine.nytimes.com /timesmachine/1905/11/19/101709385.html.

8. Ibid.

9. George Alter, Claudia Goldin, and Elyce Rotella, "The Savings of Ordinary Americans: The Philadelphia Saving Fund Society in the Mid-Nineteenth Century," *Journal of Economic History* 54, no. 4 (December 1994): 736–738.

10. Ibid., 757–760.

11. Chulhee Lee, "Sectoral Shift and the Labor-Force Participation of Older Males in the United States, 1880–1940," *Journal of Economic History* 62, no. 2 (June 2002): 520.

12. Ibid., 521.

13. Dora L. Costa, "Pensions and Retirement: Evidence from Union Army Veterans," *Quarterly Journal of Economics* 110, no. 2 (May 1995): 315–317.

14. Chulhee Lee, "The Expected Length of Male Retirement in the United States, 1850–1990," *Journal of Population Economics* 14, no. 4 (December 2001): 641–647.

15. Ibid., 647.

16. Steven A. Sass, *The Promise of Private Pensions: The First Hundred Years* (Cambridge, MA: Harvard University Press, 1997), 145–146.

17. Ibid.

18. Ibid., 145–147.

19. Social Security Administration, "Social Insurance Movement," accessed January 2015, http://www.socialsecurity.gov/history/trinfo.html.

20. Mary-Lou Weisman, "The History of Retirement, from Early Man to A.A.R.P.," *New York Times*, March 21, 1999, http://www.nytimes .com/1999/03/21/jobs/the-history-of-retirement-from-early-man-to -aarp.html.

21. Social Welfare History Project, "Townsend, Dr. Francis," accessed 2013, http://www.socialwelfarehistory.com/eras/townsend-dr-francis; Larry DeWitt, "The Townsend Plan's Pension Scheme," Social Security Administration, December 2001, http://www.ssa.gov/history /townsendproblems.html; Sass, *Promise of Private Pensions,* 94.
22. Larry DeWitt, "The 1937 Supreme Court Rulings on the Social Security Act," Social Security Administration, 1999, http://www.ssa.gov /history/court.html.
23. Social Security Administration, "Otto von Bismarck," accessed 2013, http://www.ssa.gov/history/ottob.html; Weisman, "History of Retirement."
24. Social Security Administration, "Historical Background and Development of Social Security," accessed December 2014, http://www.ssa .gov/history/briefhistory3.html; "Age 65 Retirement," Social Security Administration, accessed 2013, http://www.ssa.gov/history/age65 .html; Weisman, "History of Retirement."
25. "Age 65 Retirement."
26. Sass, *Promise of Private Pensions,* 113–115.
27. Patrick Purcell and Jennifer Staman, "Summary of the Employee Retirement Income Security Act (ERISA)," Congressional Research Service, Library of Congress, Washington, DC, April 10, 2008, http:// digitalcommons.ilr.cornell.edu/key_workplace/505, 2.
28. James Wooten, *The Employee Retirement Income Security Act of 1974: A Political History* (Berkeley: University of California Press, 2005), 51–52.
29. Ibid., 62.
30. Ibid., 183–185.
31. Ibid., 58–59.
32. Ibid., 52 and 251.
33. Charles D. Ellis, *Capital: The Story of Long-Term Investment Excellence* (Hoboken, NJ: Wiley, 2004), 146–147.
34. Ibid., 149.
35. Ibid., 148–149.
36. Ibid., 150–151.
37. Purcell and Staman, "Summary of ERISA," 3–5.
38. LIMRA Security Retirement Institute, "Retirement Plans."
39. Jim Saxton, "The Roots of Broadened Stock Ownership," Joint Economic Committee, US Congress, April 2000, http://cog.kent.edu/lib /Hall&Congress-RootsOfBroadenedStockOwnership.pdf, 4–14.
40. Ibid., 6.
41. Matteo Iacoviello, "Housing Wealth and Consumption" (working paper, Department of Economics, Boston College, Boston, MA, June 13, 2010), https://www2.bc.edu/matteo-iacoviello/research_files/HWAC.pdf, 4.

42. Brigitte C. Madrian and Dennis F. Shea, "The Power of Suggestion: Inertia in 401(k) Participation and Savings Behavior," *Quarterly Journal of Economics* 116, no. 4 (November 2001): 1150–1153 and 1160.

43. Ibid., 1184–1185.

44. "The U.S. Retirement Market, First Quarter 2011," Investment Company Institute, June 29, 2011, http://www.ici.org/pdf/ret_11_q1_data .pdf, 2.

45. Robert Steyer, "ICI: U.S. Retirement Assets Hit Record $20.8 Trillion," Pensions & Investments, June 26, 2013, http://www.pionline.com /article/20130626/ONLINE/130629908/ici-us-retirement -assets-hit-record-208-trillion.

46. "Retirement Market, First Quarter 2011," 2.

47. James M. Poterba, Steven F. Venti, and David A. Wise, "The Transition to Personal Accounts and Increasing Retirement Wealth: Macro and Micro Evidence" (NBER Working Paper 8610, National Bureau of Economic Research, Cambridge, MA, November 2001), http://www.nber .org/papers/w8610.pdf, Abstract.

4. NEW CLIENTS AND NEW INVESTMENTS

1. Nobel Media AB, "The Prize in Economics 1985—Press Release," 1985, accessed 2013, http://www.nobelprize.org/nobel_prizes/economic -sciences/laureates/1985/press.html. For the original work and quote provided, see John Maynard Keynes, *The General Theory of Employment, Interest and Money* (London: Macmillan, 1936), 96.

2. Nobel Media AB, "Prize in Economics 1985—Press Release;" Angus Deaton, "Franco Modigliani and the Life Cycle Theory of Consumption" (speech, Convegno Internazionale Franco Modgliani, Accademia Nazionale dei Lincei, Rome, February 17–18, 2005), https://www .princeton.edu/~deaton/downloads/romelecture.pdf, 1–2 and 6. For the original works, see Franco Modigliani and Richard H. Brumberg, "Utility Analysis and the Consumption Function: An Interpretation of Cross-Section Data," in *Post-Keynesian Economics*, ed. Kenneth K. Kurihara (New Brunswick, NJ: Rutgers University Press, 1954), 388–436; Franco Modigliani and Richard H. Brumberg, "Utility Analysis and Aggregate Consumption Functions: An Attempt at Integration," in *The Collected Papers of Franco Modigliani*, ed. Andrew Abel, vol. 2, *The Life Cycle Hypothesis of Saving* (Cambridge, MA: MIT Press, 1990), 128–197.

3. Nobel Media AB, "Prize in Economics 1985—Press Release;" Deaton, "Modigliani and the Life Cycle Theory," 9. For the original work,

see Milton Friedman, *A Theory of the Consumption Function* (Princeton, NJ: Princeton University Press, 1957).

4. Deaton, "Modigliani and the Life Cycle Theory," 7–8 and 16–18.

5. Investment Company Institute, *2013 Investment Company Fact Book*, accessed 2014, http://www.ici.org/pdf/2013_factbook.pdf, 117; James Wooten, *The Employee Retirement Income Security Act of 1974: A Political History* (Berkeley: University of California Press, 2005), 51–52 and 251.

6. Matteo Tonello and Stephan Rabimov, "The 2010 Institutional Investment Report: Trends in Asset Allocation and Portfolio Composition" (Research Report R-1468-10-RR, The Conference Board, New York, NY, 2010), http://papers.ssrn.com/sol3/papers.cfm?abstract_id=1707512, 22.

7. David Swensen, *Pioneering Portfolio Management: An Unconventional Approach to Institutional Investment*, rev. ed. (New York: Free Press, 2009), 17.

8. Ibid.

9. National Association of College and University Business Officers (NACUBO), and Commonfund Institute, "Average Annual Effective Spending Rates, 2011 to 2002," 2011 NACUBO-Commonfund Study of Endowments, 2012, http://www.nacubo.org/Documents/research/2011_NCSE_Public_Tables_Spending_Rates_Final_January_18_2012.pdf.

10. Uniform Law Commission, "Prudent Management of Institutional Funds Act Summary," accessed 2014, http://uniformlaws.org/ActSummary.aspx?title=Prudent%20Management%20of%20Institutional%20Funds%20Act.

11. Swensen, *Pioneering Portfolio Management*, 63.

12. National Association of College and University Business Officers (NACUBO) and Commonfund Institute, "Educational Endowments Returned an Average of 19.2% in FY2011," January 31, 2012, http://www.nacubo.org/Documents/research/2011_NCSE_Press_Release_Final_Embargo_1_31_12.pdf, 7.

13. Paul Arnsberger et al., "A History of the Tax-Exempt Sector: An SOI Perspective," *Statistics of Income Bulletin* (Internal Revenue Service, US Department of the Treasury), Winter 2008, http://www.irs.gov/pub/irs-soi/tehistory.pdf, 105.

14. Encyclopaedia Britannica, "Margaret Olivia Slocum Sage," accessed January 2015, http://www.britannica.com/EBchecked/topic/516233/Margaret-Olivia-Slocum-Sage; Encyclopaedia Britannica, "Russell Sage," accessed January 2015, http://www.britannica.com/EBchecked/topic/516237/Russell-Sage; "Working Women, 1800–1930: The Russell Sage Foundation and the Pittsburgh Survey," Harvard Library

Collections, accessed January 2015, http://ocp.hul.harvard.edu/ww
/rsf.html.

15. Carnegie Corporation of New York, "Founding and Early Years," accessed
2014, http://carnegie.org/about-us/foundation-history/founding-and
-early-years; Carnegie Corporation of New York, "Foundation History," accessed 2015, http://carnegie.org/about-us/mission-and-vision
/foundation-history; Carnegie Corporation of New York, "Programs,"
accessed 2015, http://carnegie.org/programs.

16. Rockefeller Foundation, "Our History: A Powerful Legacy," accessed July 8,
2014, http://www.rockefellerfoundation.org/about-us/our-history.

17. Arnsberger et al., "History of the Tax-Exempt Sector," 107.

18. Ibid., 107–108 and 110.

19. Amy S. Blackwood, Katie L. Roeger, and Sarah L. Pettijohn, "The
Nonprofit Sector in Brief: Public Charities, Giving, and Volunteer-
ing, 2012," Urban Institute, accessed 2014, http://www.urban.org
/UploadedPDF/412674-The-Nonprofit-Sector-in-Brief.pdf, 5.

20. Richard Sansing and Robert Yetman, "Distribution Policies of Private
Foundations" (working paper 02-20, McGladrey Institute of Accounting Education and Research, Tippie College of Business, University of Iowa, Iowa City, IA, October 2002), http://tippie.uiowa.edu
/accounting/mcgladrey/workingpapers/02-20.pdf, 1–2.

21. Charles Piller, "Foundations Align Investments with Their Charitable
Goals," *Los Angeles Times*, December 29, 2007, http://articles.latimes
.com/2007/dec/29/business/fi-foundation29.

22. Steven Lawrence and Reina Mukai, "Key Facts on Mission Investing," Foundation Center, October 2011, http://foundationcenter.org
/gainknowledge/research/pdf/keyfacts_missioninvesting2011.pdf, 1.

23. Foundation Center, "Quick Facts on U.S. Non-Profits," accessed 2015,
http://foundationcenter.org/gainknowledge/research/keyfacts2014
/foundation-focus.html.

24. Gokhan Afyonoglu et al., "The Brave New World of Sovereign
Wealth Funds," Lauder Institute of Management & International
Studies, University of Pennsylvania, 2010, http://d1c25a6gwz7q5e
.cloudfront.net/papers/download/052810_Lauder_Sovereign_Wealth
_Fund_report_2010.pdf, 1n2.

25. Sovereign Wealth Fund Institute, "Sovereign Wealth Funds Make Up
More than 25% of U.S. Retirement Assets," March 27, 2014, http://
www.swfinstitute.org/swf-article/sovereign-wealth-funds-make
-up-more-than-25-of-u-s-retirement-assets.

26. Afyonoglu et al., "Brave New World," 10.

27. Ashby H. B. Monk, "Is CalPERS a Sovereign Wealth Fund?" (working
paper 8-21, Center for Retirement Research, Boston College, Boston, MA,

December 2008), http://crr.bc.edu/wp-content/uploads/2008/12/IB_8-21.pdf, 4.

28. Afyonoglu et al., "Brave New World," 10–11.
29. Sovereign Wealth Center, "Kuwait Investment Authority," *Institutional Investor*, accessed July 8, 2014, http://www.sovereignwealthcenter.com/fund/17/Kuwait-Investment-Authority.html.
30. Afyonoglu et al., "Brave New World," 11.
31. Ibid., 12.
32. Sovereign Wealth Fund Institute, "What Is a SWF?," accessed July 8, 2014, http://www.swfinstitute.org/sovereign-wealth-fund.
33. Lixia Loh, *Sovereign Wealth Funds: States Buying the World* (Cranbrook, UK: Global Professional Publishing, 2010), 72–73.
34. Jerry W. Markham, *A Financial History of the United States*, vol. 1, *From Christopher Columbus to the Robber Barons (1492–1900)* (Armonk, NY: Sharpe, 2002), 182.
35. Thomas Kabele, "James Dodson, First Lecture on Insurances, 1757: Discussion," Kabele and Associates (New Canaan, CT), May 2, 2008, http://www.kabele.us/papers/dodsonms2.pdf, 1.
36. Aviva, "Amicable Society: Company History," accessed January 2015, http://www.aviva.com/about-us/heritage/companies/amicable-society; M. E. Ogborn, "Professional Name of the Actuary," *Journal of the Institute of the Actuaries* 82, no. 2 (September 1956): 235.
37. Encyclopaedia Britannica, "Married Women's Property Acts," accessed January 2015, http://www.britannica.com/EBchecked/topic/366305/Married-Womens-Property-Acts; Sharon Ann Murphy, "Life Insurance in the United States through World War I," in *Encyclopedia of Economic and Business History*, ed. Robert Whaples, Economic History Association, August 14, 2002, http://eh.net/encyclopedia/life-insurance-in-the-united-states-through-world-war-i.
38. Murphy, "Life Insurance in the United States."
39. American Council of Life Insurers (ACLI), *2011 Life Insurers Fact Book* (Washington, DC: American Council of Life Insurers, 2011), 63.
40. ACLI, *2011 Life Insurers Fact Book*, 1–3.
41. Ibid., 9.
42. Federal Deposit Insurance Corporation (FDIC), *An Examination of the Banking Crises of the 1980s and Early 1990s*, vol. 1 of *History of the Eighties: Lessons for the Future* (Washington, DC: Federal Deposit Insurance Corporation, 1997), 211–212.
43. FDIC, *Examination of the Banking Crises*, 230; Congressional Budget Office (CBO), *The Economic Effects of the Savings and Loan Crisis* (Washington, DC: Congressional Budget Office, 1992), 7.
44. FDIC, *Examination of the Banking Crises*, 221–222.

45. CBO, *Effects of the Crisis*, 7–8.
46. FDIC, *Examination of the Banking Crises*, 231.
47. Ibid., 225–227.
48. Ibid., 232.
49. Timothy Curry and Lynn Shibut, "The Cost of the Savings and Loan Crisis: Truth and Consequences," *FDIC Banking Review* 13, no. 2 (2000): 30–33.
50. Board of Governors of the Federal Reserve System, "Money Stock Measures—H.6," July 3, 2014, http://www.federalreserve.gov/RELEASES/h6/20140703; R. Alton Gilbert, "Requiem for Regulation Q: What It Did and Why It Passed Away," *Federal Reserve Bank of St. Louis Review*, February 1986, https://research.stlouisfed.org/publications/review/86/02/Requiem_Feb1986.pdf, 34–35.
51. Board of Governors of the Federal Reserve System, "Money Stock Measures—H.6."
52. Mike Martinez et al., *Vault Career Guide to Private Wealth Management* (New York: Vault, 2006), 10.
53. Kopin Tan, "An Upbeat View from JPMorgan's Private Bank," *Barron's*, May 19, 2012, http://online.barrons.com/news/articles/SB50001424053111904370004577392260986818168.
54. Ibid.; Geraldine Fabrikant, "Making Sure the Rich Stay Rich, Even in Crisis," *New York Times*, October 7, 2001, http://www.nytimes.com/2001/10/07/business/making-sure-the-rich-stay-rich-even-in-crisis.html.
55. JPMorgan Chase & Co., *Annual Report 2013*, April 9, 2014, http://investor.shareholder.com/jpmorganchase/annual.cfm.
56. K. Geert Rouwenhorst, "The Origins of Mutual Funds" (working paper 04-48, International Center for Finance, Yale School of Management, Yale University, New Haven, CT, December 2004), http://ssrn.com/abstract=636146, 15.
57. K. Geert Rouwenhorst, "The Origins of Mutual Funds," in *The Origins of Value: The Financial Innovations That Created Modern Capital Markets*, eds. William N. Goetzmann and K. Geert Rouwenhorst (New York: Oxford University Press, 2005), 254.
58. Rouwenhorst, "Origins of Mutual Funds" (2004), 11.
59. Morningstar, "MFS Massachusetts Investors Tr A (MITTX): Performance," accessed 2014, http://performance.morningstar.com/fund/performance-return.action?t=MITTX.
60. Jason Zweig, "Risks and Riches," *Money* 28, no. 4 (April 1999): 94–101.
61. Wharton School of Finance and Commerce, *A Study of Mutual Funds*, H.R. Rep. No. 87-2274 (1962), 37.
62. Ibid., 38.

63. Investment Company Institute, "Appendix A: How Mutual Funds and Investment Companies Operate: The Origins of Pooled Investing," in *2006 Investment Company Fact Book*, accessed 2014, http://www .icifactbook.org/2006/06_fb_appa.html.

64. Clifford E. Kirsch and Bibb L. Strench, "Mutual Funds," in *Financial Product Fundamentals: Law, Business, Compliance*, ed. Clifford E. Kirsch, 2nd ed. (New York: Practising Law Institute, 2013), 6-4.

65. Investment Company Institute, "Appendix A."

66. W. John McGuire, "The Investment Company Act of 1940," Morgan, Lewis & Bockius, 2005, http://www.morganlewis.com/pubs /Investment%20Company%20Act%20Powerpoint.pdf, slides 11–12.

67. Ibid., slide 10.

68. Matthew P. Fink, *The Rise of Mutual Funds: An Insider's View*, 2nd ed. (Oxford: Oxford University Press, 2011), 57.

69. Hugh Bullock, *The Story of Investment Companies* (New York: Columbia University Press, 1959), 101.

70. Donald Christensen, *Surviving the Coming Mutual Fund Crisis* (New York: Little, Brown, 1995), 60.

71. Barry P. Barbash, "Remembering the Past: Mutual Funds and the Lessons of the Wonder Years" (speech, ICI Securities Law Procedures Conference, Washington, DC, December 4, 1997), www.sec.gov/news /speech/speecharchive/1997/spch199.txt.

72. Fink, *Rise of Mutual Funds*, 80–81.

73. Investment Company Institute, *2013 Investment Company Fact Book*, 24–25.

74. Investment Company Institute, "Recent Mutual Fund Trends," in *2014 Investment Company Fact Book*, accessed 2014, http://www.icifactbook. org/fb_ch2.html.

5. FRAUD, MARKET MANIPULATION, AND INSIDER TRADING

1. Steve Fishman, "The Monster Mensch," *New York*, February 22, 2009, http://nymag.com/news/businessfinance/54703; Aaron Smith, "Madoff Arrives at N.C. Prison," CNN Money, July 14, 2009, http:// money.cnn.com/2009/07/14/news/economy/madoff_prison _transfer; Patricia Hurtado, "Andrew, Ruth Madoff Say Were Unaware of $65 Billion Fraud Until Confession," *Bloomberg Businessweek*, November 8, 2011, http://www.businessweek.com/news/2011-11-08 /andrew-ruth-madoff-say-they-were-unaware-of-65-billion-fraud.html.

2. Hurtado, "Andrew, Ruth Madoff Say Were Unaware."

3. Andrew Clark, "Bernard Madoff's Sons Say: We're Victims Too," *The Guardian*, March 17, 2010, http://www.theguardian.com /business/2010/mar/17/bernard-madoff-usa; Christopher Matthews, "Five Former Employees of Bernie Madoff Found Guilty of Fraud," *Wall Street Journal*, March 25, 2014, http://online.wsj.com/news/articles /SB10001424052702304679404579459551977535482.

4. Alison Gendar, "Bernie Madoff Baffled by SEC Blunders: Compares Agency's Bumbling Actions to Lt. Colombo," *Daily News* (New York), October 30, 2009, http://www.nydailynews.com/news/crime/bernie -madoff-baffled-sec-blunders-compares-agency-bumbling-actions-lt -colombo-article-1.382446.

5. Hurtado, "Andrew, Ruth Madoff Say Were Unaware."

6. Bernard Madoff, "Text of Bernard Madoff's Court Statement," National Public Radio, March 12, 2009, http://www.npr.org/templates/story /story.php?storyId=101816470.

7. David S. Hilzenrath, "Former Madoff Trader David Kugel Pleads Guilty to Fraud," *Washington Post*, November 21, 2011, http://www .washingtonpost.com/business/economy/former-madoff-trader-david -kugel-pleads-guilty-to-fraud/2011/11/21/gIQATSFLjN_story.html.

8. Brian Ross, *The Madoff Chronicles: Inside the Secret World of Bernie and Ruth* (New York: Hyperion, 2009), 25.

9. Harry Markopolos, Harry Markopolos to US Securities and Exchange Commission, "The World's Largest Hedge Fund Is a Fraud," November 7, 2005, http://online.wsj.com/documents/Madoff_SECdocs_20081217. pdf, 2.

10. "Jewish Reaction to Madoff Scandal" (transcript), *Religion and Ethics Newsweekly*, produced by Thirteen/WNET New York, PBS, March 20, 2009, http://www.pbs.org/wnet/religionandethics/2009/03/20 /march-20-2009-jewish-reaction-to-madoff-scandal/2474.

11. David Glovin, "Bernard Madoff's Accountant Friehling Pleads Guilty (Update 2)," Bloomberg News, November 3, 2009, http:// www.bloomberg.com/apps/news?pid=newsarchive&sid =ah_xWloo7TTE.

12. Ibid.; Alyssa Abkowitz, "Madoff's Auditor . . . Doesn't Audit?," CNN Money, December 19, 2008, http://archive.fortune.com/2008/12/17 /news/companies/madoff.auditor.fortune/index.htm.

13. Glovin, "Friehling Pleads Guilty."

14. Ross Kerber, "The Whistleblower," *Boston Globe*, January 8, 2009, http:// www.boston.com/business/articles/2009/01/08/the_whistleblower.

15. Harry Markopolos to US Securities and Exchange Commission, 5.

16. Carole Bernard and Phelim Boyle, "Mr. Madoff's Amazing Returns: An Analysis of the Split-Strike Conversion Strategy," *Journal of Derivatives* 17, no. 1 (Fall 2009): 62–76.

17. Harry Markopolos to US Securities and Exchange Commission, 1–2.

18. Ibid., 1.

19. Ibid.

20. Securities and Exchange Commission, "Investigation of Failure of the SEC to Uncover Bernard Madoff's Ponzi Scheme—Public Version" (Report No. OIG-509), Office of Investigations, US Securities and Exchange Commission, August 31, 2009, http://www.sec.gov/news /studies/2009/oig-509.pdf, 21–22.

21. Securities and Exchange Commission, "Post-Madoff Reforms," accessed September 2014, http://www.sec.gov/spotlight/secpostmadoffreforms .htm.

22. Ibid.

23. Jeanine Ibrahim, "Allen Stanford: Descent from Billionaire to Inmate #35017-183," CNBC, October 5, 2012, http://www.cnbc.com/id /49276842.

24. Matthew Goldstein, "Stanford's Failed Health Club," *Unstructured Finance* (blog), *Bloomberg Businessweek*, February 13, 2009, http://www.busi- nessweek.com/investing/wall_street_news_blog/archives/2009/02 /stanfords_faile.html; Matthew Goldstein, "Stanford's Rocky Start," *Bloomberg Businessweek*, March 3, 2009, http://www.businessweek .com/bwdaily/dnflash/content/mar2009/db2009033_601499.htm.

25. Goldstein, "Stanford's Rocky Start."

26. Ibrahim, "Allen Stanford: Descent."

27. Anna Driver and Eileen O'Grady, "Allen Stanford Sentenced to 110 Years in Prison," Reuters, June 14, 2012, http://www.reuters.com/article /2012/06/14/us-stanford-sentencing-idUSBRE85D17720120614.

28. Ibrahim, "Allen Stanford: Descent."

29. Goldstein, "Stanford's Rocky Start."

30. Clifford Krauss, "Stanford Sentenced to 110-Year Term in $7 Billion Ponzi Case," *New York Times*, June 14, 2012, http://www.nytimes .com/2012/06/15/business/stanford-sentenced-to-110-years-in-jail-in -fraud-case.html.

31. Ibrahim, "Allen Stanford: Descent."

32. Driver and O'Grady, "Allen Stanford Sentenced."

33. Krauss, "Stanford Sentenced to 110-Year Term."

34. Mary Darby, "In Ponzi We Trust," *Smithsonian Magazine*, Decem- ber 1998, http://www.smithsonianmag.com/people-places/in-ponzi -we-trust-64016168; Louis L. Straney, *Securities Fraud: Detection, Preven- tion and Control* (Hoboken, NJ: Wiley, 2010), 81; William Nana Wiafe Jr., *The New Competitive Strategy: The Ultimate Business Strategy That Gets Superior Results and Builds Business Empires* (n.p.: Xlibris, 2011), 39.

35. Straney, *Securities Fraud*, 81.

36. Darby, "In Ponzi We Trust;" Straney, *Securities Fraud*, 82–83.

37. Ibid., 83.

38. Darby, "In Ponzi We Trust."

39. Ibid.

40. Straney, *Securities Fraud*, 83.

41. *Ponzi v. Fessenden*, 258 U.S. 254 (1922).

42. Erin Skarda, "William Miller, the Original Schemer," *Time*, March 7, 2012, http://content.time.com/time/specials/packages/article/0,288 04,2104982_2104983_2104992,00.html.

43. "A Century of Ponzi Schemes," *DealBook* (blog), *New York Times*, December 15, 2008, http://dealbook.nytimes.com/2008/12/15/a-century-of -ponzi-schemes.

44. Skarda, "William Miller."

45. Darby, "In Ponzi We Trust."

46. John Steele Gordon, "Pyramid Schemes Are as American as Apple Pie," *Wall Street Journal*, December 17, 2008, http://online.wsj.com/news /articles/SB122948144507313073.

47. Ibid.

48. Ibid.

49. Ibid.

50. Ibid.

51. Ibid.

52. "The Match King," *Economist*, December 19, 2007, http://www.economist .com/node/10278667.

53. Torsten Kreuger, *The Truth about Ivar Kreuger* (Stuttgart: Seewald, 1968), 50.

54. Paul M. Clikeman, "The Greatest Frauds of the (Last) Century" (working paper, Robins School of Business, University of Richmond, Richmond, VA, May 2003), http://www.newaccountantusa.com/newsFeat /wealthManagement/Clikeman_Greatest_Frauds.pdf, 2.

55. Ibid.

56. Ibid.

57. Ibid., 2–3.

58. "The Match King."

59. Ibid.; Kreuger, *Truth about Ivar Kreuger*, 63–64.

60. Clikeman, "Greatest Frauds," 3.

61. Paul M. Clikeman, *Called to Account: Financial Frauds That Shaped the Accounting Profession*, 2nd ed. (New York: Routledge, 2013), 38.

62. Kenneth L. Fisher, *How to Smell a Rat: The Five Signs of Financial Fraud*, with Lara Hoffmans (Hoboken, NJ: Wiley, 2009), 167.

63. Cabell Phillips, *From the Crash to the Blitz, 1929–1939* (New York: Fordham University Press, 2000), 30–31; Fisher, *How to Smell a Rat*, 167.

64. Fisher, *How to Smell a Rat*, 167.

65. Ibid., 167–168.
66. Ibid., 168–169.
67. Ibid., 167–69; John Brooks, *Once in Golconda: A True Drama of Wall Street, 1920–1938* (New York: Harper & Row, 1969), 258.
68. James Bandler and Doris Burke, "70 Years before Madoff, There Was Whitney," CNN Money, December 16, 2008, http://money.cnn.com/2008/12/16/news/madoff.whitney.fortune.
69. Fisher, *How to Smell a Rat*, 169.
70. Kurt A. Hohenstein, ed., "William O. Douglas and the Growing Power of the SEC," Securities and Exchange Commission Historical Society, December 1, 2005, http://www.sechistorical.org/museum/galleries/douglas/index.php.
71. Ibid.
72. Ibid.
73. Kathleen M. Middleton, *Bayonne Passages*, Images of America (Charleston, SC: Arcadia, 2000), 146.
74. Norman C. Miller, *The Great Salad Oil Swindle* (New York: Coward McCann, 1965), 16–22.
75. Ibid., 17–18.
76. Middleton, *Bayonne Passages*, 146.
77. Miller, *Salad Oil Swindle*, 18.
78. George Childs Kohn, ed., *The New Encyclopedia of American Scandal*, rev. ed. (New York: Infobase, 2001), 161.
79. Miller, *Salad Oil Swindle*, 70–73.
80. Middleton, *Bayonne Passages*, 147–148.
81. Ibid.
82. Miller, *Salad Oil Swindle*, 142–146 and 183.
83. Kohn, *Encyclopedia of American Scandal*, 161.
84. Middleton, *Bayonne Passages*, 148.
85. Chris Barth, "Warren Buffett: Clairvoyant or Crazy?," *Forbes*, June 12, 2012, http://www.forbes.com/sites/chrisbarth/2012/06/12/warren-buffett-clairvoyant-or-crazy.
86. Kohn, *Encyclopedia of American Scandal*, 162.
87. Stephen G. Dimmock and William C. Gerken, "Finding Bernie Madoff: Detecting Fraud by Investment Managers" (working paper, 2011).
88. Stephen J. Brown and Onno W. Steenbeek, "Doubling: Nick Leeson's Trading Strategy," *Pacific-Basin Finance Journal* 9, no. 2 (April 2001): 85–86.
89. Ibid., 86.
90. Nick Leeson, "Biography," NickLeeson.com, accessed January 2015, http://www.nickleeson.com/biography/full_biography_02.html.

91. Martin Arnold et al., "How Kerviel Exposed Lax Controls at Société Générale," *Financial Times*, February 7, 2008, http://www.ft.com /intl/cms/s/0/927fe998-d5b2-11dc-8b56-0000779fd2ac.html.

92. Ibid.

93. Ibid.

94. Sebastian Fritz-Morgenthal and Hagen Rafeld, "Breaking Down the Biggest Trading Fraud in the History of Banking," *Risk Professional*, June 2010, 47–52, http://www.academia.edu/9042700/Breaking _Down_the_Biggest_Trading_Fraud_in_the_History_of_Banking.

95. Scott B. MacDonald and Jane E. Hughes, *Separating Fools from Their Money: A History of American Financial Scandals* (New Brunswick, NJ: Transaction, 2007), 16–17.

96. David J. Cowen, "William Duer and America's First Financial Scandal," *Financial History* 97 (Spring 2010): 20–21.

97. Ibid., 21–22.

98. Ibid., 22.

99. Ibid., 23 and 35.

100. David J. Cowen, Richard Sylla, and Robert E. Wright, "The US Panic of 1792: Financial Crisis Management and the Lender of Last Resort" (paper presented at the XIV International Economic History Congress, Helsinki, Finland, August 2006), http://www.helsinki.fi /iehc2006/papers1/Sylla.pdf, 12–19.

101. Cowen, "William Duer," 35.

102. Timothy Starr, *Railroad Wars of New York State* (Charleston, SC: History Press, 2012), 112.

103. Ibid., 114.

104. Ibid., 114–116.

105. Robert C. Kennedy, "On This Day: March 30, 1872," The Learning Network, *New York Times*, March 30, 2001, http://www.nytimes.com /learning/general/onthisday/harp/0330.html.

106. Starr, *Railroad Wars*, 123–130.

107. Kenneth L. Fisher, *100 Minds That Made the Market* (Hoboken, NJ: Wiley, 2007), 250.

108. Ibid., 252–253.

109. Ibid., 252.

110. Robert Sobel, *The Big Board: A History of the New York Stock Market*, (New York, NY: Free Press, 1965), 329.

111. Fisher, *100 Minds*, 251–252.

112. Ibid., 252.

113. Rajesh K. Aggarwal and Guojun Wu, "Stock Market Manipulations," *Journal of Business* 79, no. 4 (July 2006): 1917.

114. Steve Lohr, "Guinness Scandal Roils Britain," *New York Times*, January 30, 1987, http://www.nytimes.com/1987/01/30/business

/guinness-scandal-roils-britain.html; Lynne Curry, "Guinness Brew-Haha in the City Lapping at Thatcher Government," *Christian Science Monitor*, January 29, 1987, http://www.csmonitor.com/1987/0129/fmark29 .html.

115. Steve Lohr, "Hostile Offer by Argyll for Distillers," *New York Times*, December 2, 1985, http://www.nytimes.com/1985/12/03/business /hostile-offer-by-argyll-for-distillers.html; Steve Lohr, "Guinness Offers to Buy Distillers for $3.2 Billion," *New York Times*, January 20, 1986, http://www.nytimes.com/1986/01/21/business/guinness-offers-to -buy-distillers-for-3.2-billion.html.

116. "'Guinness Four' Guilty," BBC News, August 27, 1990, http:// news.bbc.co.uk/onthisday/hi/dates/stories/august/27 /newsid_2536000/2536035.stm.

117. Lohr, "Guinness Scandal Roils Britain."

118. Travers Smith, "The Takeovers Regime Under the Companies Act 2006: AIM-Listed Companies," May 2007, http://www.traverssmith.com /media/602015/takeovers_regime_under_the_companies _act_2006_-_aim-listed_companies_-_may_2007.pdf.

119. "Timeline: LIBOR-Fixing Scandal," BBC News, February 6, 2013, http://www.bbc.com/news/business-18671255.

120. Michael J. de la Merced, "Q. and A.: Understanding LIBOR," *Deal-Book* (blog), *New York Times*, July 10, 2012, http://dealbook.nytimes .com/2012/07/10/q-and-a-understanding-libor.

121. Ibid.

122. Christopher Matthews, "LIBOR Scandal: Yep, It's as Bad as We Thought," *Time*, December 20, 2012, http://business.time.com/2012 /12/20/libor-scandal-yep-its-as-bad-as-we-thought.

123. Andrea Tan, Gavin Finch, and Liam Vaughan, "RBS Instant Messages Show LIBOR Rates Skewed for Traders," Bloomberg News, September 26, 2012, http://www.bloomberg.com/news/2012-09-25/rbs-instant-messages-show-libor-rates-skewed-for-traders.html.

124. Vikas Shah, "Andrew Lo on the LIBOR Scandal and What's Next," AllAboutAlpha.com, November 8, 2012, http://allaboutalpha.com /blog/2012/11/08/andrew-lo-on-the-libor-scandal-and-whats-next.

125. Liam Vaughan and Gavin Finch, "LIBOR Lies Revealed in Rigging of $300 Trillion Benchmark," Bloomberg News, January 28, 2013, http:// www.bloomberg.com/news/2013-01-28/libor-lies-revealed-in-rigging -of-300-trillion-benchmark.html.

126. Dacher Keltner and Paul Piff, "Greed on Wall Street Prevents Good from Happening," *Room for Debate* (blog), *New York Times*, March 16, 2012, http://www.nytimes.com/roomfordebate /2012/03/15/does-morality-have-a-place-on-wall-street /greed-on-wall-street-prevents-good-from-happening.

127. Bob Greene, "A $100 Million Idea: Use Greed for Good," *Chicago Tribune*, December 15, 1986, http://articles.chicagotribune.com/1986-12-15/features/8604030634_1_ivan-boeskys-greed-fund.

128. Bryan K. Ulmer, "Boesky, Ivan," in *Encyclopedia of White-Collar and Corporate Crime*, ed. Lawrence M. Salinger (Thousand Oaks, CA: Sage, 2005), 1:96.

129. Stephen Koepp, "'Money Was the Only Way,'" *Time*, June 24, 2001, http://content.time.com/time/magazine/article/0,9171,144026,00.html.

130. Ulmer, "Boesky, Ivan," 1:97.

131. Koepp, "'Money Was the Only Way;'" Ulmer, "Boesky, Ivan," 1:96.

132. Keith M. Moore, *Risk Arbitrage: An Investor's Guide* (Hoboken, NJ: Wiley, 1999), 7–10.

133. Koepp, "'Money Was the Only Way.'"

134. James B. Stewart, *Den of Thieves* (New York: Simon and Schuster, 1992), 18–20.

135. Ibid., 164–165.

136. Ibid., 12 and 340.

137. Robert K. D. Colby, ed., "Wrestling with Reform: Financial Scandals and the Legislation They Inspired," Securities and Exchange Commission Historical Society, May 1, 2013, http://www.sechistorical.org/museum/galleries/wwr/index.php.

138. Ulmer, "Boesky, Ivan," 1:97.

139. Stewart, *Den of Thieves*, 431.

140. Susan Pulliam and Chad Bray, "Trader Draws Record Sentence," *Wall Street Journal*, October 14, 2011, http://online.wsj.com/news/articles/SB10001424052970203914304576627191081876286.

141. Katherine Burton and Saijel Kishan, "Raj Rajaratnam Became Billionaire Demanding Edge," Bloomberg News, October 19, 2009, http://www.bloomberg.com/apps/news?pid=newsarchive&sid=aDg9U7NGeNv4.

142. Michael J. de la Merced, "Taped Calls about Akamai Earnings Guidance Heard at Galleon Trial," *DealBook* (blog), *New York Times*, April 4, 2011, http://dealbook.nytimes.com/2011/04/04/focus-shifts-to-google-trade-at-galleon-trial.

143. Barney Gimbel, "Partners in Crime," CNN Money, October 4, 2006, http://money.cnn.com/magazines/fortune/fortune_archive/2006/10/02/8387505/index.htm.

144. Ibid.

145. Ibid.

146. Ibid.

147. Ibid.

148. Ferdinand Pecora, *Wall Street Under Oath* (New York: A. M. Kelley, 1939), quoted in Charles D. Ellis and James R. Vertin, *True Stories of the Great Barons of Finance*, vol. 2 of *Wall Street People* (Hoboken, NJ: Wiley, 2003), 182–183.

149. Senate Committee on Banking and Currency, "Stock Exchange Practices" (S. Rep. No. 73-1455) (Washington, DC: Government Printing Office, 1934), https://www.senate.gov/artandhistory/history/common/investigations/pdf/Pecora_FinalReport.pdf, 187–189.

150. Ellis and Vertin, *True Stories*, 182.

151. Pecora, *Wall Street Under Oath*, quoted in Ellis and Vertin, *True Stories*, 188.

152. Jerry W. Markham, *A Financial History of Modern US Corporate Scandals: From Enron to Reform* (Armonk, NY: Sharpe, 2006), 377.

153. Kurt A. Hohenstein, ed., "Fair to All People: The SEC and the Regulation of Insider Trading," Securities and Exchange Commission Historical Society, November 1, 2006, http://www.sechistorical.org/museum/galleries/it.

154. David Margolick, "William Carey [*sic*], Former S.E.C. Chairman, Dies at 72," *New York Times*, February 9, 1983, http://www.nytimes.com/1983/02/09/obituaries/william-carey-former-sec-chairman-dies-at-72.html.

155. Ibid.

156. Donald C. Langevoort, "Rereading *Cady, Roberts*: The Ideology and Practice of Insider Trading Regulation," *Columbia Law Review* 99, no. 5 (June 1999): 1319.

157. Stephen M. Bainbridge, ed., *Research Handbook on Insider Trading* (Cheltenham, UK: Edward Elgar, 2013), 3.

158. Ibid.

159. Philip McBride Johnson and Thomas Lee Hazen, *Derivatives Regulation* (New York: Aspen, 2004), 3:1522–1523.

160. Markham, *Financial History*, 378–379.

161. Bainbridge, *Research Handbook*, 3.

162. Hohenstein, "Fair to All People."

163. Ibid.

164. Robert Schmidt and Jesse Hamilton, "SEC 'Capacity Gap' Risks Oversight Lapses as Regulator's Targets Multiply," Bloomberg News, March 7, 2011, http://www.bloomberg.com/news/2011-03-07/sec-capacity-gap-risks-oversight-lapses-as-regulator-s-targets-multiply.html.

165. James B. Stewart, "As a Watchdog Starves, Wall Street Is Tossed a Bone," *New York Times*, July 15, 2011, http://www.nytimes.com/2011/07/16/business/budget-cuts-to-sec-reduce-its-effectiveness.html.

166. Ibid.

6. PROGRESS IN MANAGING CYCLICAL CRISES

1. Philip S. Bagwell and G. E. Mingay, *Britain and America, 1850–1939: A Study of Economic Change* (New York: Praeger, 1970), 244–246.
2. J. R. Vernon, "The 1920–21 Deflation: The Role of Aggregate Supply," *Economic Inquiry* 29, no. 3 (July 1991): 572–573.
3. Ibid., 573–574.
4. Charles H. Feinstein, Peter Temin, and Gianni Toniolo, *The World Economy Between the World Wars* (New York: Oxford University Press, 2008), 56.
5. Bagwell and Mingay, *Britain and America*, 246.
6. J. Bradford DeLong, "The Roaring Twenties," in *Slouching Towards Utopia?: The Economic History of the Twentieth Century*, February 1997, http://holtz.org/Library/Social%20Science/Economics/Slouching %20Towards%20Utopia%20by%20DeLong/Slouch_roaring13.html; Henry Cabot Lodge, "League of Nations," American Memory, Library of Congress, accessed 2015, http://memory.loc.gov; Immigration Act of 1924, Pub. L. No. 68-139, 43 Stat. 153, http://library.uwb.edu/guides /usimmigration/43%20stat%20153.pdf.
7. DeLong, "Roaring Twenties."
8. Ibid.
9. Kenneth L. Fisher, *100 Minds That Made the Market* (Hoboken, NJ: Wiley, 2007), 183–184; "The 1907 Crisis in Historical Perspective," Center for History and Economics, Harvard University, accessed 2015, http://www.fas.harvard.edu/~histecon/crisis-next/1907.
10. Fisher, *100 Minds*, 184.
11. Anthony D'Agostino, *The Rise of Global Powers: International Politics in the Era of the World Wars* (Cambridge: Cambridge University Press, 2012), 225.
12. Ibid., 226.
13. Federal Reserve Bank of New York, "George L. Harrison," accessed January 2015, http://www.newyorkfed.org/aboutthefed/GHarrisonbio .html.
14. Claire Suddath, "The Crash of 1929," *Time*, October 29, 2008, http:// content.time.com/time/nation/article/0,8599,1854569,00.html.
15. Karen Blumenthal, *Six Days in October: The Stock Market Crash of 1929* (New York: Simon and Schuster, 2002), 88.
16. Ibid., 88–89; "Exchange to Close for Two Days of Rest," *New York Times*, October 31, 1929, http://partners.nytimes.com/library/financial /103129crash-close.html.

17. Harold Bierman Jr., *The Causes of the 1929 Stock Market Crash: A Speculative Orgy or a New Era?* (Westport, CT: Greenwood, 1998), 4; Harold Bierman, "The 1929 Stock Market Crash," in *Encyclopedia of Economic and Business History*, ed. Robert Whaples, Economic History Association, March 26, 2008, http://eh.net/encyclopedia /the-1929-stock-market-crash.

18. Capital Finance International, "Jesse Lauriston Livermore: The Boy Plunger," February 20, 2014, http://cfi.co/banking/2014/02/jesse -lauriston-livermore-the-boy-plunger.

19. Bierman, *Causes of the Crash*, 6–7 and 13.

20. Gene Smiley, *The American Economy in the Twentieth Century* (Cincinnati: South-Western, 1994), 148–150.

21. D'Agostino, *Rise of Global Powers*, 227; Charles P. Kindleberger, *The World in Depression, 1929–1939*, rev. ed. (Berkeley: University of California Press, 1986), 295–296.

22. Smiley, *American Economy*, 158–161.

23. Ibid., 151–154.

24. Ben S. Bernanke, "The Financial Accelerator and the Credit Channel" (speech, The Credit Channel of Monetary Policy in the Twenty-First Century Conference, Federal Reserve Bank of Atlanta, Atlanta, GA, June 15, 2007), http://www.federalreserve.gov/newsevents/speech /bernanke20070615a.htm.

25. Franklin D. Roosevelt Presidential Library and Museum (FDR Library), "FDR: From Budget Balancer to Keynesian: A President's Evolving Approach to Fiscal Policy in Times of Crisis," accessed 2013, http:// www.fdrlibrary.marist.edu/aboutfdr/budget.html.

26. Herbert Hoover, "Statement on Efforts to Balance the Budget," March 8, 1932, The American Presidency Project, http://www.presidency.ucsb. edu/ws/?pid=23478.

27. FDR Library, "Budget Balancer to Keynesian."

28. Bruce Bartlett, "How Deficit Hawks Could Derail the Recovery," *Forbes*, January 8, 2010, http://www.forbes.com/2010/01/07/deficit-great -depression-recovery-opinions-columnists-bruce-bartlett.html; FDR Library, "Budget Balancer to Keynesian.

29. FDR Library, "Budget Balancer to Keynesian."

30. Securities and Exchange Commission Historical Society, "431 Days: Joseph P. Kennedy and the Creation of the SEC (1934–35)," accessed 2013, http://www.sechistorical.org/museum/galleries/kennedy /politicians_b.php; US Securities and Exchange Commission (SEC), "Laws That Govern the Securities Industry," accessed January 2015, http://www.sec.gov/about/laws.shtml.

31. Matthew P. Fink, *The Rise of Mutual Funds: An Insider's View*, 2nd ed. (Oxford: Oxford University Press, 2011), 23–24.

32. SEC, "Laws That Govern the Securities Industry."

33. "Topics: Glass-Steagall Act (1933)," *New York Times*, accessed January 2015, http://topics.nytimes.com/top/reference/timestopics/subjects/g /glass_steagall_act_1933/index.html.

34. Hyman P. Minsky, *Stabilizing an Unstable Economy* (New Haven, CT: Yale University Press, 1986).

35. William Seyfried, "Monetary Policy and Housing Bubbles: A Multinational Perspective," *Research in Business and Economics Journal* 2 (March 2010), http://www.aabri.com/manuscripts/09351.pdf, 1–2.

36. Kathryn J. Byun, "The US Housing Bubble and Bust: Impacts on Employment," *Monthly Labor Review* (Bureau of Labor Statistics, US Department of Labor), December 2010, http://www.bls.gov/opub /mlr/2010/12/art1full.pdf, 7.

37. Robert J. Shiller, "Understanding Recent Trends in House Prices and Home Ownership" (working paper 13553, National Bureau of Economic Research, Cambridge, MA, October 2007), http://www.nber.org /papers/w13553.pdf, 3–7.

38. Walter Bagehot, *Lombard Street: A Description of the Money Market* (London: King, 1873).

39. Board of Governors of the Federal Reserve System, "Ben S. Bernanke," accessed January 2015, http://www.federalreservehistory.org/People /DetailView/12; Phillip Y. Lipscy and Hirofumi Takinami, "The Politics of Financial Crisis Response in Japan and the United States," *Japanese Journal of Political Science* 14, no. 3 (September 2013): 331–335.

40. Baird Webel, "Troubled Asset Relief Program (TARP): Implementation and Status," Congressional Research Service, Library of Congress, Washington, DC, June 27, 2013, https://www.fas.org/sgp/crs/misc /R41427.pdf, 1; "Treasury's Bailout Proposal," CNN Money, September 20, 2008, http://money.cnn.com/2008/09/20/news/economy /treasury_proposal; US Department of the Treasury, "TARP Programs," accessed January 2015, http://www.treasury.gov/initiatives/financial -stability/TARP-Programs/Pages/default.aspx; Congressional Budget Office, "Report on the Troubled Asset Relief Program—October 2012," October 11, 2012, http://www.cbo.gov/sites/default/files/TARP10 -2012_0.pdf, 1.

41. Michael A. Fletcher, "Obama Leaves D.C. to Sign Stimulus Bill," *Washington Post*, February 18, 2009, http://www.washingtonpost.com/wp -dyn/content/article/2009/02/17/AR2009021700221.html; Council of Economic Advisers, Executive Office of the President, "The Economic Impact of the American Recovery and Reinvestment Act Five

Years Later: Final Report to Congress," February 2014, http://www .whitehouse.gov/sites/default/files/docs/cea_arra_report.pdf, i.

42. Paul Krugman, "Too Little, Gone Too Soon," *Conscience of a Liberal* (blog), *New York Times*, August 30, 2013, http://krugman.blogs .nytimes.com/2013/08/30/too-little-gone-too-soon,

43. Paul Wiseman and Pallavi Gogoi, "FDIC Chief: Small Banks Can't Compete with Bailed-Out Giants," *USA Today*, October 20, 2009, http:// usatoday30.usatoday.com/money/industries/banking/2009-10-19 -FDIC-chief-sheila-bair-banking_N.htm.

44. Frederic A. Schweikhard and Zoe Tsesmelidakis, "The Impact of Government Interventions on CDS and Equity Markets" (working paper, November 2012), http://papers.ssrn.com/sol3/papers.cfm?abstract _id=1573377, 1–2.

45. Dodd-Frank Wall Street Reform and Consumer Protection Act, Pub. L. No. 111-203, 124 Stat. 1376–2223, "Title I: Financial Stability," http:// www.law.cornell.edu/wex/dodd-frank; US Department of the Treasury, "Financial Stability Oversight Council: Who Is on the Council?," accessed January 2015, http://www.treasury.gov/initiatives/fsoc/about /council/Pages/default.aspx.

46. Board of Governors of the Federal Reserve System, "Press Release," October 23, 2014, http://www.federalreserve.gov/newsevents/press /bcreg/20141023a.htm.

47. Simon Johnson, "Sadly, Too Big to Fail Is Not Over," *Economix* (blog), *New York Times*, August 1, 2013, http://economix.blogs.nytimes .com/2013/08/01/sadly-too-big-to-fail-is-not-over.

48. James B. Stewart, "Volcker Rule, Once Simple, Now Boggles," *New York Times*, October 21, 2011, http://www.nytimes.com/2011/10/22 /business/volcker-rule-grows-from-simple-to-complex.html.

49. Ibid.; Dan Kedmey, "2 Years and 900 Pages Later, the Volcker Rule Gets the Green Light," TIME.com, December 11, 2013, http://business.time .com/2013/12/11/2-years-and-900-pages-later-the-volcker-rule-gets -the-green-light.

50. Carmen M. Reinhart and Kenneth S. Rogoff, *This Time Is Different: Eight Centuries of Financial Folly* (Princeton, NJ: Princeton University Press, 2011), xliv–xlv and 238–239.

7. THE EMERGENCE OF INVESTMENT THEORY

1. Jean-Michel Courtault et al., "Louis Bachelier on the Centenary of *Théorie de la Spéculation*," *Mathematical Finance* 10, no. 3 (July 2000): 342–343.

2. Ibid., 341–344.
3. Ibid., 346–347.
4. "Fisher, Irving" in *Concise Encyclopedia of Economics*, ed. David R. Henderson, Library of Economics and Liberty, 2008, http://www.econlib.org/library/Enc/bios/Fisher.html.
5. Irving Fisher, "Out of Keynes's Shadow," *Economist*, February 14, 2009, http://www.economist.com/node/13104022; David J. Lynch, "Economists Evoke the Spirit of Irving Fisher," Bloomberg News, January 12, 2012, http://www.bloomberg.com/bw/magazine/economists-evoke-the-spirit-of-irving-fisher-01122012.html.
6. Irving Fisher, *The Theory of Interest as Determined by Impatience to Spend Income and Opportunity to Invest It* (New York: Macmillan, 1930), 151.
7. Ibid., 152.
8. Ibid., 155.
9. Peter L. Bernstein, *Capital Ideas: The Improbable Origins of Modern Wall Street* (New York: Free Press, 1992), 150–151.
10. Ibid., 153–154.
11. Ibid., 151–152. For the original work, see John Burr Williams, *The Theory of Investment Value* (Cambridge, MA: Harvard University Press, 1938).
12. K. P. Gupta, *Cost Management: Measuring, Monitoring & Motivating Performance* (Delhi: Global India Publications, 2009), 55.
13. Franco Modigliani and Merton H. Miller, "The Cost of Capital, Corporation Finance and the Theory of Investment," *American Economic Review* 48, no. 3 (June 1958): 261–297.
14. Nobel Media AB, "The Prize in Economics 1985—Press Release," 1985, accessed 2013, http://www.nobelprize.org/nobel_prizes/economic-sciences/laureates/1985/press.html; Nobel Media AB, "The Prize in Economics 1990—Press Release," 1990, accessed 2013, http://www.nobelprize.org/nobel_prizes/economic-sciences/laureates/1990/press.html.
15. Avinash Dixit, "Paul Samuelson's Legacy," *Annual Reviews of Economics* 4 (2012): 3–4. For the original work, see Paul A. Samuelson, *Foundations of Economic Analysis* (Cambridge, MA: Harvard University Press, 1947).
16. Bernstein, *Capital Ideas*, 22–23.
17. Donald MacKenzie, *An Engine, Not a Camera: How Financial Models Shape Markets* (Cambridge, MA: MIT Press, 2006), 64.
18. Dixit, "Samuelson's Legacy," 19–20. For the original works, see Paul A. Samuelson, "Rational Theory of Warrant Pricing," *Industrial Management Review* 6, no. 2 (Spring 1965): 13–39; Paul A. Samuelson and Robert C. Merton, "A Complete Model of Warrant Pricing That Maximizes Utility," *Industrial Management Review* 10, no. 2 (Winter 1969): 17–46.

19. Fischer Black and Myron Scholes, "The Pricing of Options and Corporate Liabilities," *Journal of Political Economy* 81, no. 3 (May–June 1973): 637–654.

20. A. James Boness, "Elements of a Theory of Stock-Option Value," *Journal of Political Economy* 72, no. 2 (April 1964): 163–175.

21. Marion A. Brach, *Real Options in Practice* (Hoboken, NJ: Wiley, 2003), 24.

22. Robert C. Merton, "Option Pricing When Underlying Stock Returns Are Discontinuous," *Journal of Financial Economics* 3, no. 1–2 (January–March 1976): 125–144.

23. Steven G. Krantz and Harold R. Parks, *A Mathematical Odyssey: Journey from the Real to the Complex* (New York: Springer, 2014), 55.

24. Ecclesiastes 11:1–2 (New International Version).

25. Bruce A. Valentine, "Shakespeare Revisited," *Financial Analysts Journal* 21, no. 3 (May–June 1965), 91.

26. Harry Markowitz, "Harry M. Markowitz—Biographical," Nobel Media AB, 1990, accessed 2013, http://www.nobelprize.org/nobel_prizes/economic-sciences/laureates/1990/markowitz-bio.html.

27. Bernstein, *Capital Ideas*, 46.

28. Markowitz, "Biographical."

29. Ibid.

30. Harry Markowitz, "Portfolio Selection," *Journal of Finance* 7, no. 1 (March 1952).

31. James Tobin, "Liquidity Preference as Behavior Towards Risk," *Review of Economic Studies* 25, no. 2 (February 1958).

32. William F. Sharpe, "Capital Asset Prices: A Theory of Market Equilibrium under Conditions of Risk," *Journal of Finance* 19, no. 3 (September 1964): 425–442; John Lintner, "The Valuation of Risk Assets and the Selection of Risky Investments in Stock Portfolios and Capital Budgets," *Review of Economics and Statistics* 47, no. 1 (February 1965): 13–37.

33. Eugene F. Fama and Kenneth R. French, "The Capital Asset Pricing Model: Theory and Evidence," *Journal of Economic Perspectives* 18, no. 3 (Summer 2004): 25–28.

34. Eugene F. Fama and Kenneth R. French, "The Cross-Section of Expected Stock Returns," *Journal of Finance* 47, no. 2 (June 1992): 445–446.

35. Ibid.

36. Cowles Foundation for Research in Economics, "Alfred Cowles, 3rd (1891–1984)," Yale University, accessed 2013, http://cowles.econ.yale.edu/archive/people/directors/cowles.htm.

37. Alfred Cowles III, "Can Stock Market Forecasters Forecast?," *Econometrica* 1, no. 3 (July 1933): 309–323.

38. Ibid., 323.

39. Michael C. Jensen, "The Performance of Mutual Funds in the Period 1945–1964," *Journal of Finance* 23, no. 2 (May 1968).

40. Ibid.

41. Eugene F. Fama, "Efficient Capital Markets: A Review of Theory and Empirical Work," *Journal of Finance* 25, no. 2 (May 1970): 383.

42. Benjamin Graham and David L. Dodd, *Security Analysis* (New York: McGraw-Hill, 1934).

43. Benjamin Graham, *The Intelligent Investor* (New York: Harper, 1949).

44. Benjamin Graham, "A Conversation with Benjamin Graham," *Financial Analysts Journal* 32, no. 5 (September–October 1976): 22.

45. Warren Buffett, "The Superinvestors of Graham-and-Doddsville," *Hermes* (Columbia Business School), Fall 1984, 4–15.

46. Daniel Kahneman and Amos Tversky, "Prospect Theory: An Analysis of Decision under Risk," *Econometrica* 47, no. 2 (March 1979): 265–278.

47. Rajnish Mehra and Edward C. Prescott, "The Equity Premium: A Problem," *Journal of Monetary Economics* 15, no. 2 (March 1985): 145–161.

48. Stephen J. Brown, William N. Goetzmann, and Stephen A. Ross, "Survival," *Journal of Finance* 50, no. 3 (July 1995): 853–873.

49. Shlomo Benartzi and Richard H. Thaler, "Myopic Loss Aversion and the Equity Premium Puzzle," *Quarterly Journal of Economics* 110, no. 1 (February 1995): 73–92.

50. Burton G. Malkiel, "The Efficient Market Hypothesis and Its Critics," *Journal of Economic Perspectives* 17, no. 1 (Winter 2003): 61–62.

8. MORE NEW INVESTMENT FORMS

1. Towers Watson and *Financial Times*, "Global Alternatives Survey 2012," last modified July 2012, http://www.towerswatson.com/en-US /Insights/IC-Types/Survey-Research-Results/2012/07/Global -Alternatives-Survey-2012, 7–8.

2. Thomas J. Healey and Donald J. Hardy, "Growth in Alternative Investments," *Financial Analysts Journal* 53, no. 4 (July–August 1997): 58–59.

3. C. P. Chandrasekhar, "Private Equity: A New Role for Finance?," International Development Economics Associates, last modified May 22, 2007, http://www.networkideas.org/featart/may2007/Private_Equity .pdf, 2.

4. Healey and Hardy, "Growth in Alternative Investments," 59.

5. William H. Gross, "The Lending Lindy," PIMCO, September 2012, http://www.pimco.com/EN/Insights/Pages/The-Lending-Lindy .aspx.

6. US Securities and Exchange Commission, "Investor Bulletin: Accredited Investors," accessed 2015, http://www.sec.gov/investor/alerts /ib_accreditedinvestors.pdf, 1.

7. Jesse Hamilton and Margaret Collins, "Hedge Funds Cleared to Advertise under SEC Proposal," *Bloomberg Businessweek*, August 29, 2012, http://www.bloomberg.com/news/articles/2012-08-28/hedge -fund-marketing-could-begin-new-era-as-sec-set-for-proposal.

8. Michael E. Kitces, "What Makes Something an Alternative Asset Class, Anyway?," *Journal of Financial Planning* 25, no. 9 (September 2012): 22–23.

9. US Securities and Exchange Commission, "Hedge Funds," accessed 2015, http://investor.gov/investing-basics/investment-products/hedge-funds; "How Hedge Funds Are Structured," Hedge Fund Fundamentals, accessed January 2015, http://www.hedgefundfundamentals.com /wp-content/uploads/2012/12/HFF_HFStructured_12-2012.pdf, 14.

10. A. W. Jones Advisers, "History of the Firm," accessed 2014, http:// www.awjones.com/historyofthefirm.html; John Russell, "Alfred W. Jones, 88, Sociologist and Investment Fund Innovator," *New York Times*, June 3, 1989, http://www.nytimes.com/1989/06/03 /obituaries/alfred-w-jones-88-sociologist-and-investment-fund -innovator.html.

11. A. W. Jones Advisers, "History of the Firm".

12. Carol J. Loomis, "The Jones Nobody Keeps Up With," *Fortune*, April 1966, 247.

13. Sebastian Mallaby, "Learning to Love Hedge Funds," *Wall Street Journal*, June 11, 2010, http://online.wsj.com/news/articles/SB10001424 052748703302604575294983666012928.

14. Mario J. Gabelli, "The History of Hedge Funds—The Millionaire's Club," Gabelli Funds, last modified October 25, 2000, http://www .gabelli.com/news/mario-hedge_102500.html.

15. Loomis, "Jones Nobody Keeps Up With," 247.

16. Gabelli, "History of Hedge Funds."

17. Loomis, "Jones Nobody Keeps Up With," 237.

18. Gabelli, "History of Hedge Funds."

19. Ibid.; David Litterick, "Billionaire Who Broke the Bank of England," *Telegraph*, September 13, 2002, http://www.telegraph.co.uk/finance /2773265/Billionaire-who-broke-the-Bank-of-England.html.

20. "Hedge Fund Industry—Assets Under Management: Historical Growth of Assets," BarclayHedge Alternative Investment Databases, accessed 2015, http://www.barclayhedge.com/research/indices/ghs/mum/Hedge _Fund.html.

21. Ibid.

22. Michael Benhamou, "Betting Against the Street," *MarketWatch*, June 9, 2005, http://www.marketwatch.com/story/taking-advantage-of -convertible-arbs.

23. Azam Ahmed, "John Paulson's Long, Hot Summer," *DealBook* (blog), *New York Times*, August 4, 2011, http://dealbook.nytimes .com/2011/08/04/john-paulsons-long-hot-summer.

24. Landon Thomas Jr., "Too Big to Profit, a Hedge Fund Plans to Get Smaller," *DealBook* (blog), *New York Times*, August 1, 2012, http://dealbook.nytimes.com/2012/08/01/hedge-fund-titan-plans -to-return-2-billion-to-investors.

25. Robert Mirsky, Anthony Cowell, and Andrew Baker, "The Value of the Hedge Fund Industry to Investors, Markets, and the Broader Economy," KPMG and Centre for Hedge Fund Research, Imperial College, London, last modified April 2012, http://www.kpmg.com/KY/en/Documents /the-value-of-the-hedge-fund-industry-part-1.pdf, 11.

26. Nicole M. Boyson, "Hedge Fund Performance Persistence: A New Approach," *Financial Analysts Journal* 64, no. 6 (November–December 2008): 28–29, 42.

27. Chris Jones, *Hedge Funds of Funds: A Guide for Investors* (Hoboken, NJ: Wiley, 2007), 1.3 ("What Are Hedge Funds of Funds?").

28. Ibid.

29. Jones, *Hedge Funds of Funds*, 3.5 ("The Downsides of Investing in Hedge Funds").

30. Ibid., 1.3.

31. Serge Darolles and Mathieu Vaissie, "Do Funds of Hedge Funds Really Add Value? A Post-Crisis Analysis" (working paper, EDHEC-Risk Institute, EDHEC Business School, Lille, France, September 2010), http://www.edhec-risk.com/edhec_publications/all_publications /RISKReview.2010-10-08.0141/attachments/EDHEC_Working _Paper_Do_FoHF_Really_Add_Value_F.pdf, 7–8 and 18.

32. Melvyn Teo, "The Liquidity Risk of Liquid Hedge Funds," *Journal of Financial Economics* 100, no. 1 (April 2011): 24–26.

33. Keith C. Brown, W. V. Harlow, and Laura T. Starks, "Of Tournaments and Temptations: An Analysis of Managerial Incentives in the Mutual Fund Industry," *Journal of Finance* 51, no. 1 (March 1996): 85–90 and 108–109.

34. Ibid., 88–89.

35. Ilia D. Dichev and Gwen Yu, "Higher Risk, Lower Returns: What Hedge Fund Investors Really Earn," *Journal of Financial Economics* 100, no. 2 (May 2011): 250 and 261.

36. Daniel A. Wingerd, "The Private Equity Market: History and Prospects," *Investment Policy* 1, no. 2 (September–October 1997): 29; "Georges F. Doriot," Baker Library Historical Collections, Harvard Business

School, accessed January 2015, http://www.library.hbs.edu/hc/doriot /innovation-vc/ard.

37. Wingerd, "Private Equity Market," 30–32.

38. Ibid., 32.

39. John Steele Gordon, "A Short (Sometimes Profitable) History of Private Equity," *Wall Street Journal*, January 17, 2012, http://online.wsj.com /news/articles/SB10001424052970204468004577166850222785654.

40. Ibid.; Jon Friedman, "'Barbarians at the Gate' Authors Reflect," *MarketWatch*, November 21, 2008, http://www.marketwatch.com/story /barbarians-at-the-gate-authors-reflect-on-wall-streets-madness.

41. Wingerd, "Private Equity Market," 36–38.

42. Deborah Perry Piscione, *Secrets of Silicon Valley: What Everyone Else Can Learn from the Innovation Capital of the World* (New York: Palgrave, 2013), 43 and 132–133; National Venture Capital Association and Thomson Reuters, "2012 National Venture Capital Association Yearbook," last modified 2012, http://www.finansedlainnowacji.pl/wp-content /uploads/2012/08/NVCA-Yearbook-2012.pdf, 13.

43. National Venture Capital Association and Thomson Reuters, "2012 National Venture Capital Association Yearbook," 25 and 119.

44. Preqin, *The 2014 Preqin Global Private Equity Report: Sample Pages*, accessed 2014, https://www.preqin.com/docs/samples/The_2014 _Preqin_Global_Private_Equity_Report_Sample_Pages.pdf, 50.

45. National Venture Capital Association and Thomson Reuters, "2012 National Venture Capital Association Yearbook," 7.

46. Noshua Watson, "REITs Rising," *NYSE Magazine*, October 2003, http://www.ventasreit.com/sites/all/themes/ventasreit/images /stories/pdf/news/ventas_reit_spotlight_nov_dec03.pdf, 1.

47. Carly Schulaka, "Advisers Embrace Alternative Investments," *Journal of Financial Planning* 24, no. 9 (September 2011): 32.

48. Adam Dunsby and Kurt Nelson, "A Brief History of Commodities Indexes: An Evolution from Passive to Active Indexes," *Journal of Indexes* 13, no. 3 (May–June 2010): 37.

49. Kimberly A. Stockton, "Understanding Alternative Investments: The Role of Commodities in a Portfolio," Vanguard Investment Counseling & Research, Vanguard, last modified 2007, http://www.vanguard.com /pdf/s552.pdf, 1.

50. Chung-Hong Fu, "Timberland Investments: A Primer," Timberland Investment Resources, last modified June 2012, http://www.tirllc.com /wp-content/themes/tirllc/docs/TIR_A-Primer-2012-06-11-02.pdf, 2.

51. Jim Rinehart, "U.S. Timberland Post-Recession: Is It the Same Asset?," R&A Investment Forestry, last modified April 2010, http:// investmentforestry.com/resources/1%20-%20Post-Recession%20 Timberland.pdf, 1.

52. Ibid., 12–13.

53. Preqin, "Preqin Investor Outlook: Alternative Investments," 2014, https://www.preqin.com/docs/reports/Preqin-Investor-Outlook -Alternative-Assets-H2-2014.pdf, 4–6.

54. Investment Company Institute, *2013 Investment Company Fact Book*, accessed 2014, http://www.ici.org/pdf/2013_factbook.pdf, 36 and 47.

55. Dan Culloton, "A Brief History of Indexing," *Fund Spy* (blog), Morningstar, August 9, 2011, http://news.morningstar.com/articlenet/article .aspx?id=390749.

56. John C. Bogle, "The First Index Mutual Fund: A History of Vanguard Index Trust and the Vanguard Index Strategy," Bogle Financial Markets Research Center, Vanguard, last modified 1997, http://www.vanguard .com/bogle_site/lib/sp19970401.html.

57. Ibid.

58. Ibid.

59. Investment Company Institute, *2013 Investment Company Fact Book*, 36 and 47.

60. Ibid., 46–48.

61. Ibid., 46.

62. Ibid., 54.

63. Anthony Cowell et al., "Transformation: The Future of Alternative Investments," KPMG International and International Fund Investment, last modified June 2010, http://www.kpmg.com/TW/zh /IssuesAndInsights/Documents/FS/KPMG-Transformation.pdf, 39.

9. INNOVATION CREATES A NEW ELITE

1. US Department of Labor, "Frequently Asked Questions about Retirement Plans and ERISA," accessed 2013, http://www.dol.gov/ebsa /faqs/faq_compliance_pension.html.

2. Gary Furukawa, Randall Buck, and Gary Smart, "Money Manager Interview: Gary Furukawa, Randall Buck & Gary Smart," *Wall Street Transcript*, October 25, 2004, https://www.twst.com/interview/19635.

3. Joseph H. Spigelman, "What Basis for Superior Performance?," *Financial Analysis Journal* 30, no. 3 (May–June 1974): 32.

4. Douglas Appell, "Turning a New Page: Morgan Stanley's Gregory J. Fleming," *Pensions & Investments*, March 7, 2011, http:// www.pionline.com/article/20110307/PRINT/110309949 /turning-a-new-page-morgan-stanleys-gregory-j-fleming.

5. David A. Latzko, "Economies of Scale in Mutual Fund Administration" (working paper, York Campus, Pennsylvania State University, York, PA,

n.d.), http://www.personal.psu.edu/~dxl31/research/articles/mutual .pdf, 4–5.

6. "US Retirement Assets Hit $18 Trillion Again," *Retirement Income Journal*, July 6, 2011, http://retirementincomejournal.com/issue /july-6-2011/article/u-s-retirement-assets-hit-18-trillion-again-ici.

7. Investment Company Institute, "Retirement Assets Total $24.0 Trillion in Second Quarter 2014," September 25, 2014, http://www.ici.org /research/stats/retirement/ret_14_q2.

8. Investment Company Institute, *2012 Investment Company Fact Book*, accessed 2014, http://www.ici.org/pdf/2012_factbook.pdf, 9–11.

9. Burton G. Malkiel, "Asset Management Fees and the Growth of Finance," *Journal of Economic Perspectives* 27, no. 2 (Spring 2013): 99.

10. Daniel Golden, "Cash Me If You Can," *Upstart Business Journal*, March 18, 2009, http://upstart.bizjournals.com/executives/2009/03 /18/David-Swensen-and-the-Yale-Model.html.

11. Oregon State Treasury, "Oregon Investment Council (OIC)," accessed 2013, http://www.oregon.gov/treasury/Divisions/Investment/Pages /Oregon-Investment-Council-(OIC).aspx.

12. Russell Parker, "Boutique Asset Managers Offer Competitive Advantages," *InvestmentNews*, May 30, 2010, http://www.investmentnews.com /article/20100530/REG/305309998/boutique-asset-managers -offer-competitive-advantages.

13. Sonia Kolesnikov-Jessop, "Independent Asset Managers Thrive in Crisis," *New York Times*, April 28, 2013, http://www.nytimes.com/2013/04/29 /business/global/29iht-nwindies29.html.

14. "America's Top 300 Money Managers," *Institutional Investor*, accessed 2014, http://www.institutionalinvestor.com/Research/4376/Americas -Top-300-Money-Managers.html.

15. Ibid.

16. Ibid.; "Ranking America's Top Money Managers," *Institutional Investor*, August 1992, 79–83. Of the top twenty-five money managers in 2013, the following firms were independent: BlackRock, Vanguard Group, Fidelity Investments, Capital Group, Franklin Templeton Investments, Wellington Management Co., Invesco, T. Rowe Price Group, Legg Mason, Ameriprise Financial, and Federated Investors. The independent firms in 1991 were as follows: Fidelity Management & Research; Capital Group; Dreyfus Group; Scudder, Stevens & Clark; Franklin Group; United Asset Management; and Wellington Management Co.

17. "America's Top 300 Money Managers."

18. "Will Invest for Food," *Economist*, May 3, 2014, http://www.economist .com/news/briefing/21601500-books-and-music-investment-industry -being-squeezed-will-invest-food.

19. Ibid.

20. "The World's Billionaires," *Forbes*, accessed 2014, http://www.forbes .com/billionaires.

21. Simone Foxman, "Ten Hedge Fund Managers Each Make More Money Than the Ten Best-Paid US CEOs Combined," Quartz, April 15, 2013, http://qz.com/74533/10-hedge-fund-managers-each-make-more -money-than-the-10-best-paid-us-ceos-combined.

22. Robert Lenzner, "The Top 25 Hedge Fund Managers Earn More Than All the 500 Top CEOs Together," *Forbes*, August 6, 2013, http://www .forbes.com/sites/robertlenzner/2013/08/06/the-top-25-hedge-fund -managers-earn-more-than-all-the-500-top-ceos-together.

23. Michelle Coffey, "Warren Buffett Made $37 Million a Day in 2013," MarketWatch, December 18, 2013, http://www.marketwatch.com/story /warren-buffett-made-37-million-a-day-in-2013-2013-12-18.

24. Nathan Vardi, "The 40 Highest-Earning Hedge Fund Managers and Traders," *Forbes*, February 26, 2013, http://www.forbes.com/sites /nathanvardi/2013/02/26/the-40-highest-earning-hedge-fund -managers-and-traders.

25. Alexandra Stevenson, "Hedge Fund Moguls' Pay Has the 1% Looking Up," *DealBook* (blog), *New York Times*, May 6, 2014, http://dealbook.nytimes .com/2014/05/06/hedge-fund-moguls-pay-has-the-1-looking-up.

26. Ibid.

27. Joseph Thorndike, "Forget Carried Interest, It's All about Taxing Capital Gains," *Forbes*, November 12, 2013, http://www.forbes.com /sites/taxanalysts/2013/11/12/forget-carried-interest-its-all-about -taxing-capital-gains.

28. Julie M. Zauzmer, "Where We Stand: The Class of 2013 Senior Survey," *Harvard Crimson*, May 28, 2013, http://www.thecrimson.com /article/2013/5/28/senior-survey-2013.

29. Julie Segal, "Beating the Market Has Become Nearly Impossible," *Institutional Investor*, September 18, 2013, http://www.institutionalinvestor .com/Article/3256074/Beating-the-Market-Has-Become-Nearly- Impossible.html.

30. "Down to 1.4 and 17," *Economist*, February 8, 2014, http://www .economist.com/news/finance-and-economics/21595942-cost -investing-alternative-assets-fallingslowly-down-14-and-17.

CONCLUSION

1. Michael S. Carliner, "Development of Federal Homeownership 'Policy,'" *Housing Policy Debate* 9, no. 2 (1998): 301.

2. Albert Monroe, "How the Federal Housing Administration Affects Homeownership" (working paper, Department of Economics, Harvard University, Cambridge, MA, November 2001), http://www.jchs.harvard.edu/sites/jchs.harvard.edu/files/monroe_w02-4.pdf, 5–6.

3. Carliner, "Development of 'Policy,'" 308.

4. Ibid., 308–309.

5. GinnieMae.gov, "Our History," Accessed 2015, http://www.ginniemae.gov/inside_gnma/company_overview/Pages/our_history.aspx.

Bibliography

A. W. Jones Advisers. "History of the Firm." Accessed 2014. http://www
.awjones.com/historyofthefirm.html.

Abkowitz, Alyssa. "Madoff's Auditor . . . Doesn't Audit?" CNN Money, December 19, 2008. http://archive.fortune.com/2008/12/17/news/companies
/madoff.auditor.fortune/index.htm.

Adams, Colin. "Transport." In *The Cambridge Companion to the Roman Economy*, ed. Walter Scheidel, 218–240. Cambridge: Cambridge University Press, 2012.

Afyonoglu, Gokhan, et al. "The Brave New World of Sovereign Wealth Funds." Lauder Institute of Management & International Studies, University of Pennsylvania, 2010. http://d1c25a6gwz7q5e.cloudfront.net/papers/download
/052810_Lauder_Sovereign_Wealth_Fund_report_2010.pdf.

Aggarwal, Rajesh K., and Guojun Wu. "Stock Market Manipulations." *Journal of Business* 79, no. 4 (July 2006): 1915–1953.

Ahmed, Azam. "John Paulson's Long, Hot Summer." *DealBook* (blog), *New York Times*, August 4, 2011. http://dealbook.nytimes.com/2011/08/04
/john-paulsons-long-hot-summer.

Alter, George, Claudia Goldin, and Elyce Rotella. "The Savings of Ordinary Americans: The Philadelphia Saving Fund Society in the Mid-Nineteenth Century." *Journal of Economic History* 54, no. 4 (December 1994): 735–767.

American Council of Life Insurers. *2011 Life Insurers Fact Book*. Washington, DC: American Council of Life Insurers, 2011.

"America's Top 300 Money Managers." *Institutional Investor*. Accessed 2014. http://www.institutionalinvestor.com/Research/4376/Americas-Top -300-Money-Managers.html.

Andreau, Jean. *Banking and Business in the Roman World*. Translated by Janet Lloyd. Cambridge: Cambridge University Press, 1999.

Appell, Douglas. "Turning a New Page: Morgan Stanley's Gregory J. Fleming." *Pensions & Investments*, March 7, 2011. http://www .pionline.com/article/20110307/PRINT/110309949/turning -a-new-page-morgan-stanleys-gregory-j-fleming.

Aristophanes. *The Birds*. Translated by David Barrett. London: Penguin, 2003.

Arnold, Martin, Peter Thal Larsen, Peggy Hollinger, John O'Doherty, and Richard Milne. "How Kerviel Exposed Lax Controls at Société Générale." *Financial Times*, February 7, 2008. http://www.ft.com/intl/cms/s/0 /927fe998-d5b2-11dc-8b56-0000779fd2ac.html.

Arnsberger, Paul, Melissa Ludlum, Margaret Riley, and Mark Stanton. "A History of the Tax-Exempt Sector: An SOI Perspective." *Statistics of Income Bulletin* (Internal Revenue Service, US Department of the Treasury), Winter 2008, 105–135. http://www.irs.gov/pub/irs-soi/tehistory.pdf.

Aslanian, Sebouh. "The Circulation of Men and Credit: The Role of the Commenda and the Family Firm in Julfan Society." *Journal of the Economic and Social History of the Orient* 50, no. 2–3 (2007): 124–170.

Aviva. "Amicable Society: Company History." Accessed January 2015. http:// www.aviva.com/about-us/heritage/companies/amicable-society.

Bakan, Joel. *The Corporation: The Pathological Pursuit of Profit and Power*. New York: Free Press, 2004.

Bagehot, Walter. *Lombard Street: A Description of the Money Market*. London: King, 1873.

Bagwell, Philip S., and G. E. Mingay. *Britain and America, 1850–1939: A Study of Economic Change*. New York: Praeger, 1970.

Bainbridge, Stephen M., ed. *Research Handbook on Insider Trading*. Cheltenham, UK: Edward Elgar, 2013.

Bakan, Joel. *The Corporation: The Pathological Pursuit of Profit and Power*. New York: Free Press, 2004.

Bandler, James, and Doris Burke. "70 Years before Madoff, There Was Whitney." CNN Money, December 16, 2008. http://money.cnn.com/2008/12/16 /news/madoff.whitney.fortune.

Banner, Stuart. "The Origin of the New York Stock Exchange, 1791–1860." *Journal of Legal Studies* 27, no. 1 (January 1998): 113–140.

Barbash, Barry P. "Remembering the Past: Mutual Funds and the Lessons of the Wonder Years." Speech at the ICI Securities Law Procedures

Conference, Washington, DC, December 4, 1997. www.sec.gov/news/speech /speecharchive/1997/spch199.txt.

BarclayHedge Alternative Investment Databases. "Hedge Fund Industry— Assets Under Management." Accessed 2015. http://www.barclayhedge .com/research/indices/ghs/mum/HF_Money_Under Management html

——. "Hedge Fund Industry—Assets Under Management: Historical Growth of Assets." Accessed 2014. http://www.barclayhedge.com/research/indices/ghs/mum/Hedge_Fund.html.

Barth, Chris. "Warren Buffett: Clairvoyant or Crazy?" *Forbes*, June 12, 2012. http://www.forbes.com/sites/chrisbarth/2012/06/12/warren-buffett -clairvoyant-or-crazy.

Bartlett, Bruce. "How Deficit Hawks Could Derail the Recovery." *Forbes*, January 8, 2010. http://www.forbes.com/2010/01/07/deficit-great-depression-recovery-opinions-columnists-bruce-bartlett.html.

Benartzi, Shlomo, and Richard H. Thaler. "Myopic Loss Aversion and the Equity Premium Puzzle." *Quarterly Journal of Economics* 110, no. 1 (February 1995): 73–92.

Benedict XIV (Pope). *Vix Pervenit.* [1745]. EWTN Global Catholic Network. http://www.ewtn.com/library/ENCYC/B14VIXPE.htm.

Benhamou, Michael. "Betting Against the Street." *MarketWatch*, June 9, 2005. http://www.marketwatch.com/story/taking-advantage-of-convertible-arbs.

Berger, Adolf, Barry Nicholas, and Susan M. Treggiari. "Guardianship." In *The Oxford Classical Dictionary*, eds. Simon Hornblower, Antony Spawforth, and Esther Eidinow. 4th ed. Oxford: Oxford University Press, 2012.

Bernanke, Ben S. "The Financial Accelerator and the Credit Channel." Speech at The Credit Channel of Monetary Policy in the Twenty-First Century Conference, Federal Reserve Bank of Atlanta, Atlanta, GA, June 15, 2007. http://www.federalreserve.gov/newsevents/speech /bernanke20070615a.htm.

Bernard, Carole, and Phelim Boyle. "Mr. Madoff's Amazing Returns: An Analysis of the Split-Strike Conversion Strategy." *Journal of Derivatives* 17, no. 1 (Fall 2009): 62–76.

Bernstein, Peter L. *Capital Ideas: The Improbable Origins of Modern Wall Street*. New York: Free Press, 1992.

Bierman, Harold, Jr. *The Causes of the 1929 Stock Market Crash: A Speculative Orgy or a New Era?* Westport, CT: Greenwood, 1998.

——. "The 1929 Stock Market Crash." In *Encyclopedia of Economic and Business History*, ed. Robert Whaples. Economic History Association. March 26, 2008. http://eh.net/encyclopedia/the-1929-stock-market-crash.

Black, Fischer, and Myron Scholes. "The Pricing of Options and Corporate Liabilities." *Journal of Political Economy* 81, no. 3 (May–June 1973): 637–654.

Blackwood, Amy S., Katie L. Roeger, and Sarah L. Pettijohn. "The Nonprofit Sector in Brief: Public Charities, Giving, and Volunteering, 2012." Urban Institute. Accessed 2014. http://www.urban.org/UploadedPDF/412674 -The-Nonprofit-Sector-in-Brief.pdf.

Blumenthal, Karen. *Six Days in October: The Stock Market Crash of 1929.* New York: Simon and Schuster, 2002.

Board of Governors of the Federal Reserve System. "Ben S. Bernanke." Accessed January 2015. http://www.federalreservehistory.org/People /DetailView/12.

——. "Money Stock Measures—H.6." July 3, 2014. http://www.federal reserve.gov/RELEASES/h6/20140703.

——. "Press Release." October 23, 2014. http://www.federalreserve.gov /newsevents/press/bcreg/20141023a.htm.

Bogle, John C. "The First Index Mutual Fund: A History of Vanguard Index Trust and the Vanguard Index Strategy." Bogle Financial Markets Research Center, Vanguard. Last modified 1997. http://www.vanguard.com/bogle _site/lib/sp19970401.html.

Boness, A. James. "Elements of a Theory of Stock-Option Value." *Journal of Political Economy* 72, no. 2 (April 1964): 163–175.

Bonin, Hubert. "'Blue Angels,' 'Venture Capital,' and 'Whales': Networks Financing the Takeoff of the Second Industrial Revolution in France, 1890s–1920s." *Business and Economic History On-Line* 2 (2004): 1–49. http://www.thebhc.org/publications/BEHonline/2004/Bonin.pdf.

Bose, Sutapa, and Ashok Rudra. "Quantitative Estimates of Primitive Accumulation and Its Sources." *Economic and Political Weekly* 29, no. 4 (January 22, 1994): 199–207.

Boyson, Nicole M. "Hedge Fund Performance Persistence: A New Approach." *Financial Analysts Journal* 64, no. 6 (November–December 2008): 27–44.

Brach, Marion A. *Real Options in Practice.* Hoboken, NJ: Wiley, 2003.

Bricker, Jesse, Arthur B. Kennickell, Kevin B. Moore, and John Sabelhaus. "Changes in U.S. Family Finances from 2007 to 2010: Evidence from the Survey of Consumer Finances." *Federal Reserve Bulletin* 98, no. 2 (June 2012): 1–80.

Brooks, John. *Once in Golconda: A True Drama of Wall Street, 1920–1938.* New York: Harper & Row, 1969.

Brown, Keith C., W. V. Harlow, and Laura T. Starks. "Of Tournaments and Temptations: An Analysis of Managerial Incentives in the Mutual Fund Industry." *Journal of Finance* 51, no. 1 (March 1996): 85–110.

Brown, Richard. *Society and Economy in Modern Britain, 1700–1850.* New York: Routledge, 1990.

Brown, Stephen J., William N. Goetzmann, and Stephen A. Ross. "Survival." *Journal of Finance* 50, no. 3 (July 1995): 853–873.

Brown, Stephen J., and Onno W. Steenbeek. "Doubling: Nick Leeson's Trading Strategy." *Pacific-Basin Finance Journal* 9, no. 2 (April 2001): 83–99.

Buffett, Warren. "The Superinvestors of Graham-and-Doddsville." *Hermes* (Columbia Business School), Fall 1984, 4–15.

Bullock, Hugh. *The Story of Investment Companies.* New York: Columbia University Press, 1959.

Burton, Katherine, and Saijel Kishan. "Raj Rajaratnam Became Billionaire Demanding Edge." Bloomberg News, October 19, 2009. http://www .bloomberg.com/apps/news?pid=newsarchive&sid=aDg9U7NGeNv4.

Byun, Kathryn J. "The U.S. Housing Bubble and Bust: Impacts on Employment." *Monthly Labor Review* (Bureau of Labor Statistics, US Department of Labor), December 2010, 3–17. http://www.bls.gov/opub /mlr/2010/12/art1full.pdf.

Capital Finance International. "Jesse Lauriston Livermore: The Boy Plunger." February 20, 2014. http://cfi.co/banking/2014/02/jesse-lauriston -livermore-the-boy-plunger.

Carliner, Michael S. "Development of Federal Homeownership 'Policy.'" *Housing Policy Debate* 9, no. 2 (1998): 299–321.

Carnegie Corporation of New York. "Foundation History." Accessed 2015. http://carnegie.org/about-us/mission-and-vision/foundation -history.

——. "Founding and Early Years." Accessed 2014. http://carnegie.org /about-us/foundation-history/founding-and-early-years.

——. "Programs." Accessed 2014. http://carnegie.org/programs.

Censky, Annalyn. "Federal Reserve Launches QE3." CNN Money, September 13, 2012. http://money.cnn.com/2012/09/13/news/economy /federal-reserve-qe3.

"A Century of Ponzi Schemes." *DealBook* (blog), *New York Times*, December 15, 2008. http://dealbook.nytimes.com/2008/12/15/a-century-of-ponzi -schemes.

Chandrasekhar, C. P. "Private Equity: A New Role for Finance?" International Development Economics Associates. Last modified May 22, 2007. http:// www.networkideas.org/featart/may2007/Private_Equity.pdf.

Christensen, Donald. *Surviving the Coming Mutual Fund Crisis.* New York: Little, Brown, 1995.

Cipolla, Carlo M. *Before the Industrial Revolution: European Society and Economy, 1000–1700.* Translated by Christopher Woodall. 3rd ed. New York: Norton, 1994.

Çizakça, Murat. *A Comparative Evolution of Business Partnerships: The Islamic World and Europe, with Specific Reference to the Ottoman Archives.* The Ottoman Empire and Its Heritage 8. Leiden: Brill, 1996.

Clark, Andrew. "Bernard Madoff's Sons Say: We're Victims Too." *The Guardian*, March 17, 2010. http://www.theguardian.com/business/2010/mar /17/bernard-madoff-usa.

Clark, Robert L., Lee A. Craig, and Jack W. Wilson. *A History of Public Sector Pensions in the United States.* Philadelphia: University of Pennsylvania Press, 2003.

Clikeman, Paul M. *Called to Account: Financial Frauds That Shaped the Accounting Profession.* 2nd ed. New York: Routledge, 2013.

——. "The Greatest Frauds of the (Last) Century." Working paper, Robins School of Business, University of Richmond, Richmond, VA, May 2003. http://www.newaccountantusa.com/newsFeat/wealthManagement /Clikeman_Greatest_Frauds.pdf.

Coffey, Michelle. "Warren Buffett Made $37 Million a Day in 2013." MarketWatch, December 18, 2013. http://www.marketwatch.com/story /warren-buffett-made-37-million-a-day-in-2013-2013-12-18.

Cohen, Edward E. *Athenian Economy and Society: A Banking Perspective.* Princeton, NJ: Princeton University Press, 1992.

Colby, Robert K. D., ed. "Wrestling with Reform: Financial Scandals and the Legislation They Inspired." Securities and Exchange Commission Historical Society. May 1, 2013. http://www.sechistorical.org/museum /galleries/wwr/index.php.

Collins, Michael. *Monday and Banking in the UK: A History.* New York: Routledge, 1988.

Congressional Budget Office. *The Economic Effects of the Savings and Loan Crisis.* Washington, DC: Congressional Budget Office, 1992.

——. "Report on the Troubled Asset Relief Program—October 2012." October 11, 2012. http://www.cbo.gov/sites/default/files/TARP10 -2012_0.pdf.

Cooke, Colin Arthur. *Corporation, Trust and Company: An Essay in Legal History.* Cambridge, MA: Harvard University Press, 1951.

Costa, Dora L. "Pensions and Retirement: Evidence from Union Army Veterans." *Quarterly Journal of Economics* 110, no. 2 (May 1995): 297–319.

Council of Economic Advisers, Executive Office of the President. "The Economic Impact of the American Recovery and Reinvestment Act Five Years Later: Final Report to Congress." February 2014. http://www.whitehouse .gov/sites/default/files/docs/cea_arra_report.pdf.

Courtault, Jean-Michel, Yuri Kabanov, Bernard Bru, Pierre Crépel, Isabelle Lebon, and Arnaud Le Marchand. "Louis Bachelier on the Centenary of *Théorie de la Spéculation.*" *Mathematical Finance* 10, no. 3 (July 2000): 341–353.

Cowell, Anthony, et al. "Transformation: The Future of Alternative Investments." KPMG International and International Fund Investment. Last modified June 2010. http://www.kpmg.com/TW/zh/IssuesAndInsights /Documents/FS/KPMG-Transformation.pdf.

Cowen, David J. "William Duer and America's First Financial Scandal." *Financial History* 97 (Spring 2010): 20–35.

Cowen, David J., Richard Sylla, and Robert E. Wright. "The US Panic of 1792: Financial Crisis Management and the Lender of Last Resort." Paper presented at the XIV International Economic History Congress, Helsinki, Finland, August 2006. http://www.helsinki.fi/iehc2006/papers1/Sylla.pdf.

Cowles, Alfred, III. "Can Stock Market Forecasters Forecast?" *Econometrica* 1, no. 3 (July 1933): 309–324.

Cowles Foundation for Research in Economics. "Alfred Cowles, 3rd (1891–1984)." Yale University. Accessed 2013. http://cowles.econ.yale.edu /archive/people/directors/cowles.htm.

Culloton, Dan. "A Brief History of Indexing." *Fund Spy* (blog), Morningstar, August 9, 2011. http://news.morningstar.com/articlenet/article .aspx?id=390749.

Curry, Lynne. "Guinness Brew-Haha in the City Lapping at Thatcher Government." *Christian Science Monitor*, January 29, 1987. http://www .csmonitor.com/1987/0129/fmark29.html.

Curry, Timothy, and Lynn Shibut. "The Cost of the Savings and Loan Crisis: Truth and Consequences." *FDIC Banking Review* 13, no. 2 (2000): 26–35.

D'Agostino, Anthony. *The Rise of Global Powers: International Politics in the Era of the World Wars.* Cambridge: Cambridge University Press, 2012.

Darby, Mary. "In Ponzi We Trust." *Smithsonian Magazine*, December 1998. http://www.smithsonianmag.com/people-places/in-ponzi-we-trust -64016168.

Darolles, Serge, and Mathieu Vaissie. "Do Funds of Hedge Funds Really Add Value? A Post-Crisis Analysis." Working paper, EDHEC-Risk Institute, EDHEC Business School, Lille, France, September 2010. http://www.edhec-risk.com/edhec_publications/all_publications /RISKReview.2010-10-08.0141/attachments/EDHEC_Working_Paper _Do_FoHF_Really_Add_Value_F.pdf.

Davies, Glen. *A History of Money: From Ancient Times to the Present Day.* Cardiff: University of Wales Press, 2002.

De Roover, Florence Edler. "Partnership Accounts in Twelfth Century Genoa." *Bulletin of the Business Historical Society* 15, no. 6 (December 1941): 87–92.

De Roover, Raymond. *The Medici Bank: Its Organization, Management, Operations and Decline.* New York: New York University Press, 1948.

———. *The Rise and Decline of the Medici Bank, 1397–1494.* Washington, DC: Beard Books, 1999.

———. "Scholastic Economics: Survival and Lasting Influence from the Sixteenth Century to Adam Smith." *Quarterly Journal of Economics* 69, no. 2 (May 1955): 161–190.

Deaton, Angus. "Franco Modigliani and the Life Cycle Theory of Consumption." Speech at the Convegno Internazionale Franco Modgliani, Accademia Nazionale dei Lincei, Rome, February 17–18, 2005. https://www .princeton.edu/~deaton/downloads/romelecture.pdf.

DeLong, J. Bradford. "The Roaring Twenties." In *Slouching Towards Utopia? The Economic History of the Twentieth Century.* February 1997. http://holtz.org/Library/Social%20Science/Economics/Slouching%20 Towards%20Utopia%20by%20DeLong/Slouch_roaring13.html.

Dercksen, J. G. "On the Financing of Old Assyrian Merchants." In Dercksen, *Trade and Finance in Ancient Mesopotamia*, 85–99.

Dercksen, J. G., ed. *Trade and Finance in Ancient Mesopotamia.* Leiden: Nederlands Instituut voor het Nabije Oosten, 1999.

Deutsche Börse Group. "Company History." Accessed October 2014. http://deutsche-boerse.com/dbg/dispatch/en/kir/dbg_nav /about_us/10_Deutsche_Boerse_Group/50_Company_History.

DeWitt, Larry. "The 1937 Supreme Court Rulings on the Social Security Act." Social Security Administration. 1999. http://www.ssa.gov/history/court .html.

———. "The Townsend Plan's Pension Scheme." Social Security Administration. December 2001. http://www.ssa.gov/history/townsendproblems .html.

Dichev, Ilia D., and Gwen Yu. "Higher Risk, Lower Returns: What Hedge Fund Investors Really Earn." *Journal of Financial Economics* 100, no. 2 (May 2011): 248–263.

Dimmock, Stephen G., and William C. Gerken. "Finding Bernie Madoff: Detecting Fraud by Investment Managers." Working paper, 2011.

Dixit, Avinash. "Paul Samuelson's Legacy." *Annual Reviews of Economics* 4 (2012): 1–31.

Dodd-Frank Wall Street Reform and Consumer Protection Act. Pub. L. No. 111-203, 124 Stat. 1376–2223. http://www.law.cornell.edu/wex /dodd-frank.

Dolmetsch, Chris. "Subprime Collapse to Global Financial Meltdown: Timeline." Bloomberg News, October 13, 2008. http://www.bloomberg.com /apps/news?pid=newsarchive&sid=aleqkSjAAw10.

"Down to 1.4 and 17." *Economist*, February 8, 2014. http://www.economist .com/news/finance-and-economics/21595942-cost-investing-alternative -assets-fallingslowly-down-1.4-and-17.

Driver, Anna, and Eileen O'Grady. "Allen Stanford Sentenced to 110 Years in Prision." Reuters, June 14, 2012. http://www.reuters.com/article/2012/06/14/us-stanford-sentencing-idUSBRE85D17720120614.

Dunsby, Adam, and Kurt Nelson. "A Brief History of Commodities Indexes: An Evolution from Passive to Active Indexes," *Journal of Indexes* 13, no 3 (May–June 2010): 36–39 and 55.

Durga, P. S. Kanaka. "Identity and Symbols of Sustenance: Explorations in Social Mobility of Medieval South India." *Journal of the Economic and Social History of the Orient* 44, no. 2 (2001): 141–174.

EDinformatics. "The Capital Asset Pricing Model—Fundamental Analysis." Accessed 2013. http://edinformatics.com/investor_education/capital_asset_pricing_model.htm.

Ellis, Charles D. *Capital: The Story of Long-Term Investment Excellence.* Hoboken, NJ: Wiley, 2004.

Ellis, Charles D., and James R. Vertin. *True Stories of the Great Barons of Finance.* Vol. 2 of *Wall Street People.* Hoboken, NJ: Wiley, 2003.

Ellis, Joseph J. *His Excellency: George Washington.* New York: Knopf, 2004.

Ellis, Maria deJ. *Agriculture and the State in Ancient Mesopotamia: An Introduction to the Problems of Land Tenure.* Occasional Publications of the Babylonian Fund 1. Philadelphia: University Museum, 1976.

Encyclopaedia Britannica. "Margaret Olivia Slocum Sage." Accessed January 2015. http://www.britannica.com/EBchecked/topic/516233/Margaret-Olivia-Slocum-Sage.

——. "Married Women's Property Acts." Accessed January 2015. http://www.britannica.com/EBchecked/topic/366305/Married-Womens-Property-Acts.

——. "Russell Sage." Accessed January 2015. http://www.britannica.com/EBchecked/topic/516237/Russell-Sage.

"The Endangered Public Company." *Economist*, May 19, 2012. http://www.economist.com/node/21555562.

"Exchange to Close for Two Days of Rest." *New York Times*, October 31, 1929. http://partners.nytimes.com/library/financial/103129crash-close.html.

Fabrikant, Geraldine. "Making Sure the Rich Stay Rich, Even in Crisis." *New York Times*, October 7, 2001. http://www.nytimes.com/2001/10/07/business/making-sure-the-rich-stay-rich-even-in-crisis.html.

Fama, Eugene F. "Efficient Capital Markets: A Review of Theory and Empirical Work." *Journal of Finance* 25, no. 2 (May 1970): 383–417.

Fama, Eugene F., and Kenneth R. French. "The Capital Asset Pricing Model: Theory and Evidence." *Journal of Economic Perspectives* 18, no. 3 (Summer 2004): 25–46.

——. "The Cross-Section of Expected Stock Returns." *Journal of Finance* 47, no. 2 (June 1992): 427–465.

Federal Deposit Insurance Corporation. *An Examination of the Banking Crises of the 1980s and Early 1990s.* Vol. 1 of *History of the Eighties: Lessons for the Future.* Washington, DC: Federal Deposit Insurance Corporation, 1997.

Federal Reserve Bank of New York. "George L. Harrison." Accessed January 2015. http://www.newyorkfed.org/aboutthefed/GHarrisonbio.html.

Federal Reserve Bank of St. Louis. "The Financial Crisis: A Timeline of Events and Policy Actions." Accessed 2015. https://www.stlouisfed.org/financial-crisis/full-timeline.

Feinstein, Charles H., Peter Temin, and Gianni Toniolo. *The World Economy Between the World Wars.* New York: Oxford University Press, 2008.

Fink, Matthew P. *The Rise of Mutual Funds: An Insider's View.* 2nd ed. Oxford: Oxford University Press, 2011.

Finley, M. I. *The Ancient Economy.* Sather Classical Lectures 43. Berkeley: University of California Press, 1999.

Fisher, Irving. *The Theory of Interest as Determined by Impatience to Spend Income and Opportunity to Invest It.* New York: Macmillan, 1930.

"Fisher, Irving." In *Concise Encyclopedia of Economics,* ed. David R. Henderson. Library of Economics and Liberty. 2008. http://www.econlib.org/library/Enc/bios/Fisher.html.

Fisher, Kenneth L. *How to Smell a Rat: The Five Signs of Financial Fraud.* With Lara Hoffmans. Hoboken, NJ: Wiley, 2009.

——. *100 Minds That Made the Market.* Hoboken, NJ: Wiley, 2007.

Fishman, Steve. "The Monster Mensch." *New York,* February 22, 2009. http://nymag.com/news/businessfinance/54703.

Fletcher, Michael A. "Obama Leaves D.C. to Sign Stimulus Bill." *Washington Post,* February 18, 2009. http://www.washingtonpost.com/wp-dyn/content/article/2009/02/17/AR2009021700221.html.

Foster, Benjamin. "A New Look at the Sumerian Temple State." *Journal of the Economic and Social History of the Orient* 24, no. 3 (October 1981): 225–241.

Foundation Center. "Quick Facts on U.S. Non-Profits." Accessed 2015. http://foundationcenter.org/gainknowledge/research/keyfacts2014/foundation-focus.html.

Foxman, Simone. "Ten Hedge Fund Managers Each Make More Money Than the Ten Best-Paid US CEOs Combined." Quartz, April 15, 2013. http://qz.com/74533/10-hedge-fund-managers-each-make-more-money-than-the-10-best-paid-us-ceos-combined.

Frank, Tenney. *Rome and Italy of the Republic.* Vol. 1 of *An Economic Survey of Ancient Rome.* Paterson, NJ: Pageant, 1959.

Franklin D. Roosevelt Presidential Library and Museum. "FDR: From Budget Balancer to Keynesian: A President's Evolving Approach to Fiscal

Policy in Times of Crisis." Accessed 2013. http://www.fdrlibrary.marist.edu
/aboutfdr/budget.html.

Frazzini, Andrea, David Kabiller, and Lasse H. Pedersen. "Buffett's Alpha."
NBER Working Paper 19681, National Bureau of Economic Research,
Cambridge, MA, November 2013. http://www.nber.org/papers/w19681.

Friedman, Jon. "'Barbarians at the Gate' Authors Reflect." *Market-
Watch*, November 21, 2008. http://www.marketwatch.com/story
/barbarians-at-the-gate-authors-reflect-on-wall-streets-madness.

Friedman, Milton. *A Theory of the Consumption Function*. Princeton, NJ:
Princeton University Press, 1957.

Fritz-Morgenthal, Sebastian, and Hagen Rafeld. "Breaking Down the Biggest Trading Fraud in the History of Banking." *Risk Professional*, June
2010, 47–52. http://www.academia.edu/9042700/Breaking_Down_the
_Biggest_Trading_Fraud_in_the_History_of_Banking.

Fu, Chung-Hong. "Timberland Investments: A Primer." Timberland Investment Resources. Last modified June 2012. http://www.tirllc.com/wp
-content/themes/tirllc/docs/TIR_A-Primer-2012-06-11-02.pdf.

Furukawa, Gary, Randall Buck, and Gary Smart. "Money Manager Interview:
Gary Furukawa, Randall Buck & Gary Smart." *Wall Street Transcript*,
October 25, 2004. https://www.twst.com/interview/19635.

Gabelli, Mario J. "The History of Hedge Funds—The Millionaire's Club."
Gabelli Funds. Last modified October 25, 2000. http://www.gabelli
.com/news/mario-hedge_102500.html.

Gay, Suzanne. "The Lamp-Oil Merchants of Iwashimizu Shrine: Transregional Commerce in Medieval Japan." *Monumenta Nipponica* 64, no. 1
(Spring 2009): 1–51.

———. *The Moneylenders of Late Medieval Kyoto*. Honolulu: University of
Hawaii Press, 2001.

Gendar, Alison. "Bernie Madoff Baffled by SEC Blunders: Compares
Agency's Bumbling Actions to Lt. Colombo." *Daily News* (New
York), October 30, 2009. http://www.nydailynews.com/news/crime
/bernie-madoff-baffled-sec-blunders-compares-agency-bumbling
-actions-lt-colombo-article-1.382446.

"Georges F. Doriot." Baker Library Historical Collections, Harvard Business
School. Accessed January 2015. http://www.library.hbs.edu/hc/doriot
/innovation-vc/ard.

Gibson-Jarvie, Robert. *The City of London: A Financial and Commercial History*. Cambridge: Woodhead-Faulkner, 1979.

Gilbert, R. Alton. "Requiem for Regulation Q: What It Did and Why It Passed
Away." *Federal Reserve Bank of St. Louis Review*, February 1986, 22–37.
https://research.stlouisfed.org/publications/review/86/02/Requiem
_Feb1986.pdf.

Gimbel, Barney. "Partners in Crime." CNN Money, October 4, 2006. http://money.cnn.com/magazines/fortune/fortune_archive/2006/10/02/8387505/index.htm.

GinnieMae.gov, "Our History," Accessed 2015, http://www.ginniemae.gov/inside_gnma/company_overview/Pages/our_history.aspx.

Glovin, David. "Bernard Madoff's Accountant Friehling Pleads Guilty (Update 2)." Bloomberg News, November 3, 2009. http://www.bloomberg.com/apps/news?pid=newsarchive&sid=ah_xWloo7TTE.

Golden, Daniel. "Cash Me If You Can." *Upstart Business Journal*, March 18, 2009. http://upstart.bizjournals.com/executives/2009/03/18/David-Swenson-and-the-Yale-Model.html

Goldstein, Matthew. "Stanford's Failed Health Club." *Unstructured Finance* (blog), *Bloomberg Businessweek*, February 13, 2009. http://www.businessweek.com/investing/wall_street_news_blog/archives/2009/02/stanfords_faile.html.

——. "Stanford's Rocky Start." *Bloomberg Businessweek*, March 3, 2009. http://www.businessweek.com/bwdaily/dnflash/content/mar2009/db2009033_601499.htm.

Goldthwaite, Richard A. *The Economy of Renaissance Florence*. Baltimore: Johns Hopkins University Press, 2009.

Gordon, John Steele. "Pyramid Schemes Are as American as Apple Pie." *Wall Street Journal*, December 17, 2008. http://online.wsj.com/news/articles/SB122948144507313073.

——. "A Short (Sometimes Profitable) History of Private Equity." *Wall Street Journal*, January 17, 2012. http://online.wsj.com/news/articles/SB10001424052970204468004577166850222785654.

Gorham, Michael, and Nidhi Singh. *Electronic Exchanges: The Global Transformation from Pits to Bits*. Burlington, MA: Elsevier, 2009.

Graham, Benjamin. "A Conversation with Benjamin Graham." *Financial Analysts Journal* 32, no. 5 (September–October 1976): 20–23.

——. *The Intelligent Investor*. New York: Harper, 1949.

Graham, Benjamin, and David L. Dodd. *Security Analysis*. New York: McGraw-Hill, 1934.

Greene, Bob. "A $100 Million Idea: Use Greed for Good." *Chicago Tribune*, December 15, 1986. http://articles.chicagotribune.com/1986-12-15/features/8604030634_1_ivan-boeskys-greed-fund.

Gross, William H. "The Lending Lindy." PIMCO. September 2012. http://www.pimco.com/EN/Insights/Pages/The-Lending-Lindy.aspx.

"'Guinness Four' Guilty." BBC News, August 27, 1990. http://news.bbc.co.uk/onthisday/hi/dates/stories/august/27/newsid_2536000/2536035.stm.

Gupta, K. P. *Cost Management: Measuring, Monitoring & Motivating Performance*. Delhi: Global India Publications, 2009.

Haber, Carole, and Brian Gratton. *Old Age and the Search for Security: An American Social History.* Bloomington: Indiana University Press, 1994.

Hagstrom, Robert G. *The Warren Buffett Way.* New York: Wiley, 1994.

Hamilton, Jesse, and Margaret Collins. "Hedge Funds Cleared to Advertise under SEC Proposal." *Bloomberg Businessweek,* August 29, 2012. http://www.bloomberg.com/news/articles/2012-08-28/hedge-fund-marketing-could-begin-new-era-as-sec-set-for-proposal.

Hansen, Valerie, and Ana Mata-Fink. "Records from a Seventh-Century Pawnshop in China." In *The Origins of Value: The Financial Innovations That Created Modern Capital Markets,* eds. William N. Goetzmann and K. Geert Rouwenhorst, 54–64. Oxford: Oxford University Press, 2005.

Haron, Sudin, and Wan Nursofiza Wan Azmi. *Islamic Finance and Banking System: Philosophies, Principles and Practices.* New York: McGraw-Hill, 2009.

Harrison, A. R. W. *The Law of Athens.* Vol. 1, *The Family and Property.* 2nd ed. Indianapolis: Hackett, 1998.

Healey, Thomas J., and Donald J. Hardy. "Growth in Alternative Investments." *Financial Analysts Journal* 53, no. 4 (July–August 1997): 58–65.

Hilzenrath, David S. "Former Madoff Trader David Kugel Pleads Guilty to Fraud." *Washington Post,* November 21, 2011. http://www.washingtonpost.com/business/economy/former-madoff-trader-david-kugel-pleads-guilty-to-fraud/2011/11/21/gIQATSFLjN_story.html.

Historical Center of the Presbyterian Church in America. "January 11: Presbyterian Ministers Fund." January 11, 2012. http://www.thisday.pcahistory.org/2012/01/january-11.

Hobsbawm, Eric. *Industry and Empire: From 1750 to the Present Day.* Rev. ed. London: Penguin, 1999.

Hochfelder, David. "How Bucket Shops Lured the Masses into the Market." BloombergView, January 10, 2013. http://www.bloombergview.com/articles/2013-01-10/how-bucket-shops-lured-the-masses-into-the-market.

Hohenstein, Kurt A., ed. "Fair to All People: The SEC and the Regulation of Insider Trading." Securities and Exchange Commission Historical Society. November 1, 2006. http://www.sechistorical.org/museum/galleries/it.

——. "William O. Douglas and the Growing Power of the SEC." Securities and Exchange Commission Historical Society. December 1, 2005. http://www.sechistorical.org/museum/galleries/douglas/index.php.

Homer, Sidney, and Richard Sylla. *A History of Interest Rates.* 4th ed. Hoboken, NJ: Wiley, 2005.

Honan, Edith, and Dan Wilchins. "Bernard Madoff Arrested over Alleged $50 Billion Fraud." Reuters, December 12, 2008. http://www.reuters.com/article/2008/12/12/us-madoff-arrest-idUSTRE4BA7IK20081212.

Hong, Jiaguan. 中国金融史 [*A financial history of China*]. Chengdu, 1993.

Hoover, Herbert. "Statement on Efforts to Balance the Budget." March 8, 1932. The American Presidency Project. http://www.presidency.ucsb.edu /ws/?pid=23478.

"How Hedge Funds Are Structured." Hedge Fund Fundamentals. Accessed January2015.http://www.hedgefundfundamentals.com/wp-content/uploads /2012/12/HFF_HFStructured_12-2012.pdf.

Howe, Christopher. *The Origins of Japanese Trade Supremacy: Development and Technology in Asia from 1540 to the Pacific War.* Chicago: University of Chicago Press, 1996.

Hunt, Edwin S. "A New Look at the Dealings of the Bardi and Peruzzi with Edward III." *Journal of Economic History* 50, no. 1 (March 1990): 149–162.

Hurtado, Patricia. "Andrew, Ruth Madoff Say Were Unaware of $65 Billion Fraud Until Confession." *Bloomberg Businessweek*, November 8, 2011. http://www.businessweek.com/news/2011-11-08/andrew-ruth-madoff -say-they-were-unaware-of-65-billion-fraud.html.

Iacoviello, Matteo. "Housing Wealth and Consumption." Working paper, Department of Economics, Boston College, Boston, MA, June 13, 2010. https://www2.bc.edu/matteo-iacoviello/research_files/HWAC.pdf.

Ibrahim, Jeanine. "Allen Stanford: Descent from Billionaire to Inmate #35017-183." CNBC, October 5, 2012. http://www.cnbc.com/id/49276842.

Immigration Act of 1924. Pub. L. No. 68-139, 43 Stat. 153. http://library .uwb.edu/guides/usimmigration/43%20stat%20153.pdf.

Inikori, Joseph E. *Africans and the Industrial Revolution in England: A Study in International Trade and Economic Development.* Cambridge: Cambridge University Press, 2002.

Investment Company Institute. "Appendix A: How Mutual Funds and Investment Companies Operate: The Origins of Pooled Investing." In *2006 Investment Company Fact Book.* Accessed 2014. http://www.icifactbook .org/2006/06_fb_appa.html.

——. "Recent Mutual Fund Trends." In *2014 Investment Company Fact Book.* Accessed 2014. http://www.icifactbook.org/fb_ch2.html.

——. "Retirement Assets Total $24.0 Trillion in Second Quarter 2014." September 25, 2014. http://www.ici.org/research/stats/retirement/ret_14_q2.

——. *2012 Investment Company Fact Book.* Accessed 2014. http://www.ici .org/pdf/2012_factbook.pdf.

——. *2013 Investment Company Fact Book.* Accessed 2014. http://www.ici .org/pdf/2013_factbook.pdf.

——. "The U.S. Retirement Market, First Quarter 2011." June 29, 2011. http://www.ici.org/pdf/ret_11_q1_data.pdf.

Isidore, Chris. "Chrysler Files for Bankruptcy." CNN Money, May 1, 2009. http://money.cnn.com/2009/04/30/news/companies/chrysler _bankruptcy.

Jefferies, Julie. "The UK Population: Past, Present and Future." Office for National Statistics (UK). Last modified December 2005. http://www.ons.gov.uk/ons/rel/fertility-analysis/focus-on-people-and-migration/december-2005/focus-on-people-and-migration---focus-on-people-and-migration---chapter-1.pdf.

Jensen, Michael C. "The Performance of Mutual Funds in the Period 1945–1964." *Journal of Finance* 23, no. 2 (May 1968): 389–416.

"Jewish Reaction to Madoff Scandal" (transcript). *Religion and Ethics Newsweekly*. Produced by Thirteen/WNET New York, PBS. March 20, 2009. http://www.pbs.org/wnet/religionandethics/2009/03/20/march-20-2009-jewish-reaction-to-madoff-scandal/2474.

Johnson, Philip McBride, and Thomas Lee Hazen. *Derivatives Regulation*. Vol. 3. New York: Aspen, 2004.

Johnson, Simon. "Sadly, Too Big to Fail Is Not Over." *Economix* (blog), *New York Times*, August 1, 2013. http://economix.blogs.nytimes.com/2013/08/01/sadly-too-big-to-fail-is-not-over.

Jones, Chris. *Hedge Funds of Funds: A Guide for Investors*. Hoboken, NJ: Wiley, 2007.

Jones, Norman. "Usury." In *Encyclopedia of Economic and Business History*, ed. Robert Whaples. Economic History Association. February 10, 2008. http://eh.net/encyclopedia/usury.

J. P. Morgan Chase & Co. *Annual Report 2013*. April 9, 2014. http://investor.shareholder.com/jpmorganchase/annual.cfm.

Kabele, Thomas. "James Dodson, First Lecture on Insurances, 1757: Discussion." Kabele and Associates (New Canaan, CT), May 2, 2008. http://www.kabele.us/papers/dodsonms2.pdf.

Kahneman, Daniel, and Amos Tversky. "Prospect Theory: An Analysis of Decision under Risk." *Econometrica* 47, no. 2 (March 1979): 263–292.

Kaul, Chandrika. "From Empire to Independence: The British Raj in India, 1858–1947." BBC. Last modified March 3, 2011. http://www.bbc.co.uk/history/british/modern/independence1947_01.shtml.

Kedmey, Dan. "2 Years and 900 Pages Later, the Volcker Rule Gets the Green Light." TIME.com, December 11, 2013. http://business.time.com/2013/12/11/2-years-and-900-pages-later-the-volcker-rule-gets-the-green-light.

Kehoe, Dennis P. *Investment, Profit, and Tenancy: The Jurists and the Roman Agrarian Economy*. Ann Arbor: University of Michigan Press, 1997.

——. *Management and Investment on Estates in Roman Egypt during the Early Empire*. Bonn: Habelt, 1992.

Keltner, Dacher, and Paul Piff. "Greed on Wall Street Prevents Good from Happening." *Room for Debate* (blog), *New York Times*, March 16, 2012. http://www.nytimes.com/roomfordebate/2012/03/15/does-morality

-have-a-place-on-wall-street/greed-on-wall-street-prevents-good-from
-happening.

Kennedy, Lawrence W. *Planning the City upon a Hill: Boston since 1630.*
Amherst: University of Massachusetts Press, 1992.

Kennedy, Robert C. "On This Day: March 30, 1872." The Learning Network,
New York Times, March 30, 2001. http://www.nytimes.com/learning
/general/onthisday/harp/0330.html.

Kerber, Ross. "The Whistleblower." *Boston Globe*, January 8, 2009. http://
www.boston.com/business/articles/2009/01/08/the_whistleblower.

Keynes, John Maynard. *The General Theory of Employment, Interest and
Money.* London: Macmillan, 1936.

Kimmel, Lewis Henry. *Share Ownership in the United States.* Washington,
DC: Brookings Institution, 1952.

Kindleberger, Charles P. *The World in Depression, 1929–1939.* Rev. ed. Berkeley:
University of California Press, 1986.

Kirsch, Clifford E., and Bibb L. Strench. "Mutual Funds." In *Financial Product Fundamentals: Law, Business, Compliance*, ed. Clifford E. Kirsch. 2nd
ed. New York: Practising Law Institute, 2013.

Kitces, Michael E. "What Makes Something an Alternative Asset Class,
Anyway?" *Journal of Financial Planning* 25, no. 9 (September 2012):
22–23.

Kitchen, Martin. *A History of Modern Germany, 1800–2000.* Malden, MA:
Blackwell, 2006.

Koepp, Stephen. "'Money Was the Only Way.'" *Time*, June 24, 2001.
http://content.time.com/time/magazine/article/0,9171,144026,00
.html.

Kohn, George Childs, ed. *The New Encyclopedia of American Scandal.* Rev.
ed. New York: Infobase, 2001.

Kohn, Meir. "The Capital Market before 1600." Working paper 99-06,
Department of Economics, Dartmouth College, Hanover, NH, February
1999. http://www.dartmouth.edu/~mkohn/Papers/99-06.pdf.

——. "Finance before the Industrial Revolution: An Introduction."
Working paper 99-01, Department of Economics, Dartmouth College,
Hanover, NH, February 1999. http://www.dartmouth.edu/~mkohn
/Papers/99-01.pdf.

Kolesnikov-Jessop, Sonia. "Independent Asset Managers Thrive in Crisis."
New York Times, April 28, 2013. http://www.nytimes.com/2013/04/29
/business/global/29iht-nwindies29.html.

Kosambi, D. D. "Indian Feudal Trade Charters." *Journal of the Economic and
Social History of the Orient* 2, no. 3 (December 1959): 281–293.

Krantz, Steven G., and Harold R. Parks. *A Mathematical Odyssey: Journey
from the Real to the Complex.* New York: Springer, 2014.

Krauss, Clifford. "Stanford Sentenced to 110-Year Term in $7 Billion Ponzi Case." *New York Times*, June 14, 2012. http://www.nytimes .com/2012/06/15/business/stanford-sentenced-to-110-years-in-jail-in -fraud-case.html.

Kreuger, Torsten. *The Truth about Ivar Kreuger.* Stuttgart: Seewald, 1968.

Krugman, Paul. "Too Little, Gone Too Soon." *Conscience of a Liberal* (blog), *New York Times*, August 30, 2013. http://krugman.blogs.nytimes .com/2013/08/30/too-little-gone-too-soon.

Lamoreaux, Naomi R., Margaret Levenstein, and Kenneth L. Sokoloff. "Financing Invention during the Second Industrial Revolution: Cleveland, Ohio, 1870–1920." NBER Working Paper 10923, National Bureau of Economic Research, Cambridge, MA, November 2004. http://www.nber .org/papers/w10923.pdf.

Lane, Frederic C. *Venice and History: Collected Papers of F. C. Lane.* Baltimore: Johns Hopkins University Press, 1966.

Langevoort, Donald C. "Rereading *Cady, Roberts*: The Ideology and Practice of Insider Trading Regulation." *Columbia Law Review* 99, no. 5 (June 1999): 1319–1343.

Latzko, David A. "Economies of Scale in Mutual Fund Administration." Working paper, York Campus, Pennsylvania State University, York, PA, n.d. http://www.personal.psu.edu/~dxl31/research/articles/mutual.pdf.

Lawrence, Steven, and Reina Mukai. "Key Facts on Mission Investing." Foundation Center, October 2011. http://foundationcenter.org /gainknowledge/research/pdf/keyfacts_missioninvesting2011.pdf.

Lee, Chulhee. "The Expected Length of Male Retirement in the United States, 1850–1990." *Journal of Population Economics* 14, no. 4 (December 2001): 641–650.

——. "Sectoral Shift and the Labor-Force Participation of Older Males in the United States, 1880–1940." *Journal of Economic History* 62, no. 2 (June 2002): 512–523.

Leemans, W. F. "The Role of Landlease in Mesopotamia in the Early Second Millennium B.C." *Journal of the Economic and Social History of the Orient* 18, no. 2 (June 1975): 134–145.

Leeson, Nick. "Biography." NickLeeson.com. Accessed January 2015. http:// www.nickleeson.com/biography/full_biography_02.html.

Legal Information Institute. "Dodd-Frank: Title I—Financial Stability." Accessed January 2015. http://www.law.cornell.edu/wex/dodd-frank _title_I.

Lenzner, Robert. "The Top 25 Hedge Fund Managers Earn More Than All the 500 Top CEOs Together." *Forbes*, August 6, 2013. http://www.forbes .com/sites/robertlenzner/2013/08/06/the-top-25-hedge-fund -managers-earn-more-than-all-the-500-top-ceos-together.

LIMRA Secure Retirement Institute. "Retirement Plans—Investment Company Institute: Retirement Assets on the Rise in 2014." October 2014. http://www.limra.com/Secure_Retirement_Institute/News_Center /Retirement_Industry_Report/Retirement_Plans_-_Investment _Company_Institute__Retirement_Assets_on_the_Rise_in_2014.aspx.

Lindert, Peter H., and Jeffrey G. Williamson. "English Workers' Living Standards during the Industrial Revolution: A New Look." *Economic History Review*, n.s., 36, no. 1 (February 1983): 1–25.

Lintner, John. "The Valuation of Risk Assets and the Selection of Risky Investments in Stock Portfolios and Capital Budgets." *Review of Economics and Statistics* 47, no. 1 (February 1965): 13–37.

Lipscy, Phillip Y., and Hirofumi Takinami. "The Politics of Financial Crisis Response in Japan and the United States." *Japanese Journal of Political Science* 14, no. 3 (September 2013): 321–353.

Litterick, David. "Billionaire Who Broke the Bank of England." *Telegraph*, September 13, 2002. http://www.telegraph.co.uk/finance/2773265 /Billionaire-who-broke-the-Bank-of-England.html.

Liu, Jinyu. "The Economy of Endowments: The Case of the Roman Collegia." In *Pistoi Dia Tèn Technèn: Studies in Honour of Raymond Bogaert*, Studia Hellenistica 44, eds. Koenraad Verboven, Katelijn Vandorpe, and Véronique Chankowski, 231–256. Leuven: Peeters, 2008.

Liu, Qiugen. "两宋私营高利贷资本初探" [A first look at usury capital in the Song dynasty]. *Philosophy and Social Sciences* (Hebei University), no. 3 (1987): 11–17.

——. "论中国古代商业、高利贷资本组织中的'合资'与'合伙'" [Joint-stock partnerships in business and usury capital organization in ancient China]. *Hebei Academic Journal* (Hebei University), no. 5 (1994): 86–91.

Lo Cascio, Elio. "The Early Roman Empire: The State and the Economy." In *The Cambridge Economic History of the Greco-Roman World*, eds. Walter Scheidel, Ian Morris, and Richard P. Saller, 619–647. Cambridge: Cambridge University Press, 2007.

Lodge, Henry Cabot. "League of Nations." American Memory, Library of Congress. Accessed 2015. http://memory.loc.gov.

Loh, Lixia. *Sovereign Wealth Funds: States Buying the World*. Cranbrook, UK: Global Professional Publishing, 2010.

Lohr, Steve. "Guinness Offers to Buy Distillers for $3.2 Billion." *New York Times*, January 20, 1986. http://www.nytimes.com/1986/01/21 /business/guinness-offers-to-buy-distillers-for-3.2-billion.html.

——. "Guinness Scandal Roils Britain." *New York Times*, January 30, 1987. http://www.nytimes.com/1987/01/30/business/guinness-scandal-roils -britain.html.

——. "Hostile Offer by Argyll for Distillers." *New York Times*, December 2, 1985. http://www.nytimes.com/1985/12/03/business/hostile-offer-by -argyll-for-distillers.html.

London Stock Exchange. "Our History." Accessed October 2014. http:// www.londonstockexchange.com/about-the-exchange/company -overview/our-history/our-history.htm.

Loomis, Carol J. "The Jones Nobody Keeps Up With." *Fortune*, April 1966, 237–247.

Lopez, Robert S. *The Commercial Revolution of the Middle Ages, 950–1350.* Cambridge: Cambridge University Press, 1976.

Lowenstein, Roger. *When Genius Failed: The Rise and Fall of Long-Term Capital Management.* New York: Random House, 2000.

Lynch, David J. "Economists Evoke the Spirit of Irving Fisher." Bloomberg News, January 12, 2012. http://www.bloomberg.com/bw/magazine /economists-evoke-the-spirit-of-irving-fisher-01122012.html.

MacDonald, Scott B., and Jane E. Hughes. *Separating Fools from Their Money: A History of American Financial Scandals.* New Brunswick, NJ: Transaction, 2007.

MacKenzie, Donald. *An Engine, Not a Camera: How Financial Models Shape Markets.* Cambridge, MA: MIT Press, 2006.

Maddison, Angus. *Contours of the World Economy, 1–2030 AD: Essays in Macro-Economic History.* Oxford: Oxford University Press, 2007.

——. *The World Economy: Historical Statistics.* Paris: Development Centre of the Organisation for Economic Co-operation and Development, 2003.

Madoff, Bernard. "Text of Bernard Madoff's Court Statement." National Public Radio, March 12, 2009. http://www.npr.org/templates/story /story.php?storyId=101816470.

Madrian, Brigitte C., and Dennis F. Shea. "The Power of Suggestion: Inertia in 401(k) Participation and Savings Behavior." *Quarterly Journal of Economics* 116, no. 4 (November 2001): 1149–1187.

Malkiel, Burton G. "Asset Management Fees and the Growth of Finance." *Journal of Economic Perspectives* 27, no. 2 (Spring 2013): 97–108.

——. "The Efficient Market Hypothesis and Its Critics." *Journal of Economic Perspectives* 17, no. 1 (Winter 2003): 59–82.

Mallaby, Sebastian. "Learning to Love Hedge Funds." *Wall Street Journal*, June 11, 2010. http://online.wsj.com/news/articles/SB10001424052748 703302604575294983666012928.

Malmendier, Ulrike. "Law and Finance 'at the Origin.'" *Journal of Economic Literature* 47, no. 4 (December 2009): 1076–1108.

——. "Roman Shares." In *The Origins of Value: The Financial Innovations That Created Modern Capital Markets*, eds. William N. Goetzmann and K. Geert Rouwenhorst, 31–42. Oxford: Oxford University Press, 2005.

——. "Societas." Working paper, Department of Economics, University of California, Berkeley, CA, n.d. http://eml.berkeley.edu/~ulrike/Papers /Societas_Article_v3.pdf.

Manning, Joseph. "Demotic Papyri (664–30 B.C.E.)." In *Security for Debt in Ancient Near Eastern Law*, eds. Raymond Westbrook and Richard Jasnow, 307–324. Leiden: Brill, 2001.

Margolick, David. "William Carey [*sic*], Former S.E.C. Chairman, Dies at 72." *New York Times*, February 9, 1983. http://www.nytimes.com /1983/02/09/obituaries/william-carey-former-sec-chairman-dies-at-72 .html.

Maridaki-Karatza, Olga. "Legal Aspects of the Financing of Trade." In *The Economic History of Byzantium*, ed. Angeliki E. Laiou, 3:1105–1120. Washington, DC: Dumbarton Oaks Research Library and Collection, 2002.

Markham, Jerry W. *A Financial History of Modern US Corporate Scandals: From Enron to Reform*. Armonk, NY: Sharpe, 2006.

——. *A Financial History of the United States*. Vol. 1, *From Christopher Columbus to the Robber Barons (1492–1900)*. Armonk, NY: Sharpe, 2002.

——. *A Financial History of the United States*. Vol. 2, *From J. P. Morgan to the Institutional Investor (1900–1970)*. Armonk, NY: Sharpe, 2002.

Markopolos, Harry. Harry Markopolos to US Securities and Exchange Commission, "The World's Largest Hedge Fund Is a Fraud," November 7, 2005. http://online.wsj.com/documents/Madoff_SECdocs_20081217.pdf.

Markowitz, Harry. "Harry M. Markowitz—Biographical." Nobel Media AB. 1990. Accessed 2013. http://www.nobelprize.org/nobel_prizes /economic-sciences/laureates/1990/markowitz-bio.html.

——. "Portfolio Selection." *Journal of Finance* 7, no. 1 (March 1952): 77–91.

Martinez, Mike, et al. *Vault Career Guide to Private Wealth Management*. New York: Vault, 2006.

"The Match King." *Economist*, December 19, 2007. http://www.economist .com/node/10278667.

Matthews, Christopher. "Five Former Employees of Bernie Madoff Found Guilty of Fraud." *Wall Street Journal*, March 25, 2014. http://online.wsj .com/news/articles/SB10001424052702304679404579459551977535 482.

——. "LIBOR Scandal: Yep, It's as Bad as We Thought." *Time*, December 20, 2012. http://business.time.com/2012/12/20/libor-scandal-yep -its-as-bad-as-we-thought.

McAndrews, James, and Chris Stefanadis. "The Consolidation of European Stock Exchanges." *Current Issues in Economics and Finance* 8, no. 6 (June 2002): 1–6.

McGuire, W. John. "The Investment Company Act of 1940." Morgan, Lewis & Bockius. 2005. http://www.morganlewis.com/pubs/Investment%20 Company%20Act%20Powerpoint.pdf.

McIntosh, Jane R. *Ancient Mesopotamia: New Perspectives*. Santa Barbara, CA: ABC-CLIO, 2005.

McMorran, David. *The Origin of Investment Securities*. Detroit: First National Company of Detroit, 1925.

McNally, David. *Political Economy and the Rise of Capitalism: A Reinterpretation*. Berkeley: University of California Press, 1988.

Mehra, Rajnish, and Edward C. Prescott. "The Equity Premium: A Problem." *Journal of Monetary Economics* 15, no. 2 (March 1985): 145–161.

Meikle, Scott. *Aristotle's Economic Thought*. Oxford: Clarendon Press, 1995.

Merced, Michael J. de la. "Q. and A.: Understanding LIBOR." *DealBook* (blog), *New York Times*, July 10, 2012. http://dealbook.nytimes.com/2012/07/10/q-and-a-understanding-libor.

——. "Taped Calls about Akamai Earnings Guidance Heard at Galleon Trial." *DealBook* (blog), *New York Times*, April 4, 2011. http://dealbook.nytimes.com/2011/04/04/focus-shifts-to-google-trade-at-galleon-trial.

Merton, Robert C. "Option Pricing When Underlying Stock Returns Are Discontinuous." *Journal of Financial Economics* 3, no. 1–2 (January–March 1976): 125–144.

Michell, Humfrey. *Economics of Ancient Greece*. 2nd ed. Cambridge: Heffer, 1957.

Michie, Ranald C. "Development of Stock Markets." In *The New Palgrave Dictionary of Money and Finance*, eds. Peter Newman, Murray Milgate, and John Eatwell, 662–668. London: Macmillan, 1992.

——. *The Global Securities Market: A History*. Oxford: Oxford University Press, 2006.

Middleton, Kathleen M. *Bayonne Passages*. Images of America. Charleston, SC: Arcadia, 2000.

Miller, Norman C. *The Great Salad Oil Swindle*. New York: Coward McCann, 1965.

Millett, Paul. *Lending and Borrowing in Ancient Athens*. Cambridge: Cambridge University Press, 1991.

Milton, Giles. *Samurai William: The Adventurer Who Unlocked Japan*. London: Hodder & Stoughton, 2002.

Minsky, Hyman P. *Stabilizing an Unstable Economy*. New Haven, CT: Yale University Press, 1986.

Mirsky, Robert, Anthony Cowell, and Andrew Baker. "The Value of the Hedge Fund Industry to Investors, Markets, and the Broader Economy." KPMG and Centre for Hedge Fund Research, Imperial College, London. Last modified April 2012. http://www.kpmg.com/KY/en/Documents/the-value-of-the-hedge-fund-industry-part-1.pdf.

Modigliani, Franco, and Richard H. Brumberg. "Utility Analysis and the Consumption Function: An Interpretation of Cross-Section Data." In *Post-Keynesian Economics*, ed. Kenneth K. Kurihara, 388–436. New Brunswick, NJ: Rutgers University Press, 1954.

———. "Utility Analysis and Aggregate Consumption Functions: An Attempt at Integration." In *The Collected Papers of Franco Modigliani*, ed. Andrew Abel, 2:128–197. Cambridge, MA: MIT Press, 1990.

Modigliani, Franco, and Merton H. Miller. "The Cost of Capital, Corporation Finance and the Theory of Investment." *American Economic Review* 48, no. 3 (June 1958): 261–297.

Monk, Ashby H. B. "Is CalPERS a Sovereign Wealth Fund?" Working paper 8-21, Center for Retirement Research, Boston College, Boston, MA, December 2008. http://crr.bc.edu/wp-content/uploads/2008/12/IB_8-21.pdf.

Monroe, Albert. "How the Federal Housing Administration Affects Homeownership." Working paper, Department of Economics, Harvard University, Cambridge, MA, November 2001. http://www.jchs.harvard.edu/sites/jchs.harvard.edu/files/monroe_w02-4.pdf.

Moore, Keith M. *Risk Arbitrage: An Investor's Guide*. Hoboken, NJ: Wiley, 1999.

Moosvi, Shireen. "The Medieval State and Caste." *Social Scientist* 39, no. 7–8 (July–August 2011): 3–8.

Morningstar. "MFS Massachusetts Investors Tr A (MITTX): Performance." Accessed 2014. http://performance.morningstar.com/fund/performance-return.action?t=MITTX.

Morris, Morris D. "Towards a Reinterpretation of Nineteenth-Century Indian Economic History." *Journal of Economic History* 23, no. 4 (December 1963): 606–618.

Mugasha, Agasha. *The Law of Letters of Credit and Bank Guarantees*. Sydney: Federation Press, 2003.

Murphy, Sharon Ann. "Life Insurance in the United States through World War I." In *Encyclopedia of Economic and Business History*, ed. Robert Whaples. Economic History Association. August 14, 2002. http://eh.net/encyclopedia/life-insurance-in-the-united-states-through-world-war-i.

Murray, J. B.C. *The History of Usury*. Philadelphia: J. B. Lippincott, 1866.

National Association of College and University Business Officers (NACUBO) and Commonfund Institute. "Average Annual Effective Spending Rates, 2011 to 2002." 2011 NACUBO-Commonfund Study of Endowments, 2012. http://www.nacubo.org/Documents/research/2011_NCSE_Public_Tables_Spending_Rates_Final_January_18_2012.pdf.

———. "Educational Endowments Returned an Average of 19.2% in FY2011." 2011 NACUBO-Commonfund Study of Endowments, 2012. http://www.nacubo.org/Documents/research/2011_NCSE_Press_Release_Final_Embargo_1_31_12.pdf.

National Venture Capital Association and Thomson Reuters. "2012 National Venture Capital Association Yearbook." Last modified 2012. http://

www.finansedlainnowacji.pl/wp-content/uploads/2012/08/NVCA
-Yearbook-2012.pdf.

Neal, Larry. "On the Historical Development of Stock Markets." In *The Emergence and Evolution of Markets*, eds. Horst Brezinski and Michael Fritsch, 59–79. Cheltenham, UK: Edward Elgar, 1997.

Neumann, Hans. "Ur-Dumuzida and Ur-DUN: Reflections on the Relationship Between State-Initiated Foreign Trade and Private Economic Activity in Mesopotamia Towards the End of the Third Millennium B.C." In Dercksen, *Trade and Finance in Ancient Mesopotamia*, 43–53.

New York Stock Exchange. "Highlights of NYSE Shareowner Census Reports (1952–1990)." Accessed October 2014. http://www.nyxdata.com/nysedata/asp/factbook/viewer_edition.asp?mode=table&key=2312&category=11.

——. "Major Sources of NYSE Volume." Accessed October 2014. http://www.nyxdata.com/nysedata/asp/factbook/viewer_edition.asp?mode=table&key=2641&category=11.

——. "New York Stock Exchange Ends Member Seat Sales Today." December 30, 2013. http://www1.nyse.com/press/1135856420824.html.

——. "Selected Characteristics of Individual Shareowners." Accessed October 2014. http://www.nyxdata.com/nysedata/asp/factbook/viewer_edition.asp?mode=chart&key=51&category=11.

——. "Timeline—Events." Accessed October 2014. http://www1.nyse.com/about/history/timeline_events.html.

——. "Timeline—Technology." Accessed October 2014. http://www1.nyse.com/about/history/timeline_technology.html.

——. Transactions, Statistics and Data Library. Accessed 2014. http://www.nyse.com/financials/1022221393023.html.

"The 1907 Crisis in Historical Perspective." Center for History and Economics, Harvard University. Accessed 2015. http://www.fas.harvard.edu/~histecon/crisis-next/1907.

Nobel Media AB. "The Prize in Economics 1985—Press Release." 1985. Accessed 2013. http://www.nobelprize.org/nobel_prizes/economic-sciences/laureates/1985/press.html.

——. "The Prize in Economics 1990—Press Release." 1990. Accessed 2013. http://www.nobelprize.org/nobel_prizes/economic-sciences/laureates/1990/press.html.

Nobuhiko, Nakai, and James L. McClain. "Commercial Change and Urban Growth in Early Modern Japan." In *The Cambridge History of Japan*. Vol. 4, *Early Modern Japan*, ed. John Whitney Hall, 519–595. Cambridge: Cambridge University Press, 1991.

Obama, Barack. "President Obama on GM IPO." The White House, November 18, 2010. http://www.whitehouse.gov/photos-and-video/video/2010/11/18/president-obama-gm-ipo.

——. "Remarks by the President at Signing of Dodd-Frank Wall Street Reform and Consumer Protection Act." The White House, July 21, 2010. http://www.whitehouse.gov/the-press-office/remarks-president-signing -dodd-frank-wall-street-reform-and-consumer-protection-act.

Obstfeld, Maurice, and Alan M. Taylor. *Global Capital Markets: Integration, Crisis, and Growth.* Cambridge: Cambridge University Press, 2004.

Ogborn, M. E. "Professional Name of the Actuary." *Journal of the Institute of the Actuaries* 82, no. 2 (September 1956): 233–246.

O'Hanlon, Rosalind. *Caste, Conflict, and Ideology: Mahatma Jotirao Phule and Low Caste Protest in Nineteenth-Century Western India.* Cambridge South Asian Studies 30. Cambridge: Cambridge University Press, 1985.

"The Oldest Life Insurance Company in the United States." *New York Times,* November 19, 1905. http://timesmachine.nytimes.com/timesmachine /1905/11/19/101709385.html.

Oppenheim, A. Leo. *Ancient Mesopotamia: Portrait of a Dead Civilization.* Chicago: University of Chicago Press, 1977.

Oregon State Treasury. "Oregon Investment Council (OIC)." Accessed 2013. http://www.oregon.gov/treasury/Divisions/Investment/Pages /Oregon-Investment-Council-(OIC).aspx.

"Out of Keynes's Shadow." *Economist,* February 14, 2009. http://www .economist.com/node/13104022.

Parker, Russell. "Boutique Asset Managers Offer Competitive Advantages." *InvestmentNews,* May 30, 2010. http://www.investmentnews.com /article/20100530/REG/305309998/boutique-asset-managers-offer -competitive-advantages.

Parks, Tim. *Medici Money: Banking, Metaphysics, and Art in Fifteenth-Century Florence.* New York: Norton, 2005.

Pecora, Ferdinand. *Wall Street Under Oath.* New York: A. M. Kelley, 1939.

Persky, Joseph. "Retrospectives: From Usury to Interest." *Journal of Economic Perspectives* 21, no. 2 (Winter 2007): 227–236.

Phillips, Cabell. *From the Crash to the Blitz, 1929–1939.* New York: Fordham University Press, 2000.

Piller, Charles. "Foundations Align Investments with Their Charitable Goals." *Los Angeles Times,* December 29, 2007. http://articles.latimes .com/2007/dec/29/business/fi-foundation29.

Pirenne, Henri. *Medieval Cities: Their Origins and the Revival of Trade.* Translated by Frank D. Halsey. Princeton, NJ: Princeton University Press, 1952.

Piscione, Deborah Perry. *Secrets of Silicon Valley: What Everyone Else Can Learn from the Innovation Capital of the World.* New York: Palgrave, 2013.

Ponzi v. Fessenden. 258 U.S. 254 (1922).

Postal, Matthew A. "New York Curb Exchange (Incorporating the New York Curb Market Building), Later Known as the American Stock Exchange." New York City Landmarks Preservation Commission. June 26, 2012. http://www.nyc.gov/html/lpc/downloads/pdf/reports/2515.pdf.

Poterba, James M., Steven F. Venti, and David A. Wise. "The Transition to Personal Accounts and Increasing Retirement Wealth: Macro and Micro Evidence." NBER Working Paper 8610, National Bureau of Economic Research, Cambridge, MA, November 2001. http://www.nber.org/papers/w8610.pdf.

Preqin. "Preqin Investor Outlook: Alternative Investments." 2014. https://www.preqin.com/docs/reports/Preqin-Investor-Outlook-Alternative-Assets-H2-2014.pdf.

——. *The 2014 Preqin Global Private Equity Report: Sample Pages.* Accessed 2014. https://www.preqin.com/docs/samples/The_2014_Preqin_Global_Private_Equity_Report_Sample_Pages.pdf.

Price, Richard. *British Society, 1680–1880: Dynamism, Containment, and Change.* Cambridge: Cambridge University Press, 1999.

Pulliam, Susan, and Chad Bray. "Trader Draws Record Sentence." *Wall Street Journal,* October 14, 2011. http://online.wsj.com/news/articles/SB10001424052970203914304576627191081876286.

Purcell, Patrick, and Jennifer Staman. "Summary of the Employee Retirement Income Security Act (ERISA)." Congressional Research Service, Library of Congress, Washington, DC. April 10, 2008. http://digitalcommons.ilr.cornell.edu/key_workplace/505.

Qureshi, Anwar Iqbal. *Islam and the Theory of Interest.* Lahore: Shaikh Muhammad Ashraf, 1946.

"Ranking America's Top Money Managers." *Institutional Investor.* August 1992, 75–101.

Rathbone, Dominic. *Economic Rationalism and Rural Society in Third-Century A.D. Egypt: The Heroninos Archive and the Appianus Estate.* Cambridge: Cambridge University Press, 1991.

Reinhart, Carmen M., and Kenneth S. Rogoff. *This Time Is Different: Eight Centuries of Financial Folly.* Princeton, NJ: Princeton University Press, 2011.

Ricketts, Lowell R. "Quantitative Easing Explained." *Liber8 Economic Information Newsletter* (Federal Reserve Bank of St. Louis), April 2011. http://research.stlouisfed.org/pageone-economics/uploads/newsletter/2011/201104_ClassroomEdition.pdf.

Rinehart, Jim. "U.S. Timberland Post-Recession: Is It the Same Asset?" R&A Investment Forestry. Last modified April 2010. http://investmentforestry.com/resources/1%20-%20Post-Recession%20Timberland.pdf.

Riu, Manuel. "Banking and Society in Late Medieval and Early Modern Aragon." In *The Dawn of Modern Banking*, 131–167. New Haven, CT: Yale University Press, 1979.

Rockefeller Foundation. "Our History: A Powerful Legacy." Accessed July 8, 2014. http://www.rockefellerfoundation.org/about-us/our-history.

Ross, Brian. *The Madoff Chronicles: Inside the Secret World of Bernie and Ruth.* New York: Hyperion, 2009.

Rouwenhorst, K. Geert. "The Origins of Mutual Funds." Working paper 04-48, International Center for Finance, Yale School of Management, Yale University, New Haven, CT, December 2004. http://ssrn.com /abstract=636146.

——. "The Origins of Mutual Funds." In *The Origins of Value: The Financial Innovations That Created Modern Capital Markets*, eds. William N. Goetzmann and K. Geert Rouwenhorst, 249–269. New York: Oxford University Press, 2005.

Rubin, Jared. "The Lender's Curse: A New Look at the Origin and Persistence of Interest Bans in Islam and Christianity." PhD diss., Stanford University, 2007. ProQuest (AAT 3267615).

Russell, John. "Alfred W. Jones, 88, Sociologist and Investment Fund Innovator." *New York Times*, June 3, 1989. http://www.nytimes.com /1989/06/03/obituaries/alfred-w-jones-88-sociologist-and-investment -fund-innovator.html.

Ryan, Franklin W. *Usury and Usury Laws: A Juristic-Economic Study of the Effects of State Statutory Maximums for Loan Charges upon Lending Operations in the United States.* Boston: Houghton Mifflin, 1924.

Sahai, Nandita P. "Crafts in Eighteenth-Century Jodhpur: Questions of Class, Caste, and Community Identities." *Journal of the Economic and Social History of the Orient* 48, no. 4 (2005): 524–551.

Samuelson, Paul A. *Foundations of Economic Analysis.* Cambridge, MA: Harvard University Press, 1947.

——. "Rational Theory of Warrant Pricing." *Industrial Management Review* 6, no. 2 (Spring 1965): 13–39.

Samuelson, Paul A., and Robert C. Merton. "A Complete Model of Warrant Pricing That Maximizes Utility." *Industrial Management Review* 10, no. 2 (Winter 1969): 17–46.

Sansing, Richard, and Robert Yetman. "Distribution Policies of Private Foundations." Working paper 02-20, McGladrey Institute of Accounting Education and Research, Tippie College of Business, University of Iowa, Iowa City, IA, October 2002. http://tippie.uiowa.edu/accounting /mcgladrey/workingpapers/02-20.pdf.

Sass, Steven A. *The Promise of Private Pensions: The First Hundred Years.* Cambridge, MA: Harvard University Press, 1997.

Saxton, Jim. "The Roots of Broadened Stock Ownership." Joint Economic Committee, US Congress. April 2000. http://cog.kent.edu/lib/Hall&Congress-RootsOfBroadenedStockOwnership.pdf.

Schmidt, Robert, and Jesse Hamilton. "SEC 'Capacity Gap' Risks Oversight Lapses as Regulator's Targets Multiply." Bloomberg News, March 7, 2011. http://www.bloomberg.com/news/2011-03-07/sec-capacity-gap-risks-oversight-lapses-as-regulator-s-targets-multiply.html.

Schulaka, Carly. "Advisers Embrace Alternative Investments." *Journal of Financial Planning* 24, no. 9 (September 2011): 30–33.

Schweikhard, Frederic A., and Zoe Tsesmelidakis. "The Impact of Government Interventions on CDS and Equity Markets." Working paper, November 2012. http://papers.ssrn.com/sol3/papers.cfm?abstract_id=1573377.

Securities and Exchange Commission. "Investigation of Failure of the SEC to Uncover Bernard Madoff's Ponzi Scheme—Public Version" (Report No. OIG-509). Office of Investigations, US Securities and Exchange Commission, August 31, 2009. http://www.sec.gov/news/studies/2009/oig-509.pdf.

——. "Post-Madoff Reforms." Accessed September 2014. http://www.sec.gov/spotlight/secpostmadoffreforms.htm.

Securities and Exchange Commission Historical Society. "431 Days: Joseph P. Kennedy and the Creation of the SEC (1934–35)." Accessed 2013. http://www.sechistorical.org/museum/galleries/kennedy/politicians_b.php.

Segal, Julie. "Beating the Market Has Become Nearly Impossible." *Institutional Investor*, September 18, 2013. http://www.institutionalinvestor.com/Article/3256074/Beating-the-Market-Has-Become-Nearly-Impossible.html.

Senate Committee on Banking and Currency. "Stock Exchange Practices" (S. Rep. No. 73-1455). Washington, DC: Government Printing Office, 1934. https://www.senate.gov/artandhistory/history/common/investigations/pdf/Pecora_FinalReport.pdf.

Seyfried, William. "Monetary Policy and Housing Bubbles: A Multinational Perspective." *Research in Business and Economics Journal* 2 (March 2010). http://www.aabri.com/manuscripts/09351.pdf.

Shah, Vikas. "Andrew Lo on the LIBOR Scandal and What's Next." AllAboutAlpha.com, November 8, 2012. http://allaboutalpha.com/blog/2012/11/08/andrew-lo-on-the-libor-scandal-and-whats-next.

Sharpe, William F. "Capital Asset Prices: A Theory of Market Equilibrium under Conditions of Risk." *Journal of Finance* 19, no. 3 (September 1964): 425–442.

Shiller, Robert J. "Understanding Recent Trends in House Prices and Home Ownership." Working paper 13553, National Bureau of Economic Research, Cambridge, MA, October 2007. http://www.nber.org/papers/w13553.pdf.

Siddiqui, Shahid Hasan. *Islamic Banking: Genesis & Rationale, Evaluation & Review, Prospects & Challenges.* Karachi: Royal Book, 1994.

Skarda, Erin. "William Miller, the Original Schemer." *Time*, March 7, 2012. http://content.time.com/time/specials/packages/article/0,28804, 2104982_2104983_2104992,00.html.

Skully, Michael T. "The Development of the Pawnshop Industry in East Asia." In *Financial Landscapes Reconstructed: The Fine Art of Mapping Development*, eds. F. J. A. Bouman and Otto Hospes, 357–374. Boulder, CO: Westview, 1994.

Smart401k. "Modern Portfolio Theory and the Efficient Frontier." Accessed 2013. http://www.smart401k.com/Content/retail/resource-center /advanced-investing/modern-portfolio-theory-and-the-efficient-frontier.

Smiley, Gene. *The American Economy in the Twentieth Century.* Cincinnati: South-Western, 1994.

Smith, Aaron. "Madoff Arrives at N.C. Prison." CNN Money, July 14, 2009. http://money.cnn.com/2009/07/14/news/economy/madoff _prison_transfer.

Smith, Adam. *An Inquiry into the Nature and Causes of the Wealth of Nations.* New York: Modern Library, 1937.

Sobel, Robert. *The Big Board: A History of the New York Stock Market.* New York: Free Press, 1965.

——. *The Curbstone Brokers: The Origins of the American Stock Exchange.* London: Macmillan, 1970.

Social Security Administration. "Age 65 Retirement." Accessed 2013. http:// www.ssa.gov/history/age65.html.

——. "Historical Background and Development of Social Security." Accessed December 2014. http://www.ssa.gov/history/briefhistory3.html.

——. "Otto von Bismarck." Accessed 2013. http://www.ssa.gov/history /ottob.html.

——. "Social Insurance Movement." Accessed January 2015. http://www .socialsecurity.gov/history/trinfo.html.

Social Welfare History Project. "Townsend, Dr. Francis." Accessed 2013. http://www.socialwelfarehistory.com/eras/townsend-dr-francis.

Sosin, Joshua. "Perpetual Endowments in the Hellenistic World: A Case-Study in Economic Rationalism." PhD diss., Duke University, 2000. ProQuest (AAT 9977683).

"South Sea Bubble Short History." Baker Library, Harvard Business School. Accessed 2014. http://www.library.hbs.edu/hc/ssb/history.html.

Sovereign Wealth Center. "Kuwait Investment Authority." *Institutional Investor.* Accessed July 8, 2014. http://www.sovereignwealthcenter.com /fund/17/Kuwait-Investment-Authority.html.

Sovereign Wealth Fund Institute. "Sovereign Wealth Funds Make Up More than 25% of U.S. Retirement Assets." March 27, 2014. http://www.swfinstitute.org/swf-article/sovereign-wealth-funds-make-up-more-than-25-of-u-s-retirement-assets.

——. "What Is a SWF?" Accessed July 8, 2014. http://www.swfinstitute.org/sovereign-wealth-fund.

Spigelman, Joseph H. "What Basis for Superior Performance?" *Financial Analysis Journal* 30, no. 3 (May–June 1974): 32–86.

Starr, Timothy. *Railroad Wars of New York State*. Charleston, SC: History Press, 2012.

Stearns, Peter N. *The Industrial Revolution in World History*. 3rd ed. Boulder, CO: Westview, 2007.

Stevenson, Alexandra. "Hedge Fund Moguls' Pay Has the 1% Looking Up." *DealBook* (blog), *New York Times*, May 6, 2014. http://dealbook.nytimes.com/2014/05/06/hedge-fund-moguls-pay-has-the-1-looking-up.

Stewart, James B. "As a Watchdog Starves, Wall Street Is Tossed a Bone." *New York Times*, July 15, 2011. http://www.nytimes.com/2011/07/16/business/budget-cuts-to-sec-reduce-its-effectiveness.html.

——. *Den of Thieves*. New York: Simon and Schuster, 1992.

——. "Volcker Rule, Once Simple, Now Boggles." *New York Times*, October 21, 2011. http://www.nytimes.com/2011/10/22/business/volcker-rule-grows-from-simple-to-complex.html.

Steyer, Robert. "ICI: U.S. Retirement Assets Hit Record $20.8 Trillion." *Pensions & Investments*, June 26, 2013. http://www.pionline.com/article/20130626/ONLINE/130629908/ici-us-retirement-assets-hit-record-208-trillion.

Stockton, Kimberly A. "Understanding Alternative Investments: The Role of Commodities in a Portfolio." Vanguard Investment Counseling & Research, Vanguard. Last modified 2007. http://www.vanguard.com/pdf/s552.pdf.

Straney, Louis L. *Securities Fraud: Detection, Prevention and Control*. Hoboken, NJ: Wiley, 2010.

Suddath, Claire. "The Crash of 1929." *Time*, October 29, 2008. http://content.time.com/time/nation/article/0,8599,1854569,00.html.

Swensen, David. *Pioneering Portfolio Management: An Unconventional Approach to Institutional Investment*. Rev. ed. New York: Free Press, 2009.

Tan, Andrea, Gavin Finch, and Liam Vaughan. "RBS Instant Messages Show LIBOR Rates Skewed for Traders." Bloomberg News, September 26, 2012. http://www.bloomberg.com/news/2012-09-25/rbs-instant-messages-show-libor-rates-skewed-for-traders.html.

Tan, Kopin. "An Upbeat View from J. P. Morgan's Private Bank." *Barron's*, May 19, 2012. http://online.barrons.com/news/articles/SB5000142405 31119043700045773922260986818168.

Temin, Peter. "Two Views of the British Industrial Revolution." *Journal of Economic History* 57, no. 1 (March 1997): 63–82.

Teo, Melvyn. "The Liquidity Risk of Liquid Hedge Funds." *Journal of Financial Economics* 100, no. 1 (April 2011): 24–44.

Thomas, Landon, Jr. "Too Big to Profit, a Hedge Fund Plans to Get Smaller." *DealBook* (blog), *New York Times*, August 1, 2012. http:// dealbook.nytimes.com/2012/08/01/hedge-fund-titan-plans-to -return-2-billion-to-investors.

Thorndike, Joseph. "Forget Carried Interest, It's All about Taxing Capital Gains." *Forbes*, November 12, 2013. http://www.forbes.com/sites/taxanalysts /2013/11/12/forget-carried-interest-its-all-about-taxing-capital-gains.

Thorndike, William. Introduction to *The Outsiders: Eight Unconventional CEOs and Their Radically Rational Blueprint for Success*. Boston: Harvard Business Review Press, 2012.

"Timeline: Inside the Meltdown." PBS, February 17, 2009. http://www.pbs .org/wgbh/pages/frontline/meltdown/cron.

"Timeline: LIBOR-Fixing Scandal." BBC News, February 6, 2013. http:// www.bbc.com/news/business-18671255.

Tobin, James. "Liquidity Preference as Behavior Towards Risk." *Review of Economic Studies* 25, no. 2 (February 1958): 65–86.

Tonello, Matteo, and Stephan Rabimov. "The 2010 Institutional Investment Report: Trends in Asset Allocation and Portfolio Composition." Research Report R-1468-10-RR, The Conference Board, New York, NY, 2010. http://papers.ssrn.com/sol3/papers.cfm?abstract_id=1707512.

"Topics: Glass-Steagall Act (1933)." *New York Times*, accessed January 2015. http://topics.nytimes.com/top/reference/timestopics/subjects/g /glass_steagall_act_1933/index.html.

Toutain, Jules. *The Economic Life of the Ancient World*. Translated by M. R. Dobie. Abingdon, UK: Routledge, 1996.

Towers Watson and *Financial Times*. "Global Alternatives Survey 2012." Last modified July 2012. http://www.towerswatson.com/en-US/Insights /IC-Types/Survey-Research-Results/2012/07/Global-Alternatives -Survey-2012.

Traflet, Janice M. *A Nation of Small Shareholders: Marketing Wall Street after World War II*. Studies in Industry and Society. Baltimore: Johns Hopkins University Press, 2013.

Travers Smith. "The Takeovers Regime under the Companies Act 2006: AIM-Listed Companies." May 2007. http://www.traverssmith.com

/media/602015/takeovers_regime_under_the_companies_act_2006
_-_aim-listed_companies_-_may_2007.pdf.

"Treasury's Bailout Proposal." CNN Money, September 20, 2008. http://
money.cnn.com/2008/09/20/news/economy/treasury_proposal.

Udovitch, Abraham L. "At the Origins of the Western Commenda: Islam,
Israel, Byzantium?" *Speculum* 37, no. 2 (April 1962): 198–207.

Ulmer, Bryan K. "Boesky, Ivan." In *Encyclopedia of White-Collar and Corporate Crime*, ed. Lawrence M. Salinger, 1:96–98. Thousand Oaks, CA:
Sage, 2005.

Uniform Law Commission. "Prudent Management of Institutional Funds
Act Summary." Accessed 2014. http://uniformlaws.org/ActSummary.
aspx?title=Prudent%20Management%20of%20Institutional%20Funds%
20Act.

US Department of Labor. "Frequently Asked Questions about Retirement
Plans and ERISA." Accessed 2013. http://www.dol.gov/ebsa/faqs/faq
_compliance_pension.html.

US Department of the Treasury. "Financial Stability Oversight Council: Who
Is on the Council?" Accessed January 2015. http://www.treasury.gov
/initiatives/fsoc/about/council/Pages/default.aspx.

——. "TARP Programs." Accessed January 2015. http://www.treasury.gov
/initiatives/financial-stability/TARP-Programs/Pages/default.aspx.

"US Retirement Assets Hit $18 Trillion Again." *Retirement Income Journal*,
July 6, 2011. http://retirementincomejournal.com/issue/july-6-2011
/article/u-s-retirement-assets-hit-18-trillion-again-ici.

US Securities and Exchange Commission. "Hedge Funds." Accessed 2015.
http://investor.gov/investing-basics/investment-products/hedge-funds.

——. "Investor Bulletin: Accredited Investors." Accessed 2015. http://www
.sec.gov/investor/alerts/ib_accreditedinvestors.pdf.

——. "Laws That Govern the Securities Industry." Accessed January 2015.
http://www.sec.gov/about/laws.shtml.

Valentine, Bruce A. "Shakespeare Revisited." *Financial Analysts Journal* 21,
no. 3 (May–June 1965): 91–97.

Van De Mieroop, Marc. *The Ancient Mesopotamian City*. New York: Oxford
University Press, 1999.

Van Driel, G. "Capital Formation and Investment in an Institutional Context
in Ancient Mesopotamia." In Dercksen, *Trade and Finance in Ancient
Mesopotamia*, 25–42.

Vardi, Nathan. "The 40 Highest-Earning Hedge Fund Managers
and Traders." *Forbes*, February 26, 2013. http://www.forbes.com
/sites/nathanvardi/2013/02/26/the-40-highest-earning-hedge
-fund-managers-and-traders.

Vaughan, Liam, and Gavin Finch. "LIBOR Lies Revealed in Rigging of $300 Trillion Benchmark." Bloomberg News, January 28, 2013. http://www .bloomberg.com/news/2013-01-28/libor-lies-revealed-in-rigging-of -300-trillion-benchmark.html.

Verdier, Daniel. "Financial Capital Mobility and the Origins of Stock Markets." Working paper, European University Institute, San Domenico, Italy, February 1999.

Vernon, J. R. "The 1920–21 Deflation: The Role of Aggregate Supply." *Economic Inquiry* 29, no. 3 (July 1991): 572–580.

Visser, Wayne A. M., and Alastair MacIntosh. "A Short Review of the Historical Critique of Usury." *Accounting, Business & Financial History* 8, no. 2 (1998): 175–189.

Von Reden, Sitta. *Money in Ptolemaic Egypt: From the Macedonian Conquest to the End of the Third Century* B.C. Cambridge: Cambridge University Press, 2007.

Von Tunzelmann, G. N. "The Standard of Living Debate and Optimal Economic Growth." In *The Economics of the Industrial Revolution*, ed. Joel Mokyr, 207–226. London: Allen & Unwin, 1985.

Watson, Noshua. "REITs Rising." *NYSE Magazine*, October 2003. http:// www.ventasreit.com/sites/all/themes/ventasreit/images/stories/pdf /news/ventas_reit_spotlight_nov_dec03.pdf.

Webel, Baird. "Troubled Asset Relief Program (TARP): Implementation and Status." Congressional Research Service, Library of Congress, Washington, DC. June 27, 2013. https://www.fas.org/sgp/crs/misc/R41427 .pdf.

Weber, Max. *The History of Commercial Partnerships in the Middle Ages*. Translated by Lutz Kaelber. Lanham, MD: Rowman & Littlefield, 2003.

Webster, Richard. *A History of the Presbyterian Church in America, from Its Origin to the Year 1760*. Philadelphia: Joseph M. Wilson, 1857.

Weisman, Mary-Lou. "The History of Retirement, from Early Man to A.A.R.P." *New York Times*, March 21, 1999. http://www.nytimes .com/1999/03/21/jobs/the-history-of-retirement-from-early-man-to -aarp.html.

Wharton School of Finance and Commerce. *A Study of Mutual Funds*. H. R. Rep. No. 87-2274 (1962).

Wiafe, William Nana, Jr. *The New Competitive Strategy: The Ultimate Business Strategy That Gets Superior Results and Builds Business Empires*. N.p.: Xlibris, 2011.

Wilkins, Mira. *The History of Foreign Investment in the United States to 1914*. Harvard Studies in Business History 41. Cambridge, MA: Harvard University Press, 1989.

"Will Invest for Food." *Economist*, May 3, 2014. http://www.economist .com/news/briefing/21601500-books-and-music-investment-industry -being-squeezed-will-invest-food.

Williams, John Burr. *The Theory of Investment Value*. Cambridge, MA: Harvard University Press, 1938.

Wingerd, Daniel A. "The Private Equity Market: History and Prospects." *Investment Policy* 1, no. 2 (September–October 1997): 26–41.

Wiseman, Paul, and Pallavi Gogol. "FDIC Chief: Small Banks Can't Compete with Bailed-Out Giants." *USA Today*, October 20, 2009. http:// usatoday30.usatoday.com/money/industries/banking/2009-10-19 -FDIC-chief-sheila-bair-banking_N.htm.

Wolpert, Stanley. *India*. Rev. ed. Berkeley: University of California Press, 1999.

Wooten, James. *The Employee Retirement Income Security Act of 1974: A Political History*. Berkeley: University of California Press, 2005.

"Working Women, 1800–1930: The Russell Sage Foundation and the Pittsburgh Survey." Harvard Library Collections. Accessed January 2015. http://ocp.hul.harvard.edu/ww/rsf.html.

"The World's Billionaires." *Forbes*. Accessed 2014. http://www.forbes.com /billionaires.

Wright, Robert E. "The NYSE's Long History of Mergers and Rivalries." Bloomberg View, January 8, 2013. http://www.bloombergview.com /articles/2013-01-08/nyse-s-long-history-of-mergers-and-rivalries.

Xenophon. *Oeconomicus*. Translated by Carnes Lord. In *The Shorter Socratic Writings:* Apology of Socrates to the Jury, Oeconomicus, *and* Symposium, ed. Robert C. Bartlett, 39–101. Ithaca, NY: Cornell University Press, 1996.

Zauzmer, Julie M. "Where We Stand: The Class of 2013 Senior Survey." *Harvard Crimson*, May 28, 2013. http://www.thecrimson.com /article/2013/5/28/senior-survey-2013.

Zweig, Jason. "Risks and Riches." *Money* 28, no. 4 (April 1999): 94–101.

Index

Milton Keynes UK
Ingram Content Group UK Ltd.
UKHW010104161223
434462UK00007B/505